The Right Thing to Do

The Right Thing to Do

Readings in Moral Philosophy

Eighth Edition

Edited by
James Rachels and Stuart Rachels

ROWMAN & LITTLEFIELD
Lanham • Boulder • New York • London

Published by Rowman & Littlefield
An imprint of The Rowman & Littlefield Publishing Group, Inc.
4501 Forbes Boulevard, Suite 200, Lanham, Maryland 20706
www.rowman.com

6 Tinworth Street, London SE11 5AL, United Kingdom

British Library Cataloguing in Publication Information Available

Library of Congress Cataloging-in-Publication Data
Names: Rachels, James, 1941–2003. editor. | Rachels, Stuart, 1969– editor.
Title: The right thing to do : readings in moral philosophy / edited by James
    Rachels and Stuart Rachels.
Description: Eighth Edition. | Lanham : Rowman & Littlefield Publishing Group,
    Inc., 2019. | Includes bibliographical references and index.
Identifiers: LCCN 2019002744 (print) | LCCN 2019022261 (ebook) |
    ISBN 9781538127926 (pbk. : alk. paper) | ISBN 9781538129487 (electronic)
Subjects: LCSH: Ethics—Textbooks.
Classification: LCC BJ1012 .R5 2019 (print) | LCC BJ1012 (ebook) |
    DDC 170—dc23
LC record available at https://lccn.loc.gov/2019002744
LC ebook record available at https://lccn.loc.gov/2019022261

♾™ The paper used in this publication meets the minimum requirements of
American National Standard for Information Sciences—Permanence of Paper for
Printed Library Materials, ANSI/NISO Z39.48-1992.

Printed in the United States of America

Contents

Preface

Moral philosophy is the study of how one should live. This anthology introduces that great subject. The readings cover the main moral theories and present a wealth of ideas about various practical matters.

In selecting the pieces for this volume, I looked for articles on serious moral topics that are deftly argued and pleasant to read, that lend themselves to lively discussion, and that reward careful study. I believe that the selections chosen are not merely good articles on suitable topics; they are first-rate essays on compelling issues. Students who read this book will want to read more, I think, unless the subject is simply not for them.

This eighth edition contains eight new essays, on eight new topics: the opioid crisis, hazing, the meaning of life, the ethics of taxation, guns, doping in sports, end-of-life care, and the history of racism in America. Seven selections from the seventh edition were cut: the essays on organ-selling and eugenics (because instructors made less use of them), the pieces by Martin Luther King Jr. and Douglas Lackey (due to high permissions fees), and the selections on same-sex marriage (because that issue has been satisfactorily resolved in American law, in a way that most college-age Americans support).

For their help in preparing the new edition, I thank David Connelly, Glenda Elliott, Heather Elliott, Sean McAleer, Jake Osachy, Jada Posey, and Carol Rachels. I also thank my new publisher—Rowman & Littlefield—and in particular Natalie Mandziuk.

To learn more about James Rachels, visit www.jamesrachels.org.

If you have suggestions for the next edition, please let me know!

—Stuart Rachels

INTRODUCTION

Chapter 1

A Short Introduction to Moral Philosophy

James Rachels

An ancient legend tells the story of Gyges, a poor shepherd who found a magic ring in a fissure opened by an earthquake. The ring would make its wearer invisible, so he could go anywhere and do anything undetected. Gyges was an unscrupulous fellow, and he quickly realized that the ring could be put to good advantage. We are told that he used its power to gain entry to the royal palace, where he seduced the queen, murdered the king, and seized the throne. (It is not explained how invisibility helped him to seduce the queen—but let that pass.) In no time at all, he went from being a poor shepherd to being king of all the land.

This story is recounted in Book II of Plato's *Republic*. Like all of Plato's works, *The Republic* is written in the form of a dialogue between Socrates and his companions. Glaucon, who is having an argument with Socrates, uses the story of Gyges's ring to make a point.

Glaucon asks us to imagine that there are two such rings, one given to a man of virtue and the other given to a rogue. How might we expect them to behave? The rogue, of course, will do anything necessary to increase his own wealth and power. Since the cloak of invisibility will protect him from discovery, he can do anything he pleases without fear of being caught. Therefore, he will recognize no moral constraints on his conduct, and there will be no end to the mischief he will do.

But how will the so-called virtuous man behave? Glaucon suggests that he will do no better than the rogue:

No one, it is commonly believed, would have such iron strength of mind as to stand fast in doing right or keep his hands off other men's goods, when he could go to the marketplace and fearlessly help himself to anything he wanted, enter houses and sleep with any woman he chose, set prisoners free and kill men at his pleasure, and in a word go about among men with the powers of a god. He would behave no better than the other; both would take the same course.

Moreover, Glaucon asks, why shouldn't he? Once he is freed from the fear of reprisal, why shouldn't a person simply do what he pleases, or what he thinks is best for himself? Why should he care at all about "morality"?

The Republic, written more than 2,300 years ago, was one of the first great works of moral philosophy in Western history. Since then, philosophers have formulated theories to explain what morality is, why it is important, and why it has the peculiar hold on us that it does. What, if anything, justifies our belief that we *morally ought* to act in one way rather than another?

RELATIVISM

Perhaps the oldest philosophical theory about morality is that right and wrong are relative to the customs of one's society—on this view, there is nothing behind the demands of morality except social convention. Herodotus, the first of the great Greek historians, lived at about the time of Socrates. His *History* is full of wonderful anecdotes that illustrate his belief that "right" and "wrong" are little more than names for social conventions. Of the Massagetae, a tribe in Central Asia, he writes:

The following are some of their customs—Each man has but one wife, yet all the wives are held in common. . . . Human life does not come to its natural close with these people; but when a man grows very old, all his kinsfolk collect together and offer him up in sacrifice; offering at the same time some cattle also. After the sacrifice they boil the flesh and feast on it; and those who thus end their days are reckoned the happiest. If a man dies of disease they do not eat him, but bury him in the ground, bewailing his ill-fortune that he did not come to be sacrificed. They sow no grain, but live on their herds, and on fish, of which there is great plenty in the Araxes. Milk is what they chiefly drink. The only god they worship is the

sun, and to him they offer the horse in sacrifice, under the notion of giving
the swiftest of the gods the swiftest of all mortal creatures.

Herodotus did not think the Massagetae were to be criticized for such
practices. Their customs were neither better nor worse than those of
other peoples; they were merely different. The Greeks, who considered
themselves more "civilized," might have thought that their customs
were superior, but, Herodotus says, that is only because everyone
believes the customs of his own society to be the best. The "truth"
depends on one's point of view—that is, on the society in which one
happens to have been raised.

Relativists think that Herodotus was obviously on to something and
that those who believe in "objective" right and wrong are merely naive.
Critics, however, object to the theory on a number of grounds. First, it
is exceedingly conservative, in that the theory endorses whatever moral
views happen to be current in a society. Consider our own society.
Many people believe that our society's moral code is mistaken, at least
on some points—for example, they may disagree with the dominant
social view regarding capital punishment or gay rights or the treatment
of nonhuman animals. Must we conclude that these would-be reformers
are wrong, merely because they oppose the majority view? Why must
the majority always be right?

But there is a deeper problem with Relativism, emphasized by
Socrates. Some social customs are, indeed, merely arbitrary, and when
these customs are at issue it is fruitless to insist that one of society's
practices are better than another's. Funerary practices are a good
example. The Greeks burned their dead, while the Callatians ate their
dead, but neither practice is better than the other. However, it does not
follow from this that *all* social practices are arbitrary in the same way.
Some are, and some are not. The Greeks and the Callatians were free
to accept whatever funerary practices they liked because no objective
reason could be given why one practice was superior to the other. In
the case of other practices, however, there may be good reasons why
some are superior. It is not hard, for example, to explain why honesty
and respect for human life are socially desirable, and similarly it is not
hard to explain why slavery and racism are undesirable. Because we can
support our judgments about these matters with rational arguments, we
do not have to regard those judgments as "merely" the expression of our
particular society's moral code.

DIVINE COMMANDS

A second ancient idea, also familiar to Socrates, was that moral living consists in obedience to divine commands. If this were true, then we could easily answer the challenge of Gyges's ring—even if we had the power of invisibility, we would still be subject to divine retribution, so ultimately we could not "get away with" doing whatever we wanted.

But Socrates did not believe that right living could consist merely in trying to please the gods. In the *Euthyphro*, another of Plato's dialogues, Socrates is shown considering at some length whether "right" can be the same as "what the gods command." Now we may notice, to begin with, that there are considerable practical difficulties with this as a general theory of ethics. How, for example, are we supposed to *know* what the gods command? There are those who claim to have spoken with God about the matter and who therefore claim to be in a position to pass on his instructions to the rest of us. But people who claim to speak for God are not the most trustworthy folks—hearing voices can be a sign of schizophrenia or megalomania just as easily as an instance of divine communication. Others, more modestly, rely on scripture or church tradition for guidance. But those sources are notoriously ambiguous—they give vague and often contradictory instructions—so, when people consult these authorities, they typically rely on whatever elements of scripture or church tradition support the moral views they are already inclined to agree with. Moreover, because scripture and church tradition have been handed down from earlier times, they provide little direct help in addressing distinctively contemporary problems: the problem of environmental preservation, for example, or the problem of how much of our resources should be allocated to cancer research as opposed to other worthy endeavors.

Still, it may be thought that God's commands provide the ultimate *authority* for ethics, and that is the issue Socrates addressed. Socrates accepted that the gods exist and that they may issue instructions. But he showed that this cannot be the ultimate basis of ethics. He pointed out that we have to distinguish two possibilities: Either the gods have some reason for the instructions they issue, or they do not. If they do not, then their commands are merely arbitrary—the gods are like petty tyrants who demand that we act in this way and that, even though there is no good reason for it. But this is an impious view that religious people will not want to accept. On the other hand, if we say that the gods do have good reasons for their instructions, then we have admitted that there is a standard of rightness independent of their commands—namely, the standard to which the gods themselves refer in deciding what to require of us.

It follows, then, that even if one accepts a religious picture of the world, the rightness or wrongness of actions cannot be understood merely in terms of their conformity to divine prescriptions. We may always ask why the gods command what they do, and the answer to *that* question will reveal why right actions are right and why wrong actions are wrong.

ARISTOTLE

Although Relativism and the Divine Command Theory have always had supporters, they have never been popular among serious students of moral philosophy. The first extended, systematic treatise on moral philosophy, produced two generations after Socrates, was Aristotle's *Nicomachean Ethics* (ca. 330 BC), and Aristotle wasted no time on such notions. Instead, Aristotle offered a detailed account of the virtues—the qualities of character that people need to do well in life. The virtues include courage, prudence, generosity, honesty, and many more; Aristotle sought to explain what each one is and why it is important. His answer to the question of Gyges's ring was that virtue is necessary for human beings to achieve happiness; therefore, the man of virtue is ultimately better off *because* he is virtuous.

Aristotle's view of the virtuous life was connected with his overall way of understanding the world and our place in it. Aristotle's conception of what the world is like was enormously influential; it dominated Western thinking for more than 1,700 years. A central feature of this conception was that *everything in nature exists for a purpose.* "Nature," Aristotle said, "belongs to the class of causes which act for the sake of something."

It seems obvious that artifacts such as knives and chariots have purposes, because we have their purposes in mind when we make them. But what about natural objects that we do not make? Do they have purposes too? Aristotle thought so. One of his examples was that we have teeth so that we can chew. Such biological examples are quite persuasive; the parts of our bodies do seem, intuitively, to have particular purposes—eyes are for seeing, the heart is for pumping blood, and so on. But Aristotle's thesis was not limited to organic beings. According to him, *everything* in nature has a purpose. He also thought, to take a different sort of example, that rain falls so that plants can grow. As odd as it may seem to a modern reader, Aristotle was perfectly serious about this. He considered other alternatives, such as that the rain falls "of necessity" and that this helps the plants only "by coincidence," and rejected them. His considered view was that plants and animals are what they are, and that the rain falls as it does, "because it is better so."

The world, therefore, is an orderly, rational system, with each thing having its own proper place and serving its own special purpose. There is a neat hierarchy: The rain exists for the sake of the plants, the plants exist for the sake of the animals, and the animals exist—of course—for the sake of people. Aristotle says: "If then we are right in believing that nature makes nothing without some end in view, nothing to no purpose, it must be that nature has made all things specifically for the sake of man." This worldview is stunningly anthropocentric, or human-centered. But Aristotle was hardly alone in having such thoughts; almost every important thinker in human history has advanced such a thesis. Humans are a remarkably vain species.

NATURAL LAW

The Christian thinkers who came later found Aristotle's view of the world appealing. There was only one thing missing: God. Thus, the Christian thinkers said that the rain falls to help the plants because *that is what the Creator intended*, and the animals are for human use because *that is what God made them for*. Values and purposes were, therefore, conceived to be a fundamental part of the nature of things, because the world was believed to have been created according to a divine plan.

This view of the world had a number of consequences for ethics. On the most general level, it affirmed the supreme value of human life, and it explained why humans are entitled to do whatever they please with the rest of nature. The basic moral arrangement—human beings, whose lives are sacred, dominating a world made for their benefit—was enshrined as the Natural Order of Things.

At a more detailed level, a corollary of this outlook was that the "laws of nature" specify how things *ought to be*, as well as describing how things *are*. In turn, knowing how things ought to be enables us to evaluate states of affairs as objectively good or bad. Things are as they ought to be when they are serving their natural purposes; when they do not or cannot serve those purposes, things have gone wrong. Thus, teeth that have decayed and cannot be used for chewing are defective; and drought, which deprives plants of the rain they need, is a natural, objective evil.

There are also implications for human action: On this view, moral rules are one type of law of nature. The key idea here is that some forms of human behavior are "natural" while others are not; and "unnatural" acts are said to be wrong. Beneficence, for example, is natural for us because God has made us as social creatures. We want and need the friendship of other people, and we have natural affections for them; hence, behaving brutishly toward them is unnatural. Or to take a different sort of example, the purpose of the sex organs is procreation. Thus, any use of them for other purposes is "contrary to nature"—which is why the Christian church has traditionally regarded any form of sexual activity that cannot result in pregnancy, such as masturbation, gay sex, or sex with contraceptives, as impermissible.

This combination of ideas, together with others like them, formed the core of an outlook known as natural-law ethics. The Theory of Natural Law was developed most fully by Saint Thomas Aquinas (1225–1274), who lived at a time when the Aristotelian worldview was unchallenged. Aquinas was the foremost thinker among traditional Catholic theologians. Today natural-law theory still has adherents inside the Catholic Church, but few outside. The reason is that the Aristotelian worldview, on which natural-law ethics depends, has been replaced by the outlook of modern science.

Galileo, Newton, Darwin, and others developed ways of understanding natural phenomena that made no use of evaluative notions. In their way of thinking, the rain has no purpose. It does not fall in order to help the plants grow. Plants typically get the amount of water they need because each species has evolved, by natural selection, in the environment in which that amount of water is available. Natural selection produces an orderly arrangement that *appears* to have been designed, but that is only an illusion. To explain nature there is no need to assume purpose-involving principles, as Aristotle and the Christians had done. This new outlook was threatening to the Catholic Church, and they condemned it.

Modern science transformed people's view of what the world is like. But part of the transformation, inseparable from the rest, was an altered view of the nature of ethics. Right and wrong could no longer be deduced from the nature of things, for on the new view the natural world does not, in and of itself, manifest value and purpose. The *inhabitants* of the world may have needs and desires that generate values special to them, but that is all. The world apart from those inhabitants knows and cares nothing for their values, and it has no values of its own. A hundred and fifty years before Nietzsche declared, "There are no moral facts," the Scottish philosopher David Hume had come to the same conclusion. Hume summed up the moral implications of the new worldview in his *Treatise of Human Nature* (1739) when he wrote:

> Take any action allow'd to be vicious: Willful murder, for instance. Examine it in all lights, and see if you can find that matter of fact, or real existence, which you call *vice*. In whichever way you take it, you find only certain passions, motives, volitions and thoughts. There is no other matter of fact in the case.

To Aristotle's idea that "nature has made all things for the sake of man," Hume replied: "The life of a man is of no greater importance to the universe than that of an oyster."

THE SOCIAL CONTRACT

If morality cannot be based on God's commands, nor on the idea of natural purpose, then what can it be based on? Ethics must somehow be understood as a purely human phenomenon—as the product of human needs, interests, and desires—and nothing else. Figuring out how to do this has been the basic project of moral philosophy from the seventeenth century on.

Thomas Hobbes, the foremost English philosopher of the seventeenth century, suggested one way in which ethics might be understood in purely human terms. Hobbes assumed that "good" and "bad" are just names we give to things we like and dislike. Thus, because we may like different things, we may disagree about what is good or bad. However, Hobbes said, in our fundamental psychological makeup we are all very much alike. We are all basically self-interested creatures who want to live and to live as well as possible. This is the key to understanding ethics. Ethics arises when people realize *what they must do* to live well.

Hobbes was the first important modern thinker to provide a secular, naturalistic basis for ethics. He pointed out that each of us is enormously better off living in a mutually cooperative society than we would be if we tried to make it on our own. The benefits of social living go far beyond companionship: Social cooperation makes it possible to have schools, hospitals, and highways; houses with electricity and central heating; airplanes and telephones; websites and books; movies, opera, and bingo; science and agriculture. Without social cooperation we would lose these benefits and more. Therefore, it is to the advantage of each of us to do whatever is necessary to establish and maintain a cooperative society.

But it turns out that a mutually cooperative society can exist only if we adopt certain rules of behavior—rules that require telling the truth, keeping our promises, respecting one another's lives and property, and so on:

Without the presumption that people will tell the truth, there would be no reason for people to pay any attention to what other people say. Communication would be impossible. And without communication among its members, society would collapse.

Without the requirement that people keep their promises, there could be no division of labor—workers could not count on getting paid, retailers could not rely on their agreements with suppliers, and so on—and the economy would collapse. There could be no business, no building, no agriculture, no medicine.

Without assurances against assault, murder, and theft, no one could feel secure; everyone would have to be constantly on guard against everyone else, and social cooperation would be impossible.

Thus, to obtain the benefits of social living, we must strike a bargain with one another, with each of us agreeing to obey these rules, provided others do likewise. We must also establish mechanisms for enforcing these rules—such as legal sanctions and other, less formal methods of enforcement—so that we can *count on* one another to obey them. This "social contract" is the basis of morality. Indeed, morality can be defined as nothing more or less than *the set of rules that rational people will agree to obey, for their mutual benefit, provided that other people will obey them as well.*

This way of understanding morality has a number of appealing features. First, it takes the mystery out of ethics and makes it a practical, down-to-earth business. Living morally is not a matter of blind obedience to the mysterious dictates of a supernatural being; nor is it a matter of fidelity to lofty but pointless abstract rules. Instead, it is a matter of doing what it takes to make social living possible.

Second, the Social Contract Theory explains why we should *care* about ethics—it offers at least a partial response to the problem of Gyges's ring. If there is no God to punish us, why should we bother to do what is "right," especially when it is not to our advantage? The answer is that it *is* to our advantage to live in a society where people behave morally—thus, it is rational for us to accept moral restrictions on our conduct as part of a bargain we make with other people. We benefit directly from the ethical conduct of others, and our own compliance with the moral rules is the price we pay to secure their compliance.

Third, the Social Contract approach gives us a sensible and mature way of determining what our ethical duties really are. When "morality" is mentioned, the first thing that pops into many people's minds is an attempt to restrict their sex lives. It is unfortunate that the word *morals* has come to have such a connotation. The whole purpose of having a system of morality, according to Social Contract Theory, is to make it possible for people to live their individual lives in a setting of social cooperation. Its purpose is *not* to tell people what kinds of lives they should lead (except insofar as it is necessary to restrict conduct in the interests of maintaining social cooperation). Therefore, an ethic based on the Social Contract would have little interest in what people do in their bedrooms.

Finally, we may note again that the Social Contract Theory assumes relatively little about human nature. It treats human beings as self-interested creatures and does not assume that they are naturally altruistic, even to the slightest degree. One of the theory's charms is that it can reach the conclusion that we ought, often, to *behave* altruistically, without assuming that we *are* naturally altruistic. We want to live as well as possible, and moral obligations are created as we band together with other people to form the cooperative societies that are necessary for us to achieve this fundamentally self-interested goal.

ALTRUISM AND SELF-INTEREST

Are people essentially self-interested? Although the Social Contract Theory continues to attract supporters, not many philosophers and psychologists today would accept Hobbes's egoistic view of human nature. It seems evident that humans have at least *some* altruistic feelings, if only for their family and friends. We have evolved as social creatures just as surely as we have evolved as creatures with legs—caring for our kin and members of our local group is as natural for us as walking.

If humans do have some degree of natural altruism, does this have any significance for morals? Hume thought so. Hume agreed with Hobbes that our moral opinions are expressions of our feelings. In 1739, when he invited his readers to consider "willful murder" and see if they could find that "matter of fact" called "vice," Hume concluded:

> You can never find it, till you turn your reflexion into your own breast, and find a sentiment of [disapproval], which arises in you, towards this action. Here is a matter of fact; but 'tis the object of feeling. . . . It lies in yourself, not in the object. So that when you pronounce any action or character to be vicious, you mean nothing, but that from the constitution of your nature you have a feeling or sentiment of blame from the contemplation of it.

And what, exactly, is "the constitution of our nature"? Of course, it is part of our nature to care about ourselves and our own welfare. But Hume added that we also have "*social* sentiments"—feelings that connect us with other people and make us concerned about their welfare. That is why, Hume said, we measure right and wrong by "the true interests of mankind":

> In all determinations of morality, this circumstance of public utility is ever principally in view; and wherever disputes arise, either in philosophy or common life, concerning the bounds of duty, the question cannot, by

any means, be decided with greater certainty than by ascertaining, on any side, the true interests of mankind.

This view came to be known as Utilitarianism. In modern moral philosophy, it is the chief alternative to the Social Contract Theory.

UTILITARIANISM

Utilitarians believe that one principle sums up all of our moral duties. The precept is that *we should always do whatever will produce the greatest possible balance of happiness over unhappiness for everyone who will be affected by our action.* This "principle of utility" is deceptively simple. It is actually a combination of three ideas: First, in determining what to do, we should be guided by the expected consequences of our actions—we should do whatever will have the best consequences. Second, in determining which consequences are best, we should give the greatest possible weight to the happiness or unhappiness that would be caused—we should do whatever will cause the most happiness or the least unhappiness. And finally, the principle of utility assumes that each individual's happiness is equally as important as anyone else's.

Although Hume expressed the basic idea of Utilitarianism, two other philosophers elaborated it in greater detail. Jeremy Bentham, an Englishman who lived in the late eighteenth and early nineteenth centuries, was the leader of a group of philosophical radicals who aimed to reform the laws of Britain along utilitarian lines. This group was remarkably successful in advancing such causes as prison reform and restrictions on the use of child labor. John Stuart Mill, the son of one of Bentham's original followers, gave the theory its most popular and influential defense in his book *Utilitarianism*, published in 1861.

The Utilitarian movement attracted critics from the start. It was an easy target because it ignored conventional religious notions. The point of morality, according to the Utilitarians, had nothing to do with obeying God or gaining credit in Heaven. Rather, the point was just to make life in this world as comfortable and happy as possible. So some critics condemned Utilitarianism as a godless doctrine. To this Mill replied:

[T]he question depends upon what idea we have formed of the moral character of the Deity. If it be a true belief that God desires, above all things, the happiness of his creatures, and that this was his purpose in their creation, utility is not only not a godless doctrine, but more profoundly religious than any other.

Utilitarianism was also an easy target because it was (and still is) a *subversive* theory, in that it turned many traditional moral ideas upside down. Bentham argued, for example, that the purpose of the criminal justice system cannot be understood in the traditional way as "paying back" wrongdoers for their wicked deeds—that only piles misery upon misery. Instead, the social response to crime should be threefold: to identify and deal with the causes of criminal behavior; where possible, to reform individual lawbreakers and make them into productive citizens; and to "punish" people only insofar as it is necessary to deter others from committing similar crimes. Or, to take a different example, by insisting that everyone's happiness is equally important, the Utilitarians offended various elitist notions of group superiority. According to the Utilitarian standard, neither race, sex, nor social class makes a difference to one's moral status. Mill himself wrote a book on *The Subjection of Women* that became a classic of the nineteenth-century suffragist movement.

Finally, Utilitarianism was controversial because it had no use for "absolute" moral rules. The Utilitarians regarded the traditional rules—against killing, lying, breaking one's promises, and so on—as "rules of thumb," useful because following them will generally be for the best. But they are not absolute—whenever breaking such a rule will have better results for everyone concerned, the rule should be broken. The rule against killing, for example, might be suspended in the case of voluntary euthanasia for someone dying of a painful illness. Moreover, the Utilitarians regarded some traditional rules as dubious, even as rules of thumb. For example, Christian moralists had traditionally said that masturbation is evil because it violates the Natural Law; but from the point of view of the Principle of Utility, it appears to be harmless. A more serious matter is the traditional religious condemnation of homosexuality, which has resulted in misery for countless people. Utilitarianism implies that if an activity makes people happy, without harming anyone, it cannot be wrong.

But it is one thing to describe a moral view; it is another thing to justify it. Utilitarianism says that our moral duty is to "promote the general happiness." Why should we do that? How can the challenge of Gyges's ring be answered? As Mill puts it:

> I feel that I am bound not to rob or murder, betray or deceive; but why am I bound to promote the general happiness? If my own happiness lies in something else, why may I not give that the preference?

Aside from the "external sanctions" of law and public opinion, Mill thinks there is only one possible reason for accepting this or any other moral standard. The "internal sanction" of morality must always be "a feeling in our minds," regardless of what sort of ethic this feeling endorses. The kind of morality we accept will, therefore, depend on the nature of our feelings: If human beings have "social feelings," then Mill says that utilitarian morality will be the natural standard for them:

> The firm foundation [of utilitarian morality] is that of the social feelings of mankind—the desire to be in unity with our fellow creatures, which is already a powerful principle in human nature, and happily one of those which tend to become stronger, even without express inculcation, from the influences of advancing civilization.

IMPARTIALITY

Utilitarianism, as we have seen, has implications that are at odds with traditional morality. Much the same could be said about the Social Contract Theory. In most of the practical matters that have been mentioned—punishment, racial discrimination, women's rights, euthanasia, gay rights—the two theories have similar implications. But there is one matter on which they differ dramatically. Utilitarians believe that we have a very extensive moral duty to help other people. Social Contract theorists deny this.

Suppose, for example, you are thinking of spending $1,000 for a new living room carpet. Should you do this? What are the alternatives? One alternative is to give the money to an agency such as the United Nations Children's Fund (UNICEF). Each year millions of third-world children die of easily preventable diseases because there isn't enough money to provide the vitamin-A capsules, antibiotics, and oral rehydration treatments they need. By giving the money to UNICEF, and making do a while longer with your old carpet, you could provide much-needed medical care for dozens of children. From the point of view of utility—seeking the best overall outcome for everyone concerned—there is no doubt you should give the money to UNICEF. Obviously, the medicine will help the kids a lot more than the new rug will help you.

But from the point of view of the Social Contract, things look very different. If morality rests on an agreement between people—remember, an agreement they enter into *to promote their own interests*—what would the agreement say about helping other people? Certainly, we would want the contract to impose a duty not to harm other people, even strangers. Each of us would obviously benefit from that. And it might be in our best interests to accept a mutual obligation to provide aid to others when it is easy and convenient to do so. But would rational people accept a general duty to provide virtually unlimited aid to strangers, even at great cost to themselves? From the standpoint of self-interest, that sounds crazy. Jan Narveson, a contract theorist, writes in his book *Moral Matters* (1993):

> [M]orals, if they are to be rational, must amount to agreements among people—people of all kinds, each pursuing his or her own interests, which are various and do not necessarily include much concern for others and their interests. But people . . . have a broad repertoire of powers including some that can make them exceedingly dangerous, as well as others that can make them very helpful. This gives us reason to agree with each other that we will refrain from harming others in the pursuit of our interests, to respect each other's property and grant extensive civil rights, but not necessarily to go very far out of our way to be very helpful to those we don't know and may not particularly care for.

Unlike many philosophers who prefer to keep things abstract, Narveson is good about spelling out the implications of his view in a way that leaves no room for misunderstanding:

> What about parting with the means for making your sweet little daughter's birthday party a memorable one, in order to keep a dozen strangers alive on the other side of the world? Is this something you are morally required to do? Indeed not. She may well *matter* to you more than they. This illustrates again the fact that people do *not* "count equally" for most of us. Normal people care more about some people than others, and build their very lives around those carings.

Which view is correct? Do we have a moral duty to provide extensive aid to strangers, or not? Both views appeal ultimately to our
emotions. A striking feature of Narveson's argument is its appeal to
the fact that we *care more* for some people than others. This is certainly true: As he says, we care more for our own children than for
"strangers on the other side of the world." But does this really mean
that I may choose some trivial benefit for my children over the very
lives of the strangers? Suppose there are two buttons on my desk at
this moment, and by pressing button A, I can provide my son with a
nice party; by pressing B, I can save the lives of a dozen strangers. Is
it really all right for me to press A, just because I "care more" for my
son? Mill agrees that the issue must be decided on the basis of feelings
(how else could it be?), but for him it is not these small-scale personal
feelings that have the final say. Instead, it is one's "conscientious
feelings"—the feelings that prevail after everything has been thought
through—that finally determine one's obligations. Mill assumes that
we cannot, when we are thoughtful and reflective, approve of pushing
button A.

However, some contemporary Utilitarians have argued that the matter need not be left to the uncertainties of individual feeling. It may be
true, they say, that we all care more for ourselves, our family, and our
friends than we care for strangers. But we have rational capacities as
well as feelings, and if we think objectively about the matter, we will
realize that other people are no different. Others, even strangers, also
care about themselves, their families, and their friends, in the same way
that we do. Their needs and interests are comparable to our own. In
fact, *there is nothing of this general sort that makes anyone different
from anyone else*—and if we are in all relevant respects similar to one
another, then there is no justification for anyone taking his or her own
interests to be more important. Peter Singer, a utilitarian philosopher,
writes in his book *How Are We to Live?* (1995):

> Reason makes it possible for us to see ourselves in this way. . . . I am able
> to see that I am just one being among others, with interests and desires
> like others. I have a personal perspective on the world, from which my
> interests are at the front and center of the stage, the interests of my fam-
> ily and friends are close behind, and the interests of strangers are pushed
> to the back and sides. But reason enables me to see that others have
> similarly subjective perspectives, and that from "the point of view of the

universe" my perspective is no more privileged than theirs. Thus my ability to reason shows me the possibility of detaching myself from my own perspective, and shows me what the universe might look like if I had no personal perspective.

So, from an objective viewpoint, each of us must acknowledge that our own perspective—our own particular set of needs, interests, likes, and dislikes—is only one among many and has no special status.

KANT

The idea of impartiality is also central to the third major alternative in modern moral philosophy, the system of ethical ideas devised by the great German philosopher Immanuel Kant (1724–1804). Like the Social Contract theorists and the Utilitarians, Kant sought to explain ethics without appealing to divine commands or "moral facts." Kant's solution was to see morality as a product of "pure reason." Just as we must do some things because of our *desires*—for example, because I desire to go to a concert, I must buy a ticket—the moral law is binding on us because of our *reason.*

Like the Utilitarians, Kant believed that morality can be summed up in one ultimate principle, from which all our duties and obligations are derived. But his version of the "ultimate moral principle" was very different from the Principle of Utility, because Kant did not emphasize the outcomes of actions. What was important for him was "doing one's duty," and he held that a person's duty is not determined by calculating consequences.

Kant called his ultimate moral principle the "Categorical Imperative." But he gave this principle two very different formulations. The first version of the Categorical Imperative, as expressed in his *Fundamental Principles of the Metaphysics of Morals* (1785), goes like this:

> Act only according to that maxim by which you can at the same time will that it should become a universal law.

Stated in this way, Kant's principle summarizes a procedure for deciding whether an act is morally permissible. When you are contemplating a particular action, you are to ask what rule you would be following if you were to do it. (This will be the "maxim" of the act.) Then you are to ask whether you would be willing for that rule to be followed by everyone all the time. (That would make it a "universal law" in the relevant sense.) If so, the rule may be followed, and the act is permissible. However, if you would not be willing for everyone to follow the rule, then you may not follow it, and the act is morally impermissible.

This explains why the Moral Law is binding on us simply by virtue of our rationality. The first requirement of rationality is that we be consistent, and it would not be consistent to act on a maxim that we could not want others to adopt as well. Kant believed, in addition, that consistency requires us to interpret moral rules as having no exceptions. For this reason, he endorsed a whole range of absolute prohibitions, covering everything from lying to suicide.

However, Kant also gave another formulation of the Categorical Imperative. Later in the same book, he said that the ultimate moral principle may be understood as saying:

> So act that you treat humanity, whether in your own person or in that of another, always as an end and never as means only.

What does it mean to say that persons are to be treated as "ends" and never as a "means only"? Kant gives this example: Suppose you need money, and so you want a "loan," but you know you could not repay it. In desperation, you consider making a false promise (to repay) in order to trick a friend into giving you the money. May you do this? Perhaps you need the money for a good purpose—so good, in fact, that you might convince yourself that the lie would be justified. Nevertheless, if you lied to your friend, you would merely be manipulating him and using him "as a means."

On the other hand, what would it be like to treat your friend "as an end"? Suppose you told the truth—that you need the money for a certain purpose but could not repay it. Then your friend could make up his own mind about whether to let you have it. He could exercise his own powers of reason, consulting his own values and wishes, and make a free, autonomous choice. If he did decide to give the money for this purpose, he would be choosing to make that purpose his own. Thus, you would not merely be using him as a means to achieving your goal.

CONCLUSION

Our purpose here is not to reach any firm conclusion about which of these approaches, if any, is correct. But we may end with an observation about how that project might be undertaken.

Philosophical ideas are often very abstract, and it is difficult to see what sort of evidence counts for or against them. It is easy enough to appreciate, intuitively, the ideas behind each of these theories, but how do we determine which, if any, is correct? It is a daunting question. Faced with this problem, people are tempted to accept or reject philosophical ideas on the basis of their intuitive appeal—if an idea sounds good, one may embrace it; or if it rubs one the wrong way, it may be discarded. But this is hardly a satisfactory way to proceed if we want to discover the truth. How an idea strikes us is not a reliable guide, for our "intuitions" may be mistaken.

Happily, there is an alternative. An idea is no better than the arguments that support it. So, to evaluate a philosophical idea, we may examine the reasoning behind it. The great philosophers knew this: They did not simply announce their philosophical opinions; instead, they presented arguments in support of their views. The leading idea, from the time of Socrates to the present, has been that truth is discovered by considering the reasons for and against the various alternatives. So the correct theory is the one supported by the best arguments. Thus, philosophical thinking consists, to a large extent, of formulating and assessing arguments. This is not the whole of philosophy, but it is a big part of it. It is what makes philosophy a rational enterprise.

Chapter 2

Some Basic Points about Arguments

James Rachels

Philosophy without argument would be a lifeless exercise. What good would it be to produce a theory if there were no reasons for thinking it correct? And of what interest is the rejection of a theory if there are no good reasons for thinking it incorrect? A philosophical idea is exactly as good as the arguments in its support.

Therefore, if we want to think clearly about philosophical matters, we have to learn something about the evaluation of arguments. We have to learn to distinguish the sound ones from the unsound ones. This can be a tedious business, but it is indispensable if we want to discover the truth.

ARGUMENTS

In ordinary English, the word *argument* often means a fight, and there is a hint of unpleasantness in the word. That is not the way the word is used here. In the logician's sense, an argument is a chain of reasoning designed to prove something. It consists of one or more *premises* and a *conclusion,* together with the claim that the conclusion *follows from* the premises. Here is a simple argument. This example is not particularly interesting in itself, but it is short and clear, and it will help us grasp the main points.

(1) All men are mortal.
   Socrates is a man.
   Therefore, Socrates is mortal.

The first two statements are the premises; the third statement is the conclusion; and the word *therefore* indicates that the conclusion is supposed to follow from the premises.

What does it mean to say that the conclusion "follows from" the premises? It means that a certain logical relation exists between the premises and the conclusion, namely, that *if* the premises are true, then the conclusion must be true also. (Another way to put the same point is: The conclusion follows from the premises if, and only if, it is impossible for the premises to be true and the conclusion false at the same time.) In example (1), we can see that the conclusion does follow from the premises. If it is true that all men are mortal, and Socrates is a man, then it must be true that Socrates is mortal. (Or, it is impossible for it to be true that all men are mortal, and for Socrates to be a man, and be false that Socrates is mortal.)

In example (1), the conclusion follows from the premises, *and* the premises are in fact true. However, the conclusion of an argument may follow from the premises even if the premises are not actually true. Consider this argument:

(2) All people from Georgia are famous.
    Jimmy Carter is from Georgia.
    Therefore, Jimmy Carter is famous.

Clearly, the conclusion of this argument does follow from the premises: *If* it were true that all Georgians are famous, and Jimmy Carter is from Georgia, then it would follow that Jimmy Carter is famous. This logical relation holds between the premises and conclusion even though one of the premises is in fact false.

At this point, logicians customarily introduce a bit of terminology. They say that an argument is *valid* just in case its conclusion follows from its premises. Both of the examples given above are valid arguments in this technical sense.

In order to be a *sound* argument, however, two things are necessary: The argument must be valid, *and* its premises must be true. Thus, the argument about Socrates is a sound argument, but the argument about Jimmy Carter is not sound, because even though it is valid, its premises are not all true.

It is important to notice that an argument may be unsound even though its premises and conclusion are both true. Consider the following silly example:

(3) The earth has one moon.
John F. Kennedy was assassinated.
Therefore, snow is white.

The premises of this "argument" are both true, and the conclusion is true as well. Yet it is obviously a bad argument, because it is not valid—the conclusion does not follow from the premises. The point is that *when we ask whether an argument is valid, we are not asking whether the premises actually are true, or whether the conclusion actually is true. We are only asking whether, if the premises were true, the conclusion would really follow from them.*

I have used these trivial examples because they permit us to make the essential logical points clearly and uncontroversially. But these points are applicable to the analysis of any argument, trivial or not. To illustrate, let us consider how these points can be used to analyze a more important and controversial issue. We will look at the arguments for Moral Skepticism in some detail.

MORAL SKEPTICISM

Moral Skepticism is the idea that *there is no such thing as objective moral truth.* It is not merely the idea that we cannot *know* the truth about right and wrong. It is the more radical idea that, where ethics is concerned, "truth" does not exist. The essential point may be put in several different ways. It may be said that:

Morality is subjective; it is a matter of how we feel about things, not a matter of how things *are.*
Morality is only a matter of opinion, and one person's opinion is just as good as another's.
Values exist only in our minds, not in the world outside us.

However the point is put, the underlying thought is the same: The idea of "objective moral truth" is only a fiction; in reality, there is no such thing.

We want to know whether Moral Skepticism is correct. Is the idea of moral "truth" only an illusion? What arguments can be given in favor of this idea? In order to determine whether it is correct, we need to ask what arguments can be given for it and whether those arguments are sound.

The Cultural Differences Argument

One argument for Moral Skepticism might be based on the observation that in different cultures people have different ideas concerning right and wrong. For example, in traditional Eskimo society, infanticide was thought to be morally acceptable—if a family already had too many children, a new baby might be left to die in the snow. In our own society, however, this would be considered wrong. There are many other examples of the same kind. Different cultures have different moral codes.

Reflecting on such facts, many people have concluded that there is no such thing as objective right and wrong. Thus, they advance the following argument:

> (4) In some societies, such as among the Eskimos, infanticide is thought to be morally acceptable.
>
> In other societies, such as our own, infanticide is thought to be morally vile.
>
> Therefore, infanticide is neither objectively right nor objectively wrong; it is merely a matter of opinion that varies from culture to culture.

We may call this the "Cultural Differences Argument." This kind of argument has been tremendously influential; it has persuaded many people to be skeptical of the whole idea of "moral truth." But is it a *sound* argument? We may ask two questions about it: First, are the premises true, and second, does the conclusion really follow from them? If the answer to either question is no, then the argument must be rejected. In this case, the premises seem to be correct—there have been many cultures in which infanticide was accepted. Therefore, our attention must focus on the second matter: Is the argument *valid*?

To figure this out, we may begin by noting that the premises concern *what people believe*. In some societies, people think infanticide is all right. In others, people believe it is immoral. The conclusion, however, concerns not what people believe, but whether infanticide *really is* immoral. The problem is that this sort of conclusion does not follow from those sorts of premises. It does not follow, from the mere fact that people have different beliefs about something, that there is no "truth" in the matter. Therefore, the Cultural Differences Argument is not valid.

To make this point clearer, consider this analogous argument:

(5) In some societies, the world is thought to be flat.
   In other societies, the world is thought to be round.
   Therefore, objectively speaking, the world is neither flat nor round. It
is merely a matter of opinion that varies from culture to culture.

Clearly, *this* argument is not valid. We cannot conclude that the world is shapeless simply because not everyone agrees what shape it has. But exactly the same can be said about the Cultural Differences Argument: We cannot validly move from premises about what people believe to a conclusion about what is so, because people—even whole societies— may be wrong. The world has a definite shape, and those who think it is flat are mistaken. Similarly, infanticide might be objectively wrong (or not wrong), and those who think differently might be mistaken. There- fore, the Cultural Differences Argument is not valid, and so it provides no legitimate support for the idea that "moral truth" is only an illusion.

There are two common reactions to this analysis. These reactions illustrate traps that people often fall into.

1. The first reaction goes like this: Many people find the conclusion of the Cultural Differences Argument very appealing. This makes it hard for them to believe that the argument is invalid—when the argument is shown to be fallacious, they tend to respond: "But right and wrong really *are* only matters of opinion!" They make the mistake of thinking that if we reject an argument, we are somehow impugning the truth of its conclusion. But that is not so. Remember example (3) above; it illustrates how an argument may have a true conclusion and still be a bad argument. If an argument is unsound, then it fails to provide any reason for thinking the conclusion is true. The conclusion may still be true—that remains an open question— but the point is just that the unsound argument gives it no support.
2. One may object that it is unfair to compare morality with an obvi- ously objective matter like the shape of the earth, because we can prove what shape the earth has by scientific methods. Therefore, we know that the flat-earthers are simply wrong. But morality is differ- ent. There is no way to prove that a moral opinion is true or false.

This objection misses the point. The Cultural Differences Argument tries to derive the skeptical conclusion about morality *from a certain set of facts,* namely, the facts about cultural disagreements. This objection suggests that the conclusion might be derived from a *different* set of facts, namely, facts about what is and what is not provable. It suggests, in effect, a different argument, which might be formulated like this:

> **(6)** If infanticide (or anything else, for that matter) is objectively right or wrong, then it should be possible to *prove* that it is right or wrong.
>
> But it is not possible to prove that infanticide is right or wrong.
>
> Therefore, infanticide is neither objectively right nor objectively wrong. It is merely a matter of opinion that varies from culture to culture.

This argument is fundamentally different from the Cultural Differences Argument, even though the two arguments have the same conclusion. They are different because they appeal to different considerations in trying to prove that conclusion—in other words, they have different premises. Therefore, the question of whether argument (6) is sound is separate from the question of whether the Cultural Differences Argument is sound. The Cultural Differences Argument is not valid (and, therefore, is not sound), for the reason given above.

We should emphasize the importance of *keeping arguments separate.* It is easy to slide from one argument to another without realizing what one is doing. It is easy to think that if moral judgments are "unprovable," then the Cultural Differences Argument is strengthened. But it is not. Argument (6) merely introduces a different set of issues. It is important to pin down an argument and evaluate *it* as carefully as possible, before moving on to different considerations.

The Provability Argument

Now let us consider in more detail the question of whether it is possible to prove a moral judgment true or false. The following argument, which we might call the "Provability Argument," is a more general form of argument (6):

> **(7)** If there were any such thing as objective truth in ethics, we should be able to prove that some moral opinions are true and others false.

But, in fact, we cannot prove which moral opinions are true and which
are false.

Therefore, there is no such thing as objective truth in ethics.

Once again, we have an argument with a certain superficial appeal.
But are the premises true? And does the conclusion really follow from
them? It seems that the conclusion does follow. Therefore, the crucial
question will be whether the premises are in fact true.

The general claim that moral judgments can't be proven *sounds* right:
Anyone who has ever argued about a matter like abortion knows how
frustrating it can be to try to "prove" that one's point of view is correct. However, if we inspect this claim more closely, it turns out to be
questionable.

Suppose we consider a matter that is simpler than abortion. A student
says that a test given by a teacher was unfair. This is clearly a moral judgment—fairness is a basic moral value. Can the student prove the test was
unfair? She might point out that the test was so long that not even the
best students could complete it in the time allowed (and the test was to be
graded on the assumption that it should be completed). Moreover, the test
covered trivial matters while ignoring matters the teacher had stressed as
important. And finally, the test included questions about some matters that
were not covered in either the assigned readings or the class discussions.

Suppose all this is true. And further suppose that the teacher, when
asked to explain, has no defense to offer. (In fact, the teacher seems
confused about the whole thing and doesn't seem to have any idea what
he was doing.) Now, hasn't the student proved the test was unfair?
What more in the way of proof could we possibly want?

It is easy to think of other examples that make the same point:

Jones is a bad man. To prove this, one might point out that Jones is a
    habitual liar; he manipulates people; he cheats when he thinks he can
    get away with it; he is cruel to other people; and so on.
Dr. Smith is irresponsible. She bases her diagnoses on superficial
    considerations; she drinks Budweiser before performing delicate sur-
    gery; she refuses to listen to other doctors' advice; and so on.
A certain used-car salesman is unethical. He conceals defects in his
    cars; he takes advantage of poor people by pressuring them into pay-
    ing high prices for cars he knows are defective; he runs false adver-
    tisements on the web; and so on.

The point is that we can, and often do, back up our ethical judgments with good reasons. Thus, it does not seem right to say that they are all unprovable, as though they were nothing more than "mere opinions." If a person has good reasons for his judgments, then he is not *merely* giving "his opinion." On the contrary, he may be making a judgment which any reasonable person would have to agree with.

If we can sometimes give good reasons for our moral judgments, what accounts for the persistent impression that they are "unprovable"? There are two reasons why the Provability Argument appears better than it is.

First, there is a tendency to focus attention only on the most difficult moral issues. The question of abortion, for example, is an enormously difficult and complicated matter. If we think only of questions like *this,* it is easy to believe that "proof" in ethics is impossible. The same could be said of the sciences. There are many complicated matters that physicists cannot agree on; if we focused our attention entirely on *them,* we might conclude that there is no "proof" in physics. But, of course, there are many simpler matters in physics that can be proven and about which all competent physicists agree. Similarly, in ethics, there are many matters far simpler than abortion, about which all reasonable people must agree.

Second, it is easy to confuse two matters that are really very different:

1. Proving an opinion to be correct
2. Persuading someone to accept your proof

Suppose you are discussing a moral issue with a friend. You have perfectly cogent reasons in support of your position, while he has no good reasons on his side. Still, he refuses to accept your logic and continues to insist that he is right. This is a common, if frustrating, experience. You may be tempted to conclude that it is impossible to prove you are right. But this would be a mistake. Your proof may be impeccable; the trouble may be that your friend is being stubborn. (Of course, that is not the *only* possible explanation of what is going on, but it is one possible explanation.) The same thing can happen in any sort of discussion. You may be arguing about intelligent design versus evolution, and the other person may be unreasonable. But that does not necessarily mean that something is wrong with your arguments. Something may be wrong with the other person.

CONCLUSION

We have examined two of the most important arguments in support of Moral Skepticism and seen that these arguments are no good. Moral Skepticism might still turn out to be true, but if so, then other, better arguments will have to be found. Provisionally, at least, we have to conclude that Moral Skepticism is not nearly as plausible as we might have thought.

The purpose of this exercise, however, was to illustrate the process of evaluating philosophical arguments. We may summarize the main points like this:

1. Arguments are offered to provide support for a theory or idea; a philosophical theory may be regarded as acceptable only if there are sound arguments in its favor.
2. An argument is sound only if its premises are true and the conclusion follows logically from them.
   (a) A conclusion "follows from" the premises just in case the following is so: *If* the premises were true, then the conclusion would have to be true also. (An alternative way of saying the same thing: A conclusion follows from the premises just in case it is impossible for the premises to be true and the conclusion false at the same time.)
   (b) A conclusion can follow from premises even if those premises are in fact false.
   (c) A conclusion can be true and yet not follow from a given set of premises.
3. Therefore, in evaluating an argument, we ask two *separate* questions: Are the premises true? and Does the conclusion follow from them?
4. It is important to avoid two common mistakes. We should be careful to keep arguments separate, and not slide from one to the other, thereby confusing different issues. And, we should not think an argument stronger than it is simply because we happen to agree with its conclusion. Moreover, we should remember that, if an argument is unsound, that does not mean the conclusion must be false—it only means that *this* argument does nothing to show that the conclusion is true.

IS MORALITY OBJECTIVE?

Chapter 3

The Subjectivity of Values

J. L. Mackie

Everyone agrees that ethics is subjective in the sense that people have their own personal moral beliefs, and that those beliefs differ. But in this selection, John L. Mackie contends that ethics is subjective in a much more radical sense—that, really, there is no right or wrong.

Consider this analogy: The earth is round (or spherical), and not flat, because there is this thing—the earth—that has the property of being round. But when someone says abortion is wrong, according to Mackie, there can be no property of wrongness that inheres in abortion in analogy to how roundness adheres in the earth; there is just the feeling, or belief, that abortion is wrong.

In Mackie's view, the belief that Abraham Lincoln is morally better than John Wilkes Booth is similar to the cartoon character Homer Simpson's belief that syrup is better than jelly. Homer might like syrup more than jelly, but he's not "right" in feeling that way. Similarly, Mackie thinks, you might approve of the president who freed the slaves more than you approve of the man who shot him, but you are not "right" in feeling that way. It's just how you feel.

John L. Mackie (1917–1981) was born in Australia and taught at the University of Oxford. This selection is from his book *Ethics: Inventing Right and Wrong* (1977).

MORAL SCEPTICISM

There are no objective values. This is a bald statement of the thesis of this chapter, but before arguing for it I shall try to clarify and restrict it in ways that may meet some objections and prevent some misunderstanding.

The statement of this thesis is liable to provoke one of three very different reactions. Some will think it not merely false but pernicious; they will see it as a threat to morality and to everything else that is worthwhile, and they will find the presenting of such a thesis in what purports to be a book on ethics paradoxical or even outrageous. Others will regard it as a trivial truth, almost too obvious to be worth mentioning, and certainly too plain to be worth much argument. Others again will say that it is meaningless or empty, that no real issue is raised by the question whether values are or are not part of the fabric of the world. But, precisely because there can be these three different reactions, much more needs to be said.

The claim that values are not objective, are not part of the fabric of the world, is meant to include not only moral goodness, which might be most naturally equated with moral value, but also other things that could be more loosely called moral values or disvalues—rightness and wrongness, duty, obligation, an action's being rotten and contemptible, and so on. It also includes non-moral values, notably aesthetic ones, beauty and various kinds of artistic merit. I shall not discuss these explicitly, but clearly much the same considerations apply to aesthetic and to moral values, and there would be at least some initial implausibility in a view that gave the one a different status from the other.

Since it is with moral values that I am primarily concerned, the view I am adopting may be called moral scepticism. But this name is likely to be misunderstood: "moral scepticism" might also be used as a name for either of two first order views, or perhaps for an incoherent mixture of the two. A moral sceptic might be the sort of person who says "All this talk of morality is tripe," who rejects morality and will take no notice of it. Such a person may be literally rejecting all moral judgements; he is more likely to be making moral judgements of his own, expressing a positive moral condemnation of all that conventionally passes for morality; or he may be confusing these two logically incompatible views, and saying that he rejects all morality, while he is in fact reject-ing only a particular morality that is current in the society in which he has grown up. But I am not at present concerned with the merits or faults of such a position. These are first order moral views, positive or negative: the person who adopts either of them is taking a certain prac-tical, normative, stand. By contrast, what I am discussing is a second order view, a view about the status of moral values and the nature of moral valuing, about where and how they fit into the world. These first and second order views are not merely distinct but completely indepen-dent: one could be a second order moral sceptic without being a first order one, or again the other way round. A man could hold strong moral views, and indeed ones whose content was thoroughly conventional, while believing that they were simply attitudes and policies with regard to conduct that he and other people held. Conversely, a man could reject all established morality while believing it to be an objective truth that it was evil or corrupt.

With another sort of misunderstanding moral scepticism would seem not so much pernicious as absurd. How could anyone deny that there is a difference between a kind action and a cruel one, or that a coward and a brave man behave differently in the face of danger? Of course, this is undeniable; but it is not to the point. The kinds of behaviour to which moral values and disvalues are ascribed are indeed part of the furniture of the world, and so are the natural, descriptive, differences between them; but not, perhaps, their differences in value. It is a hard fact that cruel actions differ from kind ones, and hence that we can learn, as in fact we all do, to distinguish them fairly well in practice, and to use the words "cruel" and "kind" with fairly clear descriptive meanings; but is it an equally hard fact that actions which are cruel in such a descrip-tive sense are to be condemned? The present issue is with regard to the objectivity specifically of value, not with regard to the objectivity of those natural, factual, differences on the basis of which differing values are assigned. . . .

STANDARDS OF EVALUATION

One way of stating the thesis that there are no objective values is to say that value statements cannot be either true or false. But this formulation, too, lends itself to misinterpretation. For there are certain kinds of value statements which undoubtedly can be true or false, even if, in the sense I intend, there are no objective values. Evaluations of many sorts are commonly made in relation to agreed and assumed standards. The classing of wool, the grading of apples, the awarding of prizes at sheepdog trials, flower shows, skating and diving championships, and even the marking of examination papers are carried out in relation to standards of quality or merit which are peculiar to each particular subject-matter or type of contest, which may be explicitly laid down but which, even if they are nowhere explicitly stated, are fairly well understood and agreed upon by those who are recognized as judges or experts in each particular field. Given any sufficiently determinate standards, it will be an objective issue, a matter of truth and falsehood, how well any particular specimen measures up to those standards. Comparative judgements in particular will be capable of truth and falsehood: it will be a factual question whether this sheepdog has performed better than that one.

The subjectivist about values, then, is not denying that there can be objective evaluations relative to standards, and these are as possible in the aesthetic and moral fields as in any of those just mentioned. More than this, there is an objective distinction which applies in many such fields, and yet would itself be regarded as a peculiarly moral one: the distinction between justice and injustice. In one important sense of the word it is a paradigm case of injustice if a court declares someone to be guilty of an offence of which it knows him to be innocent. More generally, a finding is unjust if it is at variance with what the relevant law and the facts together require, and particularly if it is known by the court to be so. More generally still, any award of marks, prizes, or the like is unjust if it is at variance with the agreed standards for the contest in question: if one diver's performance in fact measures up better to the accepted standards for diving than another's, it will be unjust if the latter is awarded higher marks or the prize. In this way the justice or injustice of decisions relative to standards can be a thoroughly objective matter, though there may still be a subjective element in the interpretation or application of standards. But the statement that a certain decision is thus just or unjust will not be objectively prescriptive: in so far as it can be simply true it leaves open the question whether there is any objective requirement to do what is just and to refrain from what is unjust, and equally leaves open the practical decision to act in either way.

Recognizing the objectivity of justice in relation to standards, and of evaluative judgements relative to standards, then, merely shifts the question of the objectivity of values back to the standards themselves. The subjectivist may try to make his point by insisting that there is no objective validity about the choice of standards. Yet he would clearly be wrong if he said that the choice of even the most basic standards in any field was completely arbitrary. The standards used in sheepdog trials clearly bear some relation to the work that sheepdogs are kept to do, the standards for grading apples bear some relation to what people generally want in or like about apples, and so on. On the other hand, standards are not as a rule strictly validated by such purposes. The appropriateness of standards is neither fully determinate nor totally indeterminate in relation to independently specifiable aims or desires. But however determinate it is, the objective appropriateness of standards in relation to aims or desires is no more of a threat to the denial of objective values than is the objectivity of evaluation relative to standards. In fact it is logically no different from the objectivity of goodness relative to desires. Something may be called good simply in so far as it satisfies or is such as to satisfy a certain desire; but the objectivity of such relations of satisfaction does not constitute in our sense an objective value.

HYPOTHETICAL AND CATEGORICAL IMPERATIVES

We may make this issue clearer by referring to Kant's distinction between hypothetical and categorical imperatives, though what he called imperatives are more naturally expressed as "ought" statements than in the imperative mood. "If you want X, do Y" (or "You ought to do Y") will be a hypothetical imperative if it is based on the supposed fact that Y is, in the circumstances, the only (or the best) available means to X, that is, on a causal relation between Y and X. The reason for doing Y lies in its causal connection with the desired end, X; the oughtness is contingent upon the desire. But "You ought to do Y" will be a categorical imperative if you ought to do Y irrespective of any such desire for any end to which *Y* would contribute, if the oughtness is not thus contingent upon any desire.

A categorical imperative, then, would express a reason for acting which was unconditional in the sense of not being contingent upon any present desire of the agent to whose satisfaction the recommended action would contribute as a means—or more directly: "You ought to dance," if the implied reason is just that you want to dance or like dancing, is still a hypothetical imperative. Now Kant himself held that moral judgements are categorical imperatives, or perhaps are all applications of one categorical imperative, and it can plausibly be maintained at least that many moral judgements contain a categorically imperative element. So far as ethics is concerned, my thesis that there are no objective values is specifically the denial that any such categorically imperative element is objectively valid. The objective values which I am denying would be action-directing absolutely, not contingently (in the way indicated) upon the agent's desires and inclinations.

Another way of trying to clarify this issue is to refer to moral reasoning or moral arguments. In practice, of course, such reasoning is seldom fully explicit: but let us suppose that we could make explicit the reasoning that supports some evaluative conclusion, where this conclusion has some action-guiding force that is not contingent upon desires or purposes or chosen ends. Then what I am saying is that somewhere in the input to this argument—perhaps in one or more of the premises, perhaps in some part of the form of the argument—there will be something which cannot be objectively validated—some premiss which is not capable of being simply true, or some form of argument which is not valid as a matter of general logic, whose authority or cogency is not objective, but is constituted by our choosing or deciding to think in a certain way.

THE CLAIM TO OBJECTIVITY

If I have succeeded in specifying precisely enough the moral values whose objectivity I am denying, my thesis may now seem to be trivially true. Of course, some will say, valuing, preferring, choosing, recommending, rejecting, condemning, and so on, are human activities, and there is no need to look for values that are prior to and logically independent of all such activities. There may be widespread agreement in valuing, and particular value-judgements are not in general arbitrary or isolated: they typically cohere with others, or can be criticized if they do not, reasons can be given for them, and so on: but if all that the subjectivist is maintaining is that desires, ends, purposes, and the like figure somewhere in the system of reasons, and that no ends or purposes are objective as opposed to being merely intersubjective, then this may be conceded without much fuss.

But I do not think that this should be conceded so easily. As I have said, the main tradition of European moral philosophy includes the contrary claim, that there are objective values of just the sort I have denied. . . . Kant in particular holds that the categorical imperative is not only categorical and imperative but objectively so: though a rational being gives the moral law to himself, the law that he thus makes is determinate and necessary. Aristotle begins the *Nicomachean Ethics* by saying that the good is that at which all things aim, and that ethics is part of a science which he calls "politics," whose goal is not knowledge but practice; yet he does not doubt that there can be *knowledge* of what is the good for man, nor, once he has identified this as well-being or happiness, *eudaimonia*, that it can be known, rationally determined, in what happiness consists; and it is plain that he thinks that this happiness is intrinsically desirable, not good simply because it is desired. . . . Even the sentimentalist Hutcheson defines moral goodness as "some quality apprehended in actions, which procures approbation, . . ." while saying that the moral sense by which we perceive virtue and vice has been given to us (by the Author of nature) to direct our actions. Hume indeed was on the other side, but he is still a witness to the dominance of the objectivist tradition, since he claims that when we "see that the distinction of vice and virtue is not founded merely on the relations of objects, nor is perceiv'd by reason," this "wou'd subvert all the vulgar systems of morality." . . .

The prevalence of this tendency to objectify values—and not only moral ones—is confirmed by a pattern of thinking that we find in existentialists and those influenced by them. The denial of objective values can carry with it an extreme emotional reaction, a feeling that nothing matters at all, that life has lost its purpose. Of course this does not follow; the lack of objective values is not a good reason for abandoning subjective concern or for ceasing to want anything. But the abandonment of a belief in objective values can cause, at least temporarily, a decay of subjective concern and sense of purpose. That it does so is evidence that the people in whom this reaction occurs have been tending to objectify their concerns and purposes, have been giving them a fictitious external authority. A claim to objectivity has been so strongly associated with their subjective concerns and purposes that the collapse of the former seems to undermine the latter as well.

This view, that conceptual analysis would reveal a claim to objectivity, is sometimes dramatically confirmed by philosophers who are officially on the other side. Bertrand Russell, for example, says that "ethical propositions should be expressed [as desires]"; he defends himself effectively against the charge of inconsistency in both holding ultimate ethical valuations to be subjective and expressing emphatic opinions on ethical questions. Yet at the end he admits:

> Certainly there *seems* to be something more. Suppose, for example, that someone were to advocate the introduction of bullfighting in this country. In opposing the proposal, I should *feel*, not only that I was expressing my desires, but that my desires in the matter are *right*, whatever that may mean. As a matter of argument, I can, I think, show that I am not guilty of any logical inconsistency in holding to the above interpretation of ethics and at the same time expressing strong ethical preferences. But in feeling I am not satisfied.

But he concludes, reasonably enough, with the remark: "I can only say that, while my own opinions as to ethics do not satisfy me, other people's satisfy me still less."

I conclude, then, that ordinary moral judgements include a claim to objectivity, an assumption that there are objective values in just the sense in which I am concerned to deny this. And I do not think it is going too far to say that this assumption has been incorporated in the basic, conventional, meanings of moral terms. Any analysis of the meanings of moral terms which omits this claim to objective, intrinsic, prescriptivity is to that extent incomplete. . . .

If second order ethics were confined, then, to linguistic and conceptual analysis, it ought to conclude that moral values at least are objective: that they are so is part of what our ordinary moral statements mean: the traditional moral concepts of the ordinary man as well as of the main line of Western philosophers are concepts of objective value.

But it is precisely for this reason that linguistic and conceptual analysis is not enough. The claim to objectivity, however ingrained in our language and thought, is not self-validating. It can and should be questioned. But the denial of objective values will have to be put forward not as the result of an analytic approach, but as an "error theory," a theory that although most people in making moral judgements implicitly claim, among other things, to be pointing to something objectively prescriptive, these claims are all false. It is this that makes the name "moral scepticism" appropriate.

But since this is an error theory, since it goes against assumptions ingrained in our thought and built into some of the ways in which language is used, since it conflicts with what is sometimes called common sense, it needs very solid support. It is not something we can accept lightly or casually and then quietly pass on. If we are to adopt this view, we must argue explicitly for it. Traditionally it has been supported by arguments of two main kinds, which I shall call the argument from relativity and the argument from queerness, but these can, as I shall show, be supplemented in several ways.

THE ARGUMENT FROM RELATIVITY

The argument from relativity has as its premiss the well-known variation in moral codes from one society to another and from one period to another, and also the differences in moral beliefs between different groups and classes within a complex community. Such variation is in itself merely a truth of descriptive morality, a fact of anthropology which entails neither first order nor second order ethical views. Yet it may indirectly support second order subjectivism: radical differences between first order moral judgements make it difficult to treat those judgements as apprehensions of objective truths. But it is not the mere occurrence of disagreements that tells against the objectivity of values. Disagreement on questions in history or biology or cosmology does not show that there are no objective issues in these fields for investigators to disagree about. But such scientific disagreement results from speculative inferences or explanatory hypotheses based on inadequate evidence, and it is hardly plausible to interpret moral disagreement in the same way. Disagreement about moral codes seems to reflect people's adherence to and participation in different ways of life. The causal connection seems to be mainly that way round: it is that people approve of monogamy because they participate in a monogamous way of life rather than that they participate in a monogamous way of life because they approve of monogamy. Of course, the standards may be an idealization of the way of life from which they arise: the monogamy in which people participate may be less complete, less rigid, than that of which it leads them to approve. This is not to say that moral judgements are purely conventional. Of course there have been and are moral heretics and moral reformers, people who have turned against the established rules and practices of their own communities for moral reasons, and often for moral reasons that we would endorse. But this can usually be understood as the extension, in ways which, though new and unconventional, seemed to them to be required for consistency, of rules to which they already adhered as arising out of an existing way of life. In short, the argument from relativity has some force simply because the actual variations in the moral codes are more readily explained by the hypothesis that they reflect ways of life than by the hypothesis that they express perceptions, most of them seriously inadequate and badly distorted, of objective values.

But there is a well-known counter to this argument from relativity; namely to say that the items for which objective validity is in the first place to be claimed are not specific moral rules or codes but very general basic principles which are recognized at least implicitly to some extent in all society—such principles provide the foundations of what Sidgwick has called different methods of ethics: the principle of universalizability, perhaps, or the rule that one ought to conform to the specific rules of any way of life in which one takes part, from which one profits, and on which one relies, or some utilitarian principle of doing what tends, or seems likely, to promote the general happiness. It is easy to show that such general principles, married with differing concrete circumstances, different existing social patterns or different preferences, will beget different specific moral rules; and there is some plausibility in the claim that the specific rules thus generated will vary from community to community or from group to group in close agreement with the actual variations in accepted codes.

The argument from relativity can be only partly countered in this way. To take this line the moral objectivist has to say that it is only in these principles that the objective moral character attaches immediately to its descriptively specified ground or subject: other moral judgements are objectively valid or true, but only derivatively and contingently—if things had been otherwise, quite different sorts of actions would have been right. And despite the prominence in recent philosophical ethics of universalization, utilitarian principles, and the like, these are very far from constituting the whole of what is actually affirmed as basic in ordinary moral thought. Much of this is concerned rather with what Hare calls "ideals" or, less kindly, "fanaticism." That is, people judge that some things are good or right, and others are bad or wrong, not because—or at any rate not only because—they exemplify some general principle for which widespread implicit acceptance could be claimed, but because something about those things arouses certain responses immediately in them, though they would arouse radically and irresolvably different responses in others. "Moral sense" or "intuition" is an initially more plausible description of what supplies many of our basic moral judgements than "reason." With regard to all these starting points of moral thinking the argument from relativity remains in full force.

THE ARGUMENT FROM QUEERNESS

Even more important, however, and certainly more generally applicable, is the argument from queerness. This has two parts, one metaphysical, the other epistemological. If there were objective values, then they would be entities or qualities or relations of a very strange sort, utterly different from anything else in the universe. Correspondingly, if we were aware of them, it would have to be by some special faculty of moral perception or intuition, utterly different from our ordinary ways of knowing everything else. These points were recognized by Moore when he spoke of non-natural qualities, and by the intuitionists in their talk about a "faculty of moral intuition." Intuitionism has long been out of favour, and it is indeed easy to point out its implausibilities. What is not so often stressed, but is more important, is that the central thesis of intuitionism is one to which any objectivist view of values is in the end committed: intuitionism merely makes unpalatably plain what other forms of objectivism wrap up. Of course the suggestion that moral judgements are made or moral problems solved by just sitting down and having an ethical intuition is a travesty of actual moral thinking. But, however complex the real process, it will require (if it is to yield authoritatively prescriptive conclusions) some input of this distinctive sort, either premises or forms of argument or both. When we ask the awkward question, how we can be aware of this authoritative prescriptivity, of the truth of these distinctively ethical premises or of the cogency of this distinctively ethical pattern of reasoning, none of our ordinary accounts of sensory perception or introspection or the framing and confirming of explanatory hypotheses or inference or logical construction or conceptual analysis, or any combination of these, will provide a satisfactory answer; "a special sort of intuition" is a lame answer, but it is the one to which the clearheaded objectivist is compelled to resort.

Indeed, the best move for the moral objectivist is not to evade this issue, but to look for companions in guilt. For example, Richard Price argues that it is not moral knowledge alone that such an empiricism as those of Locke and Hume is unable to account for, but also our knowledge and even our ideas of essence, number, identity, diversity, solidity, inertia, substance, the necessary existence and infinite extension of time and space, necessity and possibility in general, power, and causation. If the understanding, which Price defines as the faculty within us that discerns truth, is also a source of new simple ideas of so many other sorts, may it not also be a power of immediately perceiving right and wrong, which yet are real characters of actions?

This is an important counter to the argument from queerness. The only adequate reply to it would be to show how, on empiricist foundations, we can construct an account of the ideas and beliefs and knowledge that we have of all these matters. I cannot even begin to do that here, though I have undertaken some parts of the task elsewhere. I can only state my belief that satisfactory accounts of most of these can be given in empirical terms. If some supposed metaphysical necessities or essences resist such treatment, then they too should be included, along with objective values, among the targets of the argument from queerness. . . .

Plato's Forms give a dramatic picture of what objective values would have to be. The Form of the Good is such that knowledge of it provides the knower with both a direction and an overriding motive; something's being good both tells the person who knows this to pursue it and makes him pursue it. An objective good would be sought by anyone who was acquainted with it, not because of any contingent fact that this person, or every person, is so constituted that he desires this end, but just because the end has to-be-pursuedness somehow built into it. Similarly, if there were objective principles of right and wrong, any wrong (possible) course of action would have not-to-be-doneness somehow built into it. Or we should have something like Clarke's necessary relations of fitness between situations and actions, so that a situation would have a demand for such-and-such an action somehow built into it. . . .

Another way of bringing out this queerness is to ask, about anything that is supposed to have some objective moral quality, how this is linked with its natural features. What is the connection between the natural fact that an action is a piece of deliberate cruelty—say, causing pain just for fun—and the moral fact that it is wrong? It cannot be an entailment, a logical or semantic necessity. Yet it is not merely that the two features occur together. The wrongness must somehow be "consequential" or "supervenient"; it is wrong because it is a piece of deliberate cruelty. But just what *in the world* is signified by this "because"? And how do we know the relation that it signifies, if this is something more than such actions being socially condemned, and condemned by us too, perhaps through our having absorbed attitudes from our social environment? It is not even sufficient to postulate a faculty which "sees" the wrongness: something must be postulated which can see at once the natural features that constitute the cruelty, and the wrongness, and the mysterious consequential link between the two. Alternatively, the intuition required might be the perception that wrongness is a higher order property belonging to certain natural properties; but what is this belonging of properties to other properties, and how can we discern it? How much simpler and more comprehensible the situation would be if we could replace the moral quality with some sort of subjective response which could be causally related to the detection of the natural features on which the supposed quality is said to be consequential.

Chapter 4

Our Sense of Right and Wrong

C. S. Lewis

C. S. Lewis (1898–1963), a beloved defender of Christian faith, argued that in grasping the moral law we understand something about what the world is really like. The world is not the cold, impersonal place pictured by science; rather, it includes the moral standards that bind all human beings together.

Lewis wrote dozens of books, mostly novels and short stories. His more philosophical works include *The Problem of Pain* (1940), *Surprised by Joy* (1955), and *Mere Christianity* (1952), from which this selection is taken.

THE LAW OF HUMAN NATURE

Every one has heard people quarrelling. Sometimes it sounds funny and sometimes it sounds merely unpleasant; but however it sounds, I believe we can learn something very important from listening to the kind of things they say. They say things like this: "How'd you like it if anyone did the same to you?"—"That's my seat, I was there first"—"Leave him alone, he isn't doing you any harm"—"Why should you shove in first?"—"Give me a bit of your orange, I gave you a bit of

C. S. Lewis, *Mere Christianity* (New York: HarperCollins Publishers, 1952). Copyright © C. S. Lewis Pte. Ltd. 1942, 1943, 1944, 1952.

mine"—"Come on, you promised." People say things like that every day, educated people as well as uneducated, and children as well as grown-ups.

Now what interests me about all these remarks is that the man who makes them is not merely saying that the other man's behavior does not happen to please him. He is appealing to some kind of standard of behavior which he expects the other man to know about. And the other man very seldom replies: "To hell with your standard." Nearly always he tries to make out that what he has been doing does not really go against the standard, or that if it does there is some special excuse. He pretends there is some special reason in this particular case why the person who took the seat first should not keep it, or that things were quite different when he was given the bit of orange, or that something has turned up which lets him off keeping his promise. It looks, in fact, very much as if both parties had in mind some kind of Law or Rule of fair play or decent behavior or morality or whatever you like to call it, about which they really agreed. And they have. If they had not, they might, of course, fight like animals, but they could not quarrel in the human sense of the word. Quarrelling means trying to show that the other man is in the wrong. And there would be no sense in trying to do that unless you and he had some sort of agreement as to what Right and Wrong are; just as there would be no sense in saying that a footballer had committed a foul unless there was some agreement about the rules of football.

Now this Law or Rule about Right and Wrong used to be called the Law of Nature. Nowadays, when we talk of the "laws of nature" we usually mean things like gravitation, or heredity, or the laws of chemistry. But when the older thinkers called the Law of Right and Wrong "the Law of Nature," they really meant the Law of Human Nature. The idea was that, just as all bodies are governed by the law of gravitation, and organisms by biological laws, so the creature called man also had his law—with this great difference, that a body could not choose whether it obeyed the law of gravitation or not, but a man could choose either to obey the Law of Human Nature or to disobey it.

We may put this in another way. Each man is at every moment subjected to several different sets of law but there is only one of these which he is free to disobey. As a body, he is subjected to gravitation and cannot disobey it; if you leave him unsupported in mid-air, he has no more choice about falling than a stone has. As an organism, he is subjected to various biological laws which he cannot disobey any more than an animal can. That is, he cannot disobey those laws which he shares with other things; but the law which is peculiar to his human nature, the law he does not share with animals or vegetables or inorganic things, is the one he can disobey if he chooses.

This law was called the Law of Nature because people thought that every one knew it by nature and did not need to be taught it. They did not mean, of course, that you might not find an odd individual here and there who did not know it, just as you find a few people who are color-blind or have no ear for a tune. But taking the race as a whole, they thought that the human idea of decent behavior was obvious to every one. And I believe they were right. If they were not, then all the things we said about the war were nonsense. What was the sense in saying the enemy were in the wrong unless Right is a real thing which the Nazis at bottom knew as well as we did and ought to have practiced? If they had had no notion of what we mean by right, then, though we might still have had to fight them, we could no more have blamed them for that than for the color of their hair.

I know that some people say the idea of a Law of Nature or decent behavior known to all men is unsound, because different civilizations and different ages have had quite different moralities.

But this is not true. There have been differences between their moralities, but these have never amounted to anything like a total difference. If anyone will take the trouble to compare the moral teaching of, say, the ancient Egyptians, Babylonians, Hindus, Chinese, Greeks and Romans, what will really strike him will be how very like they are to each other and to our own. Some of the evidence for this I have put together in the appendix of another book called *The Abolition of Man*; but for our present purpose I need only ask the reader to think what a totally different morality would mean. Think of a country where people were admired for running away in battle, or where a man felt proud of double-crossing all the people who had been kindest to him. You might just as well try to imagine a country where two and two made five. Men have differed as regards to what people you ought to be unselfish to—whether it was only your own family, or your fellow countrymen, or every one. But they have always agreed that you ought not to put yourself first. Selfishness has never been admired. Men have differed as to whether you should have one wife or four. But they have always agreed that you must not simply have any woman you liked.

But the most remarkable thing is this. Whenever you find a man who says he does not believe in a real Right and Wrong, you will find the same man going back on this a moment later. He may break his promise to you, but if you try breaking one to him he will be complaining "It's not fair" before you can say Jack Robinson. A nation may say treaties don't matter; but then, next minute, they spoil their case by saying that the particular treaty they want to break was an unfair one. But if treaties do not matter, and if there is no such thing as Right and Wrong—in other words, if there is no Law of Nature—what is the difference between a fair treaty and an unfair one? Have they not let the cat out of the bag and shown that, whatever they say, they really know the Law of Nature just like anyone else?

It seems, then, we are forced to believe in a real Right and Wrong. People may be sometimes mistaken about them, just as people sometimes get their sums wrong; but they are not a matter of mere taste and opinion any more than the multiplication table. Now if we are agreed about that, I go on to my next point, which is this. None of us are really keeping the Law of Nature. If there are any exceptions among you, I apologize to them. They had much better read some other book, for nothing I am going to say concerns them. And now, turning to the ordinary human beings who are left:

I hope you will not misunderstand what I am going to say. I am not preaching, and Heaven knows I do not pretend to be better than anyone else. I am only trying to call attention to a fact; the fact that this year, or this month, or, more likely, this very day, we have failed to practice ourselves the kind of behavior we expect from other people. There may be all sorts of excuses for us. That time you were so unfair to the children was when you were very tired. That slightly shady business about the money—the one you have almost forgotten—came when you were very hard-up. And what you promised to do for old so-and-so and have never done—well, you never would have promised if you had known how frightfully busy you were going to be. And as for your behavior to your wife (or husband) or sister (or brother) if I knew how irritating they could be, I would not wonder at it—and who the dickens am I, anyway? I am just the same. That is to say, I do not succeed in keeping the Law of Nature very well, and the moment anyone tells me I am not keeping it, there starts up in my mind a string of excuses as long as your arm. The question at the moment is not whether they are good excuses. The point is that they are one more proof of how deeply, whether we like it or not, we believe in the Law of Nature. If we do not believe in decent behavior, why should we be so anxious to make excuses for not having behaved decently? The truth is, we believe in decency so much—we feel the Rule of Law pressing on us so—that we cannot bear to face the fact that we are breaking it, and consequently we try to shift the responsibility. For you notice that it is only for our bad behavior that we find all these explanations. It is only our bad temper that we put down to being tired or worried or hungry; we put our good temper down to ourselves.

These, then, are the two points I wanted to make. First, that human beings, all over the earth, have this curious idea that they ought to behave in a certain way, and cannot really get rid of it. Secondly, that they do not in fact behave in that way. They know the Law of Nature; they break it. These two facts are the foundation of all clear thinking about ourselves and the universe we live in.

THEORETICAL ESSAYS

Chapter 5

Utilitarianism

John Stuart Mill

In the history of moral philosophy, the name of John Stuart Mill (1806–1873) is inevitably linked with that of Jeremy Bentham (1748–1832). Few philosophers have combined theory and practice as successfully as Bentham. A wealthy Londoner, he studied law but never practiced, instead devoting himself to writing and working for social reform. He became the leader of a group of philosophical radicals known as the Benthamites, who campaigned for causes like prison reform and restrictions on the use of child labor. Bentham was an effective member of the British establishment; almost all of the Benthamites' legislative proposals eventually became law.

Bentham was convinced that both law and morals must be based on a realistic, non-supernatural conception of human beings. The first sentence of his greatest work, *The Principles of Morals and Legislation*, declares: "Nature has placed mankind under the governance of two sovereign masters, *pain* and *pleasure*." Some things give us pleasure, and others cause us pain. This explains why we behave as we do—we seek pleasure and avoid pain—and also why we judge some things to be good and other things to be bad. Therefore, he reasoned, morality must consist in trying to bring about as much pleasure as possible, while striving to minimize pain. This moral principle, the Principle of Utility, requires us to always choose the action or social policy that provides the most happiness for all.

From John Stuart Mill, *Utilitarianism* (1861).

One of Bentham's followers was James Mill, a distinguished Scottish philosopher, historian, and economist. James Mill's son, John Stuart, would become the leading advocate of utilitarianism for the next generation. James Mill, in fact, educated his son with this in mind. He had the boy studying Greek and Latin at age three and, by age thirteen, John Stuart was already mastering the blend of subjects that the British call "political economy." He was twenty-six when Bentham died, and he knew the older man well. He was not, however, a mere follower of the master. Mill became more accomplished than Bentham, contributing to subjects that Bentham barely knew, such as the philosophy of science and the foundations of mathematical knowledge.

Unlike Bentham, the Mills were not wealthy, and John Stuart earned his living in the office of the East India Company, as had his father. In 1830, he met and fell in love with Harriet Taylor, who, alas, was married with three children. Harriet was faithful to her husband until he died in 1849. Two years later, she and Mill married. With Harriet as his partner, Mill became a leader in the women's rights movement, publishing *The Subjection of Women* in 1869.

The following excerpts are from Mill's book *Utilitarianism*, in which he develops some of the basic ideas of utilitarian moral theory.

II. WHAT UTILITARIANISM IS

The creed which accepts as the foundation of morals, Utility, or the Greatest Happiness Principle, holds that actions are right in proportion as they tend to promote happiness, wrong as they tend to produce the reverse of happiness. By happiness is intended pleasure, and the absence of pain; by unhappiness, pain, and the privation of pleasure. To give a clear view of the moral standard set up by the theory, much more requires to be said; in particular, what things it includes in the ideas of pain and pleasure; and to what extent this is left an open question. But these supplementary explanations do not affect the theory of life on which this theory of morality is grounded—namely, that pleasure, and freedom from pain, are the only things desirable as ends; and that all desirable things (which are as numerous in the utilitarian as in any other scheme) are desirable either for the pleasure inherent in themselves, or as means to the promotion of pleasure and the prevention of pain.

Now, such a theory of life excites in many minds, and among them in some of the most estimable in feeling and purpose, inveterate dislike. To suppose that life has (as they express it) no higher end than pleasure—no better and nobler object of desire and pursuit—they designate as utterly mean and grovelling; as a doctrine worthy only of swine, to whom the followers of Epicurus were, at a very early period, contemptuously likened; and modern holders of the doctrine are occasionally made the subject of equally polite comparisons by its German, French, and English assailants.

When thus attacked, the Epicureans have always answered, that it is not they, but their accusers, who represent human nature in a degrading light; since the accusation supposes human beings to be capable of no pleasures except those of which swine are capable. If this supposition were true, the charge could not be gainsaid, but would then be no longer an imputation; for if the sources of pleasure were precisely the same to human beings and to swine, the rule of life which is good enough for the one would be good enough for the other. The comparison of the Epicurean life to that of beasts is felt as degrading, precisely because a beast's pleasures do not satisfy a human being's conceptions of happiness. Human beings have faculties more elevated than the animal appetites, and when once made conscious of them, do not regard anything as happiness which does not include their gratification. I do not, indeed, consider the Epicureans to have been by any means faultless in drawing out their scheme of consequences from the utilitarian principle. To do this in any sufficient manner, many Stoic, as well as Christian elements require to be included. But there is no known Epicurean theory of life which does not assign to the pleasures of the intellect, of the feelings and imagination, and of the moral sentiments, a much higher value as pleasures than to those of mere sensation. It must be admitted, however, that utilitarian writers in general have placed the superiority of mental over bodily pleasures chiefly in the greater permanency, safety, uncostliness, etc. of the former—that is, in their circumstantial advantages rather than in their intrinsic nature. And on all these points utilitarians have fully proved their case; but they might have taken the other, and, as it may be called, higher ground, with entire consistency. It is quite compatible with the principle of utility to recognise the fact, that some *kinds* of pleasure are more desirable and more valuable than others. It would be absurd that while, in estimating all other things, quality is considered as well as quantity, the estimation of pleasures should be supposed to depend on quantity alone.

If I am asked, what I mean by difference of quality in pleasures, or what makes one pleasure more valuable than another, merely as a pleasure, except its being greater in amount, there is but one possible answer. Of two pleasures, if there be one to which all or almost all who have experience of both give a decided preference, irrespective of any feeling of moral obligation to prefer it, that is the more desirable pleasure. If one of the two is, by those who are competently acquainted with both, placed so far above the other that they prefer it, even though knowing it to be attended with a greater amount of discontent, and would not resign it for any quantity of the other pleasure which their nature is capable of, we are justified in ascribing to the preferred enjoyment a superiority in quality, so far outweighing quantity as to render it, in comparison, of small account.

Now it is an unquestionable fact that those who are equally acquainted with, and equally capable of appreciating and enjoying, both, do give a most marked preference to the manner of existence which employs their higher faculties. Few human creatures would consent to be changed into any of the lower animals, for a promise of the fullest allowance of a beast's pleasures; no intelligent human being would consent to be a fool, no instructed person would be an ignoramus, no person of feeling and conscience would be selfish and base, even though they should be persuaded that the fool, the dunce, or the rascal is better satisfied with his lot than they are with theirs. They would not resign what they possess more than he, for the most complete satisfaction of all the desires which they have in common with him. If they ever fancy they would, it is only in cases of unhappiness so extreme, that to escape from it they would exchange their lot for almost any other, however undesirable in their own eyes. A being of higher faculties requires more to make him happy, is capable probably of more acute suffering, and is certainly accessible to it at more points, than one of an inferior type; but in spite of these liabilities, he can never really wish to sink into what he feels to be a lower grade of existence. We may give what explanation we please of this unwillingness; we may attribute it to pride, a name which is given indiscriminately to some of the most and to some of the least estimable feelings of which mankind are capable; we may refer it to the love of liberty and personal independence, an appeal to which was with the Stoics one of the most effective means for the inculcation of it; to the love of power, or to the love of excitement, both of which do really enter into and contribute to it: but its most appropriate appellation is a sense of dignity, which all human beings possess in one form or other, and in some, though by no means in exact, proportion to their higher faculties, and which is so essential a part of the happiness of those in whom it is strong, that nothing which conflicts with it could be, otherwise than momentarily, an object of desire to them. Whoever supposes that this preference takes place at a sacrifice of happiness—that the superior being, in anything like the equal circumstances, is not happier than the inferior—confounds the two very different ideas, of happiness, and content. It is indisputable that the being whose capacities of enjoyment are low, has the greatest chance of having them fully satisfied; and a highly endowed being will always feel that any happiness which he can look for, as the world is constituted, is imperfect. But he can learn to bear its imperfections, if they are at all bearable; and they will not make him envy the being who is indeed unconscious of the imperfections, but only because he feels not at all the good which those imperfections qualify. It is better to be a human being dissatisfied than a pig satisfied; better to be Socrates dissatisfied than a fool satisfied. And if the fool, or the pig, is of a different opinion, it is because they only know their own side of the question. The other party to the comparison knows both sides.

It may be objected, that many who are capable of the higher pleasures, occasionally, under the influence of temptation, postpone them to the lower. But this is quite compatible with a full appreciation of the intrinsic superiority of the higher. Men often, from infirmity of character, make their election for the nearer good, though they know it to be the less valuable; and this no less when the choice is between two bodily pleasures, than when it is between bodily and mental. They pursue sensual indulgences to the injury of health, though perfectly aware that health is the greater good. It may be further objected, that many who begin with youthful enthusiasm for everything noble, as they advance in years sink into indolence and selfishness. But I do not believe that those who undergo this very common change, voluntarily choose the lower description of pleasures in preference to the higher. I believe that before they devote themselves exclusively to the one, they have already become incapable of the other. Capacity for the nobler feelings is in most natures a very tender plant, easily killed, not only by hostile influences, but by mere want of sustenance; and in the majority of young persons it speedily dies away if the occupations to which their position in life has devoted them, and the society into which it has thrown them, are not favourable to keeping that higher capacity in exercise. Men lose their high aspirations as they lose their intellectual tastes, because they have not time or opportunity for indulging them; and they addict themselves to inferior pleasures, not because they deliberately prefer them, but because they are either the only ones to which they have access, or the only ones which they are any longer capable of enjoying. It may be questioned whether any one who has remained equally susceptible to both classes of pleasures, ever knowingly and calmly preferred the lower, though many, in all ages, have broken down in an ineffectual attempt to combine both.

From this verdict of the only competent judges, I apprehend there can be no appeal. On a question which is the best worth having of two pleasures, or which of two modes of existence is the most grateful to the feelings, apart from its moral attributes and from its consequences, the judgment of those who are qualified by knowledge of both, or, if they differ, that of the majority among them, must be admitted as final. And there needs be the less hesitation to accept this judgment respecting the quality of pleasures, since there is no other tribunal to be referred to even on the question of quantity. What means are there of determining which is the acutest of two pains, or the intensest of two pleasurable sensations, except the general suffrage of those who are familiar with both? Neither pains nor pleasures are homogeneous, and pain is always heterogeneous with pleasure. What is there to decide whether a particular pleasure is worth purchasing at the cost of a particular pain, except the feelings and judgment of the experienced? When, therefore, those feelings and judgment declare the pleasures derived from the higher faculties to be preferable *in kind*, apart from the question of intensity, to those of which the animal nature, disjoined from the higher faculties, is susceptible, they are entitled on this subject to the same regard.

I have dwelt on this point, as being a necessary part of a perfectly just conception of Utility or Happiness, considered as the directive rule of human conduct. But it is by no means an indispensable condition to the acceptance of the utilitarian standard; for that standard is not the agent's own greatest happiness, but the greatest amount of happiness altogether; and if it may possibly be doubted whether a noble character is always the happier for its nobleness, there can be no doubt that it makes other people happier, and that the world in general is immensely a gainer by it. Utilitarianism, therefore, could only attain its end by the general cultivation of nobleness of character, even if each individual were only benefitted by the nobleness of others, and his own, so far as happiness is concerned, were a sheer deduction from the benefit. But the bare enunciation of such an absurdity as this last, renders refutation superfluous.

According to the Greatest Happiness Principle, as above explained, the ultimate end, with reference to and for the sake of which all other things are desirable (whether we are considering our own good or that of other people), is an existence exempt as far as possible from pain, and as rich as possible in enjoyments, both in point of quantity and quality; the test of quality, and the rule for measuring it against quantity, being the preference felt by those who, in their opportunities of experience, to which must be added their habits of self-consciousness and self-observation, are best furnished with the means of comparison. This, being, according to the utilitarian opinion, the end of human action, is necessarily also the standard of morality; which may accordingly be defined, the rules and precepts for human conduct, by the observance of which an existence such as has been described might be, to the greatest extent possible, secured to all mankind; and not to them only, but, so far as the nature of things admits, to the whole sentient creation. . . .

I must again repeat, what the assailants of utilitarianism seldom have the justice to acknowledge, that the happiness which forms the utilitarian standard of what is right in conduct, is not the agent's own happiness, but that of all concerned. As between his own happiness and that of others, utilitarianism requires him to be as strictly impartial as a disinterested and benevolent spectator. In the golden rule of Jesus of Nazareth, we read the complete spirit of the ethics of utility. To do as one would be done by, and to love one's neighbour as oneself, constitute the ideal perfection of utilitarian morality. As the means of making the nearest approach to this ideal, utility would enjoin, first, that laws and social arrangements should place the happiness, or (as speaking practically it may be called) the interest, of every individual, as nearly as possible in harmony with the interest of the whole; and secondly, that education and opinion, which have so vast a power over human character, should so use that power as to establish in the mind of every individual an indissoluble association between his own happiness and the good of the whole; especially between his own happiness and the practice of such modes of conduct, negative and positive, as regard for the universal happiness prescribes: so that not only he may be unable to conceive the possibility of happiness to himself, consistently with conduct opposed to the general good, but also that a direct impulse to promote the general good may be in every individual one of the habitual motives of action, and the sentiments connected therewith may fill a large and prominent place in every human being's sentient existence. If the impugners of the utilitarian morality represented it to their own minds in this its true character, I know not what recommendation possessed by any other morality they could possibly affirm to be wanting to it: what more beautiful or more exalted developments of human nature any other ethical system can be supposed to foster, or what springs of action, not accessible to the utilitarian, such systems rely on for giving effect to their mandates. . . .

IV. OF WHAT SORT OF PROOF THE PRINCIPLE OF UTILITY IS SUSCEPTIBLE

It has already been remarked, that questions of ultimate ends do not admit of proof, in the ordinary acceptation of the term. To be incapable of proof by reasoning is common to all first principles; to the first premises of our knowledge, as well as to those of our conduct. But the former, being matters of fact, may be the subject of a direct appeal to the faculties which judge of fact—namely, our senses, and our internal consciousness. Can an appeal be made to the same faculties on questions of practical ends? Or by what other faculty is cognizance taken of them?

Questions about ends are, in other words, questions about what things are desirable. The utilitarian doctrine is, that happiness is desirable, and the only thing desirable, as an end; all other things being only desirable as means to that end. What ought to be required of this doctrine—what conditions is it requisite that the doctrine should fulfill—to make good its claim to be believed?

The only proof capable of being given that an object is visible, is that people actually see it. The only proof that a sound is audible, is that people hear it: and so of the other sources of our experience. In like manner, I apprehend, the sole evidence it is possible to produce that any-thing is desirable, is that people do actually desire it. If the end which the utilitarian doctrine proposes to itself were not, in theory and in practice, acknowledged to be an end, nothing could ever convince any person that it was so. No reason can be given why the general happiness is desirable, except that each person, so far as he believes it to be attain-able, desires his own happiness. This, however, being a fact, we have not only all the proof which the case admits of, but all which it is pos-sible to require, that happiness is a good: that each person's happiness is a good to that person, and the general happiness, therefore, a good to the aggregate of all persons. Happiness has made out its title as *one* of the ends of conduct, and consequently one of the criteria of morality.

But it has not, by this alone, proved itself to be the sole criterion. To do that, it would seem, by the same rule, necessary to show, not only that people desire happiness, but that they never desire anything else. Now it is palpable that they do desire things which, in common language, are decidedly distinguished from happiness. They desire, for example, virtue, and the absence of vice, no less really than pleasure and the absence of pain. The desire of virtue is not as universal, but it is as authentic a fact, as the desire of happiness. And hence the opponents of the utilitarian standard deem that they have a right to infer that there are other ends of human action besides happiness, and that happiness is not the standard of approbation and disapprobation.

But does the utilitarian doctrine deny that people desire virtue, or maintain that virtue is not a thing to be desired? The very reverse. It maintains not only that virtue is to be desired, but that it is to be desired disinterestedly, for itself. Whatever may be the opinion of utilitarian moralists as to the original conditions by which virtue is made virtue; however they may believe (as they do) that actions and dispositions are only virtuous because they promote another end than virtue; yet this being granted, and it having been decided, from considerations of this description, what *is* virtuous, they not only place virtue at the very head of the things which are good as means to the ultimate end, but they also recognise as a psychological fact the possibility of its being, to the individual, a good in itself, without looking to any end beyond it; and hold, that the mind is not in a right state, not in a state comfortable to Utility, not in the state most conducive to the general happiness, unless it does love virtue in this manner—as a thing desirable in itself, even although, in the individual instance, it should not produce those other desirable consequences which it tends to produce, and on account of which it is held to be virtue. This opinion is not, in the smallest degree, a departure from the Happiness principle. The ingredients of happiness are very various, and each of them is desirable in itself, and not merely when considered as swelling an aggregate. The principle of utility does not mean that any given pleasure, as music, for instance, or any given exemption from pain, as for example health, are to be looked upon as a means to a collective something termed happiness, and to be desired on that account. They are desired and desirable in and for themselves; besides being means, they are a part of the end. Virtue, according to the utilitarian doctrine, is not naturally and originally part of the end, but it is capable of becoming so; and in those who love it disinterestedly it has become so, and is desired and cherished, not as a means to happiness, but as a part of their happiness.

To illustrate this farther, we may remember that virtue is not the only thing, originally a means, and which if it were not a means to anything else, would be and remain indifferent, but which by association with what it is a means to, comes to be desired for itself, and that too with the utmost intensity. What, for example, shall we say of the love of money? There is nothing originally more desirable about money than about any heap of glittering pebbles. Its worth is solely that of the things which it will buy; the desires for other things than itself, which it is a means of gratifying. Yet the love of money is not only one of the strongest moving forces of human life, but money is, in many cases, desired in and for itself; the desire to possess it is often stronger than the desire to use it, and goes on increasing when all the desires which point to ends beyond it, to be encompassed by it, are falling off. It may be then said truly, that money is desired not for the sake of an end, but as part of the end. From being a means to happiness, it has come to be itself a principal ingredient of the individual's conception of happiness. The same may be said of the majority of the great objects of human life—power, for example, or fame; except that to each of these there is a certain amount of immediate pleasure annexed, which has at least the semblance of being naturally inherent in them; a thing which cannot be said of money. Still, however, the strongest natural attraction, both of power and of fame, is the immense aid they give to the attainment of our other wishes; and it is the strong association thus generated between them and all our objects of desire, which gives to the direct desire of them the intensity it often assumes, so as in some characters to surpass in strength all other desires. In these cases the means have become a part of the end, and a more important part of it than any of the things which they are means to. What was once desired as an instrument for the attainment of happiness, has come to be desired for its own sake. In being desired for its own sake it is, however, desired as *part* of happiness. The person is made, or thinks he would be made, happy by its mere possession; and is made unhappy by failure to obtain it. The desire of it is not a different thing from the desire of happiness, any more than the love of music, or the desire of health. They are included in happiness. They are some of the elements of which the desire of happiness is made up. Happiness is not an abstract idea, but a concrete whole; and these are some of its parts. And the utilitarian standard sanctions and approves their being so. Life would be a poor thing, very ill provided with sources of happiness, if there were not this provision of nature, by which things originally indifferent, but conducive to, or otherwise associated with, the satisfaction of our primitive desires, become in themselves sources of pleasure more valuable than the primitive pleasures, both in permanency, in the space of human existence that they are capable of covering, and even in intensity.

Virtue, according to the utilitarian conception, is a good of this description. There was no original desire of it, or motive to it, save its conduciveness to pleasure, and especially to protection from pain. But through the association thus formed, it may be felt a good in itself, and desired as such with as great intensity as any other good; and with this difference between it and the love of money, of power, or of fame, that all of these may, and often do, render the individual noxious to the other members of the society to which he belongs, whereas there is nothing which makes him so much a blessing to them as the cultivation of the disinterested love of virtue. And consequently, the utilitarian standard, while it tolerates and approves those other acquired desires, up to the point beyond which they would be more injurious to the general happiness than promotive of it, enjoins and requires the cultivation of the love of virtue up to the greatest strength possible, as being above all things important to the general happiness.

It results from the preceding considerations, that there is in reality nothing desired except happiness. Whatever is desired otherwise than as a means to some end beyond itself, and ultimately to happiness, is desired as itself a part of happiness, and is not desired for itself until it has become so.

Chapter 6

Utilitarianism and Integrity

Bernard Williams

◆

Utilitarianism is the theory that we should always try to maximize happiness. It is hard to argue against the value of being happy, but critics are quick to point out that other things may also have value.

Sir Bernard Williams (1929–2003), one of the great critics of Utilitarianism, held professorships at both Cambridge University and Oxford University. In this selection, he considers two difficult test cases for the utilitarian theory.

(1) George, who has just taken his Ph.D. in chemistry, finds it extremely difficult to get a job. He is not very robust in health, which cuts down the number of jobs he might be able to do satisfactorily. His wife has to go out to work to support them, which itself causes a great deal of strain, since they have small children and there are severe problems about looking after them. The results of all this, especially on the children, are damaging. An older chemist, who knows about this situation, says that he can get George a decently paid job in a certain laboratory, which pursues research into chemical and biological warfare. George says that he cannot accept this, since he is opposed to chemical and biological warfare. The older man replies that he is not too keen on it

From Bernard Williams, "Utilitarianism and Integrity" in *Utilitarianism: For and Against*, J. J. C. Smart and Bernard Williams (Cambridge: Cambridge University Press, 1973), 96–107. Copyright © 1973 Cambridge University Press. Used with permission.

himself, come to that, but after all George's refusal is not going to make the job or the laboratory go away; what is more, he happens to know that if George refuses the job, it will certainly go to a contemporary of George's who is not inhibited by any such scruples and is likely if appointed to push along the research with greater zeal than George would. Indeed, it is not merely concern for George and his family, but (to speak frankly and in confidence) some alarm about this other man's excess of zeal, which has led the older man to offer to use his influence to get George the job. . . . George's wife, to whom he is deeply attached, has views (the details of which need not concern us) from which it follows that at least there is nothing particularly wrong with research into CBW. What should he do?

(2) Jim finds himself in the central square of a small South American town. Tied up against the wall are a row of twenty Indians, most terrified, a few defiant, in front of them several armed men in uniform. A heavy man in a sweat-stained khaki shirt turns out to be the captain in charge and, after a good deal of questioning of Jim which establishes that he got there by accident while on a botanical expedition, explains that the Indians are a random group of the inhabitants who, after recent acts of protest against the government, are just about to be killed to remind other possible protestors of the advantages of not protesting. However, since Jim is an honoured visitor from another land, the captain is happy to offer him a guest's privilege of killing one of the Indians himself. If Jim accepts, then as a special mark of the occasion, the other Indians will be let off. Of course, if Jim refuses, then there is no special occasion, and Pedro here will do what he was about to do when Jim arrived, and kill them all. Jim, with some desperate recollection of schoolboy fiction, wonders whether if he got hold of a gun, he could hold the captain, Pedro and the rest of the soldiers to threat, but it is quite clear from the set-up that nothing of that kind is going to work: any attempt at that sort of thing will mean that all the Indians will be killed, and himself. The men against the wall, and the other villagers, understand the situation, and are obviously begging him to accept. What should he do?

To these dilemmas, it seems to me that utilitarianism replies, in the first case, that George should accept the job, and in the second, that Jim should kill the Indian. Not only does utilitarianism give these answers but, if the situations are essentially as described and there are no further special factors, it regards them, it seems to me, as *obviously* the right answers. But many of us would certainly wonder whether, in (1), that could possibly be the right answer at all; and in the case of (2), even one who came to think that perhaps that was the answer, might well wonder whether it was obviously the answer. Nor is it just a question of the rightness or obviousness of these answers. It is also a question of what sort of considerations come into finding the answer. A feature of utilitarianism is that it cuts out a kind of consideration which for some others makes a difference to what they feel about such cases: a consideration involving the idea, as we might first and very simply put it, that each of us is specially responsible for what *he* does, rather than for what other people do. This is an idea closely connected with the value of integrity. It is often suspected that utilitarianism, at least in its direct forms, makes integrity as a value more or less unintelligible. I shall try to show that this suspicion is correct. Of course, even if that is correct, it would not necessarily follow that we should reject utilitarianism; perhaps, as utilitarians sometimes suggest, we should just forget about integrity, in favour of such things as a concern for the general good. However, if I am right, we cannot merely do that, since the reason why utilitarianism cannot understand integrity is that it cannot coherently describe the relations between a man's projects and his actions.

TWO KINDS OF REMOTER EFFECT

A lot of what we have to say about this question will be about the relations between my projects and other people's projects. But before we get on to that, we should first ask whether we are assuming too hastily what the utilitarian answers to the dilemmas will be. In terms of more direct effects of the possible decisions, there does not indeed seem much doubt about the answer in either case; but it might be said that in terms of more remote or less evident effects counterweights might be found to enter the utilitarian scales. Thus the effect on George of a decision to take the job might be invoked, or its effect on others who might know of his decision. The possibility of there being more beneficent labours in the future from which he might be barred or disqualified, might be mentioned; and so forth. Such effects—in particular, possible effects on the agent's character, and effects on the public at large—are

often invoked by utilitarian writers dealing with problems about lying
or promise-breaking, and some similar considerations might be invoked
here.

There is one very general remark that is worth making about arguments of this sort. The certainty that attaches to these hypotheses
about possible effects is usually pretty low; in some cases, indeed, the
hypothesis invoked is so implausible that it would scarcely pass if it
were not being used to deliver the respectable moral answer, as in the
standard fantasy that one of the effects of one's telling a particular lie
is to weaken the disposition of the world at large to tell the truth. The
demands on the certainty or probability of these beliefs as beliefs about
particular actions are much milder than they would be on beliefs favour-
ing the unconventional course. It may be said that this is as it should
be, since the presumption must be in favour of the conventional course:
but that scarcely seems a *utilitarian* answer, unless utilitarianism has
already taken off in the direction of not applying the consequences to
the particular act at all.

Leaving aside that very general point, I want to consider now two
types of effect that are often invoked by utilitarians, and which might be
invoked in connection with these imaginary cases. The attitude or tone
involved in invoking these effects may sometimes seem peculiar; but
that sort of peculiarity soon becomes familiar in utilitarian discussions,
and indeed it can be something of an achievement to retain a sense of it.

First, there is the psychological effect on the agent. Our descriptions of
these situations have not so far taken account of how George or Jim will
be after they have taken the one course or the other; and it might be said
that if they take the course which seemed at first the utilitarian one, the
effects on them will be in fact bad enough and extensive enough to can-
cel out the initial utilitarian advantages of that course. Now there is one
version of this effect in which, for a utilitarian, some confusion must be
involved, namely that in which the agent feels bad, his subsequent conduct and relations are crippled and so on, *because he thinks that he has
done the wrong thing*—for if the balance of outcomes was as it appeared
to be *before* invoking this effect, then he has not (from the utilitarian
point of view) done the wrong thing. So that version of the effect, for a
rational and utilitarian agent, could not possibly make any difference to
the assessment of right and wrong. However, perhaps he is not a thoroughly rational agent, and is disposed to have bad feelings, whichever

he decided to do. Now such feelings, which are from a strictly utilitarian point of view irrational—nothing, a utilitarian can point out, is advanced by having them—cannot, consistently, have any great weight in a utilitarian calculation. I shall consider in a moment an argument to suggest that they should have no weight at all in it. But short of that, the utilitarian could reasonably say that such feelings should not be encouraged, even if we accept their existence, and that to give them a lot of weight is to encourage them. Or, at the very best, even if they are straightforwardly and without any discount to be put into the calculation, their weight must be small: they are after all (and at best) one man's feelings.

That consideration might seem to have particular force in Jim's case. In George's case, his feelings represent a larger proportion of what is to be weighed, and are more commensurate in character with other items in the calculation. In Jim's case, however, his feelings might seem to be of very little weight compared with other things that are at stake. There is a powerful and recognizable appeal that can be made on this point: as that a refusal by Jim to do what he has been invited to do would be a kind of self-indulgent squeamishness. . . . If he does not see [the situation] from a utilitarian point of view, he will not see his resistance to the invitation, and the unpleasant feelings he associates with accepting it, *just* as disagreeable experiences of his; they figure rather as emotional expressions of a thought that to accept would be wrong. He may be asked, as by the appeal, to consider whether he is right, and indeed whether he is fully serious, in thinking that. But the assertion of the appeal, that he is being self-indulgently squeamish, will not itself answer that question, or even help to answer it, since it essentially tells him to regard his feelings just as unpleasant experiences of his, and he cannot, by doing that, answer the question they pose when they are precisely not so regarded, but are regarded as indications of what he thinks is right and wrong. If he does come round fully to the utilitarian point of view then of course he will regard these feelings just as unpleasant experiences of his. And once Jim—at least—has come to see them in that light, there is nothing left for the appeal to do, since *of course* his feelings, so regarded, are of virtually no weight at all in relation to the other things at stake. The "squeamishness" appeal is not an argument which adds in a hitherto neglected consideration. Rather, it is an invitation to consider the situation, and one's own feelings, from a utilitarian point of view.

The reason why the squeamishness appeal can be very unsettling, and one can be unnerved by the suggestion of self-indulgence in going against utilitarian considerations, is not that we are utilitarians who are uncertain what utilitarian value to attach to our moral feelings, but that we are partially at least not utilitarians, and cannot regard our moral feelings merely as objects of utilitarian value. Because our moral relation to the world is partly given by such feelings, and by a sense of what we can or cannot "live with," to come to regard those feelings from a purely utilitarian point of view, that is to say, as happenings outside one's moral self, is to lose a sense of one's moral identity; to lose, in the most literal way, one's integrity.

Chapter 7

The Experience Machine

Robert Nozick

Robert Nozick (1938–2002) was Joseph Pellegrino University Professor of Philosophy at Harvard University. The following selection is from his book *Anarchy, State, and Utopia*, a brilliant and entertaining defense of minimal government. In this excerpt, Nozick uses a thought experiment to explore questions about what matters to us *other than what our experiences are like*. How we answer these questions may cast light on the ethics of drug use, watching videos, and perhaps even sleeping late.

Suppose there was an experience machine that would give you any experience you desired. Superduper neuropsychologists could stimulate your brain so that you would think and feel you were writing a great novel, or making a friend, or reading an interesting book. All the time you would be floating in a tank, with electrodes attached to your brain. Should you plug into this machine for life, preprogramming your life's experiences? If you are worried about missing out on desirable experiences, we can suppose that business enterprises have researched thoroughly the lives of many others. You can pick and choose from their large library or smorgasbord of such experiences, selecting your life's experiences for, say, the next two years. After two years have passed, you will have ten minutes or ten hours out of the tank, to select the experiences of your *next* two years. Of course, while in the tank you won't know that you're there; you'll think it's all actually happening. Others can also plug in to have the experiences they want, so there's no need to stay unplugged to serve them. (Ignore problems such as who will service the machines if everyone plugs in.) Would you plug in? *What else can matter to us, other than how our lives feel from the inside?* Nor should you refrain because of the few moments of distress between the moment you've decided and the moment you're plugged. What's a few moments of distress compared to a lifetime of bliss (if that's what you choose), and why feel any distress at all if your decision *is* the best one?

What does matter to us in addition to our experiences? First, we want to *do* certain things, and not just have the experience of doing them. In the case of certain experiences, it is only because first we want to do the actions that we want the experiences of doing them or thinking we've done them. (But *why* do we want to do the activities rather than merely to experience them?) A second reason for not plugging in is that we want to *be* a certain way, to be a certain sort of person. Someone floating in a tank is an indeterminate blob. There is no answer to the question of what a person is like who has long been in the tank. Is he courageous, kind, intelligent, witty, loving? It's not merely that it's difficult to tell; there's no way he is. Plugging into the machine is a kind of suicide. It will seem to some, trapped by a picture, that nothing about what we are like can matter except as it gets reflected in our experiences. But should it be surprising that what *we are* is important to us? Why should we be concerned only with how our time is filled, but not with what we are?

Thirdly, plugging into an experience machine limits us to a manmade reality, to a world no deeper or more important than that which people can construct. There is no *actual* contact with any deeper reality, though the experience of it can be simulated. Many persons desire to leave themselves open to such contact and to a plumbing of deeper significance. This clarifies the intensity of the conflict over psychoactive drugs, which some view as mere local experience machines, and others view as avenues to a deeper reality; what some view as equivalent to surrender to the experience machine, others view as following one of the reasons *not* to surrender!

We learn that something matters to us in addition to experience by imagining an experience machine and then realizing that we would not use it. We can continue to imagine a sequence of machines each designed to fill lacks suggested for the earlier machines. For example, since the experience machine doesn't meet our desire to *be* a certain way, imagine a transformation machine which transforms us into whatever sort of person we'd like to be (compatible with our staying us). Surely one would not use the transformation machine to become as one would wish, and thereupon plug into the experience machine! So something matters in addition to one's experiences *and* what one is like. Nor is the reason merely that one's experiences are unconnected with what one is like. For the experience machine might be limited to provide only experiences possible to the sort of person plugged in. Is it that we want to make a difference in the world? Consider then the result machine, which produces in the world any result you would produce and injects your vector input into any joint activity. We shall not pursue here the fascinating details of these or other machines. What is most disturbing about them is their living of our lives for us. Is it misguided to search for *particular* additional functions beyond the competence of machines to do for us? Perhaps what we desire is to live (an active verb) ourselves, in contact with reality. (And this, machines cannot do *for* us.) Without elaborating on the implications of this, which I believe connect surprisingly with issues about free will and causal accounts of knowledge, we need merely note the intricacy of the question of what matters *for people* other than their experiences.

Chapter 8

The Categorical Imperative

Immanuel Kant

Immanuel Kant (1724–1804) led a quiet life. He never traveled
far from his home in Königsberg, a city in the German state of
East Prussia. A popular professor and much-desired dinner guest,
Kant was known for his regular habits: A bachelor, he arose
each morning at 4 AM, prepared his lectures, taught from 7 AM
until noon, read until 4 PM, took a walk, had dinner, and wrote
until bedtime. He repeated this routine day after day, for years.
Despite his modest habits, on the day he was buried, thousands of
mourners followed his coffin down the street, as the bells of all
the churches tolled.

Kant's unorthodox views on religion did cause some controversy. However, Kant was not an atheist. He was from a family
of Pietists, who distrusted organized religion. In his later years, as
the rector of his university, it was his duty to lead the faculty pro-
cession to the university chapel for religious services—which he
would. Upon reaching the chapel, however, he would stand aside
and not enter. In 1786, having become the most famous philosopher in Germany, and having argued that God's existence cannot
be proven, Kant was ordered to stop publishing on the subject.

Immanuel Kant, "Foundations of the Metaphysics of Morals" (1785) in *The Critique of Practical Reason and Other Writings in Moral Philosophy*, trans. Lewis White Beck (Chicago:
University of Chicago Press, 1949), 73–74, 80–83, 86–87. Used with permission of the Estate
of Lewis White Beck.

Today, "Kant scholarship" is an academic specialty unto itself; many scholars spend their whole lives trying to understand Kant's ideas. Every year new books appear defending new interpretations of his philosophy. The banquet of interpretations is partly due to the richness of Kant's thought. But it is also due to the fact that Kant was an exceedingly obscure writer.

Kant believed that morality can be summed up in one ultimate principle, which he called the Categorical Imperative. According to this principle, to act morally is to act from motives that everyone, everywhere could live by.

The following selection is from Kant's *Foundations of the Metaphysics of Morals*, the most accessible presentation of his ethical theory.

All imperatives command either hypothetically or categorically. . . . The hypothetical imperative . . . says only that the action is good to some purpose, possible or actual. . . . The categorical imperative, which declares the action to be of itself objectively necessary without making any reference to a purpose, that is, without having any other end, holds as an apodictical (practical) principle. . . .

If I think of a hypothetical imperative as such, I do not know what it will contain until the condition is stated [under which it is an imperative]. But if I think of a categorical imperative, I know immediately what it contains. For since the imperative contains besides the law only the necessity of the maxim of acting in accordance with this law, while the law contains no condition to which it is restricted, there is nothing remaining in it except the universality of law as such to which the maxim of the action should conform; and in effect this conformity alone is represented as necessary by the imperative.

There is, therefore, only one categorical imperative. It is: Act only according to that maxim by which you can at the same time will that it should become a universal law.

Now if all imperatives of duty can be derived from this one imperative as a principle, we can at least show what we understand by the concept of duty and what it means, even though it remains undecided whether that which is called duty is an empty concept or not.

The universality of law according to which effects are produced constitutes what is properly called nature in the most general sense (as to form), that is, the existence of things so far as it is determined by universal laws. [By analogy], then, the universal imperative of duty can be expressed as follows: Act as though the maxim of your action were by your will to become a universal law of nature.

We shall now enumerate some duties. . . .

1. A man who is reduced to despair by a series of evils feels a weariness with life but is still in possession of his reason sufficiently to ask whether it would not be contrary to his duty to himself to take his own life. Now he asks whether the maxim of his action could become a universal law of nature. His maxim, however, is: For love of myself, I make it my principle to shorten my life when by a longer duration it threatens more evil than satisfaction. But it is questionable whether this principle of self-love could become a universal law of nature. One immediately sees a contradiction in a system of nature, whose law would be to destroy life by the feeling whose special office is to impel the improvement of life. In this case it would not exist as nature; hence that maxim cannot obtain as a law of nature, and thus it wholly contradicts the supreme principle of all duty.

2. Another man finds himself forced by need to borrow money. He well knows that he will not be able to repay it, but he also sees that nothing will be loaned him if he does not firmly promise to repay it at a certain time. He desires to make such a promise, but he has enough conscience to ask himself whether it is not improper and opposed to duty to relieve his distress in such a way. Now, assuming he does decide to do so, the maxim of his action would be as follows: When I believe myself to be in need of money, I will borrow money and promise to repay it, although I know I shall never do so. Now this principle of self-love or of his own benefit may very well be compatible with his whole future welfare, but the question is whether it is right. He changes the pretension of self-love into a universal law and then puts the question: How would it be if my maxim became a universal law? He immediately sees that it could never hold as a universal law of nature and be consistent with itself; rather it must necessarily contradict itself. For the universality of a law which says that anyone who believes himself to be in need could promise what he pleased with the intention of not fulfilling it would make the promise itself and the end to be accomplished by it impossible; no one would believe what was promised to him but would only laugh at any such assertion as vain pretense.

3. A third finds in himself a talent which could, by means of some cultivation, make him in many respects a useful man. But he finds himself in comfortable circumstances and prefers indulgence in pleasure to troubling himself with broadening and improving his fortunate natural gifts. Now, however, let him ask whether his maxim of neglecting his gifts, besides agreeing with his propensity to idle amusement, agrees also with what is called duty. He sees that a system of nature could indeed exist in accordance with such a law, even though man (like the inhabitants of the South Sea Islands) should let his talents rust and resolve to devote his life merely to idleness, indulgence, and propagation—in a word, to pleasure. But he cannot possibly will that this should become a universal law of nature or that it should be implanted in us by a natural instinct. For, as a rational being, he necessarily wills that all his faculties should be developed, inasmuch as they are given to him for all sorts of possible purposes.

4. A fourth man, for whom things are going well, sees that others (whom he could help) have to struggle with great hardships, and he asks, "What concern of mine is it? Let each one be as happy as heaven wills, or as he can make himself; I will not take anything from him or even envy him; but to his welfare or to his assistance in time of need I have no desire to contribute." If such a way of thinking were a universal law of nature, certainly the human race could exist, and without doubt even better than in a state where everyone talks of sympathy and good will or even exerts himself occasionally to practice them while, on the other hand, he cheats when he can and betrays or otherwise violates the rights of man. Now although it is possible that a universal law of nature according to that maxim could exist, it is nevertheless impossible to will that such a principle should hold everywhere as a law of nature. For a will which resolved this would conflict with itself, since instances can often arise in which he would need the love and sympathy of others, and in which he would have robbed himself, by such a law of nature springing from his own will, of all hope of the aid he desires.

The foregoing are a few of the many actual duties, or at least of duties we hold to be actual, whose derivation from the one stated principle is clear. We must be able to will that a maxim of our action become a universal law; this is the canon of the moral estimation of our action generally. Some actions are of such a nature that their maxim cannot even be *thought* as a universal law of nature without contradiction, far from it being possible that one could will that it should be such. In others this internal impossibility is not found though it is still impossible to *will* that their maxim should be raised to the universality of a law of nature, because such a will would contradict itself. We easily see that the former maxim conflicts with the stricter or narrower (imprescriptable) duty, the latter with broader (meritorious) duty. Thus all duties, so far as the kind of obligation (not the object of their action) is concerned, have been completely exhibited by these examples in their dependence on the one principle.

Chapter 9

The Virtues

Aristotle

Aristotle (384–322 BC) may be the most influential thinker of all time. His theory of physics reigned for a thousand years; his system of logic was dominant until the nineteenth century; Charles Darwin called him "the greatest biologist of all time"; and his theory of ethics still has many followers.

Aristotle was born in Stagira in northern Greece and moved to Athens when he was seventeen. There he became a pupil of Plato. Aristotle left Athens after Plato's death in 347 BC; four years later, he became tutor to the boy who would become Alexander the Great. From 334 BC until his death, Aristotle headed his own school in Athens.

The following selection, from Books I and II of Aristotle's *Nicomachean Ethics*, discusses two central themes in his moral philosophy: The nature of the good life, and what it means to be virtuous.

But what is happiness? If we consider what the function of man is, we find that happiness is a virtuous activity of the soul.

But presumably to say that happiness is the supreme good seems a platitude, and some more distinctive account of it is still required. This

From Aristotle, *The Ethics of Aristotle*, trans. J. A. K. Thomson (London: Penguin Books, 1976), bks. 1, 2, pp. 75–80, 84, 91–92, 94, 100–2.

might perhaps be achieved by grasping what is the function of man. If we take a flautist or a sculptor or any artist—or in general any class of men who have a specific function or activity—his goodness and proficiency is considered to lie in the performance of that function; and the same will be true of man, assuming that man has a function. But is it likely that whereas joiners and shoemakers have certain functions or activities, man as such has none, but has been left by nature a functionless being? Just as we can see that eye and hand and foot and every one of our members has some function, should we not assume that in like manner a human being has a function over and above these particular functions? What, then, can this possibly be? Clearly life is a thing shared also by plants, and we are looking for man's *proper* function; so we must exclude from our definition the life that consists in nutrition and growth. Next in order would be a sort of sentient life; but this too we see is shared by horses and cattle and animals of all kinds. There remains, then, a practical life of the rational part. (This has two aspects: one amenable to reason, the other possessing it and initiating thought.) As this life also has two meanings, we must lay down that we intend here life determined by activity, because this is accepted as the stricter sense. Now if the function of man is an activity of the soul in accordance with, or implying, a rational principle; and if we hold that the function of an individual and of a good individual of the same kind—for example, of a harpist and of a good harpist, and so on generally—is generically the same, the latter's distinctive excellence being attached to the name of the function (because the function of the harpist is to play the harp, but that of the good harpist is to play it well); and if we assume that the function of man is a kind of life, viz., an activity or series of actions of the soul, implying a rational principle; and if the function of a good man is to perform these well and rightly; and if every function is performed well when performed in accordance with its proper excellence: if all this is so, the conclusion is that the good for man is an activity of soul in accordance with virtue, or if there are more kinds of virtue than one, in accordance with the best and most perfect kind.

There is a further qualification: in a complete lifetime. One swallow does not make a summer; neither does one day. Similarly neither can one day, or a brief space of time, make a man blessed and happy. . . .

Our view of happiness is supported by popular beliefs.

viii. We must examine our principle not only as reached logically, from a conclusion and premises, but also in the light of what is commonly said about it; because if a statement is true all the data are in harmony with it, while if it is false they soon reveal a discrepancy.

Now goods have been classified under three heads, as (*a*) external, (*b*) of the soul, and (*c*) of the body. Of these we say that goods of the soul are good in the strictest and fullest sense, and we rank actions and activities of soul as goods of the soul; so that according to this view, which is of long standing and accepted by philosophers, our definition will be correct. We are right, too, in saying that the end consists in certain actions or activities, because this puts it among goods of the soul and not among external goods. Our definition is also supported by the belief that the happy man lives and fares well; because what we have described is virtually a kind of good life or prosperity. Again, our definition seems to include all the required constituents of happiness; for some think that it is virtue, others prudence, and others wisdom; others that it is these, or one of these, with the addition of pleasure, or not in total separation from it; and others further include favourable external conditions. Some of these views are popular beliefs of long standing; others are those of a few distinguished men. It is reasonable to suppose that neither group is entirely mistaken, but is right in some respect, or even in most.

Now our definition is in harmony with those who say that happiness is virtue, or a particular virtue; because an activity in accordance with virtue implies virtue. But presumably it makes no little difference whether we think of the supreme good as consisting in the *possession* or in the *exercise* of virtue: in a state of mind or in an activity. For it is possible for the *state* to be present in a person without effecting any good result (e.g., if he is asleep or quiescent in some other way), but not for the *activity*: he will necessarily act, and act well. Just as at the Olympic Games it is not the best-looking or the strongest men present that are crowned with wreaths, but the competitors (because it is from them that the winners come), so it is those who *act* that rightly win the honours and rewards in life.

Moreover, the life of such people is in itself pleasant. For pleasure is an experience of the soul, and each individual finds pleasure in that of which he is said to be fond. For example, a horse gives pleasure to one who is fond of horses, and a spectacle to one who is fond of sight-seeing.

In the same way just acts give pleasure to a lover of justice, and virtuous conduct generally to the lover of virtue. Now most people find that the things which give them pleasure conflict, because they are not pleasant by nature; but lovers of beauty find pleasure in things that are pleasant by nature, and virtuous actions are of this kind, so that they are pleasant not only to this type of person but also in themselves. So their life does not need to have pleasure attached to it as a sort of accessory, but contains its own pleasure in itself. Indeed, we may go further and assert that anyone who does not delight in fine actions is not even a good man; for nobody would say that a man is just unless he enjoys acting justly, nor liberal unless he enjoys liberal actions, and similarly in all the other cases. If this is so, virtuous actions must be pleasurable in themselves. What is more, they are both good and fine, and each in the highest degree, assuming that the good man is right in his judgement of them; and his judgement is as we have described. So happiness is the best, the finest, the most pleasurable thing of all; and these qualities are not separated as the inscription at Delos suggests:

> Justice is loveliest, and health is best,
> But sweetest to obtain is heart's desire.

All these attributes belong to the best activities; and it is these, or the one that is best of them, that we identify with happiness.

Nevertheless it seems clear that happiness needs the addition of external goods, as we have said; for it is difficult if not impossible to do fine deeds without any resources. Many can only be done by the help of friends, or wealth, or political influence. There are also certain advantages, such as good ancestry or good children, or personal beauty, the lack of which mars our felicity; for a man is scarcely happy if he is very ugly to look at, or of low birth, or solitary and childless; and presumably even less so if he has children or friends who are quite worthless, or if he had good ones who are now dead. So, as we said, happiness seems to require this sort of prosperity too; which is why some identify it with good fortune, although others identify it with virtue. . . .

We are now in a position to define the happy man as "one who is active in accordance with complete virtue, and who is adequately furnished with external goods, and that not for some unspecified period but throughout a complete life." And probably we should add "destined both to live in this way and to die accordingly"; because the future is obscure to us, and happiness we maintain to be an *end* in every way utterly final and complete. . . .

Moral virtues, like crafts, are acquired by practice and habituation.

i. Virtue, then, is of two kinds, intellectual and moral. Intellectual virtue owes both its inception and its growth chiefly to instruction, and for this very reason needs time and experience. Moral goodness, on the other hand, is the result of habit, from which it has actually got its name, being a slight modification of the word *ethos*. This fact makes it obvious that none of the moral virtues is engendered in us by nature, since nothing that is what it is by nature can be made to behave differently by habituation. For instance, a stone, which has a natural tendency downwards, cannot be habituated to rise, however often you try to train it by throwing it into the air; nor can you train fire to burn downwards; nor can anything else that has any other natural tendency be trained to depart from it. The moral virtues, then, are engendered in us neither *by* nor *contrary to* nature; we are constituted by nature to receive them, but their full development in us is due to habit.

Again, of all those faculties with which nature endows us we first acquire the potentialities, and only later effect their actualization. (This is evident in the case of the senses. It was not from repeated acts of seeing or hearing that we acquired the senses but the other way round: we had these senses before we used them; we did not acquire them as the result of using them.) But the virtues we do acquire by first exercising them, just as happens in the arts. Anything that we have to learn to do we learn by the actual doing of it: people become builders by building and instrumentalists by playing instruments. Similarly we become just by performing just acts, temperate by performing temperate ones, brave by performing brave ones. This view is supported by what happens in city-states. Legislators make their citizens good by habituation; this is the intention of every legislator, and those who do not carry it out fail of their object. This is what makes the difference between a good constitution and a bad one.

Again, the causes or means that bring about any form of excellence are the same as those that destroy it, and similarly with art; for it is as a result of playing the harp that people become good and bad harpists. The same principle applies to builders and all other craftsmen. Men will become good builders as a result of building well, and bad ones as a result of building badly. Otherwise there would be no need of anyone to teach them: they would all be *born* either good or bad. Now this holds good also of the virtues. It is the way that we behave in our dealings with other people that makes us just or unjust, and the way that we behave in the face of danger, accustoming ourselves to be timid or confident, that makes us brave or cowardly. Similarly with situations involving desires and angry feelings: some people become temperate and patient from one kind of conduct in such situations, others licentious and choleric from another. In a word, then, like activities produce like dispositions. Hence we must give our activities a certain quality, because it is their characteristics that determine the resulting dispositions. So it is a matter of no little importance what sort of habits we form from the earliest age—it makes a vast difference, or rather all the difference in the world. . . .

A cardinal rule: right conduct is incompatible with excess or deficiency in feelings and actions.

First, then, we must consider this fact: that it is in the nature of moral qualities that they are destroyed by deficiency and excess, just as we can see (since we have to use the evidence of visible facts to throw light on those that are invisible) in the case of bodily health and strength. For both excessive and insufficient exercise destroy one's strength, and both eating and drinking too much or too little destroy health, whereas the right quantity produces, increases, and preserves it. So it is the same with temperance, courage, and the other virtues. The man who shuns and fears everything and stands up to nothing becomes a coward; the man who is afraid of nothing at all, but marches up to every danger, becomes foolhardy. Similarly the man who indulges in every pleasure and refrains from none becomes licentious; but if a man behaves like a boor and turns his back on every pleasure, he is a case of insensibility. Thus temperance and courage are destroyed by excess and deficiency and preserved by the mean. . . .

If, then, every science performs its function well only when it observes the mean and refers its products to it (which is why it is customary to say of well-executed works that nothing can be added to them or taken away, the implication being that excess and deficiency alike destroy perfection, while the mean preserves it)—if good craftsmen, as we hold, work with the mean in view; and if virtue, like nature, is more exact and more efficient than any art, it follows that virtue aims to hit the mean. By virtue I mean moral virtue since it is this that is concerned with feelings and actions, and these involve excess, deficiency and a mean. It is possible, for example, to feel fear, confidence, desire, anger, pity, and pleasure and pain generally, too much or too little; and both of these are wrong. But to have these feelings at the right times on the right grounds towards the right people for the right motive and in the right way is to feel them to an intermediate, that is to the best, degree; and this is the mark of virtue. Similarly there are excess and deficiency and a mean in the case of actions. But it is in the field of actions and feelings that virtue operates; and in them excess and deficiency are failings, whereas the mean is praised and recognized as a success: and these are both marks of virtue. Virtue, then, is a mean condition, inasmuch as it aims at hitting the mean.

Again, failure is possible in many ways (for evil, as the Pythagoreans represented it, is a form of the Unlimited, and good of the Limited), but success is only possible in one way. That is why the one is easy and the other difficult; it is easy to miss the target and difficult to hit it. Here, then, is another reason why excess and deficiency fall under evil, and the mean state under good:

For men are bad in countless ways, but good in only one.

A provisional definition of virtue

So virtue is a purposive disposition, lying in a mean that is relative to us and determined by a rational principle, and by that which a prudent man would use to determine it. It is a mean between two kinds of vice, one of excess and the other of deficiency; and also for this reason, that whereas these vices fall short of or exceed the right measure in both feelings and actions, virtue discovers the mean and chooses it. Thus from the point of view of its essence and the definition of its real nature, virtue is a mean; but in respect of what is right and best, it is an extreme.

Chapter 10

Master Morality and Slave Morality

Friedrich Nietzsche

The German philosopher Friedrich Nietzsche (1844–1900) is a
controversial figure. He expressed himself in angry, flamboyant
prose, and he hated women. After he went insane and died—
apparently from syphilis—his sister used his work to further her
own dark agenda. Under her influence, Nietzsche became the
favorite philosopher of the Nazis, including Adolph Hitler, who
was once photographed contemplating a bust of the philosopher.
However, Friedrich Nietzsche was not an anti-Semite; he called
the Jews "the strongest, toughest, and purest race" living in
Europe. Nietzsche's sister Elisabeth was the Nazi.

In this selection, Nietzsche contrasts "Master Morality" with
"Slave Morality," and there is no doubt which he prefers. Master
morality is the morality of the proud and the strong; slave morality
is the morality of the groveling and the weak. Nietzsche regards
"slave values" as pathetic. For good or for ill, Nietzsche exemplified the values he praised; his books contain sections with such titles
as "Why I Am So Clever" and "Why I Write Such Good Books."

Wandering through the many subtler and coarser moralities which have
so far been prevalent on earth, or still are prevalent, I found that certain

From Friedrich Nietzsche, *Beyond Good and Evil*, trans. Walter Kaufmann (New York:
Vintage Books, 1966), 204–7.

features recurred regularly together and were closely associated—until I finally discovered two basic types and one basic difference.

There are *master morality* and *slave morality*—I add immediately that in all the higher and more mixed cultures there also appear attempts at mediation between these two moralities, and yet more often the interpenetration and mutual misunderstanding of both, and at times they occur directly alongside each other—even in the same human being, within a *single* soul. The moral discrimination of values has originated either among a ruling group whose consciousness of its difference from the ruled group was accompanied by delight—or among the ruled, the slaves, and dependents of every degree.

In the first case, when the ruling group determines what is "good," the exalted, proud states of the soul are experienced as conferring distinction and determining the order of rank. The noble human being separates from himself those in whom the opposite of such exalted, proud states finds expression: he despises them. It should be noted immediately that in this first type of morality the opposition of "good" and *"bad"* means approximately the same as "noble" and "contemptible." (The opposition of "good" and *"evil"* has a different origin.) One feels contempt for the cowardly, the anxious, the petty, those intent on narrow utility; also for the suspicious with their unfree glances, those who humble themselves, the doglike people who allow themselves to be maltreated, the begging flatterers, above all the liars: it is part of the fundamental faith of all aristocrats that the common people lie. "We truthful ones"—thus the nobility of ancient Greece referred to itself.

It is obvious that moral designations were everywhere first applied to *human beings* and only later, derivatively, to actions. Therefore it is a gross mistake when historians of morality start from such questions as: why was the compassionate act praised? The noble type of man experiences *itself* as determining values; it does not need approval; it judges, "what is harmful to me is harmful in itself"; it knows itself to be that which first accords honor to things; it is *value-creating*. Everything it knows as part of itself it honors: such a morality is self-glorification. In the foreground there is the feeling of fullness, of power that seeks to overflow, the happiness of high tension, the consciousness of wealth that would give and bestow: the noble human being, too, helps the unfortunate, but not, or almost not, from pity, but prompted more by an urge begotten by excess of power. The noble human being honors himself as one who is powerful, also as one who has power over himself, who knows how to speak and be silent, who delights in being severe and hard with himself, and respects all severity and hardness. "A hard heart Wotan put into my breast," says an old Scandinavian saga: a fitting poetic expression, seeing that it comes from the soul of a proud Viking. Such a type of man is actually proud of the fact that he is *not* made for pity, and the hero of the saga therefore adds as a warning: "If the heart is not hard in youth it will never harden." Noble and courageous human beings who think that way are furthest removed from that morality which finds the distinction of morality precisely in pity, or in acting for others; faith in oneself, pride in oneself, a fundamental hostility and irony against "selflessness" belong just as definitely to noble morality as does a slight disdain and caution regarding compassionate feelings and a "warm heart."

It is the powerful who *understand* how to honor; this is their art, their realm of invention. The profound reverence for age and tradition—all law rests on this double reverence—the faith and prejudice in favor of ancestors and disfavor of those yet to come are typical of the morality of the powerful; and when the men of "modern ideas," conversely, believe almost instinctively in "progress" and "the future" and more and more lack respect for age, this in itself would sufficiently betray the ignoble origin of these "ideas."

A morality of the ruling group, however, is most alien and embarrassing to the present taste in the severity of its principle that one has duties only to one's peers; that against beings of a lower rank, against everything alien, one may behave as one pleases or "as the heart desires," and in any case "beyond good and evil"—here pity and like feelings may find their place. The capacity for, and the duty of, long gratitude and long revenge—both only among one's peers—refinement in repaying, the sophisticated concept of friendship, a certain necessity for having enemies (as it were, as drainage ditches for the affects of envy, quarrelsomeness, exuberance—at bottom, in order to be capable of being good *friends*): all these are typical characteristics of noble morality which, as suggested, is not the morality of "modern ideas" and therefore is hard to empathize with today, also hard to dig up and uncover.

It is different with the second type of morality, *slave morality*. Suppose the violated, oppressed, suffering, unfree, who are uncertain of themselves and weary, moralize: what will their moral valuations have in common? Probably, a pessimistic suspicion about the whole condition of man will find expression, perhaps a condemnation of man along with his condition. The slave's eye is not favorable to the virtues of the powerful: he is skeptical and suspicious, *subtly* suspicious, of all the "good" that is honored there—he would like to persuade himself that even their happiness is not genuine. Conversely, those qualities are brought out and flooded with light which serve to ease existence for those who suffer: here pity, the complaisant and obliging hand, the warm heart, patience, industry, humility, and friendliness are honored—for here these are the most useful qualities and almost the only means for enduring the pressure of existence. Slave morality is essentially a morality of utility.

Here is the place for the origin of that famous opposition of "good" and "evil": into evil one's feelings project power and dangerousness, a certain terribleness, subtlety, and strength that does not permit contempt to develop. According to slave morality, those who are "evil" thus inspire fear; according to master morality it is precisely those who are "good" that inspire, and wish to inspire, fear, while the "bad" are felt to be contemptible.

The opposition reaches its climax when, as a logical consequence of slave morality, a touch of disdain is associated also with the "good" of this morality—this may be slight and benevolent—because the good human being has to be *undangerous* in the slaves' way of thinking: he is good-natured, easy to deceive, a little stupid perhaps. Wherever slave morality becomes preponderant, language tends to bring the words "good" and "stupid" closer together.

WOMEN

Chapter 11

Caring Relations and Principles of Justice

Virginia Held

Historically, men have dominated public life, and, in the public sphere, relationships are often impersonal and contractual. Businessmen negotiate; they make deals and bargain. Moreover, public figures may make decisions that affect large numbers of people, and so they may need to calculate which decision would have the best overall outcome. Small wonder, then, that men's moral theories emphasize duty, contracts, and the calculation of costs and benefits.

A moral theory tailored to the traditional concerns of women would look very different. In the small-scale world of friends and family, bargaining and calculating are less important, while love and caring dominate. According to Virginia Held, the values of care are no less important than the values of justice.

Virginia Held (1929–) is professor emerita at the City University of New York. She wrote *The Ethics of Care: Personal, Political, and Global* (2005).

THE CONTROVERSY

The question of whether impartial, universal, and rational moral principles must always be given priority over other possible grounds for
moral motivation continues to provoke extensive debate. David Velleman has recently added his defense of Kantian ethics. . . .

Velleman concentrates on the case that Bernard Williams discusses
. . . of whether a man may justifiably save his wife rather than a stranger,
if he can save only one. Williams suggests that if the man stops to think
about whether universal principles could permit him to give special
consideration to his wife rather than treating both persons impartially,
the man is having "one thought too many." . . .

Williams's arguments are presented from the point of view of a man
with a set of projects, the sorts of projects that make life worth living
for this man. The image, like its Kantian alternative, is still that of an
individual deliberator. Williams pits the individual's particular goals—
to live life with his wife or, in another case, to be a painter—against the
individual's rational and impartial moral principles, and he doubts that
the latter should always have priority. Williams disputes the view that
our particular projects must always be constrained by universal principles requiring that we should only pursue what universal principles
permit. If a man's life would be worth living only if he put, for example,
his art ahead of his universalizable moral obligations to his family,
Williams is not willing to give priority to his moral obligations. In the
example of the man and the drowning others, the man's wife may be his
project, but the dilemma is posed in terms of an individual's own particular goals versus his universal moral obligations. At a formal level it
remains within the traditional paradigm of egoism versus universalism.
Williams is unwilling to yield the claims of the ego, especially those
that enable it to continue to be the person it is, to the requirements of
universalization. But he does not reject the traditional way of conceptu-
alizing the alternatives. . . . The problem is seen as pitting the claims of
an individual ego against those of impartial rules.

The feminist challenge to Kantian moralities does require a change
in this paradigm. It does not pit an individual ego against universal
principles, but considers a particular relationship between persons, a
caring relationship, and questions whether it should always yield to
universal principles of justice. . . . When universal principles conflict
with the claims of relationships, the feminist challenge disputes that the

principles should always have priority. The feminist critique . . . gives us reason to doubt that . . . justice should always have priority over care. . . .

DIFFERENCES AMONG FEMINISTS

. . . The feminist critique of liberalism . . . is the more fundamental one that turning everyone into a complete liberal individual leaves no one adequately attentive to relationships between persons. . . . It is possible for two strangers to have a so-called "relation" of equality between them, with nothing at all to bind them together into a friendship or a community. Liberal equality doesn't itself provide or concern itself with the more substantial components of relationship. It is in evaluating and making recommendations for the latter that an ethic of care is most appropriate. As many feminists argue, the issues for moral theory are less a matter of justice versus care than of how to appropriately integrate justice and care, or care and justice if we are wary of the traditional downgrading and marginalizing of care. And it is not satisfactory to think of care, as it is conceptualized by liberal individualism, as a mere personal preference an individual may choose or not. Neither is it satisfactory to think of caring relationships as merely what rational individuals may choose to care about as long as they give priority to universal, and impartial, moral principles.

Marilyn Friedman calls attention to when partiality is or is not morally valuable. "Personal relationships," she writes, "vary widely in their moral value. The quality of a particular relationship is profoundly important in determining the moral worth of any partiality which is necessary for sustaining that relationship." Partiality toward other white supremacists on the part of a white supremacist, for instance, does not have moral worth. When relationships cause harm, or are based on such wrongful relations as that of master and slave, we should not be partial toward them. But when a relationship has moral worth, such as a caring relationship between parents and children, or a relation of trust between friends and lovers clearly may have, the question of the priority, or not, of impartiality can arise. And as moralities of impartial rules so easily forget, and as Friedman makes clear, "close relationships call . . . for personal concern, loyalty, interest, passion, and responsiveness to the uniqueness of loved ones, to their specific needs, interests, history, and so on. In a word, personal relationships call for attitudes of partiality rather than impartiality."

Evaluating the worth of relationships does not mean that universal norms have priority after all. It means that from the perspective of justice, some relationships are to be judged unjustifiable, often to the point that they should be ended to the extent possible, although this is often a limited extent. (For instance, we will never stop being the sibling of our siblings, or the ex-friend or ex-spouse of the friends or spouse with whom we have broken a relation.) But once a relationship can be deemed to have value, moral issues can arise as to whether the claims of the relationship should or should not be subordinated to the perspective of justice. . . . Moreover, the aspects of a relationship that make it a bad relationship can often be interpreted as failures to appropriately care for particular others, rather than only as violations of impartial moral rules. Certainly, avoiding serious moral wrongs should take priority over avoiding trivial ones, and pursuing highly important moral goods should take priority over pursuing insignificant ones. But this settles nothing about caring relations versus impartial moral rules. . . . Some caring relations are of the utmost importance, . . . while some of the requirements of impartial moral rules are relatively insignificant. And sometimes it is the reverse. . . .

A LOOK AT SOME CASES

Let me now try to examine in greater detail what is at issue between an ethic of care and a morality built on impartiality, and why a satisfactory feminist morality should not accept the view that universal, impartial, liberal moral principles of justice and right should always be accorded priority over the concerns of caring relationships, which include considerations of trust, friendship, and loyalty. The argument needs to be examined both at the level of personal relationships and at the level of social policy. Advocates of an ethic of care have argued successfully against the view that care—within the bounds of what is permitted by universal principles—is admirable in personal relations, but that the core value of care is inappropriate for the impersonal relations of strangers and citizens. I will explore issues of both kinds.

Consider, first, the story of Abraham. It has been discussed by a number of defenders of an ethic of care who do not agree with the religious and moral teaching that Abraham made the right decision when he chose to obey the command of God and kill his infant son. . . . From the perspective of an ethic of care, the relationship between child and parent should not always be subordinated to the command of God or of universal moral rules. But let's consider a secular case in which there is a genuine conflict between impartialist rules and the parent-child relation. . . .

Suppose the father of a young child is by profession a teacher with a special skill in helping troubled young children succeed academically. Suppose now that on a utilitarian calculation of how much overall good will be achieved, he determines that, from the point of view of universal utilitarian rules, he ought to devote more time to his work, staying at his school after hours and so on, letting his wife and others care for his own young child. But he also thinks that from the perspective of care, he should build his relationship with his child, developing the trust and mutual consideration of which it is capable. Even if the universal rules allow him some time for family life, and even if he places appropriate utilitarian value on developing his relationship with his child—the good it will do the child, the pleasure it will give him, the good it will enable the child to do in the future, etc.—the calculation still comes out, let's say, as before: he should devote more time to his students. But the moral demands of care suggest to him that he should spend more time with his child. . . .

The argument for impartiality might go something like this: Reasoning as an abstract agent, I should act on moral rules that all could accept from a perspective of impartiality. Those rules recommend that we treat all persons equally, including our children, with respect to exercising our professional skills, and that when we have special skills we should use them for the benefit of all persons equally. For example, a teacher should not favor his own child if his child happens to be one of his students. And if one has the abilities and has had the social advantages to become a teacher, one should exercise those skills when they are needed, especially when they are seriously needed.

But the father in my example also considers the perspective of care. From this perspective his relationship with his child is of enormous and irreplaceable value. He thinks that out of concern for this particular relationship he should spend more time with his child. He experiences the relationship as one of love and trust and loyalty, and thinks in this case that he should subordinate such other considerations as exercising his professional skills to this relationship. He thinks he should free himself to help his child feel the trust and encouragement his development will require, even if this conflicts with impartial morality.

He reflects on what the motives would be in choosing between the alternatives. For one alternative, the motive would be: because universal moral rules recommend it. For the other, the motive would be: because this is my child and I am the father of this child and the relationship between us is no less important than universal rules. He reflects on whether the latter can be a moral motive and concludes that it can in the sense that he can believe it is the motive he ought to act on. And he can do this without holding that every father ought to act similarly toward his child. He can further conclude that if Kantian and utilitarian moralities deny that such a motive can be moral, then they have mistakenly defined the moral to suit their purposes, and, by arbitrary fiat, excluded whatever might challenge their universalizing requirements. He may have read Annette Baier's discussion of the possible tendency of women to resist subordinating their moral sensitivities to autonomously chosen Kantian rules. Baier writes:

> What did Kant, the great prophet of autonomy, say in his moral theory about women? He said they were incapable of legislation, not fit to vote, that they needed the guidance of more "rational" males. Autonomy was not for them; it was only for first-class, really rational persons. . . . But where Kant concludes "so much the worse for women," we can conclude "so much the worse for the male fixation on the special skill of drafting legislation, for the bureaucratic mentality of rule-worship, and for the male exaggeration of the importance of independence over mutual interdependence."

The father in my example may think fathers should join mothers in paying more attention to relationships of care and in resisting the demands of impartial rules when they are excessive.

From the perspective of all, or everyone, perhaps particular relationships should be subordinated to universal rules. But from the perspective of particular persons in relationships, it is certainly meaningful to ask: Why must we adopt the perspective of all and everyone when it is a particular relationship that we care about at least as much as "being moral" in the sense required by universal rules? . . . What I am arguing is that in the ethics of care, the moral claims of caring are no less valid than the moral claims of impartial rules. This is not to say that considerations of impartiality are unimportant; it does deny that they should always have priority. This makes care ethics a challenge to liberalism as a moral theory, not a mere supplement. . . .

MODELS OF MORALITY

At the level of morality, we need to decide which "models" are appropriate for which contexts. . . .

An ethic of care suggests that the priority of justice is at best persuasive for the legal-judicial context. It might also suggest that calculations of general utility are at best appropriate for some choices about public policy. A moral theory is still needed to show us how, within the relatedness that should exist among all persons as fellow human beings, and that does exist in many personal contexts and numerous group ones, we should apply the various possible models. We will then be able to see how we should apply the legal-judicial model of impartiality to given ranges of issues, or the utilitarian model of concern for the general welfare to another range of issues, all the time recognizing other issues, such as those that can be seen most clearly among friends and within families and in cases of group solidarity, for which these models are inappropriate or inadequate. And we will see how the model of caring relations can apply and have priority in some contexts, and how it should not be limited to the personal choices made by individuals after they have met all the requirements of justice. A comprehensive moral theory would show, I believe, how care and its related values are not less important than justice. Whether they are more important remains to be argued, but not in this paper.

Chapter 12

Homeward Bound

Linda Hirshman

The women's movement of the 1960s and 1970s markedly improved the status of women in American society. Before then, it was commonly believed that a woman's place is in the home; that women are unfit for leadership roles; that women are less intelligent than men, at least when it comes to worldly affairs; that "girls" should go to college mostly to find husbands; that sexual violence against women is shameful to its victims; and that husbands, by definition, cannot rape their own wives. Today, these views simply appear sexist. But even the notion of sexism had to be established as legitimate by the feminist movement.

It has been widely observed, however, that the feminist movement had a much greater impact on the public lives of women than on their private lives. At home, women are still expected to do most of the child care and most of the chores. In this essay, Linda Hirshman diagnoses this problem, explores its roots, and advises young women on how to avoid its clutches.

Dr. Linda Hirshman (1944–) is a widely read philosopher, lawyer, and cultural historian who has written for *Slate*, *Politico*, *The Washington Post*, the *New York Times*, *Newsweek*, and *The Daily Beast*.

I. THE TRUTH ABOUT ELITE WOMEN

Half the wealthiest, most-privileged, best-educated females in the country stay home with their babies rather than work in the market economy. . . .

I stumbled across the news three years ago when researching a book on marriage after feminism. I found that among the educated elite, who are the logical heirs of the agenda of empowering women, feminism has largely failed in its goals. There are few women in the corridors of power, and marriage is essentially unchanged. The number of women at universities exceeds the number of men. But, more than a generation after feminism, the number of women in elite jobs doesn't come close.

Why did this happen? The answer I discovered—an answer neither feminist leaders nor women themselves want to face—is that while the public world has changed, albeit imperfectly, to accommodate women among the elite, private lives have hardly budged. The real glass ceiling is at home.

Looking back, it seems obvious that the unreconstructed family was destined to re-emerge after the passage of feminism's storm of social change. Following the original impulse to address everything in the lives of women, feminism turned its focus to cracking open the doors of the public power structure. This was no small task. At the beginning, there were male juries and male Ivy League schools, sex-segregated want ads, discriminatory employers, harassing colleagues. As a result of feminist efforts—and larger economic trends—the percentage of women, even of mothers in full- or part-time employment, rose robustly through the 1980s and early 1990s.

But then the pace slowed. The census numbers for all working mothers leveled off around 1990 and have fallen modestly since 1998. In interviews, women with enough money to quit work say they are "choosing" to opt out. Their words conceal a crucial reality: the belief that women are responsible for child-rearing and homemaking was largely untouched by decades of workplace feminism. Add to this the good evidence that the upper-class workplace has become more demanding and then mix in the successful conservative cultural campaign to reinforce traditional gender roles and you've got a perfect recipe for feminism's stall. . . .

The arguments still do not explain the absence of women in elite workplaces. If these women were sticking it out in the business, law, and academic worlds, now, 30 years after feminism started filling the selective schools with women, the elite workplaces should be proportionately female. They are not. Law schools have been graduating classes around 40-percent female for decades—decades during which both schools and firms experienced enormous growth. And . . . in 2003, the major law firms had only 16-percent female partners, according to the American Bar Association. It's important to note that elite workplaces like law firms grew in size during the very years that the percentage of female graduates was growing, leading you to expect a higher female employment than the pure graduation rate would indicate. The Harvard Business School has produced classes around 30-percent female. Yet only 10.6 percent of Wall Street's corporate officers are women, and a mere nine are Fortune 500 CEOs. Harvard Business School's dean, who extolled the virtues of interrupted careers on *60 Minutes*, has a 20-percent female academic faculty.

It is possible that the workplace is discriminatory and hostile to family life. If firms had hired every childless woman lawyer available, that alone would have been enough to raise the percentage of female law partners above 16 percent in 30 years. It is also possible that women are voluntarily taking themselves out of the elite job competition for lower status and lower-paying jobs. Women must take responsibility for the consequences of their decisions. It defies reason to claim that the falloff from 40 percent of the class at law school to 16 percent of the partners at all the big law firms is unrelated to half the mothers with graduate and professional degrees leaving full-time work at childbirth and staying away for several years after that, or possibly bidding down. . . .

II. THE FAILURE OF CHOICE FEMINISM

What is going on? Most women hope to marry and have babies. If they resist the traditional female responsibilities of child-rearing and house-holding, what Arlie Hochschild called "The Second Shift," they are fixing for a fight. But elite women aren't resisting tradition. None of the stay-at-home brides I interviewed saw the second shift as unjust; they agree that the household is women's work. As one lawyer-bride put it in explaining her decision to quit practicing law after four years, "I had a wedding to plan." Another, an Ivy Leaguer with a master's degree, described it in management terms: "He's the CEO and I'm the CFO. He sees to it that the money rolls in and I decide how to spend it." . . .

Conservatives contend that the dropouts prove that feminism "failed" because it was too radical, because women didn't want what feminism had to offer. In fact, if half or more of feminism's heirs . . . are not working seriously, it's because feminism wasn't radical enough: It changed the workplace but it didn't change men, and, more importantly, it didn't fundamentally change how women related to men.

The movement did start out radical. Betty Friedan's original call to arms compared housework to animal life. In *The Feminine Mystique* she wrote, "[V]acuuming the living room floor—with or without makeup—is not work that takes enough thought or energy to challenge any woman's full capacity. . . . Down through the ages man has known that he was set apart from other animals by his mind's power to have an idea, a vision, and shape the future to it . . . when he discovers and creates and shapes a future different from his past, he is a man, a human being."

Thereafter, however, liberal feminists abandoned the judgmental starting point of the movement in favor of offering women "choices." The choice talk spilled over from people trying to avoid saying "abortion," and it provided an irresistible solution to feminists trying to duck the mommy wars. A woman could work, stay home, have 10 children or one, marry or stay single. It all counted as "feminist" as long as she *chose* it. . . .

Only the most radical fringes of feminism took on the issue of gender relations at home, and they put forth fruitless solutions like socialism and separatism. We know the story about socialism. Separatism ran right into heterosexuality and reproduction, to say nothing of the need to earn a living other than at a feminist bookstore. As feminist historian Alice Echols put it, "Rather than challenging their subordination in domestic life, the feminists of NOW committed themselves to fighting for women's integration into public life."

Great as liberal feminism was, once it retreated to choice the movement had no language to use on the gendered ideology of the family. Feminists could not say, "Housekeeping and child-rearing in the nuclear family is not interesting and not socially validated. Justice requires that it not be assigned to women on the basis of their gender and at the sacrifice of their access to money, power, and honor." . . .

III. WHAT IS TO BE DONE?

Here's the feminist moral analysis that choice avoided: The family—with its repetitious, socially invisible, physical tasks—is a necessary part of life, but it allows fewer opportunities for full human flourishing than public spheres like the market or the government. This less-flourishing sphere is not the natural or moral responsibility only of women. Therefore, assigning it to women is unjust. Women assigning it to themselves is equally unjust. To paraphrase, as Mark Twain said, "A man who chooses not to read is just as ignorant as a man who cannot read."

. . . If women's flourishing does matter, feminists must acknowledge that the family is to 2005 what the workplace was to 1964 and the vote to 1920. Like the right to work and the right to vote, the right to have a flourishing life that includes but is not limited to family cannot be addressed with language of choice.

Women who want to have sex and children with men as well as good work in interesting jobs where they may occasionally wield real social power need guidance, and they need it early. Step one is simply to begin talking about flourishing. In so doing, feminism will be returning to its early, judgmental roots. This may anger some, but it should sound the alarm before the next generation winds up in the same situation. Next, feminists will have to start offering young women not choices and not utopian dreams but *solutions* they can enact on their own. Prying women out of their traditional roles is not going to be easy. It will require rules . . . .

There are three rules: Prepare yourself to qualify for good work, treat work seriously, and don't put yourself in a position of unequal resources when you marry.

The preparation stage begins with college. It is shocking to think that girls cut off their options for a public life of work as early as college. But they do. The first pitfall is the liberal-arts curriculum, which women are good at, graduating in higher numbers than men. Although many really successful people start out studying liberal arts, the purpose of a liberal education is not, with the exception of a miniscule number of academic positions, job preparation.

So the first rule is to use your college education with an eye to career goals. Feminist organizations should produce each year a survey of the most common job opportunities for people with college degrees, along with the average lifetime earnings from each job category and the characteristics such jobs require. The point here is to help women see that yes, you can study art history, but only with the realistic understanding that one day soon you will need to use your arts education to support yourself and your family. The survey would ask young women to select what they are best suited for and give guidance on the appropriate course of study. . . .

After college comes on-the-job training or further education. . . . Every *Times* groom assumed he had to succeed in business, and was really trying. By contrast, a common thread among the women I interviewed was a self-important idealism about the kinds of intellectual, prestigious, socially meaningful, politics-free jobs worth their incalculably valuable presence. So the second rule is that women must treat the first few years after college as an opportunity to lose their capitalism virginity and prepare for good work, which they will then treat seriously.

The best way to treat work seriously is to find the money. Money is the marker of success in a market economy; it usually accompanies power, and it enables the bearer to wield power, including within the family. Almost without exception, the brides who opted out graduated with roughly the same degrees as their husbands. Yet somewhere along the way the women made decisions in the direction of less money. Part of the problem was idealism; idealism on the career trail usually leads to volunteer work, or indentured servitude in social-service jobs, which is nice but doesn't get you to money. Another big mistake involved changing jobs excessively. Without exception, the brides who eventually went home had much more job turnover than the grooms did. There's no such thing as a perfect job. . . .

If you are good at work you are in a position to address the third undertaking: the reproductive household. The rule here is to avoid taking on more than a fair share of the second shift. If this seems coldhearted, consider the survey by the Center for Work-Life Policy. Fully 40 percent of highly qualified women with spouses felt that their husbands create more work around the house than they perform. According to Phyllis Moen and Patricia Roehling's *Career Mystique*, "When couples marry, the amount of time that a woman spends doing housework increases by approximately 17 percent, while a man's decreases by 33 percent." Not a single *Times* groom was a stay-at-home dad. Several of them could hardly wait for Monday morning to come. None of my *Times* grooms took even brief paternity leave when his children were born.

How to avoid this kind of rut? You can either find a spouse with less social power than you or find one with an ideological commitment to gender equality. Taking the easier path first, marry down. Don't think of this as brutally strategic. If you are devoted to your career goals and would like a man who will support that, you're just doing what men throughout the ages have done: placing a safe bet.

In her 1995 book, *Kidding Ourselves: Babies, Breadwinning and Bargaining Power*, Rhona Mahony recommended finding a sharing spouse by marrying younger or poorer, or someone in a dependent status, like a starving artist. Because money is such a marker of status and power, it's hard to persuade women to marry poorer. So here's an easier rule: Marry young or marry much older. Younger men are potential high-status companions. Much older men are sufficiently established so that they don't have to work so hard, and they often have enough money to provide unlimited household help. By contrast, slightly older men with bigger incomes are the most dangerous, but even a pure counterpart is risky. If you both are going through the elite-job hazing rituals simultaneously while having children, someone is going to have to give. Even the most devoted lawyers with the hardest-working nannies are going to have weeks when no one can get home other than to sleep. The odds are that when this happens, the woman is going to give up her ambitions and professional potential.

It is possible that marrying a liberal might be the better course. After all, conservatives justified the unequal family in two modes: "God ordained it" and "biology is destiny." Most men (and most women), including the liberals, think women are responsible for the home. But at least the liberal men should feel squeamish about it.

If you have carefully positioned yourself either by marrying down or finding someone untainted by gender ideology, you will be in a position to resist bearing an unfair share of the family. Even then you must be vigilant. Bad deals come in two forms: economics and home economics. The economic temptation is to assign the cost of child care to the woman's income. If a woman making $50,000 per year whose husband makes $100,000 decides to have a baby, and the cost of a full-time nanny is $30,000, the couple reason that, after paying 40 percent in taxes, she makes $30,000, just enough to pay the nanny. So she might as well stay home. This totally ignores that both adults are in the enterprise together and the demonstrable future loss of income, power, and security for the woman who quits. Instead, calculate that all parents make a total of $150,000 and take home $90,000. After paying a full-time nanny, they have $60,000 left to live on.

The home-economics trap involves superior female knowledge and superior female sanitation. The solutions are ignorance and dust. Never figure out where the butter is. "Where's the butter?" Nora Ephron's legendary riff on marriage begins. In it, a man asks the question when looking directly at the butter container in the refrigerator. "Where's the butter?" actually means butter my toast, buy the butter, remember when we're out of butter. Next thing you know you're quitting your job at the law firm because you're so busy managing the butter. If women never start playing the household-manager role, the house will be dirty, but the realities of the physical world will trump the pull of gender ideology. Either the other adult in the family will take a hand or the children will grow up with robust immune systems.

If these prescriptions sound less than family-friendly, here's the last rule: Have a baby. Just don't have two. Mothers' Movement Online's Judith Statdman Tucker reports that women who opt out for child-care reasons act only after the second child arrives. A second kid pressures the mother's organizational skills, doubles the demands for appointments, wildly raises the cost of education and housing, and drives the family to the suburbs. But cities, with their Chinese carry-outs and all, are better for working mothers. It is true that if you follow this rule, your society will not reproduce itself. But if things get bad enough, who knows what social consequences will ensue? After all, the vaunted French child-care regime was actually only a response to the superior German birth rate.

IV. WHY DO WE CARE?

The privileged brides of the *Times*—and their husbands—seem happy. Why do we care what they do? After all, most people aren't rich and white and heterosexual, and they couldn't quit working if they wanted to.

We care because what they do is bad for them, is certainly bad for society, and is widely imitated, even by people who never get their weddings in the *Times*. This last is called the "regime effect," and it means that even if women don't quit their jobs for their families, they think they should and feel guilty about not doing it. . . .

As for society, elites supply the labor for the decision-making classes—the senators, the newspaper editors, the research scientists, the entrepreneurs, the policy-makers, and the policy wonks. If the ruling class is overwhelmingly male, the rulers will make mistakes that benefit males, whether from ignorance or from indifference. Media surveys reveal that if only one member of a television show's creative staff is female, the percentage of women on-screen goes up from 36 percent to 42 percent. A world of 84-percent male lawyers and 84-percent female assistants is a different place than one with women in positions of social authority. . . .

Worse, the behavior tarnishes every female with the knowledge that she is almost never going to be a ruler. Princeton President Shirley Tilghman described the elite colleges' self-image perfectly when she told her freshmen last year that they would be the nation's leaders, and she clearly did not have trophy wives in mind. Why should society spend resources educating women with only a 50-percent return rate on their stated goals? The American Conservative Union carried a column in 2004 recommending that employers stay away from such women or risk going out of business. Good psychological data show that the more women are treated with respect, the more ambition they have. And vice versa. The opt-out revolution is really a downward spiral.

Finally, these choices are bad for women individually. A good life for humans includes the classical standard of using one's capacities for speech and reason in a prudent way, the liberal requirement of having enough autonomy to direct one's own life, and the utilitarian test of doing more good than harm in the world. Measured against these time-tested standards, the expensively educated upper-class moms will be leading lesser lives. At feminism's dawning, two theorists compared gender ideology to a caste system. To borrow their insight, these daughters of the upper classes will be bearing most of the burden of the work always associated with the lowest caste: sweeping and cleaning bodily waste. . . .

When she sounded the blast that revived the feminist movement 40 years after women received the vote, Betty Friedan spoke of lives of purpose and meaning, better lives and worse lives, and feminism went a long way toward shattering the glass ceilings that limited their prospects outside the home. Now the glass ceiling begins at home. Although it is harder to shatter a ceiling that is also the roof over your head, there is no other choice.

SEX, DATE RAPE, AND HAZING

Chapter 13

Our Sexual Ethics

Bertrand Russell

Bertrand Russell (1872–1970), who won the Nobel Prize for Literature, wrote on almost every philosophical subject. Many consider him to have been the greatest philosopher of the twentieth century. "Bertie," as his friends called him, was certainly ahead of his time. In this essay, first published in 1936, Lord Russell advocates a rational approach to sexual ethics. He endorses such ideas as economic equality for women, sexual relations outside of marriage, and honest communication with one's children. Russell does not, however, offer a solution to what he sees as the greatest cause of sexual conflict, namely, the tension between wanting to have a variety of partners but wanting one's own partners to be monogamous.

I

Sex, more than any other element in human life, is still viewed by many, perhaps by most, in an irrational way. Homicide, pestilence, insanity, gold, and precious stones—all the things, in fact, that are the objects

Bertrand Russell, "Our Sexual Ethics" in *Why I Am Not a Christian*, ed. Paul Edwards (New York: Simon & Schuster, Inc., 1985). Copyright © 1957, 1985 George Allen & Unwin, Ltd. Used with permission. All rights reserved.

of passionate hopes or fears—have been seen, in the past, through a mist of magic or mythology; but the sun of reason has now dispelled the mist, except here and there. The densest cloud that remains is in the territory of sex, as is perhaps natural since sex is concerned in the most passionate part of most people's lives.

It is becoming apparent, however, that conditions in the modern world are working to effect a change in the public attitude toward sex. As to what change, or changes, this will bring about, no one can speak with any certainty; but it is possible to note some of the forces now at work, and to discuss what their results are likely to be upon the structure of society.

In so far as human nature is concerned, it cannot be said to be *impossible* to produce a society in which there is very little sexual intercourse outside of marriage. The conditions necessary for this result, however, are such as are made almost unattainable by modern life. Let us, then, consider what they are.

The greatest influence toward monogamy is immobility in a region containing few inhabitants. If a man hardly ever has occasion to leave home and seldom sees any woman but his wife, it is easy for him to be faithful; but if he travels without her or lives in a crowded urban community, the problem is proportionately more difficult. The next greatest assistance to monogamy is superstition: those who genuinely believe that "sin" leads to eternal punishment might be expected to avoid it, and to some extent they do so, although not to so great an extent as might be expected. The third support of virtue is public opinion. Where, as in agricultural societies, all that a man does is known to his neighbors, he has powerful motives for avoiding whatever convention condemns. But all these causes of correct behavior are much less potent than they used to be. Fewer people live in isolation; the belief in hell-fire is dying out; and in large towns no one knows what his neighbor does. It is, therefore, not surprising that both men and women are less monogamous than they were before the rise of modern industrialism.

Of course, it may be said that, while an increasing number of people fail to observe the moral law, that is no reason for altering our standards. Those who sin, we are sometimes told, should know and recognize that they sin, and an ethical code is none the worse for being difficult to live up to. But I should reply that the question whether a code is good or bad is the same as the question whether or not it promotes human happiness. . . .

The difficulty of arriving at a workable sexual ethic arises from the conflict between the impulse to jealousy and the impulse to polygamy. There is no doubt that jealousy, while in part instinctive, is to a very large degree conventional. In societies in which a man is considered a fit object for ridicule if his wife is unfaithful, he will be jealous where she is concerned, even if he no longer has any affection for her. Thus jealousy is intimately connected with the sense of property and is much less where this sense is absent. If faithfulness is no part of what is conventionally expected, jealousy is much diminished. But although there is more possibility of lessening jealousy than many people suppose, there are very definite limits so long as fathers have rights and duties. So long as this is the case, it is inevitable that men should desire some assurance that they are the fathers of their wives' children. If women are to have sexual freedom, fathers must fade out, and wives must no longer expect to be supported by their husbands. This may come about in time, but it will be a profound social change, and its effects, for good or ill, are incalculable.

In the meantime, if marriage and paternity are to survive as social institutions, some compromise is necessary between complete promiscuity and lifelong monogamy. To decide on the best compromise at any given moment is not easy; and the decision should vary from time to time, according to the habits of the population and the reliability of birth-control methods. Some things, however, can be said with some definiteness.

In the first place, it is undesirable, both physiologically and educationally, that women should have children before the age of twenty. Our ethics should, therefore, be such as to make this a rare occurrence.

In the second place, it is unlikely that a person without previous sexual experience, whether man or woman, will be able to distinguish between mere physical attraction and the sort of congeniality that is necessary in order to make marriage a success. Moreover, economic causes compel men, as a rule, to postpone marriage, and it is neither likely that they will remain chaste in the years from twenty to thirty nor desirable psychologically that they should do so; but it is much better that, if they have temporary relations, that they should be not with prostitutes but with girls of their own class, whose motive is affection rather than money. For both these reasons, young unmarried people should have considerable freedom as long as children are avoided.

In the third place, divorce should be possible without blame to either party and should not be regarded as in any way disgraceful. A childless marriage should be terminable at the wish of one of the partners, and any marriage should be terminable by mutual consent—a year's notice being necessary in either case. Divorce should, of course, be possible on a number of other grounds—insanity, desertion, cruelty, and so on; but mutual consent should be the most usual ground.

In the fourth place, everything possible should be done to free sexual relations from the economic taint. At present, wives, just as much as prostitutes, live by the sale of their sexual charms; and even in temporary free relations the man is usually expected to bear all the joint expenses. The result is that there is a sordid entanglement of money with sex, and that women's motives not infrequently have a mercenary element. Sex, even when blessed by the church, ought not to be a profession. It is right that a woman should be paid for housekeeping or cooking or the care of children, but not merely for having sexual relations with a man. Nor should a woman who has once loved and been loved by a man be able to live ever after on alimony when his love and hers have ceased. A woman, like a man, should work for her living, and an idle wife is no more intrinsically worthy of respect than a gigolo.

II

Two very primitive impulses have contributed, though in very different degrees, to the rise of the currently accepted code of sexual behavior. One of these is modesty and the other, as mentioned above, is jealousy. Modesty, in some form and to some degree, is almost universal in the human race and constitutes a taboo which must only be broken through in accordance with certain forms and ceremonies, or, at the least, in conformity with some recognized etiquette. Not everything may be seen, and not all facts may be mentioned. This is not, as some moderns suppose, an invention of the Victorian age; on the contrary, anthropologists have found the most elaborate forms of prudery among primitive savages. The conception of the obscene has its roots deep in human nature. We may go against it from a love of rebellion, or from loyalty to the scientific spirit, or from a wish to feel wicked, such as existed in Byron; but we do not thereby eradicate it from among our natural impulses. No doubt convention determines, in a given community, exactly what is to be considered indecent, but the universal existence of *some* convention of the kind is conclusive evidence of a source which is not merely conventional. In almost every human society, pornography and exhibitionism are reckoned as offenses, except when, as not infrequently occurs, they form part of religious ceremonies. . . .

But jealousy, I believe, has been the most potent single factor in the genesis of sexual morality. Jealousy instinctively rouses anger; and anger, rationalized, becomes moral disapproval. The purely instinctive motive must have been reinforced, at an early stage in the development of civilization, by the desire of males to be certain of paternity. Without security in this respect the patriarchal family would have been impossible, and fatherhood, with all its economic implications, could not have become the basis of social institutions. It was, accordingly, wicked to have relations with another man's wife but not even mildly reprehensible to have relations with an unmarried woman. . . . It is the claim of women to equality with men that has done most to make a new system necessary in the world today. Equality can be secured in two ways: either by exacting from men the same strict monogamy as was, in the past, exacted from women; or by allowing women, equally with men, a certain relaxation of the traditional code. The first of these ways was preferred by most of the pioneers of women's rights and is still preferred by the churches; but the second has many more adherents in practice, although most of them are in doubt as to the theoretical justifiability of their own behavior. And those who recognize that *some* new ethic is required find it difficult to know just what its precepts should be.

There is another source of novelty, and that is the effect of the scientific outlook in weakening the taboo on sexual knowledge. It has come to be understood that various evils—for example, venereal disease—cannot be effectively combated unless they are spoken of much more openly than was formerly thought permissible; and it has also been found that reticence and ignorance are apt to have injurious effects upon the psychology of the individual. Both sociology and psychoanalysis have led serious students to reject the policy of silence in regard to sexual matters, and many practical educators, from experience with children, have adopted the same position. Those who have a scientific outlook on human behavior, moreover, find it impossible to label any action as "sin"; they realize that what we do has its origin in our heredity, our education, and our environment, and that it is by control of these causes, rather than by denunciation, that conduct injurious to society is to be prevented.

In seeking a new ethic of sexual behavior, therefore, we must not ourselves be dominated by the ancient irrational passions which gave rise to the old ethic, though we should recognize that they may, by accident, have led to some sound maxims, and that, since they still exist, though perhaps in a weakened form, they are still among the data of our problem. What we have to do positively is to ask ourselves what moral rules are most likely to promote human happiness, remembering always that, whatever the rules may be, they are not likely to be universally observed. That is to say, we have to consider the effect which the rules will in fact have, not that which they would have if they were completely effective.

III

Let us look next at the question of knowledge on sexual subjects, which arises at the earliest age and is the least difficult and doubtful of the various problems with which we are concerned. There is no sound reason, of any sort or kind, for concealing facts when talking to children. Their questions should be answered and their curiosity satisfied in exactly the same way in regard to sex as in regard to the habits of fishes, or any other subject that interests them. There should be no sentiment, because young children cannot feel as adults do and see no occasion for high-flown talk. It is a mistake to begin with the loves of the bees and the flowers; there is no point in leading up to the facts of life by devious routes. The child who is told what he wants to know and allowed to see his parents naked will have no pruriency and no obsession of a sexual kind. Boys who are brought up in official ignorance think and talk much more about sex than boys who have always heard this topic treated on a level with any other. Official ignorance and actual knowledge teach them to be deceitful and hypocritical with their elders. On the other hand, real ignorance, when it is achieved, is likely to be a source of shock and anxiety, and to make adaptation to real life difficult. All ignorance is regrettable, but ignorance on so important a matter as sex is a serious danger.

When I say that children should be told about sex, I do not mean that they should be told only the bare physiological facts; they should be told whatever they wish to know. There should be no attempt to represent adults as more virtuous than they are, or sex as occurring only in marriage. There is no excuse for deceiving children. And when, as must happen in conventional families, they find that their parents have lied, they lose confidence in them and feel justified in lying to them. There are facts which I should not obtrude upon a child, but I would tell him anything sooner than say what is not true. Virtue which is based upon a false view of the facts is not real virtue. Speaking not only from theory but from practical experience, I am convinced that complete openness on sexual subjects is the best way to prevent children from thinking about them excessively, nastily, or unwholesomely, and also the almost indispensable preliminary to an enlightened sexual morality.

Where adult sexual behavior is concerned, it is by no means easy to arrive at a rational compromise between the antagonistic considerations that have each their own validity. The fundamental difficulty is, of course, the conflict between the impulse to jealousy and the impulse to sexual variety. Neither impulse, it is true, is universal: there are those (though they are few) who are never jealous, and there are those (among men as well as among women) whose affections never wander from the chosen partner. If either of these types could be made universal, it would be easy to devise a satisfactory code. It must be admitted, however, that either type can be made more common by conventions designed to that end.

Much ground remains to be covered by a complete sexual ethic, but I do not think we can say anything very positive until we have more experience, both of the effects of various systems and of the changes resulting from a rational education in matters of sex. . . .

In the meantime, it would be well if men and women could remember, in sexual relations, in marriage, and in divorce, to practice the ordinary virtues of tolerance, kindness, truthfulness, and justice. Those who, by conventional standards, are sexually virtuous too often consider themselves thereby absolved from behaving like decent human beings. Most moralists have been so obsessed by sex that they have laid much too little emphasis on other more socially useful kinds of ethically commendable conduct.

Chapter 14

Alcohol and Rape

Nicholas Dixon

The black-and-white cases are easy to assess: if a man has consensual sex with a woman who is slightly tipsy, it is not rape; if a man has sex with a woman who has passed out from drunkenness, it is rape. Real life, however, is peppered with grey. What if a woman slurs her words and remembers little the next day? Was it sexual assault even if she initiated the encounter and seemed rational, despite the slurring? This kind of case is difficult to assess, for many reasons.

Nicholas Dixon is a professor of philosophy at Alma College in Michigan.

Many date or acquaintance rapes, especially those that occur in a college setting, involve the use of alcohol by both rapist and victim. To what extent, if any, should the fact that a woman has been drinking alcohol before she has sexual relations affect our determination of whether or not she has been raped? I will consider the impact of the woman's intake of alcohol on both the *actus reus* ("guilty act") and *mens rea* ("guilty mind") elements of rape. A man is guilty of rape only if he not only commits the *actus reus* of rape—sex without his partner's consent—but does so with the requisite guilty mind, that

Nicholas Dixon, "Alcohol and Rape" in *Public Affairs Quarterly*, vol. 15, no. 4 (October 2001): 341–54. Copyright © 2001. Used with permission.

is, intentionally, knowingly, recklessly, or negligently. I will take for granted that, regardless of a woman's alcoholic intake, she has been raped whenever a man forces himself on her after she says "no" or otherwise resists. I will focus instead on situations when women who have been drinking provide varying levels of acquiescence to sex. Let us begin by considering two relatively straightforward examples, which we can use as limiting cases, of sexual encounters involving alcohol.

I. TWO LIMITING CASES

A. Fraternity Gang Rape

In 1988 four Florida State University fraternity members allegedly had sex with an 18-year-old female student after she had passed out with an almost lethal blood alcohol level of .349 percent. Afterwards, she was allegedly "dumped" in a different fraternity house.

If these events, which led to a five-year ban on the fraternity chapter, really happened, the woman was certainly raped. Since a woman who is unconscious after heavy drinking is unable to consent, the fraternity members committed the *actus reus* of rape. Moreover, any claim that they were unaware of her lack of consent, thus potentially negating the *mens rea* requirement, would ring hollow. We may extrapolate beyond this extreme case to situations where a person is so drunk that, while she is conscious, she is barely aware of where she is and who her partner is, and she has no recollection of what has happened the following day. She may acquiesce and give the physiological responses that indicate consent, and she may even say "yes" when asked whether she wants to have sex, but her mental state is so impaired by alcohol that she cannot give a sufficiently meaningful level of consent to rebut rape charges against the man with whom she has sexual relations.

B. A Regretted Sexual Encounter

A male and female college student go on a dinner date, and both drink a relatively small amount of alcohol, say a glass of wine or beer. The conversation flows freely, and she agrees to go back to his place to continue the evening. They have one more drink there, start kissing and making out, and he asks her to spend the night. She is not drunk and, impressed by his gentle and communicative manner, accepts his offer. However, she is not used to drinking, and, although she is not significantly cognitively impaired—her speech is not slurred and her conversation is lucid—her inhibitions have been markedly lowered by the alcohol. When she wakes up alongside him the following morning, she bitterly regrets their lovemaking.

No rape has occurred. While she now regrets having spent the night with her date, and would quite likely not have agreed to do so had she not drunk any alcohol, her consent at the time was sufficiently voluntary to rule out any question of rape. While their sexual encounter violated her more lasting values, this no more entails that she did not "really" consent than the fact that my overeating at dinner violates my long-term plan to diet entails that my indulgence was not an autonomous action. Moreover, even if we granted for the sake of argument the far-fetched claim that the *actus reus* of rape occurred, his belief that she did consent was perfectly reasonable, so he would still fail to exhibit the requisite *mens rea*. . . . A distinction exists between rape and bad sex. Unwisely having sex after unwisely drinking alcohol is not necessarily rape. We do a lot of unwise things when drinking, like *continuing* to drink too long and getting a bad hangover, and staying up too late when we have to work the next day. In neither case would we question our consent to our act of continuing to drink or staying up late. Why should a person's consent to sex after moderate amounts of drinking be any more suspect?

II. PROBLEMATIC INTERMEDIATE CASES: IMPAIRED SEX

Real sexual encounters involving alcohol tend to fall in between these two limiting cases. Imagine, for instance, a college student who gets very drunk at a party. Her blood alcohol level is well above the legal limit for driving. She is slurring her words and is unsteady on her feet, but she knows where she is and with whom she is speaking or dancing. She ends up spending the night with a guy at the party—perhaps someone she has just met, perhaps an acquaintance, but no one with whom she is in an ongoing relationship. She willingly responds to his sexual advances, but, like the woman in case IB, horribly regrets her sexual encounter the next day. Although she remembers going home with the guy from the party, she cannot recall much else from the evening and night. Let us call this intermediate case, in which the woman's judgment is significantly impaired by alcohol, "impaired sex." Has she been raped?

In the next two subsections I will examine two competing analyses of impaired sex, each one suggested by one of the limiting cases in section I. First, though, I pause to consider how relevant the degree to which the man has helped to bring about the woman's impaired state is to the question of whether rape has occurred. Suppose that he has deliberately got her drunk, cajoling her to down drink after drink, with the intention of lowering her resistance to his planned sexual advances? The very fact that he uses such a strategy implies that he doubts that she would agree to have sex with him if she were sober. Should she bring rape charges, on the ground that her acquiescence to sex when she was drunk was invalid, his claim that he believed that she voluntarily consented would appear disingenuous. His recklessness in disregarding doubts about the voluntariness of her consent arguably meets the *mens rea* requirement. (Remember that in this section we are discussing women who are very drunk to the point of slurring their words and being unsteady on their feet, not those who are less inhibited after drinking a moderate amount of alcohol.)

For the remainder of this paper, I will focus instead on the more difficult variant of impaired sex in which the man does not use alcohol as a tool for seduction. Instead, he meets the woman when she is already drunk, or else he drinks with her with no designs on getting her drunk. In either case, he spontaneously takes advantage of the situation in which he finds himself. Is he guilty of rape?

A. Women's Responsibility for Their Own Actions

Few would deny that the woman in section IB is responsible for her own unwise decision to engage in a sexual encounter that she now regrets. Katie Roiphe and Camille Paglia would extend this approach to impaired sex, involving a woman who is very drunk but not incoherent. Roiphe insists that women are autonomous adults who are responsible for the consequences of their use of alcohol and other drugs.[1] And Paglia argues that sex is an inherently risky business, in which rape is an ever-present danger. Rather than complain about sexual assault, women who desire to be sexually active should take steps to minimize its danger, by being alert to warning signs, learning self-defense, and avoiding getting drunk when doing so would put them at risk for rape.[2] . . .

Both Roiphe and Paglia are vulnerable to powerful criticisms. . . . However, we can isolate from their more dubious views a relatively uncontroversial underlying principle, which is surely congenial to liberal and most other types of feminists: namely, that we should respect women's status as agents, and we should not degrade them by treating them as incapable of making autonomous decisions about alcohol and sexuality. We should, instead, hold women at least partly responsible for the consequences of their voluntary decision to drink large amounts of alcohol, made in full knowledge that it may result in choices that they will later regret. This principle would count against regarding impaired sex as rape. A plausible corollary of this principle is that women, as autonomous beings, have a duty to make their wishes about sex clear to their partners. When a woman drinks heavily and ends up having a sexual encounter that she later regrets, she has failed to exercise this positive duty of autonomous people. Her actions have sent the wrong message to her partner, and to blame him for the sex in which she willingly engages but that she later regrets seems unfair. Even if we allow that her consent is so impaired that the *actus reus* of rape has occurred, on this view he does not fulfill the *mens rea* element of the crime of rape. The onus is on the woman to communicate her lack of consent and, in the absence of such communication, his belief in her consent is quite reasonable. In sum, proponents of this approach hesitate to regard impaired sex as rape, because doing so suggests that women are unable to make autonomous decisions about alcohol and sexuality, and because it ignores women's positive duty to exercise their autonomy by clearly communicating their considered preferences (and not just their momentary passion) about sex.

B. Communicative Sexuality: Men's Duty to Ensure That Women Consent

The "women's responsibility for sex" approach is very plausible in case IB, where a woman later regrets sex in which she willingly engaged after moderate drinking. However, men's accountability for unwanted sex becomes unavoidable in the gang rape described in subsection IA. Granted, the female student may have voluntarily and very unwisely chosen to drink massive amounts of alcohol, but once she had passed out, the four fraternity members who allegedly had intercourse with her had absolutely no reason to believe that she consented to sex.

Regardless of whether they deliberately got her drunk or, on the other hand, took advantage of her after finding her in this condition, they are guilty of recklessly ignoring the evident risk that she did not consent, and hence fulfill the *mens rea* requirement for rape.

In cases such as this, Lois Pineau's model of "communicative sexuality" becomes enormously plausible.[3] . . . Its central tenet is that men too are responsible for ensuring that effective communication occurs. In particular, the burden is on men to ensure that their female partners really do consent to sexual intimacy, and they should refrain from sexual activity if they are not sure of this consent. A reasonable belief that a woman consented to sex will still count as a defense against rape, but the reasonableness of this belief will itself be judged on whether it would have been reasonable, from the woman's point of view, to consent to sex. Since virtually no woman would want four men to have sex with her after she has passed into an alcoholic coma, in the absence of some miraculous evidence that the female student actually wanted sex in such unpleasant circumstances, the four fraternity members blatantly violated their duty to be sure of the woman's consent, and are indeed guilty of rape.

More generally, Pineau argues that it is never reasonable to assume that a woman consents to "aggressive non-communicative sex." Not only does her approach regard the extreme case of sex with an unconscious person as rape, but it would put any man who fails to take reasonable precautions to ensure that a woman consents to sex at risk for a rape conviction should she later declare that she did not consent. When doubt exists about consent, the burden is on the man to *ask*. The much-discussed Antioch University "Sexual Offense Policy," which requires explicit consent to each new level of sexual intimacy every time it occurs, is a quasi-legal enactment of Pineau's model of communicative sexuality.

Pineau's approach entails a very different analysis of our central case of impaired sex than the "women's responsibility for sex" model discussed in the previous section. At first blush, one might think that all that Pineau would require of a man would be to ask the woman whether she is really sure that she wants to continue with sexual intimacy. If he boldly forges ahead without even asking the woman this question, and if the woman later claims that she was too drunk for her acquiescence to sex to constitute genuine consent, he risks being found guilty of Pineau's proposed category of "non-aggravated sexual assault," which would carry a lighter penalty than "standard" rape when a woman communicates her lack of consent by saying "no" or otherwise resisting.

But even explicitly asking the woman for consent may be insufficient to protect him from blame and liability under the communicative sexuality model. The issue is precisely whether the word "yes," when spoken by a woman who is very drunk, is sufficient evidence of her consent. Being very drunk means that her judgment is impaired, as is evident from her horror and regret the following morning when she realizes what she has done. Given that we are only too aware of our propensity to do things that we later regret when we are very drunk, the man in this situation has good reason to doubt whether the woman's acquiescence to his advances and her "yes" to his explicit question is a fully autonomous reflection of lasting values and desires. Since he cannot be reasonably sure that the woman consents, he should refrain from sexual intercourse. Even if he is unaware of the danger that she does not consent, he *should* be aware and is, therefore, guilty of negligence. His belief that she consents may be sincere, but it is unreasonable and does not provide a defense to charges of non-aggravated sexual assault. On Pineau's "communicative sexuality" model, then, the man who proceeds with impaired sex meets both the *actus reus* and *mens rea* requirements of non-aggravated sexual assault.

III. SHOULD WE PUNISH MEN FOR IMPAIRED SEX?

Pineau's claim that men have a *moral obligation* to ensure that their partners consent to sex is very plausible. Given alcohol's tendency to cloud people's judgment, men should be especially careful to ensure that a woman consents to sex when she is very drunk. In most circumstances, this requires simply refraining from sexual activity. Imposing this relatively minor restriction on men's sexual freedom seems amply justified by the goal of preventing the enormous harm of rape. However, whether we should find men who fail to meet this duty and proceed to have sex with very drunk women guilty of rape—or even of non-aggravated sexual assault or a similar felony carrying a lighter penalty than "standard" rape—is much more controversial.

A. The Importance of Context

Alan Soble criticizes the Antioch University policy on the ground that it fails to distinguish between different types of sexual encounter.[4] Its demand that people obtain explicit verbal consent to each new level of sexual activity during each sexual encounter may be appropriate for one-night stands with strangers. However, it seems unduly intrusive in the context of an ongoing, committed relationship, when the partners may be sufficiently well attuned to one another's body language to be reasonably sure that both people consent to sex. Under Antioch's policy, "[t]he history of the relationship, let alone the history of the evening, counts for nothing."[5]

A similar criticism applies to the demand that men always refrain from impaired sex. While the existence of a long-term, committed relationship does not provide a man with immunity from charges of sexual misconduct—marital rape, after all, can occur—men may reasonably proceed with sexual intimacy with long-term partners who are very drunk when doing so with a stranger would be wrong. In the case of a stranger, the only clue to her wishes that he has is her current, drunken acquiescence, whereas his history of consenting lovemaking with his partner, presumably often when both are sober, gives him every reason to believe that her current consent is fully voluntary and reflective of her ongoing desires. Another exception that could apply even in the case of one-night stands would be when a woman, while sober, gives her advance consent to consuming large amounts of alcohol followed by sexual activity. So if we do criminalize sex with women whose judgment is impaired by large amounts of alcohol, we need to build in exceptions for ongoing relationships and advance consent. . . .

B. Imprecise Distinctions and Fairness to Men

Because of the risk of the substantial harm of sex without a woman's fully voluntary consent, men should normally not have impaired sex. And, provided that we widely publicize the change in rape law and allow exceptions for established relationships and advance consent, criminalizing impaired sex would not be inherently unfair to men. The strongest reason against doing so is that implementing such a law would be a logistical nightmare that would indeed create the risk of unjustly convicting men.

Distinctions that are morally significant are difficult to translate into law. For instance, whether a man deliberately encourages a woman to drink large amounts of alcohol in order to make her more responsive to his sexual advances or, on the other hand, encounters her when she is already drunk or else innocently drinks with her with no intention of taking advantage of her, is relevant to our judgment of his actions. However, proving such subtle differences in intention would be extremely difficult, especially when the prosecution's star witness, the woman who was allegedly assaulted, was drunk at the crucial time.

The biggest logistical problem of all concerns drawing boundaries. The only clear cases are of the type discussed in section I: sex with a woman who is unconscious or incoherent due to alcohol (rape), and communicative sex with a lucid, slightly tipsy woman who later regrets it (no rape). In between these limiting cases is a vast array of situations, whose diversity is concealed by my use of the blanket category of impaired sex. Just how impaired does a woman's judgment have to be to fall into this category? At what point does a woman progress from being merely tipsy, and responsible for any poor judgments that she makes as a result of her condition, to being so impaired that a man who proceeds to have sex with her recklessly or negligently runs the risk of sex without her fully voluntary consent? . . . But the vagueness of the meaning of "significantly impaired" does indeed create doubts about whether men would have fair warning about how to conform their behavior to this new law. Saying that when in doubt, men should err on the side of caution is fair enough, but the only way to be completely sure of avoiding conviction for this felony would be to completely abstain from sex with women who have drunk any alcohol, and this would be an unreasonable restriction on sexual freedom. A law that gives fair warning requires a certain amount of precision about forbidden behavior, and this is hard to come by in matters of impairment due to alcohol. Setting a certain blood alcohol level as the cutoff point seems arbitrary, and requiring a man to be aware of his partner's reading on this scale seems unreasonable and even absurd.

In defense of criminalizing impaired sex, one might argue that making judgment calls about how a legal rule applies to a particular case is precisely what courts are supposed to do. This approach works well when courts are asked to determine how a clear-cut rule applies to the often messy details of a case. The problem here, though, is that the distinction on which impaired sex is based is itself fuzzy, making judgments about whether rape has occurred doubly difficult.

Those who would make impaired sex a felony might point out the analogy with drunk driving laws, in which we set a more or less arbitrary blood alcohol level as the legally acceptable limit, in full knowledge that this limit corresponds only approximately with drivers' level of impairment. The overwhelmingly good overall consequences of a law that deters drunk driving help us to accept the occasional minor injustice of convicting a person whose driving ability was, despite his or her illegal blood alcohol level, not significantly affected. In this light, my dismissal of a blood alcohol level as a cutoff point for impaired sex may have been premature. Such a law would give men a strong incentive to refrain from sex when they have any doubts that their potential partner may be too impaired to give fully voluntary consent.

However, criminalizing impaired sex when the woman's blood alcohol level is above a certain limit is unacceptable for several reasons. First, it places an onerous burden on the man to know his partner's blood alcohol level, in contrast to drunk driving laws, which require us to monitor our *own* intake of intoxicants. Even a man who accompanies his partner throughout her drinking may be unaware of her tolerance level, which may be unusually low. Men who meet women who have already been drinking would have even less reason to be sure that their blood alcohol level is within the legal limit. To be sure of escaping conviction for rape, men in these circumstances would have to either administer portable breathalyzer tests to their partners or else simply abstain from sex. Now showing such restraint may be precisely the kind of caring, thoughtful behavior that we, following Pineau's communicative sexuality model, want to encourage. But to require men to do so, on pain of criminal sanctions (typically imprisonment), seems to be an unduly heavy-handed intrusion into the sex lives of two adults.

Second, measuring a woman's blood alcohol level in order to secure convictions for rape will very likely not be feasible in most cases. Courts need to know her level of impairment at the time of the alleged rape, but in very few cases will a woman be available for a blood test immediately after the sexual encounter. Even an hour afterwards may be too late, in that her blood alcohol level may have dropped below the legal limit for her partner to be at risk for impaired sex. Due to the emotional trauma or the effects of alcohol, many women will not report the incident until several hours afterwards or even the next day, by which time most or all of the alcohol will have worked its way through her system.

In sum, making impaired sex a felony would be unfair to men, in that the concept "significantly impaired" is too vague for (1) courts to be able to make non-arbitrary judgments to distinguish the guilty from the innocent or (2) men to have fair warning to enable them to conform their behavior to the law. If, on the other hand, we make the law more precise and objective by specifying a blood alcohol content above which a woman's sexual partner would be liable for prosecution for impaired sex, we are placing an undue burden on men whose potential sexual partners have been drinking. Moreover, few women who believe that they have been raped will submit to blood alcohol tests early enough to secure convictions for impaired sex.

One way we might soften the blow of concerns with fair warning would be to make impaired sex a misdemeanor rather than a felony. Such a law would protect women, while the occasional injustice done to men who are convicted though they reasonably believe that their partners consent would result only in such minimal penalties as suspended sentences, fines, or community service. Granted, these minimal penalties might provide little deterrence to men, but they would at least send the desired message that men should exercise care in sexual intimacy when alcohol is involved. And the fact that the penalties are light would minimize whatever danger might exist of frivolous or vindictive complaints against men. However, even if we reduce it to a misdemeanor, we would be hard pressed to rid impaired sex of the connotations of moral turpitude that currently attach to rape and other sexual offenses, so the issue of fair warning would remain significant. Moreover, even though the penalties for a misdemeanor would be slight, we should hesitate to involve courts in prosecuting cases that are very difficult to prove and that people may well sometimes justly perceive as unfair to defendants.

IV. CONCLUSION

Existing rape laws probably suffice to convict men for clear cases of sexual misconduct involving alcohol, such as sex with unconscious women or with women who are drunk to the point of incoherence. In jurisdictions where such laws do not exist, we should create a category of rape—on the lines of "sex with a partner who is incapable of consent"—that would criminalize such cases. Granted, complications would arise. We would probably have to allow for exceptions for advance consent and for ongoing relationships. And, as in all rape cases, proving guilt may often be difficult, often reducing to "her word against his." But the harm done by men who take advantage of women in such circumstances is great enough to justify taking on these problems.

However, we would do better to deal with impaired sex by means of moral disapproval and educational measures rather than legal sanctions. The dangers of unjustly convicting men on the basis of unworkable distinctions, and of simultaneously degrading women (however inadvertently) and being unfair to men by underestimating women's ability to take responsibility for their alcohol intake and sexuality, are too great. Instead, we should regard impaired sex as a moral wrong on the lines of obtaining sexual gratification by means of trickery, such as concealing the fact that one has a spouse or significant other, or declaring one's undying love when all one wants is a brief fling. In the case of both impaired sex and trickery, one's partner is prevented from making a fully autonomous decision about her sexual activity: either because her judgment is clouded by alcohol, or because she has been denied vital information. Both are wrong, and both are better dealt with by informal sanctions than by inevitably heavy-handed and sometimes unfair legal interventions.

NOTES

1. Katie Roiphe, "The Morning After" in Robert Trevas, Arthur Zucker, and Donald Borchert (eds.), *Philosophy of Sex and Love: A Reader* (Upper Saddle River, NJ: Prentice Hall, 1997), p. 365.

2. Camille Paglia, "Date Rape: Another Perspective" in William H. Shaw (ed.), *Social and Personal Ethics,* 2nd edition (Belmont, CA: Wadsworth Publishing Co., 1996).

3. Lois Pineau, "Date Rape: A Feminist Analysis," *Law and Philosophy* 8 (1989), pp. 217–43.

4. Alan Soble, "Antioch's 'Sexual Offense Policy': A Philosophical Exploration" *Journal of Social Philosophy,* vol. 28, no. 1 (spring 1997), pp. 30–32.

5. Ibid., p. 30.

Chapter 15

A Death at Penn State

Caitlin Flanagan

Each year, there are a small number of hazing deaths in the United States. In 2017, four college students died in incidents that involved binge drinking, peer pressure, and fraternity ritual: Maxwell Gruver of Louisiana State University (LSU), who died at age eighteen; Tim Piazza of Pennsylvania State University (Penn State), who died at age nineteen; and Matthew Ellis (of Texas State) and Andrew Coffey (of FSU) who died at age twenty. Despite the publicity created by such tragedies, the fraternity culture hasn't changed. The case of Tim Piazza, however, promises to have the most impact. Over two dozen people were criminally charged in Piazza's death, and the Beta Theta Pi national fraternity has agreed, as part of a court settlement, to make its chapter houses alcohol free by August 2020.

I

At about 3 p.m. on Friday, February 3, Tim Piazza, a sophomore at Penn State University, arrived at Hershey Medical Center by helicopter. Eighteen hours earlier, he had been in the kind of raging good health that only teenagers enjoy. He was a handsome, redheaded kid with a shy smile, a hometown girlfriend, and a family who loved him very much. Now he had a lacerated spleen, an abdomen full of blood, and multiple traumatic brain injuries. He had fallen down a flight of stairs during a hazing event at his fraternity, Beta Theta Pi, but the members had waited nearly 12 hours before calling 911, relenting only when their pledge "looked fucking dead." Tim underwent surgery shortly after arriving at Hershey, but it was too late. He died early the next morning.

Every year or so brings another such death, another healthy young college man a victim of hazing at the hands of one of the nation's storied social fraternities. And with each new death, the various stakeholders perform in ways that are so ritualized, it's almost as though they are completing the second half of the same hazing rite that killed the boy.

The fraternity enters a "period of reflection"; it may appoint a "blue-ribbon panel." It will announce reforms that look significant to anyone outside the system, but that are essentially cosmetic. Its most dramatic act will be to shut down the chapter, and the house will stand empty for a time, its legend growing ever more thrilling to students who walk past and talk of a fraternity so off the chain that it killed a guy. In short order it will "recolonize" on the campus, and in a few years the house will be back in business.

The president of the college or university where the tragedy occurred will make bold statements about ensuring there is never another fraternity death at his institution. But he knows—or will soon discover—that fraternity executives do not serve at the pleasure of college presidents. He will be forced into announcing his own set of limp reforms. He may "ban" the fraternity from campus, but since the fraternity will have probably closed the chapter already, he will be revealed as weak.

The media will feast on the story, which provides an excuse to pay an unwarranted amount of attention to something viewers are always interested in: the death of a relatively affluent white suburban kid. Because the culprits are also relatively affluent white suburban kids, there is no need to fear pandering to the racial bias that favors stories about this type of victim. The story is ultimately about the callousness and even cruelty of white men.

The grieving parents will appear on television. In their anger and sorrow, they will hope to press criminal charges. Usually they will also sue the fraternity, at which point they will discover how thoroughly these organizations have indemnified themselves against culpability in such deaths. The parents will try to turn their grief into meaningful purpose, but they will discover how intractable a system they are up against, and how draining the process of chipping away at it is. They will be worn down by the endless civil case that forces them to relive their son's passing over and over. The ritual will begin to slow down, but then a brand-new pair of parents—filled with the energy and outrage of early grief—will emerge, and the cycle will begin again.

Tim Piazza's case, however, has something we've never seen before. This time the dead student left a final testimony, a vivid, horrifying, and inescapable account of what happened to him and why. The house where he was so savagely treated had been outfitted with security cameras, which recorded his long ordeal. Put together with the texts and group chats of the fraternity brothers as they delayed seeking medical treatment and then cleaned up any traces of a wild party—and with the 65-page report released by a Centre County grand jury, which recommended 1,098 criminal charges against 18 former members and against the fraternity itself—the footage reveals a more complete picture of certain dark realities than we have previously had.

II

In 2004, a Penn State alumnus from the class of 1970 named Donald Abbey visited his old fraternity house, Beta Theta Pi. He had been a star fullback in the early years of the Joe Paterno era, and gone on to become a billionaire real-estate investor and builder in California who remembered the Beta house as a central part of his college experience. But when he visited, he was shocked—it was, he recalled, "repulsive," and he felt compelled to bring his experience in "repositioning properties" to bear on 220 North Burrowes Road. He would spend a total of $8.5 million on what would be the most extensive renovation of an American fraternity house in history.

Abbey's taste does not run to the economic or the practical. One of the mansions he built for himself in California, in the San Gabriel Valley, has an underground firing range; a million-gallon, temperature-controlled trout pond; an oak-paneled elevator; and "Venetian plaster masterpieces throughout." Similarly, his vision for the refurbished Beta house was like something out of a movie about college. (*Exterior: the frat where the rich bastards live.*) The bathrooms had heated floors, the two kitchens had copper ceilings, the tables were hand-carved mahogany imported from Colombia. At the entrances were biometric fingerprint scanners.

Abbey seems not to have considered why the house might have become so "repulsive" in the first place. A simple trip through the archives of *The Daily Collegian* might have revealed to him that the Alpha Upsilon chapter of Beta Theta Pi was hardly the Garrick Club. This was an outfit in which a warm day might bring the sight of a brother sitting, with his pants pulled down, on the edge of a balcony, while a pledge stood on the ground below, his hands raised as though to catch the other man's feces. At the very least, this might not have been the crowd for anything requiring a fingerprint.

The renovations were largely complete by the winter of 2007, and almost immediately the members began to trash the house. Abbey was justly furious, and at some point he had at least 14 security cameras installed throughout the public rooms, an astonishing and perhaps unprecedented step. The cameras were in no way secret, and yet the brothers continued to engage in a variety of forbidden acts, including hazing, in clear view of them. In late January 2009, the national fraternity put the chapter on probation. But the young men continued to break the rules. A few weeks later, the chapter's probation was converted to the more serious "interim suspension." Incredibly, with the pressure on and the cameras still recording, the behavior continued. By the end of February, the chapter had been disbanded.

The public often interprets the "closing" of a fraternity as a decisive action. In fact, it is really more of a "reopening under new management" kind of process. The national organization grooms a new set of brothers—a "colony"—and trains them carefully so that the bad behavior of the previous group will not be replicated. The first few years typically go very well. Indeed, not two years after the Penn State chapter of Beta Theta Pi reopened in the fall of 2010, it won a Sisson Award, one of the highest honors the national fraternity can confer. But just as typically, the chapter reverts to its previous behavior. Alumni visit their old house and explain how things ought to be done; private Facebook groups and GroupMe chats are initiated among brothers of different chapters, and information about secret hazing rituals is exchanged. This time, when the brothers of the newly reconstituted Beta chapter reverted to type and started hazing, the national organization did not intervene.

I wanted to learn more about the cameras, and also about something called the "Shep Test," so in June I called the North-American Interfraternity Conference, the trade association for social fraternities, which is located in Carmel, Indiana. I asked to schedule an interview with the CEO, Jud Horras, who was also a Beta, a former assistant secretary of the fraternity's national organization, and someone who had been intimately involved in the disbanding and recolonization of the Penn State chapter.

III

In 1998, a year after Tim Piazza was born, Beta Theta Pi launched something it called Men of Principle, intended to be a "culture-reversing initiative." What culture was it seeking to reverse? This was best answered in the four planks of the campaign. The first was administrative: create "a five-person trained and active advisory team." The other three were the crux of the matter: commit "to a 100% hazing-free pledge program," institute "alcohol-free recruitment," and eliminate the "Shep Test," which it described as "the rogue National Test."

The last one caught my attention, so I Googled around to find out what it was. Most fraternity secrets—their handshakes and members' manuals and rituals—have gone the way of everything else in the time of the internet, and even those customs that members want to hide aren't too hard to track down. But there really wasn't anything at all about the Shep Test—except for this, from the national Beta organization:

> Some chapters conduct the "Shep Test." If Francis W. Shepardson, Denison 1882, one of the greatest leaders in our great and good fraternity knew that this practice was named after him he would be disgraced. This act is in direct violation of our third principle and second and third obligations. It contradicts everything Beta Theta Pi stands for.

It seemed to me—based on the fact that I could find nothing else about it—that the Shep Test had truly been eliminated. Or so I thought, until I read the grand jury's presentment of the Piazza case. Text messages from members' cellphones had been entered into evidence, and included this exchange between two brothers at the time of the fall 2016 initiation:

CASEY: We were setting up
TORRYE: Setting what up?
CASEY: Like the shep test and the fake branding
TORRYE: Ohh
CASEY: I in charge of administering the shep test
TORRYE: What happens first?
CASEY: Fake branding

And from the next night:

CASEY: It starting . . . We have them wait in the boiler room after the shep
test until we set up paddling

As people have since explained it to me, the Shep Test itself is little more than a quiz about Beta Theta Pi history, but it's one part of a night of mind games and physical punishments. A former Beta told me that pledges were held down on a table as a red-hot poker was brought close to their bare feet and they were told they were going to be branded. With pillowcases over their heads, they were paddled, leaving bruises and, on at least one occasion, breaking the skin. They were forced to eat and drink disgusting things, denied sleep, and terrorized in a variety of other ways.

Jud Horras called me back and proposed something surprising: He would fly to Los Angeles for a day to meet with me in the lobby of an airport hotel. I said it was a pity to come all that way and not see the beach, so I would pick him up and take him to breakfast at Hermosa Beach, where he couldn't shake me if my questions got too difficult. He was coming out to show that he had nothing to hide, but I knew he was not prepared for the hardest question I had for him, which I would return to over and over again: Why hadn't Beta Theta Pi taken the simple, obvious steps that would have saved Tim Piazza's life?

Jud Horras is a young man with a wife and a small son and daughter, and if Tim Piazza were alive and well—if he'd gone home to his apartment that night plastered but with a story to tell—I would have fully enjoyed my time with him. He grew up in Ames, Iowa, and spent summers working on a farm—rare for fraternity members, who are more often suburban kids of relative affluence. His parents divorced, and he lived with his father and brother; by his own estimation, he "made mistakes" in high school. When he began at Iowa State, he was a lost young man, arrogant and insecure. But Beta Theta Pi turned his life around.

He learned—via, of all things, a college fraternity—how to exert self-control. Mentors—among them Senator Richard Lugar, a fellow Beta, who brought him to Washington as an intern the summer before his senior year—took him under their wing, and Horras's gratitude to these men is immense. He loves his fraternity the way some men love their church or their country.

Horras was eager to walk me through a list of talking points that he had written on a yellow legal pad during his flight. He wanted me to understand that changes were coming to the fraternity industry, that the wild drinking could not go on indefinitely. In many regards, our conversation was like other such conversations I've had with fraternity executives over the years. He was willing to acknowledge problems in the fraternity, but not to connect certain of its customs to any particular death. At the national level, all fraternities vehemently prohibit hazing, and spend tremendous energy and money trying to combat it. But according to the most comprehensive study of college hazing, published in 2008 by a University of Maine professor named Elizabeth Allan, a full 80 percent of fraternity members report being hazed. It's not an aberration; it's the norm.

I asked Horras why no one at Beta Theta Pi had done anything about all the bad behavior those cameras must have recorded over the years since the reopening of the chapter. He said that no one could be expected to watch every single minute of film. He said that at some point, you have to trust young men to make the right decisions. What Beta Theta Pi had done for him as a young man, he suggested, was allow him to make some poor decisions until he started to turn around and become the man he wanted to be. Giving members the freedom to do that was part of what the fraternity was about. If they screwed up and got caught—well, that was on them. As for the death of Tim Piazza, while it constituted "a tragedy for him and his family," it would provide the industry with the impetus needed to make some necessary reforms. In fact, his death was a "golden opportunity."

Then I asked Horras about the Shep Test, and why it endured, despite the effort that had gone into eradicating it. He interrupted me: "Wait a minute. That test doesn't happen anymore. We have testimonials instead, where pledges can—"

"But it's in the presentment" I said, and he looked at me, baffled. "One kid asks where the pledges were, and the other one says they're waiting in the boiler room after the Shep Test."

It was clear in that moment—and as he affirmed in a later email—that Horras hadn't read the presentment very closely.

In my notebook, I wrote:

Long pause
Long pause—
Long pause

Finally he said, with consummate feeling, "I'm fucking mad that that stuff is going on."

And then I realized why Horras was able to see the torture and death of a 19-year-old kid as a golden opportunity: He didn't really know that much about it. I started to ask him another question, but for a few moments he seemed lost.

"Am I just fighting for a bunch of idiots?" he asked.

IV

I visited Jim and Evelyn Piazza on a lush New Jersey evening in July, when a summer rain was falling on the wide lawns and large houses of their neighborhood in Hunterdon County, one of the wealthiest areas in the United States.

Jim and Evelyn, who are both accountants, had been at work. Jim is tall and balding and was still dressed for the office, in shirtsleeves and trousers. Evelyn, who is petite and has long, ringleted hair—a lighter shade of red than Tim's—was in shorts and a T–shirt. Their house, where Tim had grown up since the age of six months, was silent and immaculate. We sat around their kitchen table with bottles of cold water and talked.

A fraternity death is, in some ways, like any other traumatic death of a young person. There is the horrifying telephone call, the race to the hospital, the stunned inability to comprehend basic information. (During cellphone calls on the two-hour drive, the doctor kept telling Evelyn that her son was "a very sick boy.") But a fraternity death also brings multiple other levels of shock: The young person was killed because of something his friends did to him; his own university quickly backs away from any responsibility for his death; his parents become pariahs to the other members' parents as they seek justice for their lost son.

In an effort to learn more about fraternities, the Piazzas—who had not taken part in Greek life when they were college students—had attended an information session while at a Penn State parents' weekend in the fall of 2014 for their older son, Mike, who was then a freshman. Evelyn recalled that a university official told the crowd of parents that there was no hazing at the university. An uncomfortable silence followed, until one by one, parents informed the man that their sons were currently being hazed.

When I tried to confirm this incident with Penn State, the university denied, in a series of baffling phone calls and emails, that it could have happened. "We don't doubt the Piazzas' sincerity," one of the exchanges begins, before heaping doubt on their assertion. I brought up all of this at the Piazzas' table.

"We got a letter from another parent who was there," Jim said. "He remembered it just the way we did." I now have a copy of that letter, and have spoken with the parent who wrote it; the account verifies everything the Piazzas remember and identifies the man who made the remarks as the university's then-head of Greek life, Roy Baker.

This is what the past nine months have been like for the Piazzas as they try to get justice for their son: simple requests for information and action on their part, the strangled responses of a massive, inelegant, and transparently self-protecting bureaucracy in reply. When Jim Piazza met with Penn State President Eric Barron a week after Tim's death, he slid the program from his son's funeral across the desk: "Since no one had the time to come," he said.

The Piazzas are still easily unraveled by memories of their son. When I asked whether a spare car in the driveway had been Tim's, Jim said yes and then suddenly struggled for composure; he had driven it back to the house after Tim's death. Evelyn told me about a time, not long before Tim died, when the two of them were alone in the house at dinnertime, and he suggested that they go to a restaurant. They did, and they had a typically fun time together; when the check came, Tim reached over and picked it up. "I thought he was kidding around," Evelyn told me. "But he said, 'I think I can afford to take my mother out to dinner.'"

The Piazzas and I talked for close to an hour. As they walked me out, I thought of the Catholic funeral that Evelyn had so carefully planned for her son, and the grace with which both had withstood this horror.

"You must have a very strong faith," I said, and Jim winced a little and glanced at his wife.

"They stole my son," she said. "And they stole my faith."

Jim opened the front door for me. It was full night now, and the rain had stopped. The leaves and grass were wet, and soft lights illuminated the trees. I walked out onto the porch, and then Jim took a sudden step toward me. I thought he was going to ask me something, or tell me one last thing.

"Be careful on the street," he said. At my puzzled look, he explained that there were deer in the area and that they were hard to see at night. And then I got in my car, armed with a father's good counsel about avoiding the dangers that hid in an ordinary night.

V

When I talked with people about Tim Piazza's death, many brought up an earlier Penn State crisis, the Jerry Sandusky scandal, in which the longtime assistant football coach was convicted for a decades-long practice of sexually abusing young boys, and the university's head coach, Joe Paterno, was abruptly fired. Both cases gestured to a common theme: that of dark events that had taken place on or near the campus for years, with some kind of tacit knowledge on the part of the university. There is also the sense that at Penn State, both the fraternities and the football team operate as they please. To the extent that this is true, the person responsible is Joe Paterno.

It's hard to think of a single person with a greater influence on a modern university than Paterno, who died in 2012. Because of his football team—which he coached for half a century—Penn State went from an institution best known as a regional agricultural school to a vast university with a national reputation. He was Catholic, old-school, elaborately respectful of players' mothers—and eager to wrest their sons away and turn them into men, via the time-honored, noncoddling, masculine processes of football.

To say he was a beloved figure doesn't begin to suggest the role he played on campus. He was Heaney at Harvard, Chomsky at MIT. That he was not a scholar but a football coach and yet was the final authority on almost every aspect of Penn State life says a great deal about the institution. He was also a proud Delta Kappa Epsilon man and a tremendous booster of the fraternity system, and—as was typical for men of his generation—he understood hazing to be an accepted part of Greek life.

In 2007, he gave the practice his implicit endorsement. Photographs had surfaced of some members of the wrestling team apparently being hazed: They were in their underwear with 40-ounce beer bottles duct-taped to their hands. "What'd they do?" he asked during an open football practice that week. "When I was in college, when you got in a fraternity house, they hazed you. They made you stay up all night and played records until you went nuts, and you woke in the morning and all of a sudden they got you before a tribunal and question you as to whether you have the credentials to be a fraternity brother. I didn't even know where I was. That was hazing. I don't know what hazing is today." He wasn't upset that the wrestlers had engaged in hazing; he was scornful of them for doing it wrong.

Looking back at the past two decades at Penn State, we see a university grappling with its fraternity problem in ways that pitted concerned administrators against a powerful system, and achieving little change. In 1997, five members of a fraternity showed up at University Health Services with what the physician there strongly suspected were hazing injuries; in the ominous phrase of the director of Health Services, the injuries had been caused by "something that someone else was doing to them." The president of the university at the time, Graham Spanier (who is currently fighting a jail sentence resulting from his role in the Sandusky scandal), became involved. "We will not tolerate hazing at Penn State," he said. Yet an investigation into the fraternity resulted in its complete exoneration, most likely because the pledges refused to report what the brothers had done to them, which is typical. The episode, which was covered in the student newspaper, reinforced a message that would have tragic consequences for Tim Piazza: that seeking medical help for an injured pledge invites scrutiny and perhaps serious trouble.

In 2004, the university initiated a program called Greek Pride: A Return to Glory, which was intended "to eliminate negative behavior within Greek organizations." Many meetings were held, but nothing much seems to have come of them. Then, in 2009, after a freshman named Joseph Dado got so drunk at a fraternity party that he fell down a set of concrete stairs and died, the university's student-run Interfraternity Council made what seemed to be a game-changing decision. It contracted with an outside security firm called St. Moritz. The firm would send employees to fraternity parties for unscheduled checks to make sure that they were in compliance with various safety policies. It was a system that should have saved Tim Piazza's life. Two checkers arrived minutes before he fell down the stairs, and inspected a house rife with policy violations, yet no alarm was raised, and the night raged on.

Who were these checkers, and how could they have missed the obvious violations that were taking place? The IFC claims that neither it nor St. Moritz retains any records from that night. Nor will it comment on a fact that *The Daily Collegian* reported: that the checkers were not full-time security guards, but Penn State kids who were working part-time for St. Moritz. (The company declined to comment.) In the words of Stacy Parks Miller, the district attorney who brought the charges against the Beta brothers, the whole system was an elaborate "sham," one that was exposed only after Tim Piazza died.

In 2015, a former pledge of Kappa Delta Rho's Penn State chapter, James Vivenzio, made national news. He told police that his fraternity had kept a secret Facebook page where members could post naked pictures of female students, some of whom were unconscious or being sexually assaulted. He also said that he had been severely hazed two years earlier, and had reported the hazing to the Office of Student Conduct. Danny Shaha, the head of that office, took the report seriously enough to visit Vivenzio in his Virginia home. Tellingly, his fraternity was the same one that had been investigated after the five injured students went to Health Services 18 years earlier. Yet Vivenzio claims that Student Conduct did not investigate his allegations until he went to the police.

Vivenzio is currently suing both the fraternity and the university. His suit describes the hazing he endured: cigarette burns; "late-night line-ups that featured force-feeding bucketfuls of liquor mixed with urine, vomit, hot sauce and other liquid and semi-solid ingredients"; being told to "guzzle hard liquor without stopping until vomiting was induced." (Penn State claims that it could not address Vivenzio's hazing because he declined to provide documentation or pursue a formal disciplinary process, an assertion Vivenzio's attorney disputes. After he went to the police, the university suspended the fraternity for three years.)

Another piece of ongoing Penn State litigation involves a student at the Altoona campus named Marquise Braham, who pledged Phi Sigma Kappa as a freshman in 2013. His parents' civil suit describes what he experienced:

> Among other things, being forced to consume gross amounts of alcohol, chug bottles of Listerine, swallow live fish, fight fellow pledges; being

burned with candle wax, deprived of sleep for 89 hours, locked in a room with other pledges, alcohol, and a trashcan to catch their vomit; having a gun held to his head; and being forced to kill, gut, and skin animals.

Braham had texted with his residence-hall adviser, a young woman, desperately seeking help in understanding what was happening to him, but she only endorsed the system. "Yes it will get worse," she wrote. "I'm sorry to say hahaha but it will."

He made it through the hazing, but the next semester he was expected to haze other pledges, which broke him. He went home to New York for spring break, saying that he needed to see a priest. At lunch with his mother the day before he was to return, he excused himself from the table, climbed to the top of a nearby building, and jumped to his death. A grand jury found no link between his death and the hazing he had endured. Penn State suspended Phi Sigma Kappa's charter for six years.

VI

After Tim Piazza fell, four fraternity brothers carried him, unconscious, to a couch. He was in obvious need of medical attention, yet the fraternity brothers treated him with a callousness bordering on the sadistic. They slapped and punched him, threw his shoes at him, poured beer on him, sat two abreast on his twitching legs. Precious minutes and hours passed by, the difference between Tim's life and death.

Two hours into the nightmarish security footage, something extraordinary happens. A young man walks into the frame and approaches the couch where Tim is lying, still unconscious. This is Kordel Davis, a recently initiated freshman brother and the chapter's only black member at the time. According to the presentment, he "leans over Timothy's head. Davis then turns to the Beta brothers near Timothy and becomes very animated, again pointing at his head and then at Tim."

The presentment states that when the brothers told Davis that Tim had fallen down the basement stairs, he became

even more concerned—now for Timothy's life. He stressed to them that Timothy needed to go to the hospital since he could have a concussion. Davis told them that if Tim was sleeping they needed to wake him up and call 911 immediately. He screamed at them to get help. In response

[Beta brother] Jonah Neuman rose from the couch and shoved Davis into
the opposite wall. Neuman instructed Davis to leave and that they had it
under control.

Davis then sought out Ed Gilmartin, the vice president of the chapter:
"The camera captures Davis gesturing once more, referring repeatedly
to his head and pointing at Timothy." Davis testified that Gilmartin told
him he was crazy and "claimed the other brothers were kinesiology
and biology majors," so Davis's word "meant nothing to him when
compared to theirs."

I sat with Kordel Davis this summer in the cacophonous food court
in Philadelphia's Reading Terminal Market, and we talked about that
moment. "They made you doubt yourself," I said, and—in as pure an
expression of teenage-male anguish as I've ever seen, tears welling in
his eyes—he said, "Like I've doubted myself my whole life."

Kordel was born to a 16-year-old single mother in Reading, Pennsylvania, and was removed from her care and placed in two successive foster homes. At age 3, he was adopted by a white couple who had already
adopted 9-year-old white twins from foster care, and who would adopt a
black infant the next year; they divorced soon after that, at which point
family life was further complicated by frequent moves, and the eventual introduction of new stepparents and stepsiblings. Kordel attended a
majority-white high school, where he made good friends and had many
caring teachers, and where he found a mentor in the football coach. Yet
he also says that he was hazed as a freshman on that team, including by
an older white player who beat him in front of others, and that he was
called a racist nickname by his teammates. When the nickname came to
the attention of a teacher and his coach, the other players claimed that
it was meant to be affectionate.

"After all that," I asked him, "why would you join an all-white fraternity with these privileged kids?"

"Because I've been around kids like that all my life," he said. "I
know how to handle them."

Or at least he thought he did.

The story of black members of historically white fraternities is a
complex one. Although the clubs started opening their ranks to African-
Americans in the 1950s and 1960s, they have few black members;
nationally, only 3 percent of Beta Theta Pi's members are black, for
example. There is reason to believe that official membership policy and

actual practice diverge. In 2015, cellphone video of some Sigma Alpha Epsilon members from the University of Oklahoma singing a fraternity song became public:

There will never be a n— SAE
There will never be a n— SAE
You can hang him from a tree
But he'll never sing with me
There will never be a n— SAE

Any hope that this was the local custom of one rogue chapter disappeared when authorities discovered where the brothers had learned the lyrics: on a 2011 "national leadership cruise" that brought together hundreds of active and alumni members.

When Kordel Davis was interviewed by a police detective after Tim Piazza's death, he had a scar on his forehead, which was still there when I met with him over the summer. It was from an injury sustained during his own bid-acceptance night the previous semester, when he, too, had fallen after drinking heavily. "My shirt, my phone—they were covered in so much blood," he told me. His fraternity brothers put him to bed, he survived the night, and the next morning they took him for medical care—at a privately owned urgent-care clinic instead of University Health Services, where hazing might have been suspected. Keeping that incident secret was one of the costs of membership. Yet after Kordel was initiated, he did not seem to have the full measure of brotherhood that the others enjoyed. Once, he brought some friends to a party—to which other brothers had also brought guests—but was told he was not allowed to have guests, and so he had to leave, embarrassed, with his friends.

Kordel seemed rootless when I talked with him over the summer. "I lost my future," he told me. He was seized by remorse over what had happened to Tim, and he had decided not to return to Penn State, although he had loved it there and had been awarded a significant financial-aid package. He'd read enough on online message boards to know what fraternity members on campus thought of him: that he had ratted out his brothers by talking so openly to the police, and thereby ruined Greek life for everyone.

I thought about the summons he had received from the police department, about the day he had gone there, alone, a 19-year-old black kid in a county that is 90 percent white, to report on events surrounding the death of a white college student. Still, the police were kind to him. They had a nickname for him, based on his actions on the tape: the Good Samaritan.

When I dropped Kordel off at his father's home, I wondered whether this experience would indeed cost him his future. But he is resilient, incredibly so. By summer's end he had been accepted at Rutgers, and had taken out student loans to pay his tuition. Perhaps he won't have to pay them back himself. I asked a lawyer with extensive knowledge of fraternity litigation whether Kordel might have his own civil claim against Beta Theta Pi, and he affirmed that—given the hazing he had experienced as well as the scarring—he could indeed have a "deep-six-figure claim."

VII

In late May, shortly after the grand jury's harrowing presentment was released to the public, Jud Horras appeared on *CBS This Morning*. In a conversation with Gayle King, Charlie Rose, and Norah O'Donnell, he was measured, calm, and so ungraspable—always separating the thugs of one rogue chapter from the larger entity of the fraternity industry—that midway through the interview, O'Donnell lost her patience and interrupted him.

"There have been 60 deaths over eight years involving fraternity activities," she said angrily. "There should be *zero tolerance*. There should be immediate action on this. It is *unacceptable*. This is murder."

Her sentiment was one shared by many people when they learned about what had happened to Tim Piazza, but it revealed a common misunderstanding: Fraternities *do* have a zero-tolerance policy regarding hazing. And that's probably one of the reasons Tim Piazza is dead.

For most of their long history, fraternities pretty much did as they pleased. But in the 1980s, parents of injured and dead children began to fight back: They sued the organizations and began to recover huge sums in damages. Insurance companies dropped fraternities en masse. Because of this crisis, the modern fraternity industry was born, one that is essentially self-insured, with fraternities pooling their money to create a fund from which damages are paid.

The executives realized that even if they couldn't change members' behavior, they had to indemnify themselves against it, which they did by creating an incredibly strict set of rules, named for a term of art in the insurance industry: risk-management policies. These policies forbid not just the egregious behaviors of hazing and sexual assault, but also a vast range of activities that comprise normal fraternity life in the majority of chapters. You can't play beer pong in a fraternity house. You can't have a sip of alcohol if you're under the age of 21, or allow anyone else who's underage to have a sip of alcohol. During a party, alcohol consumption must be tightly regulated. Either the chapter can hire a third-party vendor to sell drinks—and to assume all liability for what happens after guests consume them—or members and guests may each bring a small amount of alcohol for personal use and hand it over to a monitor who labels it, and then metes it back to the owner in a slow trickle.

In an emergency, when the police and an ambulance show up, the national organization will easily be able to prove that the members were in violation of its policies, and will therefore be able to cut them loose and deny them any of the benefits—including the payment of attorneys' fees and damages—that come with the fraternity insurance the members themselves have paid for.

Fraternity members live under the shadow of giant sanctions and lawsuits that can result even from what seem like minor incidents. The strict policies promote a culture of secrecy, and when something really does go terribly wrong, the young men usually start scrambling to protect themselves. Doug Fierberg, a Washington, D.C., lawyer whose practice is built on representing plaintiffs in fraternity lawsuits, told me that "in virtually every hazing death, there is a critical three or four hours after the injury when the brothers try to figure out what to do. It is during those hours that many victims pass the point of no return."

All of these dynamics came into play the night Tim Piazza was fatally injured. The chapter president, Brendan Young, was—get this—*majoring* in risk management. He fully understood that officers of the fraternity face greater liability than do regular members. He became the president in November 2016, and shortly before rush began, in January 2017, he texted Daniel Casey, the pledge master: "I know you know this. If anything goes wrong with the pledges this semester then both of us are fucked." He wasn't suggesting they scrap hazing; he was reminding his subordinate that they had better not get caught doing it. (Young's lawyer declined to comment.)

Even a full day after Tim died, some members were, amazingly, still focused on the consequences that could befall them. "Between you and me," a member texted Young, "what are the chances the house gets shut down?"

"I think very high," Young replied. "I just hope none of us get into any lawsuits."

"You think they are going to sue?" asked the brother, to which Young responded in a way that is chilling and that reveals a sophisticated knowledge of how such events play out: "It depends if they want to go through with it, or just distance themselves from us all together."

VIII

In fact, Jim and Evelyn Piazza have not chosen to distance themselves from the men who hazed their late son and left him to a fate that Jim compares to a crucifixion. They attended every day of the pretrial hearings that determined which of the charges against the brothers would go to trial, a grueling process that—with its many continuances and breaks—lasted the entire summer.

It ended, finally, with what looked like a significant defeat: The most-serious charges—of involuntary manslaughter and aggravated assault—were dropped. In the courtroom, the 16 fraternity brothers (two had waived their right to a preliminary hearing) backslapped one another and exchanged fist bumps. The Piazzas quietly left.

Still, 14 of the Beta brothers will face a total of 328 criminal charges—jury selection is scheduled to begin in December—and the Piazzas also plan to file a civil suit after the trial ends. (When asked for comment, the national Beta fraternity stated that members of the Penn State chapter had not met its "expectations of friendship and brotherhood" and that it had "moved to close the chapter in February and expel men charged in the case." An attorney for the chapter did not respond to a request for comment.)

The university has responded to the crisis with some significant steps: It has wrested discipline of the fraternities from the IFC, a group run entirely by frat brothers, and put it firmly in the hands of the Office of Student Conduct; checks on fraternity parties will be conducted not by

St. Moritz, but by university employees. It has also permanently banned Beta Theta Pi from campus. The motivation behind these changes may lie as much in an earnest desire for reform as in a panicked need to contain what could become an ever-widening scandal, one with the potential to be as newsworthy as the Sandusky scandal.

At the end of the Piazza presentment, the grand jury issues a stunning condemnation of Penn State's fraternity culture:

> The Penn State Greek community nurtured an environment so permissive of excessive drinking and hazing that it emboldened its members to repeatedly act with reckless disregard to human life. . . . Timothy Piazza died as a direct result of the extremely reckless conduct of members of the Beta Fraternity who operated within the permissive atmosphere fostered by the Pennsylvania State University Interfraternity Council.

The grand jury is now investigating the broader issue of hazing at Penn State and may recommend criminal charges. It is also reviewing the James Vivenzio and Marquise Braham cases. The presentment that could emanate from those horrific cases will surely be the subject of intense media scrutiny.

As for the university's permanent ban of Beta Theta Pi from campus, a week after the most-serious charges against the former brothers were dropped, Beta alumni received an email inviting them to stay at their beloved house during football weekends this fall.

The Greek system has powerful allies at Penn State. After Tim Piazza's death, several prominent trustees of the university vouched for fraternities, which they felt should be reformed but not hobbled. Their logic was sometimes tortured. William Oldsey told *The Philadelphia Inquirer* in May that the story of Tim Piazza—whose parents he pitied mightily—offered not an indictment but an endorsement of Greek life: "This is a good-enough system that it attracted a kid of the high caliber and character of Tim Piazza."

IX

So let us now imagine all the forces arrayed against 19-year-old Tim Piazza as he gets dressed in his jacket and tie, preparing to go to his new chapter house and accept the bid the brothers have offered him.

He is up against a university that has allowed hazing to go on for decades; a fraternity chapter that has hazed pledge classes at least twice in the previous 12 months; a set of rules that so harshly punishes hazing that the brothers will think it better to take a chance with his life than to face the consequences of having made him get drunk; and a "checking system" provided by a security firm that is, in many regards, a sham. He thinks he is going to join a club that his college endorses, and that is true. But it is also true that he is setting off to get jumped by a gang, and he won't survive.

So here is Tim, reaching for his good jacket—in a closet that his mother will soon visit to select the clothes he will wear in his coffin—a little bit excited and a little bit nervous.

"They're going to get me fucked up," he texts his girlfriend, and then he pulls closed the door of his college apartment for the last time.

He has been told to show up at exactly 9:07. Inside, the 14 pledges are lined up, each with his right hand on the right shoulder of the one in front of him, and taken into the living room, where they are welcomed into the fraternity with songs and skits. And then it is time for the first act of hazing in their pledge period: quickly drinking a massive amount of alcohol in an obstacle course, the "gauntlet." Court documents and the security footage provide excruciating detail about what comes next.

About an hour after the gauntlet begins, the pledges return to the living room, all of them showing signs of drunkenness. At 10:40, Tim appears on one of the security cameras, assisted by one of the brothers. The forensic pathologist will later describe his level of intoxication at this point as "stuporous." He is staggering, hunched over, and he sits down heavily on the couch and doesn't want to get up. But the brother encourages him to stand and walks him through the dining room and kitchen and back to the living room, where he sits down again on the couch. And then Tim tries to do something that could have saved his life.

He stands up, uncertainly, and heads toward the front door. If he makes it through that door, he may get out to the street, may find a place to sit or lie down, may come to the attention of someone who can help him—at the very least by getting him back to his apartment and away from the fraternity. He reaches the front door, but the mechanism to open it proves too complicated in his drunken state, so he turns around and staggers toward another door. Perhaps he is hoping that this door will be easier to open; perhaps he is hoping that it also leads out of the fraternity house. But it is the door to the basement, and when he opens it—perhaps expecting his foot to land on level ground—he takes a catastrophic fall.

On the security footage, a fraternity brother named Luke Visser points toward the stairs in an agitated way. Greg Rizzo clearly hears the fall and goes to the top of the steps to see what's happened. Later, he will tell the police that he saw Tim "facedown, at the bottom of the steps." Jonah Neuman will tell the police that he saw Tim lying face-down with his legs on the stairs.

Rizzo sends a group text: "Tim Piazza might actually be a problem. He fell 15 feet down a flight of steps, hair-first, going to need help." (Rizzo, who was not charged with any crimes, told the police that he later advocated for calling an ambulance.)

Four of the brothers carry Tim up the stairs. By now he has some-how lost his jacket and tie, and his white shirt has ridden up, revealing a strange, dark bruise on his torso. This is from his lacerated spleen, which has begun spilling blood into his abdomen. The brothers put him on a couch, and Rizzo performs a sternum rub—a test for consciousness used by EMTs—but Tim does not respond. Another brother throws beer in his face, but he does not respond. Someone throws his shoes at him, hard. Someone lifts his arm and it falls back, deadweight, to his chest.

At this point, the brothers have performed a series of tests to deter-mine whether Tim is merely drunk or seriously injured. He has failed all their tests. The next day, Tim's father will ask the surgeon who delivers the terrible news of Tim's prognosis whether the outcome would have been different if Tim had gotten help earlier, and the surgeon will say—unequivocally—that yes, it would have been different. That "earlier" is right now, while Tim is lying here, unresponsive to the sternum rub, the beer poured on him, the dropped arm.

A brother named Ryan Foster rolls Tim on his side, but has to catch him because he almost rolls onto the floor. Jonah Neuman straps a back-pack full of books to him to keep him from rolling over and aspirating vomit. Two brothers sit on Tim's legs to keep him from moving.

This is the moment when Kordel Davis arrives and attempts to save Tim's life, only to be thrown against the wall by Neuman. Davis disap-pears from the video, in search of an officer of the club. By now Tim is "thrashing and making weird movements," according to the grand-jury presentment.

Daniel Casey comes into the room, looks at Tim, and slaps him in the face three times. Tim does not respond. Two other brothers wrestle near the couch and end up slamming on top of Tim, whose spleen is still pouring blood into his abdomen. Tim begins to twitch and vomit.

At this point, Joseph Ems appears "frustrated" by Tim, according to the grand jury. With an open hand, he strikes the unconscious boy hard, on the abdomen, where the bruise has bloomed. This blow may be one of the reasons the forensic pathologist will find that Tim's spleen was not just lacerated, but "shattered." (EMS was originally charged with recklessly endangering another person, but that charge—the only one brought against him—has been dropped.) Still, Tim does not wake up.

Forty-five minutes later, Tim rolls onto the floor. The heavy backpack is still strapped to him. He rolls around, his legs moving. He attempts to stand up, and manages to free himself from the backpack, which falls to the floor. But the effort is too much, and he falls backwards, banging his head on the hardwood floor. A fraternity member shakes him, gets no response, and walks away.

At 3:46 in the morning, Tim is on the floor, curled up in the fetal position. At home in New Jersey, his parents are sleeping. Across campus, his older brother, Mike, has no idea that Tim is not safely in his bed.

At 3:49 a.m., Tim wakes up and struggles to his knees, cradling his head in his hands; he falls again to the hardwood floor. An hour later, he manages to stand up, and staggers toward the front door, but within seconds he falls, headfirst, into an iron railing and then onto the floor. On some level he must know: *I am dying.* He stands once again and tries to get to the door. His only hope is to get out of this house, but he falls headfirst once again.

At 5:08 a.m., Tim is on his knees, his wounded head buried in his hands. Around campus, people are beginning to wake up. The cafeteria workers are brewing coffee; athletes are rising for early practices. It's cold and still dark, but the day is beginning. Tim is dying inside the Beta house, steps away from the door he has been trying all night to open.

Around 7 o'clock, another pledge wanders into the living room, where Tim is now lying on the couch groaning, and the pledge watches as he rolls off the couch and onto the floor, and again lifts himself to his knees and cradles his head in his hands, "as if he had a really bad headache." The pledge lifts his cellphone, records Tim's anguish on

Snapchat, and then—while Tim is rocking back and forth on the floor—leaves the house. A few minutes later, Tim stands and staggers toward the basement steps, and disappears from the cameras' view.

The house begins to stir. Some fraternity members head off to class, and in the fullness of time they return. And then, at about 10 a.m., a brother named Kyle Pecci (who was not charged) arrives and asks a pledge, Daniel Erickson (who was also not charged), a question that seems to both of them a casual one: Whatever happened to that pledge who fell down the stairs at the party? They come across Tim's shoes, and realize that Tim must still be somewhere in the house, so they look for him. The search reveals him collapsed behind one of the bars in the basement. He is lying on his back, with his arms tight at his sides and his hands gripped in fists. His face is bloody and his breathing is labored. His eyes are half open; his skin is cold to the touch; he is unnaturally pale. Three men carry him upstairs and put him on the couch, but no one calls 911.

Fraternity brothers with garbage bags appear in the footage and start cleaning up the evidence. Brothers try to prop Tim up on the couch and dress him, but his limbs are too stiff and they can't do it. Someone wipes the blood off his face, and someone else tries, without luck, to pry open his clenched fingers. Clearly the brothers are trying to make this terrible situation appear a little bit better for when the authorities arrive. But they do not use their many cellphones to call 911. Instead one brother uses his phone to do a series of internet searches for terms such as *cold extremities in drunk person* and *binge drinking, alcohol, bruising or discoloration, cold feet and cold hands.*

Where is Tim right now, as his body lies on the couch? Are his soul and self still here, in the room, or have they already slipped away? He has put up a valiant, almost incredible fight for his life, but by now he has lost that fight. When he was a little boy, he used to make people laugh because he got so frustrated with board games; he didn't like playing those games, with their rules and tricks. He loved sports, and running, and playing with his friends at the beach. But his body is cold now, his legs and arms unbending.

Finally, at 10:48 a.m., a brother calls 911—perhaps realizing that it would be best to do so while the pledge is still technically alive—and Tim is delivered from the charnel house. Soon his parents will race toward him, and so will his frantic brother, who has been searching for him. They will be reunited for the few hours they have left with this redheaded boy they have loved so well, and at least it can be said that Tim did not die alone, or in the company of the men who tortured him.

On February 7, the Facebook page of the Beta Theta Pi national organization will report that "Tim Piazza, a sophomore at Penn State who had recently accepted an invitation to join the Fraternity, has passed due to injuries sustained from an accidental fall in the chapter house." Flags at the fraternity's administrative offices in Oxford, Ohio, will fly at half-mast for eight days, "representative of the eight young men of Tim's same age who founded the Fraternity." The Facebook post will encourage collegiate members around the country to "conduct Beta's official Burial Service" on Friday evening, from 4 to 8 o'clock. And with those final rituals of the fraternity, Tim Piazza's 28-hour membership in Beta Theta Pi will come to an end. "Rest in peace, Tim Piazza," ends the post. "Rest in peace."

ILLICIT DRUGS

Chapter 16

America's Unjust Drug War

Michael Huemer

Over two million Americans are currently in jail or in prison, and several million more are on probation or parole. The United States has the highest rate of incarceration of any country in the world. Despite having less than 5 percent of the world's *people*, the United States has over 20 percent of the world's prisoners.

There were not always so many inmates. In the early 1970s, the US government began waging a "war on drugs," which has led to more arrests, more convictions, and longer sentences for drug offenders. Today, more than 450,000 people are behind bars for nonviolent drug offenses.

Professor Michael Huemer (1969–) thinks we should end this war. Drug use, he says, is less harmful than smoking or being obese, but nobody wants to outlaw cigarettes or lock people up for eating French fries. Drug laws are seriously unjust, he claims, because they violate one's right to control one's own body.

Should the recreational use of drugs such as marijuana, cocaine, heroin, and LSD, be prohibited by law? *Prohibitionists* answer yes. They usually argue that drug use is extremely harmful both to drug users and to

Michael Huemer, "America's Unjust Drug War" in *The New Prohibition*, ed. Bill Masters (St. Louis, MO: Accurate Press, 2004), 133–44. Copyright © 2004. Used with permission of the author.

society in general, and possibly even immoral, and they believe that these facts provide sufficient reasons for prohibition. *Legalizers* answer no. They usually give one or more of three arguments: First, some argue that drug use is not as harmful as prohibitionists believe, and even that it is sometimes beneficial. Second, some argue that drug prohibition "does not work," in other words, it is not very successful in preventing drug use and/or has a number of very bad consequences. Lastly, some argue that drug prohibition is unjust or violates rights.

I won't attempt to discuss all these arguments here. Instead, I will focus on what seem to me the three most prominent arguments in the drug legalization debate: first, the argument that drugs should be out-lawed because of the harm they cause to drug users; second, the argument that they should be outlawed because they harm people other than the user; and third, the argument that drugs should be legalized because drug prohibition violates rights. I shall focus on the moral/philosophical issues that these arguments raise, rather than medical or sociological issues. I shall show that the two arguments for prohibition fail, while the third argument, for legalization, succeeds.

I. DRUGS AND HARM TO USERS

The first major argument for prohibition holds that drugs should be pro-hibited because drug use is extremely harmful to the users themselves, and prohibition decreases the rate of drug abuse. This argument assumes that the proper function of government includes preventing people from harming themselves. Thus, the argument is something like this:

1. Drug use is very harmful to users.
2. The government should prohibit people from doing things that harm themselves.
3. Therefore, the government should prohibit drug use.

Obviously, the second premise is essential to the argument; if I believed that drug use was very harmful, but I did *not* think that the government should prohibit people from harming themselves, then I would not take this as a reason for prohibiting drug use. But premise (2), if taken without qualification, is extremely implausible. Consider some examples of things people do that are harmful (or entail a risk of harm) to themselves: smoking tobacco, drinking alcohol, eating too much, riding motorcycles, having unprotected or promiscuous sex, maintaining relationships with inconsiderate or abusive boyfriends and girlfriends, maxing out their credit cards, working in dead-end jobs, dropping out of college, moving to New Jersey, and being rude to their bosses. Should the government prohibit all of these things?[1] Most of us would agree that the government should not prohibit *any* of these things, let alone all of them. And this is not merely for logistical or practical reasons; rather, we think that controlling those activities is not the business of government.

Perhaps the prohibitionist will argue, not that the government should prohibit *all* activities that are harmful to oneself, but that it should prohibit activities that harm oneself in a certain way, or to a certain degree, or that also have some other characteristic. It would then be up to the prohibitionist to explain how the self-inflicted harm of drug use differs from the self-inflicted harms of the other activities mentioned above. Let us consider three possibilities.

(1) One suggestion would be that drug use also harms people other than the user; we will discuss this harm to others in section II below. If, as I will contend, neither the harm to drug users nor the harm to others justifies prohibition, then there will be little plausibility in the suggestion that the combination of harms justifies prohibition. Of course, one could hold that a certain threshold level of total harm must be reached before prohibition of an activity is justified, and that the combination of the harm of drugs to users and their harm to others passes that threshold even though neither kind of harm does so by itself. But if, as I will contend, the "harm to users" and "harm to others" arguments both fail because it is not the government's business to apply criminal sanctions to prevent the kinds of harms in question, *then* the combination of the two harms will not make a convincing case for prohibition.

(2) A second suggestion is that drug use is generally *more* harmful than the other activities listed above. But there seems to be no reason to believe this. As one (admittedly limited) measure of harmfulness, consider the mortality statistics. In the year 2000, illicit drug use directly or indirectly caused an estimated 17,000 deaths in the United States.[2] By contrast, tobacco caused an estimated 435,000 deaths.[3] Of course, more people use tobacco than use illegal drugs,[4] so let us divide by the number of users: tobacco kills 4.5 people per 1000 at-risk persons per year; illegal drugs kill 0.66 people per 1000 at-risk persons per year.[5] Yet almost no one favors outlawing tobacco and putting smokers in

prison. On a similar note, obesity caused an estimated 112,000 deaths in the same year (due to increased incidence of heart disease, strokes, and so on), or 1.8 per 1000 at-risk persons.[6] Health professionals have warned about the pandemic of obesity, but no one has yet called for imprisoning obese people.

There are less tangible harms of drug use—harms to one's general quality of life. These are difficult to quantify. But compare the magnitude of the harm to one's quality of life that one can bring about by, say, dropping out of high school, working in a dead-end job for several years, or marrying a jerk—these things can cause extreme and lasting detriment to one's well-being. And yet no one proposes jailing those who drop out, work in bad jobs, or make poor marriage decisions. The idea of doing so would seem ridiculous, clearly beyond the state's prerogatives.

(3) Another suggestion is that drug use harms users *in a different way* than the other listed activities. What sorts of harms do drugs cause? First, illicit drugs may worsen users' health and, in some cases, entail a risk of death. But many other activities—including the consumption of alcohol, tobacco, and fatty foods; sex; and (on a broad construal of "health") automobiles—entail health risks, and yet almost no one believes those activities should be criminalized.

Second, drugs may damage users' relationships with others—particularly family, friends, and lovers—and prevent one from developing more satisfying personal relationships.[7] Being rude to others can also have this effect, yet no one believes you should be put in jail for being rude. Moreover, it is very implausible to suppose that people should be subject to criminal sanctions for ruining their personal relationships. I have no general theory of what sort of things people should be punished for, but consider the following example: suppose that I decide to break up with my girlfriend, stop calling my family, and push away all my friends. I do this for no good reason—I just feel like it. This would damage my personal relationships as much as anything could. Should the police now arrest me and put me in jail? If not, then why should they arrest me for doing something that only has a *chance* of indirectly bringing about a similar result? The following seems like a reasonable political principle: If it would be wrong (because not part of the government's legitimate functions) to punish people for *directly bringing about* some result, then it would also be wrong to punish people for doing some other action on the grounds that the action has a *chance* of bringing about that result indirectly. If the state may not prohibit me from *directly cutting off* my relationships with others, then the fact that my drug use *might have the result* of damaging those relationships does not provide a good reason to prohibit me from using drugs.

Third, drugs may harm users' financial lives, costing them money, causing them to lose their jobs or not find jobs, and preventing them from getting promotions. The same principle applies here: if it would be an abuse of government power to prohibit me from directly bringing about those sorts of negative financial consequences, then surely the fact that drug use might indirectly bring them about is not a good reason to prohibit drug use. Suppose that I decide to quit my job and throw all my money out the window, for no reason. Should the police arrest me and put me in prison?

Fourth and finally, drugs may damage users' moral character, as James Q. Wilson believes:

> [I]f we believe—as I do—that dependency on certain mind-altering drugs *is* a moral issue and that their illegality rests in part on their immorality, then legalizing them undercuts, if it does not eliminate altogether, the moral message. That message is at the root of the distinction between nicotine and cocaine. Both are highly addictive; both have harmful physical effects. But we treat the two drugs differently not simply because nicotine is so widely used as to be beyond the reach of effective prohibition, but because its use does not destroy the user's essential humanity. Tobacco shortens one's life, cocaine debases it. Nicotine alters one's habits, cocaine alters one's soul. The heavy use of crack, unlike the heavy use of tobacco, corrodes those natural sentiments of sympathy and duty that constitute our human nature and make possible our social life.[8]

In this passage, Wilson claims that the use of cocaine (a) is immoral, (b) destroys one's humanity, (c) alters one's soul, and (d) corrodes one's sense of sympathy and duty. One problem with Wilson's argument is the lack of evidence supporting claims (a)–(d). Before we put people in prison for corrupting their souls, we should require some objective evidence that their souls are in fact being corrupted. Before we put people in prison for being immoral, we should require some argument showing that their actions are in fact immoral. Perhaps Wilson's charges of immorality and corruption all come down to the charge that drug users lose their sense of sympathy and duty—that is, claims (a)–(c) all rest upon claim (d). It is plausible that *heavy* drug users experience a decreased sense of sympathy with others and a decreased sense of duty and responsibility. Does this provide a good reason to prohibit drug use?

Again, it seems that one should not prohibit an activity on the grounds that it may indirectly cause some result, unless it would be appropriate to prohibit the direct bringing about of that result. Would it be appropriate, and within the legitimate functions of the state, to punish people for being unsympathetic and undutiful, or for behaving in an unsympathetic and undutiful way? Suppose that Howard—though not a drug user—doesn't sympathize with others. When people try to tell Howard their problems, he just tells them to quit whining. Friends and co-workers who ask Howard for favors are rudely rebuffed. Furthermore—though he does not harm others in ways that would be against our current laws—Howard has a poor sense of duty. He doesn't bother to show up for work on time, nor does he take any pride in his work; he doesn't donate to charity; he doesn't try to improve his community. All around, Howard is an ignoble and unpleasant individual. Should he be put in jail?

If not, then why should someone be put in jail merely for doing something that would have a *chance* of causing them to become like Howard? If it would be an abuse of governmental power to punish people for being jerks, then the fact that drug use may cause one to become a jerk is not a good reason to prohibit drug use.

II. DRUGS AND HARM TO OTHERS

Some argue that drug use must be outlawed because drug use harms the user's family, friends, and co-workers, and/or society in general. A report produced by the Office of National Drug Control Policy states:

> Democracies can flourish only when their citizens value their freedom and embrace personal responsibility. Drug use erodes the individual's capacity to pursue both ideals. It diminishes the individual's capacity to operate effectively in many of life's spheres—as a student, a parent, a spouse, an employee—even as a coworker or fellow motorist. And, while some claim it represents an expression of individual autonomy, drug use is in fact inimical to personal freedom, producing a reduced capacity to participate in the life of the community and the promise of America.[9]

At least one of these alleged harms—dangerous driving—*is* clearly the business of the state. For this reason, I entirely agree that people should be prohibited from driving while under the influence of drugs. But what about the rest of the alleged harms?

Return to our hypothetical citizen Howard. Imagine that Howard—again, for reasons having nothing to do with drugs—does not value freedom, nor does he embrace personal responsibility. It is unclear exactly what this means, but, for good measure, let us suppose that Howard embraces a totalitarian political ideology and denies the existence of free will. He constantly blames other people for his problems and tries to avoid making decisions. Howard is a college student with a part-time job. However, he is a terrible student and worker. He hardly ever studies and frequently misses assignments, as a result of which he gets poor grades. As mentioned earlier, Howard comes to work late and takes no pride in his work. Though he does nothing against our current laws, he is an inattentive and inconsiderate spouse and parent. Nor does he make any effort to participate in the life of his community, or the promise of America. He would rather lie around the house, watching television and cursing the rest of the world for his problems. In short, Howard does all the bad things to his family, friends, co-workers, and society that the ONDCP says *may* result from drug use. And most of this is voluntary.

Should Congress pass laws against what Howard is doing? Should the police then arrest him, and the district attorney prosecute him, for being a loser?

Once again, it seems absurd to suppose that we would arrest and jail someone for behaving in these ways, undesirable as they may be. Since drug use only has a *chance* of causing one to behave in each of these ways, it is even more absurd to suppose that we should arrest and jail people for drug use on the grounds that drug use has these potential effects.

III. THE INJUSTICE OF DRUG PROHIBITION

Philosopher Douglas Husak has characterized drug prohibition as the greatest injustice perpetrated in the United States since slavery.[10] This is no hyperbole. If the drug laws are unjust, then America has over half a million people unjustly imprisoned.[11]

Why think the drug laws are *unjust?* Husak's argument invokes a principle with which few could disagree: it is unjust for the state to punish people without having a good reason for doing so.[12] We have seen the failure of the most common proposed rationales for drug prohibition. If nothing better is forthcoming, then we must conclude that prohibitionists have no rational justification for punishing drug users. We have deprived hundreds of thousands of people of basic liberties and subjected them to severe hardship conditions, for no good reason.

This is bad enough. But I want to say something stronger: it is not merely that we are punishing people for no good reason. We are punishing people for exercising their natural rights. Individuals have a right to use drugs. This right is neither absolute nor exceptionless; suppose, for example, that there existed a drug which, once ingested, caused a significant proportion of users, without any further free choices on their part, to attack other people without provocation. I would think that stopping the use of this drug would be the business of the government. But no existing drug satisfies this description. Indeed, though I cannot take time to delve into the matter here, I think it is clear that the drug *laws* cause far more crime than drugs themselves do.

The idea of a right to use drugs derives from the idea that individuals own their own bodies. That is, a person has the right to exercise control over his own body—including the right to decide how it should be used, and to exclude others from using it—in a manner similar to the way one may exercise control over one's (other) property. This statement is somewhat vague; nevertheless, we can see the general idea embodied in commonsense morality. Indeed, it seems that if there is *anything* one would have rights to, it would be one's own body. This explains why we think others may not physically attack you or kidnap you. It explains why we do not accept the use of unwilling human subjects for medical experiments, even if the experiments are beneficial to society—the rest of society may not decide to use your body for its own purposes without your permission. It explains why some believe that women have a right to an abortion—and why some others do not. The former believe that a woman has the right to do what she wants with her own body; the latter believe that the fetus is a distinct person, and a woman does not have the right to harm *its* body. Virtually no one disputes that, *if* a fetus is merely a part of the woman's body, *then* a woman has a right to choose whether to have an abortion; just as virtually no one disputes that, *if* a fetus is a distinct person, then a woman lacks the right to destroy it. Almost no one disputes that persons have rights over their own bodies but not over others' bodies.

The right to control one's body cannot be interpreted as implying a right to use one's body in *every* conceivable way, any more than we have the right to use our property in every conceivable way. Most importantly, we may not use our bodies to harm others in certain ways, just as we may not use our property to harm others. But drug use seems to be a paradigm case of a legitimate exercise of the right to control one's own body. Drug consumption takes place in and immediately around the user's own body; the salient effects occur *inside* the user's body. If we consider drug use merely as altering the user's own body and mind, it is hard to see how anyone who believes in rights at all could deny that it is protected by a right, for: (a) it is hard to see how anyone who believes in rights could deny that individuals have rights over their own bodies and minds, and (b) it is hard to see how anyone who believes in such rights could deny that drug use, considered merely as altering the user's body and mind, is an example of the exercise of one's rights over one's own body and mind.

Consider two ways a prohibitionist might object to this argument. First, a prohibitionist might argue that drug use does not *merely* alter the user's own body and mind, but also harms the user's family, friends, co-workers, and society. I responded to this sort of argument in section II. Not just *any* way in which an action might be said to "harm" other people makes the action worthy of criminal sanctions. Here we need not try to state a general criterion for what sorts of harms make an action worthy of criminalization; it is enough to note that there are some kinds of "harms" that virtually no one would take to warrant criminal sanctions, and that these include the "harms" I cause to others by being a poor student, an incompetent worker, or an apathetic citizen.[13] That said, I agree with the prohibitionists at least this far: no one should be permitted to drive or operate heavy machinery while under the influence of drugs that impair their ability to do those things; nor should pregnant mothers be permitted to ingest drugs, if it can be proven that those drugs cause substantial risks to their babies (I leave open the question of what the threshold level of risk should be, as well as the empirical questions concerning the actual level of risk created by illegal drugs). But, in the great majority of cases, drug use does not harm anyone in any *relevant*

ways—that is, ways that we normally take to merit criminal penalties—
and should not be outlawed.

Second, a prohibitionist might argue that drug use fails to qualify
as an exercise of the user's rights over his own body, because the
individual is not truly acting freely in deciding to use drugs. Perhaps
individuals only use drugs because they have fallen prey to some sort
of psychological compulsion, because drugs exercise a siren-like allure
that distorts users' perceptions, because users don't realize how bad
drugs are, or something of that sort. The exact form of this objection
doesn't matter; in any case, the prohibitionist faces a dilemma. If users
do not freely choose to use drugs, then it is unjust to *punish* them for
using drugs. For if users do not choose freely, then they are not morally responsible for their decision, and it is unjust to punish a person
for something he is not responsible for. But if users *do* choose freely in
deciding to use drugs, then this choice is an exercise of their rights over
their own bodies.

I have tried to think of the best arguments prohibitionists could
give, but in fact prohibitionists have remained puzzlingly silent on this
issue. When a country goes to war, it tends to focus on how to win,
sparing little thought for the rights of the victims in the enemy country. Similarly, one effect of America's declaring "war" on drug users
seems to have been that prohibitionists have given almost no thought
to the rights of drug users. Most either ignore the issue or mention it
briefly only to dismiss it without argument.[14] In an effort to discredit
legalizers, the Office of National Drug Control Policy produced the
following caricature—

> The easy cynicism that has grown up around the drug issue is no accident.
> Sowing it has been the deliberate aim of a decades-long campaign by
> proponents of legalization, critics whose mantra is "nothing works," and
> whose central insight appears to be that they can avoid having to propose
> the unmentionable—a world where drugs are ubiquitous and where use
> and addiction would skyrocket—if they can hide behind the bland man-
> agement critique that drug control efforts are "unworkable."[15]

—apparently denying the existence of the central issues I have discussed in this essay. It seems reasonable to assume that an account of
the state's right to forcibly interfere with individuals' decisions regarding their own bodies is not forthcoming from these prohibitionists.

IV. CONCLUSION

Undoubtedly, the drug war has been disastrous in many ways that others can more ably describe—in terms of its effects on crime, on police corruption, and on other civil liberties, to name a few. But more than that, the drug war is morally outrageous in its very conception. If we are to call ours a free society, we cannot deploy force to deprive people of their liberty and property for whimsical reasons. The exercise of such coercion requires a powerful and clearly stated rationale. Most of the reasons that have been proposed in the case of drug prohibition would be considered feeble if advanced in other contexts. Few would take seriously the suggestion that people should be imprisoned for harming their own health, being poor students, or failing to share in the American dream. It is still less credible that we should imprison people for an activity that only *may* lead to those consequences. Yet these and other, similarly weak arguments form the core of prohibition's defense.

Prohibitionists are likewise unable to answer the argument that individuals have a right to use drugs. Any such answer would have to deny either that persons have rights of control over their own bodies, or that consuming drugs constituted an exercise of those rights. We have seen that the sort of harms drug use allegedly causes to society do not make a case against its being an exercise of the user's rights over his own body. And the claim that drug users can't control their behavior or don't know what they are doing renders it even more mysterious why one would believe drug users deserve to be punished for what they are doing.

I will close by responding to a query posed by prohibition-advocate James Inciardi:

> The government of the United States is not going to legalize drugs anytime soon, if ever, and certainly not in this [the 20th] century. So why spend so much time, expense, and intellectual and emotional effort on a quixotic undertaking? . . . [W]e should know by now that neither politicians nor the polity respond positively to abrupt and drastic strategy alterations.[16]

The United States presently has 553,000 people unjustly imprisoned. Inciardi may—tragically—be correct that our government has no intention of stopping its flagrant violations of the rights of its people any time soon. Nevertheless, it remains the duty of citizens and of political and social theorists to identify the injustice, and not to tacitly assent to it. Imagine a slavery advocate, decades before the Civil War, arguing that abolitionists were wasting their breath and should move on to more productive activities, such as arguing for incremental changes in the way slaves are treated, since the southern states had no intention of ending slavery any time soon. The institution of slavery is a black mark on our nation's history, but our history would be even more shameful if no one at the time had spoken against the injustice.

Is this comparison overdrawn? I don't think so. The harm of being unjustly imprisoned is qualitatively comparable (though it usually ends sooner) to the harm of being enslaved. The increasingly popular scapegoating and stereotyping of drug users and sellers on the part of our nation's leaders is comparable to the racial prejudices of previous generations. Yet very few seem willing to speak on behalf of drug users. Perhaps the unwillingness of those in public life to defend drug users' rights stems from the negative image we have of drug users and the fear of being associated with them. Yet these attitudes remain baffling. I have used illegal drugs myself. I know many decent and successful individuals, both in and out of my profession, who have used illegal drugs. Two United States Presidents, one Vice-President, a Speaker of the House, and a Supreme Court Justice have all admitted to having used illegal drugs.[17] Nearly half of all Americans over the age of 11 have used illegal drugs.[18] But now leave aside the absurdity of recommending criminal sanctions for all these people. My point is this: if we are convinced of the injustice of drug prohibition, then—even if our protests should fall on deaf ears—we cannot remain silent in the face of such a large-scale injustice in our own country. And, fortunately, radical social reforms *have* occurred, more than once in our history, in response to moral arguments.

NOTES

1. Douglas Husak (*Legalize This! The Case for Decriminalizing Drugs,* London: Verso, 2002, pages 7, 101–3) makes this sort of argument. I have added my own examples of harmful activities to his list.

2. Ali Mokdad, James Marks, Donna Stroup, and Julie Gerberding, "Actual Causes of Death in the United States, 2000," *Journal of the American Medical Association* 291, no. 10 (2004): 1238–45, page 1242. The statistic includes estimated contributions of drug use to such causes of death as suicide, homicide, motor vehicle accidents, and HIV infection.

3. Mokdad et al., page 1239; the statistic includes estimated effects of secondhand smoke. The Centers for Disease Control and Prevention provides an estimate of 440,000 ("Annual Smoking-Attributable Mortality, Years of Potential Life Lost, and Economic Costs—United States, 1995–1999," *Morbidity and Mortality Weekly Report* 51, 2002: 300–3, http://www.cdc.gov/mmwr/ PDF/wk/mm5114.pdf, page 300).

4. James Inciardi ("Against Legalization of Drugs" in Arnold Trebach and James Inciardi, *Legalize It? Debating American Drug Policy,* Washington, DC: American University Press, 1993, pages 161, 165) makes this point, accusing drug legalizers of "sophism." He does not go on to calculate the number of deaths per user, however.

5. I include both current and former smokers among "at risk persons." The calculation for tobacco is based on Mokdad et al.'s report (page 1239) that 22.2% of the adult population were smokers and 24.4% were former smokers in 2000, and the U.S. Census Bureau's estimate of an adult population of 209 million in the year 2000 ("Table 2: Annual Estimates of the Population by Sex and Selected Age Groups for the United States: April 1, 2000 to July 1, 2007 [NC-EST2007-02]," release date May 1, 2008, http://www.census.gov/popest/ national/asrh/NC-EST2007/NC-EST2007-02.xls). The calculation for illicit drugs is based on the report of the Office of National Drug Control Policy (hereafter, ONDCP) that, in the year 2000, 11% of persons aged 12 and older had used illegal drugs in the previous year ("Drug Use Trends," October 2002, http://www.whitehousedrugpolicy.gov/publications/factsht/druguse/), and the U.S. Census Bureau's report of a population of about 233 million Americans aged 12 and over in 2000 ("Table 1: Annual Estimates of the Population by Sex and Five-Year Age Groups for the United States: April 1, 2000 to July 1, 2007 [NC-EST2007-01]," release date May 1, 2008, http://www.census.gov/popest/ national/asrh/NC-EST2007/NC-EST2007-02.xls). Interpolation was applied to the Census Bureau's "10 to 14" age category to estimate the number of persons aged 12 to 14. In the case of drugs, if "at risk persons" are considered to include only those who admit to having used illegal drugs in the past month, then the death rate is 1.2 per 1,000 at-risk persons.

6. Based on 112,000 premature deaths caused by obesity in 2000 (Katherine Flegal, Barry Graubard, David Williamson, and Mitchell Gail, "Excess Deaths Associated with Underweight, Overweight, and Obesity," *Journal of the American Medical Association* 293, no. 15, 2005: 1861–7), a 30.5% obesity rate among U.S. adults in 2000 (Allison Hedley, Cynthia Ogden, Clifford Johnson, Margaret Carroll, Lester Curtin, and Katherine Flegal, "Prevalence of Overweight and Obesity Among U.S. Children, Adolescents, and Adults, 1999–2002," *Journal of the American Medical Association* 291, no. 23 (2004): 2847–50) and a U.S. adult population of 209 million in 2000 (U.S. Census Bureau, "Table 2," op. cit.).

7. Inciardi, pages 167, 172.

8. James Q. Wilson, "Against the Legalization of Drugs," *Commentary* 89 (1990): 21–8, page 26.

9. ONDCP, *National Drug Control Strategy 2002,* Washington, DC: Government Printing Office, http://www.whitehousedrugpolicy.gov/publications/policy/03ndcs/, pages 1–2.

10. Husak, *Legalize This!,* page 2.

11. In 2006, there were approximately 553,000 people in American prisons and jails whose most serious offense was a drug offense. This included 93,751 federal inmates (U.S. Department of Justice, "Prisoners in 2006," December 2007, http://www.ojp.usdoj.gov/bjs/pub/pdf/p06.pdf, page 9). State prisons held another 269,596 drug inmates, based on the 2006 state prison population of 1,377,815 ("Prisoners in 2006," page 2) and the 2004 rate of 19.57% of state prisoners held on drug charges ("Prisoners in 2006," page 24). Local jails held another 189,204 drug inmates, based on the 2006 local jail population of 766,010 ("Prisoners in 2006," page 3) and the 2002 rate of 24.7% of local inmates held on drug charges (U.S. Department of Justice, "Profile of Jail Inmates 2002," published July 2004, revised October 12, 2004, http://www.ojp.usdoj.gov/bjs/pub/pdf/pji02.pdf, page 1). In all cases, I have used the latest statistics available as of this writing.

12. Husak, *Legalize This!*, page 15. See his chapter 2 for an extended discussion of various proposed rationales for drug prohibition, including many issues that I lack space to discuss here.

13. Husak (*Drugs and Rights*, Cambridge University Press, 1992, pages 166–68) similarly argues that no one has a *right* that I be a good neighbor, proficient student, and so on, and that only harms that violate rights can justify criminal sanctions.

14. See Inciardi for an instance of ignoring and Daniel Lungren ("Legalization Would Be a Mistake" in Timothy Lynch, ed., *After Prohibition*, Washington, DC: Cato Institute, 2000, page 180) for an instance of unargued dismissal. Wilson (page 24) addresses the issue, if at all, only by arguing that drug use makes users worse parents, spouses, employers, and co-workers. This fails to refute the contention that individuals have a right to use drugs.

15. ONDCP, *National Drug Control Strategy 2002*, page 3.

16. Inciardi, page 205.

17. Bill Clinton, Al Gore, Newt Gingrich, and Clarence Thomas (reported by David Phinney, "Dodging the Drug Question," ABC News, August 19, 1999, http://abcnews.go.com/sections/politics/DailyNews/prez_questions990819.html). George W. Bush has refused to state whether he has ever used illegal drugs. Barack Obama has acknowledged using cocaine and marijuana (*Dreams from My Father*, New York: Random House, 2004, page 93).

18. In 2006, 45% of Americans aged 12 and over reported having used at least one illegal drug (U.S. Department of Health and Human Services, "National Survey on Drug Use and Health," 2006, Table 1.1B, http://www .oas.samhsa.gov/NSDUH/2k6NSDUH/tabs/Sect1peTabs1to46.htm).

Chapter 17

The Opioid Crisis, as Lived in West Virginia

Margaret Talbot

In 2015, a dismal record was set, as 52,404 people in the United States died from drug overdose. The next year, however, was worse, with more than 63,600 overdose deaths. And then 2017 was even more horrific, with over 72,200 senseless fatalities. The worst drug crisis in American history is ongoing, and deepening. Overdosing on drugs is the most common way for American adults under the age of fifty-five to die—more common than from car accidents, or suicide, or anything else.

Most of these deaths involve an opioid narcotic. The opioid drugs include morphine, heroin, fentanyl, sufentanil, tramadol, oxycodone (OxyContin), and hydrocodone (Vicodin). This class of drugs is indispensible to medicine—morphine in particular has probably saved humans from more pain than any other drug in history. However, the opioids are dangerous. Sufentanil is hundreds of times more potent than morphine.

In this selection, the author describes what the drug crisis is like for those in its midst. West Virginia—one of the poorest states, and the state that went most heavily for Donald Trump in the 2016 presidential election—also has the highest rate of overdose deaths.

I

Michael Barrett and Jenna Mulligan, emergency paramedics in Berkeley County, West Virginia, recently got a call that sent them to the youth softball field in a tiny town called Hedgesville. It was the first practice of the season for the girls' Little League team, and dusk was descending. Barrett and Mulligan drove past a clubhouse with a blue-and-yellow sign that read "Home of the Lady Eagles," and stopped near a scrubby set of bleachers, where parents had gathered to watch their daughters bat and field.

Two of the parents were lying on the ground, unconscious, several yards apart. As Barrett later recalled, the couple's thirteen-year-old daughter was sitting behind a chain-link backstop with her teammates, who were hugging her and comforting her. The couple's younger children, aged ten and seven, were running back and forth between their parents, screaming, "Wake up! Wake up!" When Barrett and Mulligan knelt down to administer Narcan, a drug that reverses heroin overdoses, some of the other parents got angry. "You know, saying, 'This is bullcrap,'" Barrett told me. "'Why's my kid gotta see this? Just let 'em lay there.'" After a few minutes, the couple began to groan as they revived. Adults ushered the younger kids away. From the other side of the backstop, the older kids asked Barrett if the parents had overdosed. "I was, like, 'I'm not gonna say.' The kids aren't stupid. They know people don't just pass out for no reason." During the chaos, someone made a call to Child Protective Services.

At this stage of the American opioid epidemic, many addicts are collapsing in public—in gas stations, in restaurant bathrooms, in the aisles of big-box stores. Brian Costello, a former Army medic who is the director of the Berkeley County Emergency Medical Services, believes that more overdoses are occurring in this way because users figure that somebody will find them before they die. "To people who don't have that addiction, that sounds crazy," he said. "But, from a health-care provider's standpoint, you say to yourself, 'No, this is survival to them.' They're struggling with using but not wanting to die."

A month after the incident, the couple from the softball field, Angel Dawn Holt, who is thirty-five, and her boyfriend, Christopher Schildt, who is thirty-three, were arraigned on felony charges of child neglect. (Schildt is not the biological father of Holt's kids.) A local newspaper, the Martinsburg *Journal*, ran an article about the charges, noting that the couple's children, who had been "crying when law enforcement arrived," had been "turned over to their grandfather."

West Virginia has the highest overdose death rate in the country, and heroin has devastated the state's Eastern Panhandle, which includes Hedgesville and the larger town of Martinsburg. Like the vast majority of residents there, nearly all the addicts are white, were born in the area, and have modest incomes. Because they can't be dismissed as outsiders, some locals view them with empathy. Other residents regard addicts as community embarrassments. Many people in the Panhandle have embraced the idea of addiction as a disease, but a vocal cohort dismisses this as a fantasy disseminated by urban liberals.

These tensions were aired in online comments that amassed beneath the *Journal* article. A waitress named Sandy wrote, "Omgsh, How sad!! Shouldnt be able to have there kids back! Seems the heroin was more important to them, than watchn there kids have fun play ball, and have there parents proud of them!!" A poster named Valerie wrote, "Stop giving them Narcan! At the tax payers expense." Such views were countered by a reader named Diana: "I'm sure the parents didn't get up that morning and say hey let's scar the kids for life. I'm sure they wished they could sit through the kids practice without having to get high. The only way to understand it is to have lived it. The children need to be in a safe home and the adults need help. They are sick, I know from the outside it looks like a choice but its not. Shaming and judging will not help anyone."

II

In Berkeley County, which has a population of a hundred and fourteen thousand, when someone under sixty dies, and the cause of death isn't mentioned in the paper, locals assume that it was an overdose. It's becoming the default explanation when an ambulance stops outside a neighbor's house, and the best guess for why someone is sitting in his car on the side of the road in the middle of the afternoon. On January 18th, county officials started using a new app to record overdoses. According to this data, during the next two and a half months emergency medical personnel responded to a hundred and forty-five overdoses, eighteen of which were fatal. This underestimates the scale of the epidemic, because many overdoses do not prompt 911 calls.

Last year, the county's annual budget for emergency medication was twenty-seven thousand dollars. Narcan, which costs fifty dollars a dose, consumed two-thirds of that allotment. The medication was administered two hundred and twenty-three times in 2014, and four hundred and three times in 2016.

One Thursday in March, a few weeks before Michael Barrett responded to Angel Holt's overdose, I rode with him in his paramedic vehicle, a specially equipped S.U.V. He started his day as he often does, with bacon and eggs at the Olde Country Diner, in Martinsburg. Barrett, who is thirty-three, with a russet-colored beard and mustache, works two twenty-four-hour shifts a week, starting at 7 a.m. The diner shares a strip mall with the E.M.T. station, and, if he has to leave on a call before he can finish eating, the servers will box up his food in a hurry. Barrett's father and his uncles were volunteer firemen in the area, and, growing up, he often accompanied them in the fire truck. As they'd pull people from crumpled cars or burning buildings, he'd say to himself, "Man, they *doing* stuff—they're awesome." When Barrett became a paramedic, in his twenties, he knew that he could make a lot more money "going down the road," as people around here say, referring to Baltimore or Washington, D.C. But he liked it when older colleagues told him, "I used to hold you at the fire department when you were a baby."

Barrett's first overdose call of the day came at 8 a.m., for a twenty-year-old woman. Several family members were present at the home, and while Barrett and his colleagues worked on her they cried and blamed one another, and themselves, for not watching her more closely. The woman was given Narcan, but she was too far gone; she died after arriving at the hospital.

We stopped by a local fire station, where the men and women on duty talked about all the O.D. calls they took each week. Sometimes they knew the person from high school, or were related to the person. Barrett said that in such cases you tended "to get more angry at them—you're, like, 'Man, you got a *kid*, what the hell's wrong with you?'"

Barrett sometimes had to return several times in one day to the same house—once, a father, a mother, and a teenage daughter overdosed on heroin in succession. Such stories seemed like twisted variations on the small-town generational solidarity he admired; as Barrett put it, even if one family member wanted to get clean, it would be next to impossible unless the others did, too. He was used to O.D. calls by now, except for the ones in which kids were around. He once arrived at a home to find a seven-year-old and a five-year-old following the instructions of a 911 operator and performing C.P.R. on their parents. (They survived.)

Around three o'clock, the dispatcher reported that a man in Hedgesville was slumped over the steering wheel of a jeep. By the time we got there, the man, who appeared to be in his early thirties, had been helped out of his vehicle and into an ambulance. A skinny young sheriff's deputy on the scene showed us a half-filled syringe: the contents resembled clean sand, which suggested pure heroin. That was a good thing—these days, the narcotic is often cut with synthetic painkillers such as fentanyl, which is fifty times as powerful as heroin.

The man had floppy brown hair and a handsome face; he was wearing jeans, work boots, and a black windbreaker. He'd been revived with oxygen—he hadn't needed Narcan—but as he sat in the ambulance his eyes were only partly opened, and his pupils, when I could catch a glimpse of them, were constricted to pinpoints. Barrett asked him, "Did you take a half syringe? 'Cause there's half a syringe left." The man looked up briefly and said, "Yeah? I was trying to take it all." He said that he was sorry—he'd been clean for a month. Then he mumbled something about having a headache. "Well, sure you do," another paramedic said. "You weren't breathing there for a while. Your brain didn't have any oxygen."

The man's jeep sat, dead still, in the middle of a street that sloped sharply downhill. A woman introduced herself to me as Ethel. She had been driving behind the man when he lost consciousness. "I just rolled up, saw he was slumped over the wheel," she said. "I knew what it was right away." She beeped her horn, but he didn't move. She called 911 and stayed until the first responders showed up, "in case he started to roll forward, and maybe I could stop traffic—and to make sure he was O.K." I asked if the man's jeep had been running during this time. "Oh, yeah," she said. "He just happened to stop with his foot on the brake." Barrett shared some protocol: whenever he came across people passed out in a car, he put the transmission in park and took their keys, in case they abruptly revived. He'd heard of people driving off with E.M.T. personnel halfway inside.

The sky was a dazzling blue, with fluffy white clouds scudding overhead. The man took a sobriety test, wobbling across the neat lawn of a Methodist church. "That guy's still high as a kite," somebody said.

We were driving away from Hedgesville when the third overdose call of the day came, for a twenty-nine-year-old male. Inside a nicely kept house in a modern subdivision, the man was lying unconscious on the bathroom floor, taking intermittent gasps. He was pale, though not yet the blue-tinged gray that people turn when they've been breathing poorly for a while. Opioid overdoses usually kill people by inhibiting respiration: breathing slows and starts to sound labored, then stops altogether. Barrett began preparing a Narcan dose. Generally, the goal was to get people breathing well again, not necessarily to wake them completely. A full dose of Narcan is two milligrams, and in Berkeley County the medics administer 0.4 milligrams at a time, so as not to snatch patients' high away too abruptly: you didn't want them to go into instant withdrawal, feel terribly sick, and become belligerent. Barrett crouched next to the man and started an I.V. A minute later, the man sat up, looking bewildered and resentful. He threw up. Barrett said, "Couple more minutes and you would have died, buddy."

"Thank you," the man said.

"You're welcome—but now you need to go to the hospital."

The man's girlfriend was standing nearby, her hair in a loose bun. She responded calmly to questions: "Yeah, he does heroin"; "Yeah, he just ate." The family dog was snuffling at the front door, and one of the sheriff's deputies asked if he could let it outside. The girlfriend said, "Sure." Brian Costello had told me that family members had grown oddly comfortable with E.M.T. visits: "That's the scary part—that it's becoming the norm." The man stood up, and then, swaying in the doorway, vomited a second time.

"We're gonna take him to the hospital," Barrett told the girlfriend. "He could stop breathing again."

As we drove away, Barrett predicted that the man would check himself out of the hospital as soon as he could; most O.D. patients refused further treatment. Even a brush with death was rarely a turning point for an addict. "It's kind of hard to feel good about it," Barrett said of the intervention. "Though he did say, 'Thanks for waking me up.' Well, that's our job. But do you feel like you're really making a difference? Ninety-nine percent of the time, no." The next week, Barrett's crew was called back to the same house repeatedly. The man overdosed three times; his girlfriend, once.

It was getting dark, and Barrett stopped at a convenience store for a snack—chocolate milk and a beef stick. That evening, he dealt with one more O.D. A young woman had passed out in her car in the parking lot of a 7-Eleven, with her little girl squirming in a car seat. An older woman who happened on the scene had taken the girl, a four-year-old, into the store and bought her some hot chocolate and Skittles. After the young woman received Narcan, Barrett told her that she could have killed her daughter, and she started sobbing hysterically. Meanwhile, several guys in the parking lot were becoming agitated. They had given the woman C.P.R., but someone had called 911 and suggested that they had supplied her with the heroin. The men were black and everybody else—the overdosing woman, the older woman, the cops, the ambulance crew—was white. The men were told to remain at the scene while the cops did background checks. Barrett attempted to defuse the tension by saying, "Hey, you guys gave her C.P.R.? Thanks. We really appreciate that." The criminal checks turned up nothing; there was no reason to suspect that the men were anything but Good Samaritans. The cops let the men go, the young woman went to the E.R., and the little girl was retrieved by her father.

III

Heroin is an alluringly cheap alternative to prescription pain medication. In 1996, Purdue Pharma introduced OxyContin, marketing it as a safer form of opiate—the class of painkillers derived from the poppy plant. (The term "opioids" encompasses synthetic versions of opiates as well.) Opiates such as morphine block pain but also produce a dreamy euphoria, and over time they cause physical cravings. OxyContin was sold in time-release capsules that levelled out the high and, supposedly, diminished the risk of addiction, but people soon discovered that the capsules could be crushed into powder and then injected or snorted. Between 2000 and 2014, the number of overdose deaths in the United States jumped by 137 percent.

Some states became inundated with opiates. According to the Charleston *Gazette-Mail*, between 2007 and 2012 drug wholesalers shipped to West Virginia seven hundred and eighty million pills of hydrocodone (the generic name for Vicodin) and oxycodone (the generic name for OxyContin). That was enough to give each resident four hundred and thirty-three pills. The state has a disproportionate number of people who have jobs that cause physical pain, such as coal mining. It also has high levels of poverty and joblessness, which cause psychic pain. Mental-health services, meanwhile, are scant. Chess

Yellott, a retired family practitioner in Martinsburg, told me that many West Virginians self-medicate to mute depression, anxiety, and post-traumatic stress from sexual assault or childhood abuse. "Those things are treatable, and upper-middle-class parents generally get their kids treated," he said. "But, in families with a lot of chaos and money problems, kids don't get help."

In 2010, Purdue introduced a reformulated capsule that is harder to crush or dissolve. The Centers for Disease Control subsequently issued new guidelines stipulating that doctors should not routinely treat chronic pain with opioids, and instead should try approaches such as exercise and behavioral therapy. The number of prescriptions for opioids began to drop.

But when prescription opioids became scarcer their street price went up. Drug cartels sensed an opportunity, and began flooding rural America with heroin. Daniel Ciccarone, a professor at the U.C.-San Francisco School of Medicine, studies the heroin market. He said of the cartels, "They're multinational, savvy, borderless entities. They worked very hard to move high-quality heroin into places like rural Vermont." They also kept the price low. In West Virginia, many addicts told me, an oxycodone pill now sells for about eighty dollars; a dose of heroin can be bought for about ten. . . .

"The Changing Face of Heroin Use in the United States," a 2014 study led by Theodore Cicero, of Washington University in St. Louis, looked at some three thousand heroin addicts in substance-abuse programs. Half of those who began using heroin before 1980 were white; nearly 90 percent of those who began using in the past decade were white. This demographic shift may be connected to prescribing patterns. A 2012 study by a University of Pennsylvania researcher found that black patients were 34 percent less likely than white patients to be prescribed opioids for such chronic conditions as back pain and migraines, and 14 percent less likely to receive such prescriptions after surgery or traumatic injury.

But a larger factor, it seems, was the despair of white people in struggling small towns. Judith Feinberg, a professor at West Virginia University who studies drug addiction, described opioids as "the ultimate escape drugs." She told me, "Boredom and a sense of uselessness and inadequacy—these are human failings that lead you to just want to withdraw. On heroin, you curl up in a corner and blank out the world. It's an extremely seductive drug for dead-end towns, because it makes the world's problems go away.

Much more so than coke or meth, where you want to run around and *do* things—you get aggressive, razzed and jazzed."

Peter Callahan, a psychotherapist in Martinsburg, said that heroin "is a very tough drug to get off of, because, while it was meant to numb *physical* pain, it numbs emotional pain as well—quickly and intensely." In tight-knit Appalachian towns, heroin has become a social contagion. Nearly everyone I met in Martinsburg has ties to someone—a child, a sibling, a girlfriend, an in-law, an old high-school coach—who has struggled with opioids. As Callahan put it, "If the lady next door is using, and so are other neighbors, and people in your family are, too, the odds are good that you're going to join in."

In 2015, Berkeley County created a new position, recovery-services coordinator, to connect residents with rehab. Yet there is a chronic shortage of beds in the state for addicts who want help. Kevin Knowles, who was appointed to the job, told me, "If they have private insurance, I can hook them right up. If they're on Medicaid—and 95 percent of the people I work with are—it's going to be a long wait for them. Weeks, months." He said, "The number of beds would have to increase by a factor of three or four to make any impact."

West Virginia has an overdose death rate of 41.5 per hundred thousand people. (New Hampshire has the second-highest rate: 34.3 per hundred thousand.) This year, for the sixth straight year, West Virginia's indigent burial fund, which helps families who can't afford a funeral pay for one, ran out of money. Fred Kitchen, the president of the West Virginia Funeral Directors Association, told me that, in the funeral business, "we know the reason for that was the increase in overdose deaths." He added, "Families take out second mortgages, cash in 401(k)s, and go broke to try and save a son or daughter, who then overdoses and dies." Without the help of the burial fund, funeral directors must either give away caskets, plots, and cremation services—and risk going out of business—or, Kitchen said, look "mothers, fathers, husbands, wives, and children in the eye while they're saying, 'You have nothing to help us?'"

IV

Recently, Martinsburg has begun to treat the heroin crisis more openly as a public-health problem. The police chief, a Chicago transplant named Maurice Richards, had devised a progressive-sounding plan called the Martinsburg Initiative, which would direct support services toward children who appeared to be at risk for addiction, because their families were struggling socially or emotionally. In December, Tina Stride and several other local citizens stood up at a zoning meeting to proclaim the need for a detox center. They countered several residents who testified that such a center would bring more addicts, and more heroin, to their neighborhoods. "I'm here to say that's already here," a woman in favor of the proposal said. "It's in your neighbor's house, in the bathroom at Wendy's, in our schools." She added, "We're talking about making America great again? Well, it starts here."

That night, the Board of Zoning Appeals voted to allow a detox center, run by Peter Callahan, the psychotherapist, to occupy an unused commercial building in town. People in the hearing room cheered and cried and hugged one another. The facility will have only sixteen beds and won't be ready for patients until December, but the Hope Dealer women were thrilled about it. Now they wouldn't have to drive halfway across the state every time an addict called them up. . . .

This spring, Berkeley County started its first needle-exchange program, and other efforts are being made to help addicts survive. The new app that first responders are using to document overdoses allows them to input how many times a patient is given Narcan; when multiple doses are required, the heroin tends to be adulterated with strong synthetics. Such data can help the health department and law enforcement track dangerous batches of drugs, and help warn addicts.

Some Martinsburg residents who had been skeptical of medication-assisted treatment told me that they were coming around to the idea. A few cited the Surgeon General's report on substance abuse, released in November, which encouraged the expansion of such treatment, noting that studies have repeatedly demonstrated its efficacy in "reducing illicit drug use and overdose deaths." In Berkeley County, it felt like a turning point, though the Trump Administration was likely to resist such approaches. Tom Price, the new Secretary of Health and Human Services, has dismissed medication-assisted treatment as "substituting one opioid for another." It was also unclear how most addicts would pay for treatment if the Affordable Care Act was repealed.

Martinsburg residents, meanwhile, tried to take heart from small breakthroughs. Angel Holt, the mother who'd overdosed at the softball practice, told me that she and her boyfriend had stayed clean since that day, and she was hoping to regain custody of her children. She'd been helped by the kindness of an older couple, Karen and Ed Schildt, who lived in Thurmont, Maryland. A year earlier, the Schildts had lost their twenty-five-year-old son, Chris, to a heroin overdose. They were deeply religious, and when they heard what happened to Angel Holt and Christopher Schildt they decided to reach out to them. The fact that their son had the same name as Holt's boyfriend surely meant that God had put the couple in their path. Karen texted Holt words of encouragement almost daily.

In February, I spent an afternoon with Shawn Valentine, the *nonprofit program director*, who introduced me to Shelby, her twenty-five-year-old daughter. Shelby had become addicted to opioids at twenty-one, when she was depressed and waitressing at a Waffle House. Her co-workers always seemed to know how to get their hands on pills. When the meds got too expensive, Shelby turned to heroin.

Shelby, Valentine, and I were sitting in Valentine's kitchen, along with Shelby's sweet fifteen-year-old brother, Patrick. Shelby said, "People don't realize what the brain goes through when you're addicted—it's like a mental shutdown. Everything is gray. You have these blinders on." As she described it, the constant hunt for heroin imposed a kind of order on life's confounding open-endedness. Addiction told you what every day was for, when otherwise you might not have known.

For close to a year, Shelby had been in a program in which she put a dissolvable strip of Suboxone on her tongue every day, and attended group and individual therapy. (The word "assisted" in "medication-assisted treatment" indicates the primacy of the need for recovering addicts to figure out why they are drawn to opioids.) Shelby said that Suboxone helped curb her craving for heroin, without sedating her. "There are triggers," she said. "But the urge to run a hundred yards down the street and try to find my ex-dealer and pay him, then shove a used rig in my arm real quick? That's gone."

She can now be trusted not to sell treasured things for drug money: her little brother's video-game console, her mom's four-leaf-clover necklace. Her long auburn hair, which she used to wash and comb so seldom that her mother once spent four hours trying to untangle it, is now silky and soft.

Valentine told me that, if Shelby had to be on Suboxone all her life, "I'm absolutely on board with that." She turned to Shelby. "Whatever it takes for you to be a healthy, productive human being."

Recently, Shelby's mother told her, "O.K., I'll let you take the truck without me, to take your brother to the movies." Shelby recalled, "I was almost, like, 'Pinch me, wake me up—this can't be true.' Because without her truck there's no working. That's how she makes her living. She said, 'Here's a piece of trust. Don't throw it away.'"

Shelby and her brother drove to the mall and saw a horror movie. It was not a very good one, they agreed, but it didn't matter. They headed home in the dark, and the moment they got there Shelby placed the keys to the truck in her mother's hand.

Chapter 18

Is Doping Wrong?

Peter Singer

Athletes can take drugs to improve their strength, speed, and stamina. Should sporting associations ban all of these drugs? Or does the answer depend on the sport, and on the drug? In this selection, Peter Singer (1946–) considers a standard for answering such questions, proposed by Julian Savulescu: that athletes should be allowed to take only those drugs which are safe.

There is now a regular season for discussing drugs in sports, one that arrives every year with the Tour de France. This year, the overall leader, two other riders, and two teams were expelled or withdrew from the race as a result of failing, or missing, drug tests. The eventual winner, Alberto Contador, is himself alleged to have had a positive test result last year. So many leading cyclists have tested positive for drugs, or have admitted, from the safety of retirement, that they used them, that one can plausibly doubt that it is possible to be competitive in this event otherwise.

In the United States, the debate has been fueled by the baseball player Barry Bonds's march toward the all-time record for home runs in a career. Bonds is widely believed to have been helped by drugs and synthetic hormones. He is frequently booed and mocked by fans,

Peter Singer, "Is Doping Wrong?" in *Project Syndicate*, August 2007. © 2007 Peter Singer. Used with permission of the author.

and many thought that baseball's commissioner, Bud Selig, should not attend games at which Bonds might tie or break the record.

At the elite level, the difference between being a champion and an also-ran is so miniscule, and yet matters so much, that athletes are pressured to do whatever they can to gain the slightest edge over their competitors. It is reasonable to suspect that gold medals now go not to those who are drug-free, but to those who most successfully refine their drug use for maximum enhancement without detection.

As events like the Tour de France turn farcical, bioethics professor Julian Savulescu has offered a radical solution. Savulescu, who directs the Uehiro Centre for Practical Ethics at Oxford University and holds degrees in both medicine and bioethics, says that we should drop the ban on performance-enhancing drugs, and allow athletes to take whatever they want, as long as it is safe for them to do so.

Savulescu proposes that instead of trying to detect whether an athlete has taken drugs, we should focus on measurable indications of whether an athlete is risking his or her health. So, if an athlete has a dangerously high level of red blood cells as a result of taking erythropoietin (EPO), he or she should not be allowed to compete. The issue is the red blood cell count, not the means used to elevate it.

To those who say that this will give drug users an unfair advantage, Savulescu replies that now, without drugs, those with the best genes have an unfair advantage. They must still train, of course, but if their genes produce more EPO than ours, they are going to beat us in the Tour de France, no matter how hard we train. Unless, that is, we take EPO to make up for our genetic deficiency. Setting a maximum level of red blood cells actually levels the playing field by reducing the impact of the genetic lottery. Effort then becomes more important than having the right genes.

Some argue that taking drugs is "against the spirit of sport." But it is difficult to defend the current line between what athletes can and cannot do in order to enhance their performance.

In the Tour de France, cyclists can even use overnight intravenous nutrition and hydration to restore their bodies. Training at high altitude is permitted, though it gives those athletes who can do it an edge over competitors who must train at sea level. The World Anti-Doping Code no longer prohibits caffeine. In any case, performance-enhancement is, Savulescu says, the very spirit of sport. We should allow athletes to pursue it by any safe means.

Moreover, I would argue that sport has no single "spirit." People play sports to socialize, for exercise, to keep fit, to earn money, to become famous, to prevent boredom, to find love, and for the sheer fun of it. They may strive to improve their performance, but often they do so for its own sake, for the sense of achievement.

Popular participation in sport should be encouraged. Physical exercise makes people not only healthier, but also happier. To take drugs will usually be self-defeating. I swim for exercise, and I time myself over a set distance to give myself a goal and encourage myself to work harder. I am pleased when I swim fast, but I would get no sense of achievement from improving my time if the improvement came out of a bottle.

But elite sport, watched by millions but participated in by few, is different. For the sake of fame and glory now, athletes will be tempted to risk their long-term health. So, while Savulescu's bold suggestion may reduce drug use, it will not end it.

The problem is not with the athletes, but with us. We cheer them on. We acclaim them when they win. And no matter how blatant the drug use may be, we don't stop watching the Tour de France. Maybe we should just turn off the television and get on our own bikes.

POVERTY

Chapter 19

Famine, Affluence, and Morality

Peter Singer

The Australian philosopher Peter Singer (1946–) is the most widely read author in the field of ethics. In this essay, he considers whether it is morally defensible for well-off people to spend money on luxuries while other people starve.

As I write this, in November 1971, people are dying in East Bengal from lack of food, shelter, and medical care. The suffering and death that are occurring there now are not inevitable, not unavoidable in any fatalistic sense of the term. Constant poverty, a cyclone, and a civil war have turned at least nine million people into destitute refugees; nevertheless, it is not beyond the capacity of the richer nations to give enough assistance to reduce any further suffering to very small proportions. The decisions and actions of human beings can prevent this kind of suffering. Unfortunately, human beings have not made the necessary decisions. At the individual level, people have, with very few exceptions, not responded to the situation in any significant way. Generally speaking, people have not given large sums to relief funds; they have not written to their parliamentary representatives demanding increased government assistance; they have not demonstrated in the streets, held symbolic fasts, or done anything else directed toward providing the

Peter Singer, "Famine, Affluence, and Morality" in *Philosophy and Public Affairs*, vol. 1, no. 1 (spring 1972): 229–43. Copyright © 1972 Peter Singer. Used with permission of the author.

refugees with the means to satisfy their essential needs. At the government level, no government has given the sort of massive aid that would enable the refugees to survive for more than a few days. Britain, for instance, has given rather more than most countries. It has, to date, given £14,750,000. For comparative purposes, Britain's share of the non-recoverable development costs of the Anglo-French Concorde project is already in excess of £275,000,000, and on present estimates will reach £440,000,000. The implication is that the British government values a supersonic transport more than thirty times as highly as it values the lives of the nine million refugees. Australia is another country which, on a per capita basis, is well up in the "aid to Bengal" table. Australia's aid, however, amounts to less than one-twelfth of the cost of Sydney's new opera house. . . .

These are the essential facts about the present situation in Bengal. So far as it concerns us here, there is nothing unique about this situation except its magnitude. The Bengal emergency is just the latest and most acute of a series of major emergencies in various parts of the world, arising both from natural and from manmade causes. There are also many parts of the world in which people die from malnutrition and lack of food independent of any special emergency. I take Bengal as my example only because it is the present concern, and because the size of the problem has ensured that it has been given adequate publicity. Neither individuals nor governments can claim to be unaware of what is happening there.

What are the moral implications of a situation like this? In what follows, I shall argue that the way people in relatively affluent countries react to a situation like that in Bengal cannot be justified; indeed, the whole way we look at moral issues—our moral conceptual scheme— needs to be altered, and with it, the way of life that has come to be taken for granted in our society. . . .

I begin with the assumption that suffering and death from lack of food, shelter, and medical care are bad. I think most people will agree about this, although one may reach the same view by different routes. I shall not argue for this view. People can hold all sorts of eccentric positions, and perhaps from some of them it would not follow that death by starvation is in itself bad. It is difficult, perhaps impossible, to refute such positions, and so for brevity I will henceforth take this assumption as accepted. Those who disagree need read no further.

My next point is this: if it is in our power to prevent something bad from happening, without thereby sacrificing anything of comparable moral importance, we ought, morally, to do it. By "without sacrificing anything of comparable moral importance" I mean without causing anything else comparably bad to happen, or doing something that is wrong in itself, or failing to promote some moral good, comparable in significance to the bad thing that we can prevent. This principle seems almost as uncontroversial as the last one. It requires us only to prevent what is bad, and to promote what is good, and it requires this of us only when we can do it without sacrificing anything that is, from the moral point of view, comparably important. I could even, as far as the application of my argument to the Bengal emergency is concerned, qualify the point so as to make it: if it is in our power to prevent something very bad from happening, without thereby sacrificing anything morally significant, we ought, morally, to do it. An application of this principle would be as follows: if I am walking past a shallow pond and see a child drowning in it, I ought to wade in and pull the child out. This will mean getting my clothes muddy, but this is insignificant, while the death of the child would presumably be a very bad thing.

The uncontroversial appearance of the principle just stated is deceptive. If it were acted upon, even in its qualified form, our lives, our society, and our world would be fundamentally changed. For the principle takes, firstly, no account of proximity or distance. It makes no moral difference whether the person I can help is a neighbor's child ten yards from me or a Bengali whose name I shall never know, ten thousand miles away. Secondly, the principle makes no distinction between cases in which I am the only person who could possibly do anything and cases in which I am just one among millions in the same position.

I do not think I need to say much in defense of the refusal to take proximity and distance into account. The fact that a person is physically near to us, so that we have personal contact with him, may make it more likely that we *shall* assist him, but this does not show that we *ought* to help him rather than another who happens to be further away. If we accept any principle of impartiality, universalizability, equality, or whatever, we cannot discriminate against someone merely because he is far away from us (or we are far away from him). Admittedly, it is possible that we are in a better position to judge what needs to be done to help a person near to us than one far away, and perhaps also to provide the assistance we judge to be necessary. If this were the case, it would be a reason for helping those near to us first. This may once have been a justification for being more concerned with the poor in one's town than with famine victims in India. Unfortunately for those who like to keep their moral responsibilities limited, instant communication and swift transportation have changed the situation. From the moral point of view, the development of the world into a "global village" has made an important, though still unrecognized, difference to our moral situation. Expert observers and supervisors, sent out by famine relief organizations or permanently stationed in famine-prone areas, can direct our aid to a refugee in Bengal almost as effectively as we could get it to someone in our own block. There would seem, therefore, to be no possible justification for discriminating on geographical grounds.

There may be a greater need to defend the second implication of my principle—that the fact that there are millions of other people in the same position, in respect to the Bengali refugees, as I am, does not make the situation significantly different from a situation in which I am the only person who can prevent something very bad from occurring. Again, of course, I admit that there is a psychological difference between the cases; one feels less guilty about doing nothing if one can point to others, similarly placed, who have also done nothing. Yet this can make no real difference to our moral obligations. Should I consider that I am less obliged to pull the drowning child out of the pond if on looking around I see other people, no further away than I am, who have also noticed the child but are doing nothing? One has only to ask this question to see the absurdity of the view that numbers lessen obligation. It is a view that is an ideal excuse for inactivity; unfortunately most of the major evils—poverty, overpopulation, pollution—are problems in which everyone is almost equally involved.

The view that numbers do make a difference can be made plausible if stated in this way: if everyone in circumstances like mine gave £5 to the Bengal Relief Fund, there would be enough to provide food, shelter, and medical care for the refugees; there is no reason why I should give more than anyone else in the same circumstances as I am; therefore I have no obligation to give more than £5. Each premise in this argument is true, and the argument looks sound. It may convince us, unless we notice that it is based on a hypothetical premise, although the conclusion is not stated hypothetically. The argument would be sound if the conclusion were: if everyone in circumstances like mine were to give £5, I would have no obligation to give more than £5. If the conclusion were so stated, however, it would be obvious that the argument has no bearing on a situation in which it is not the case that everyone else gives £5. This, of course, is the actual situation. It is more or less certain that not everyone in circumstances like mine will give £5. So there will not be enough to provide the needed food, shelter, and medical care. Therefore by giving more than £5 I will prevent more suffering than I would if I gave just £5. . . .

If my argument so far has been sound, neither our distance from a preventable evil nor the number of other people who, in respect to that evil, are in the same situation as we are, lessens our obligation to mitigate or prevent that evil. I shall therefore take as established the principle I asserted earlier. As I have already said, I need to assert it only in its qualified form: if it is in our power to prevent something very bad from happening, without thereby sacrificing anything else morally significant, we ought, morally, to do it.

The outcome of this argument is that our traditional moral categories are upset. The traditional distinction between duty and charity cannot be drawn, or at least, not in the place we normally draw it. Giving money to the Bengal Relief Fund is regarded as an act of charity in our society. The bodies which collect money are known as "charities." These organizations see themselves in this way—if you send them a check, you will be thanked for your "generosity." Because giving money is regarded as an act of charity, it is not thought that there is anything wrong with not giving. The charitable man may be praised, but the man who is not charitable is not condemned. People do not feel in any way ashamed or guilty about spending money on new clothes or a new car instead of giving it to famine relief. (Indeed, the alternative does not occur to them.) This way of looking at the matter cannot be justified. When we buy new clothes not to keep ourselves warm but to look "well-dressed" we are not providing for any important need. We would not be sacrificing anything significant if we were to continue to wear our old clothes, and give the money to famine relief. By doing so, we would be preventing another person from starving. It follows from what I have said earlier that we ought to give money away, rather than spend it on clothes which we do not need to keep us warm. To do so is not charitable, or generous. Nor is it the kind of act which philosophers and theologians have called "supererogatory"—an act which it would be good to do, but not wrong not to do. On the contrary, we ought to give the money away, and it is wrong not to do so. . . .

One objection to the position I have taken might be simply that it is too drastic a revision of our moral scheme. People do not ordinarily judge in the way I have suggested they should. Most people reserve their moral condemnation for those who violate some moral norm, such as the norm against taking another person's property. They do not condemn those who indulge in luxury instead of giving to famine relief. But given that I did not set out to present a morally neutral description of the way people make moral judgments, the way people do in fact judge has nothing to do with the validity of my conclusion. My conclusion follows from the principle which I advanced earlier, and unless that principle is rejected, or the arguments are shown to be unsound, I think the conclusion must stand, however strange it appears. . . .

It has been argued by some writers, among them Sidgwick and Urmson, that we need to have a basic moral code which is not too far beyond the capacities of the ordinary man, for otherwise there will be a general breakdown of compliance with the moral code. Crudely stated, this argument suggests that if we tell people that they ought to refrain from murder and give everything they do not really need to famine relief, they will do neither, whereas if we tell them that they ought to refrain from murder and that it is good to give to famine relief but not wrong not to do so, they will at least refrain from murder. The issue here is: Where should we draw the line between conduct that is required and conduct that is good although not required, so as to get the best possible result? This would seem to be an empirical question, although a very difficult one. One objection to the Sidgwick-Urmson line of argument is that it takes insufficient account of the effect that moral standards can have on the decisions we make. Given a society in which a wealthy man who gives 5 percent of his income to famine relief is regarded as most generous, it is not surprising that a proposal that we all ought to give away half our incomes will be thought to be absurdly unrealistic. In a society which held that no man should have more than enough while others have less than they need, such a proposal might seem narrow-minded. What it is possible for a man to do and what he is likely to do are both, I think, very greatly influenced by what people around him are doing and expecting him to do. In any case, the possibility that by spreading the idea that we ought to be doing very much more than we are to relieve famine we shall bring about a general breakdown of moral behavior seems remote. If the stakes are an end to widespread starvation, it is worth the risk. Finally, it should be emphasized that these considerations are relevant only to the issue of what we should require from others, and not to what we ourselves ought to do.

The second objection to my attack on the present distinction between duty and charity is one which has from time to time been made against utilitarianism. It follows from some forms of utilitarian theory that we all ought, morally, to be working full time to increase the balance of happiness over misery. The position I have taken here would not lead to this conclusion in all circumstances, for if there were no bad occurrences that we could prevent without sacrificing something of comparable moral importance, my argument would have no application. Given the present conditions in many parts of the world, however, it does follow from my argument that we ought, morally, to be working full time to relieve great suffering of the sort that occurs as a result of famine or other disasters. Of course, mitigating circumstances can be adduced—for instance, that if we wear ourselves out through overwork, we shall be less effective than we would otherwise have been. Nevertheless, when all considerations of this sort have been taken into account, the conclusion remains: we ought to be preventing as much suffering as we can without sacrificing something else of comparable moral importance. This conclusion is one which we may be reluctant to face. I cannot see, though, why it should be regarded as a criticism of the position for which I have argued, rather than a criticism of our ordinary standards of behavior. Since most people are self-interested to some degree, very few of us are likely to do everything that we ought to do. It would, however, hardly be honest to take this as evidence that it is not the case that we ought to do it.

It may still be thought that my conclusions are so wildly out of line with what everyone else thinks and has always thought that there must be something wrong with the argument somewhere. In order to show that my conclusions, while certainly contrary to contemporary Western moral standards, would not have seemed so extraordinary at other times and in other places, I would like to quote a passage from a writer not normally thought of as a way-out radical, Thomas Aquinas.

Now, according to the natural order instituted by divine providence, material goods are provided for the satisfaction of human needs. Therefore the division and appropriation of property, which proceeds from human law, must not hinder the satisfaction of man's necessity from such goods. Equally, whatever a man has in superabundance is owed, of natural right, to the poor for their sustenance. So Ambrosius says, and it is also to be found in the *Decretum Gratiani*: "The bread which you withhold belongs to the hungry; the clothing you shut away, to the naked; and the money you bury in the earth is the redemption and freedom of the penniless."[1]

I now want to consider a number of points, more practical than philosophical, which are relevant to the application of the moral conclusion we have reached. These points challenge not the idea that we ought to be doing all we can to prevent starvation, but the idea that giving away a great deal of money is the best means to this end. . . .

Another, more serious reason for not giving to famine relief funds is that until there is effective population control, relieving famine merely postpones starvation. If we save the Bengal refugees now, others, perhaps the children of these refugees, will face starvation in a few years' time. In support of this, one may cite the now well-known facts about the population explosion and the relatively limited scope for expanded production.

. . . I accept that the earth cannot support indefinitely a population rising at the present rate. This certainly poses a problem for anyone who thinks it important to prevent famine. Again, however, one could accept the argument without drawing the conclusion that it absolves one from any obligation to do anything to prevent famine. The conclusion that should be drawn is that the best means of preventing famine, in the long run, is population control. It would then follow from the position reached earlier that one ought to be doing all one can to promote population control (unless one held that all forms of population control were wrong in themselves, or would have significantly bad consequences). Since there are organizations working specifically for population control, one would then support them rather than more orthodox methods of preventing famine.

A third point raised by the conclusion reached earlier relates to the question of just how much we all ought to be giving away. One possibility . . . is that we ought to give until we reach the level of marginal utility—that is, the level at which, by giving more, I would cause as much suffering to myself or my dependents as I would relieve by my gift. This would mean, of course, that one would reduce oneself to very near the material circumstances of a Bengali refugee. It will be recalled that earlier I put forward both a strong and a moderate version of the principle of preventing bad occurrences. The strong version, which required us to prevent bad things from happening unless in doing so we would be sacrificing something of comparable moral significance, does seem to require reducing ourselves to the level of marginal utility. I should also say that the strong version seems to me to be the correct one. I proposed the more moderate version—that we should prevent bad occurrences unless, to do so, we had to sacrifice something morally significant—only in order to show that, even on this surely undeniable principle, a great change in our way of life is required. On the more moderate principle, it may not follow that we ought to reduce ourselves to the level of marginal utility, for one might hold that to reduce oneself and one's family to this level is to cause something significantly bad to happen. Whether this is so I shall not discuss, since, as I have said, I can see no good reason for holding the moderate version of the principle rather than the strong version. Even if we accepted the principle only in its moderate form, however, it should be clear that we would have to give away enough to ensure that the consumer society, dependent as it is on people spending on trivia rather than giving to famine relief, would slow down and perhaps disappear entirely. There are several reasons why this would be desirable in itself. The value and necessity of economic growth are now being questioned not only by conservationists, but by economists as well. There is no doubt, too, that the consumer society has had a distorting effect on the goals and purposes of its members. Yet looking at the matter purely from the point of view of overseas aid, there must be a limit to the extent to which we should deliberately slow down our economy; for it might be the case that if we gave away, say, 40 percent of our Gross National Product (GNP), we would slow down the economy so much that in absolute terms we would be giving less than if we gave 25 percent of the much larger GNP that we would have if we limited our contribution to this smaller percentage.

I mention this only as an indication of the sort of factor that one would have to take into account in working out an ideal. Since Western societies generally consider 1 percent of the GNP an acceptable level for overseas aid, the matter is entirely academic. Nor does it affect the question of how much an individual should give in a society in which very few are giving substantial amounts.

... The issue is one which faces everyone who has more money than he needs to support himself and his dependents, or who is in a position to take some sort of political action. These categories must include practically every teacher and student of philosophy in the universities of the Western world. If philosophy is to deal with matters that are relevant to both teachers and students, this is an issue that philosophers should discuss.

Discussion, though, is not enough. What is the point of relating philosophy to public (and personal) affairs if we do not take our conclusions seriously? In this instance, taking our conclusion seriously means acting upon it. The philosopher will not find it any easier than anyone else to alter his attitudes and way of life to the extent that, if I am right, is involved in doing everything that we ought to be doing. At the very least, though, one can make a start. The philosopher who does so will have to sacrifice some of the benefits of the consumer society, but he can find compensation in the satisfaction of a way of life in which theory and practice, if not yet in harmony, are at least coming together.

NOTE

1. *Summa Theologica*, II-II, Question 66, Article 7, in *Aquinas, Selected Political Writings*, ed. A. P. d'Entrèves, trans. J. G. Dawson (Oxford: Basil Blackwell, 1948), p. 171.

Chapter 20

Poverty and Parenthood

Stuart Rachels

Many people believe that having a child is immoral under certain circumstances—for example, if the mother is very young, or if the child would suffer from a severe genetic disorder. Some philosophers, however, have argued that parenthood is immoral even in the usual case. This argument usually takes one of three forms: (a) *Pessimism about human life*: Human life contains more bad than good; therefore, we shouldn't create more lives. Sometimes people express this idea by saying, "I wouldn't want to bring a child into this world." (b) *An unusual rights violation*: Creating a child exposes her to all the harms of life, without her permission. Yet we cannot obtain the consent of the nonexistent. Therefore, we shouldn't make babies. (c) *Environmental strain*: Increasing the population of first-world countries adds to their overuse of scarce, depletable, and environmentally hazardous resources. Therefore, people in those countries shouldn't have children.

In this selection, however, the author takes a different approach. The *Famine Relief Argument against Having Children* appeals to what economists call "opportunity costs"—in other words, the cost of being unable to do something because you've chosen to do something else. The argument goes like this: In countries like the United States, parents typically spend over $200,000 to raise a

This originally appeared as "The Immorality of Having Children" in *Ethical Theory and Moral Practice* (published online September 17, 2013). Reprinted by permission.

child. That money would be much better spent on the poor. Therefore, people in such countries shouldn't have children. Anyone
who accepts Peter Singer's Famine Relief Argument, the author
claims, should accept this argument as well.

---

1. THE BIGGEST DECISION IN LIFE

Parenthood, Not Marriage

My father, who taught college for nearly four decades, was fond of saying that the biggest decision people face in forming their worldview is
whether to believe in God. Sometimes he put the point this way: If the
question is not what to *do*, but what to *believe*, then God's existence
matters most. Religious belief is crucial because so much turns on it. If
you embrace Christianity, for example, then this may affect your view
of anthropology, biology, cosmology, history, love, morality, metaphysics, politics, and much else.

But what if we're interested in action rather than belief? What is the
biggest *practical* decision that most of us will face at some point in our
lives? I think our culture favors a particular answer to this question,
namely: *Should I get married?* This does not mean, "Should I *ever* get
married?" or "Do I want to involve the government in my most inti-
mate relationship?" Rather, our culture's most celebrated question is,
"Should I marry [fill in the name of one's girlfriend/boyfriend]?" We
ask ourselves: Is s/he good enough? Am I ready? Am I in love? Will
it last forever? Note that our culture glorifies marriage with its biggest
ritual celebration: the wedding. . . .

However, that emphasis is misplaced. To be sure, tying the knot is a
big decision: marriage is currently supposed to last a lifetime, and if a
couple participates in the (aptly nicknamed) wedding-industrial complex, then their nuptials will be both time-consuming and expensive
(over \$25,000 on average[1]). But, to be crass, there's always divorce:
marriage has an escape hatch. It's not an easy hatch to open; divorce is
almost always emotionally traumatic. Yet once it's done, it's done. And
divorce is so common in our society that divorced individuals are not
stigmatized.

Instead, I suggest, the biggest decision that most of us will face is whether to have children. There are three reasons for this.

First, each additional person profoundly affects the world. For starters, an individual is likely to have a marked effect on the environment over the course of her life.[2] But also, each person probably impacts the social world even more: given the vagaries of social life, each of us affects whom others will meet, befriend, fall in love with, and lust for—which, in turn, will affect [who will exist in the future]. In sum, just as one's religious beliefs have logical implications that ripple across one's worldview, so one's procreative decisions have causal implications that ripple across one's world.

Second, being a parent entails drastically changing one's lifestyle for at least eighteen years. Parenting consumes vast sums of time, money, and energy. It is a monumental undertaking.

Third, parenthood has no morally viable escape hatch. You can divorce your spouse, but you can't divorce your kids—you can only neglect them. You *can* give your children up for adoption (and thus opt out of parenthood), but even that wouldn't put the genie fully back in the bottle: someone else would still have to raise your biological children, and those children would still affect the world profoundly.

So, in sum, the question of whether to have a child is more important than the question of whether to marry one's sweetheart—and, indeed, is *the* most significant question that most people will face—because every new child will profoundly affect the world in general and two parents in particular. Moreover, whereas marriage can be undone by divorce, once a baby exists, there's no turning back: a human life will unfold with all of its ramifications. The decision to beget is awesome and irrevocable.

Our Culture Downplays the Biggest Decision

Why doesn't our culture regard parenthood as being the biggest decision in life? There are several reasons. (i) Although creating a new human being will have profound effects on the world, most of those effects are unpredictable. Would the world be better in the long run if my spouse and I have a child? Would people be happier? Would justice prevail more often? Those questions dissolve into countless others, whose answers can't be known. And what we can't know, we don't mull over. . . .

(ii) Parenthood might seem like the default option in life. Having kids in our home may seem normal to us simply because we grew up in a home that had kids in it. Perhaps we learn subliminally from a young age that *When I grow up, I will be the mommy (or daddy) in the home.* Some children even play games to this effect.

(iii) In the real world, many parents didn't choose to become parents, exactly: they chose to have sex; the woman accidentally became pregnant; and then the woman chose not to abort. We call such babies "accidents"—a term that stands in contrast to choice. Many children are accidental. For example, in 1994, 31 percent of babies born in the United States were accidents.[3] Even though the specter of unintentional pregnancy makes some people think harder about whether to have kids, the frequency of such pregnancies also makes some people view parenthood as something that simply happens at a certain stage of life. And parenthood can't be a big decision if it isn't (really) a decision at all.

(iv) Sometimes, one member of a couple (or both) wants to have a child *really* badly. In such cases, we may see parenthood as automatic or inevitable—in other words, as not (really) chosen. And again, if parenthood isn't chosen, then it can't be life's biggest decision. For all these reasons, our society views begetting more lightly than it should.

Our Culture Commends Begetting

Yet I want to emphasize a further reason, (v): Our culture downplays the importance of the critical decision by viewing the choice to conceive as being obviously respectable so long as certain minimal conditions are fulfilled (e.g., the mother is not in extreme poverty, neither parent is dying, and the parents are not on the verge of divorce). In other words, we view begetting as an obviously good thing. In our culture, nothing seems more natural than to congratulate someone who has just had a baby: "What a blessing!" "It's a little miracle!" "What a bundle of joy!" We've all seen someone react to the presence of a baby like Frances McDormand's character in the movie *Raising Arizona* (1987): "He's an angel! He's an angel straight from Heaven!" Our own parents are likely to foster a positive view of parenthood in us, first because they may want grandchildren; and second, because emphasizing the advantages of parenting to one's children is a way of expressing love to them—it is a way of saying, *I'm glad I had you*. In general, almost no parent wants to talk publicly about the disadvantages of parenthood, for fear of looking like a bad parent or uncaring person. Thus, we tend to hear mostly positive things. Furthermore, many of us want to be like our parents, and one way to do that is to become parents ourselves. Further still, some subcultures put a special premium on large families: Italian-Americans, Catholics, Jews, and Mormons, for example, all traditionally prize big families. Finally, most people in our society are either Christians or Jews, and the Book of Genesis quotes God as saying, "Be fruitful and multiply and fill the earth . . ."[4]—a clear directive to make babies. Thus, people in our culture tend to view parenthood favorably.

However, few people in our culture see parenthood as obligatory; these days, a young couple is unlikely to be pressured by outsiders to start a family. Instead of censuring the childless, we are more likely to pity them. We may suspect, for example, that an older couple who have no kids tried and failed, and we assume that their lives are the poorer for it. So, we feel sorry for them. The upshot is that our culture views parenthood as a no-pressure dilemma: if you choose to have kids, great; but if you don't, no one will complain. Again, we view the decision surprisingly lightly.

On the whole, then, our culture regards the decision to procreate as being both less important and less controversial than it should. I have emphasized these points in order to say to the reader: I expect this essay to rub you wrong; please keep an open mind. In what follows, I will argue that it is immoral to have a child, by which I mean *it is immoral to conceive and rear a child*. The argument will be limited in two ways. First, it will say nothing about adoption. Adoptive parents do not conceive their children and thus do not "have children" in the sense relevant to my argument. (In another, perfectly normal sense, adoptive parents do of course have children.) Second, I won't argue that it is always, in every conceivable circumstance, immoral to have children; rather, I will assume some background conditions, which almost always hold true in contemporary Western society. The argument itself is simple. As I've said, parenting consumes vast sums of time, money, and energy. It would be much better to direct those resources elsewhere—so much better, that having a child must be considered immoral.

2. THE FAMINE RELIEF ARGUMENT AGAINST HAVING CHILDREN

How much does raising a child cost in the United States? Each year, the U.S. Department of Agriculture answers this question in its *Expenditures on Children by Families*. The latest report estimates that a middle-income family with a child born in 2010 will spend about $226,920 on child rearing.[5] That figure, however, doesn't represent the full price of having children, because it ignores all the costs that accrue after the child turns 18—for example, the cost of college tuition. Also, many young adults live at home where they can receive routine assistance from Mom and Dad.[6] Robert Schoeni and Karen Ross estimate that children between the ages of 18 and 34 receive an average of $38,000 from their parents (plus a lot of free labor!).[7] Thus, the overall (average) cost of parenthood might be closer to $226,920 + $38,000 = $264,920. However, I can't offer a total estimate because I don't know what financial arrangements hold, on average, between children over the age of 34 and their parents. On the one hand, the children may continue to receive support (here and there, and eventually via inheritance); on the other hand, the parents may increasingly depend on their grown children as they get older. But we needn't settle on a final figure; my argument will merely assume that having a child is so expensive that a significant amount of moral good could be accomplished by using that money for other purposes. In what follows, I'll assume that having a child costs around $227,000, although I suspect that the true figure is even higher.

Now let's consider how much good could be accomplished by giving $227,000 to humanitarian causes. I'm not asking the utopian question, how much good would $227,000 accomplish *if spent optimally*? Rather, I am asking how much good would likely result from giving $227,000 to a smattering of reputable poverty relief organizations over the next 20 years. Even that question, however, requires philosophical clarification, because there are two ways to understand the notion of accomplishing good. On the *simple causal interpretation*, I do good by bringing about a valuable state of affairs. For example, I do good by helping an old woman carry her groceries into her home. On the *causal / counterfactual interpretation*, I do good by bringing about a better state of affairs than would have existed without my action. On that understanding, I do good by helping the old woman only if no one else would have helped her. For reasons I'll explain later, I'll employ the causal / counterfactual interpretation. Thus, I am asking: how much better would things be if we gave $227,000 to charity than if we gave none?

It would be easy to assess the value of charitable giving if it worked like this: you send a $20 bill to a large organization (UNICEF, say); that organization uses your $20 bill to achieve a specific, short-term goal (feeding a particular child, say); and your donation "makes the difference" in the sense that the goal would not have been achieved without your donation. Under those conditions, your donation has the value of the accomplished goal. In the real world, however, it is typical for contributions to simply be added to the large operating budgets of charities. Thus, to assess the value of a donation, we must know what the charity would have done differently without the amount of one's donation. And we never know that. Even employees at the charity will not know the answer to questions like this: how would the Hunger Eradication Initiative have differed with $710,861 in its budget instead of $710,881? Moreover, let's not forget that charitable organizations often pursue long-term economic development projects alongside short-term assistance programs. And long-term endeavors are hard to assess.

The upshot is that we rarely know what difference we make when we give to large charities. That fact may dishearten us, but it doesn't mean that our efforts are wasted. The major charities provide birth control to millions of women; vaccinate multitudes of infants; educate legions of children; feed vast camps of refugees; and so on. They need money to do these things. Giving $227,000 to such groups is likely to make a wonderful difference, even if we don't know exactly what that difference will be.

Let's now consider the main argument. Having a child costs hundreds of thousands of dollars; that money would be *much* better spent on famine relief; therefore, it is immoral to have children. This is essentially an expected-utility argument: we shouldn't have children because having a child is a poor way to squeeze benefit out of $227,000. If the language of expected utility seems cold, then we might say: *We should immunize, feed and clothe impoverished children who already exist rather than spend hundreds of thousands of dollars on having one child of our own.* I will call this the *Famine Relief Argument against Having Children.* It applies almost across-the-board within our culture. However, it would not apply in cultures that expect children to economically benefit their parents—where, for example, children work on the family farm from a young age and then support their parents later in life. In such cases, remaining childless might make one poorer and thus *diminish* one's ability to give.

Before continuing, let me say [two] things about the argument.

1. We can now see why we need the "causal/counterfactual" conception of doing good rather than the "simple causal" conception. The Famine Relief Argument against Having Children urges us to remain childless in order to be more generous. However, for many people, remaining childless would be a sacrifice, and I would not urge anyone to sacrifice anything unless the sacrifice paid off counterfactually. Suppose, for example, that you gave $227,000 to a charity that eventually vaccinated 10,000 children against the rotavirus. Further suppose that the same children would have been vaccinated without your donation, because a wealthy benefactor was waiting in the wings, poised to donate whatever the charity needed in the end. If you knew all this in advance, then I can't see why you'd give $227,000 to that charity, unless you simply preferred for the wealthy benefactor to have an extra $227,000 rather than you. The Famine Relief Argument against Having Children urges us to sacrifice for others only if those others would be worse off without our sacrifice.

2. Although the argument concludes that it is immoral to have children, I do not believe that parents should be punished, admonished, or blamed in any way, simply for being parents. Blame is usually irritating and unwelcome to the blamed, and in this case, I doubt that blaming parents would do any good. Would chastising parents make them less likely to have more children and more likely to give to charity? Would it deter potential parents from having children? Casting blame on parents would probably have little effect other than bothering the parents and pointlessly diminishing the world's limited appetite for moral ideas and moral debate. Also, I reject the Kantian idea that people should be punished simply because they have done something wrong. Thus, I oppose parenthood *and* the blaming of parents. . . .

3. CONNECTIONS TO SINGER'S ARGUMENT

The great philosophical advocate of generosity in our time is Peter Singer. My argument is named after Singer's "Famine Relief Argument."[8] One version of Singer's argument goes like this: "If we can

prevent something very bad from happening, without sacrificing anything of comparable or nearly comparable moral significance, then we
ought, morally, to do it; we *can* prevent something very bad from happening, without sacrificing anything of comparable or nearly comparable moral significance, by foregoing our luxuries and giving our money
to famine relief instead. Therefore, we ought to do so." Like Singer,
I use the phrase "famine relief" as a stand-in for whatever charitable
causes make sense. Feeding the hungry is one excellent charitable idea,
but of course there are others.

My argument relates to Singer's in two key ways. First, my argument
might merely be a special case of his. Singer says that we should forego
our luxuries in favor of generosity, and having children might be one
of those luxuries. Thus, we might amplify Singer's second premise to
read: "We can prevent something very bad from happening, without
sacrificing anything of comparable or nearly comparable moral significance, by foregoing our luxuries (for example, by foregoing having
children) and giving our money to famine relief instead."

Admittedly, it seems odd to call children a "luxury." We think of
luxuries as things typically enjoyed by the rich—diamond earrings,
Ferraris, and summer holidays in the South of France, for example. But
people of all economic classes have children. Also, we contrast "luxury" with "necessity," and children are necessary for the continuation
of our species. Yet, despite these observations, we might still consider
children luxuries. After all, having kids is expensive and isn't necessary
for the parents' health or survival. . . .

The second connection may be deeper. Before stating it, let me fill
in some background. Singer's argument is part of a moral worldview
that sees suffering as the greatest evil and the prevention of suffering
as the greatest good. The morally best life that a person of wealth and
opportunity can lead, on this view, is a life of saintly self-sacrifice—she
sacrifices everything to combat the causes of suffering, where those
causes are things like factory farming, depression, poverty, microbial
illness, and political repression. Even if perfect beneficence is unrealistic for creatures like us, it is at least a noble ideal: we can always strive
to be more generous, and we can morally assess people by seeing how
close they come to this benevolent endpoint.

Most people don't come very close. Money is easy to spend, and
many people feel like their expected lifestyle leaves little room for
giving. In the United States, even the wealthy may find themselves in

credit-card debt after making only "normal" purchases. "I don't know where all my money goes," they might say, as though their money had hotwired their Lexus and driven off, whereas in fact they made concrete choices that resulted in their money's going to the mortgage company, the school, the car dealership, the airline, the clothing designer, the online electronics store, and so on. If we can admit that we choose our lifestyle, then we can honestly address the question: What are the biggest decisions we make that affect how much we give to charity?

Our relevant decisions fall into two groups: those that affect our own level of wealth, and those that affect how much of our wealth we donate. I'll consider these topics, briefly, in turn.

How can we affect our own wealth-level? Naturally, there's a lot of advice out there, most of it bad. The most common route to wealth is being born into a rich family, but we can't choose our lineage. Instead, the biggest wealth-affecting decision we make is probably that of career choice. And certainly, one attains brighter economic prospects by choosing to go to law school than by choosing to become a dishwasher. However, I wish to emphasize the extent to which luck and circumstance, rather than choice, influences our ultimate income level. Let me make three observations about this.

First, the idea that a person has a variety of career options representing a variety of possible income levels largely assumes the perspective of the well off. Most people don't have the personal connections or educational background to compete for *any* high-paying job. Indeed, they may be lucky to be employed. Choice is not irrelevant here; one can try to network and to maximize the educational opportunities one has. However, choice can only do so much. Second, people's employment options are limited by their talents, interests, and personality traits. To some extent, we can shape these things through our decisions; but to some extent, we cannot. Third, pure luck often determines how well a person's career goes. Did a good job open up at the right time and place? Did the interview go well? Did the market unexpectedly turn? Did you get a good boss? Did you join a well-run or poorly-run company? No career protects a person from the vagaries of life. Many lawyers are unemployed or underemployed; businesses fail; banking is risky. Perhaps the best bet is medicine—doctors can always make good money. However, becoming a physician is notoriously difficult; it requires having a knack for science, a strong work ethic, a tolerance for blood and needles, an ability to function on little sleep, and a general high intelligence—high enough to secure a spot in a medical school, anyway. Thus, I am impressed by the extent to which luck and happenstance contribute to a person's ultimate level of wealth.

Choice matters more when we examine *what we do with the money we have*. The best advice for rich people who strive to be more generous is captured by the cliché, *Live simply so that others can simply live*. For example, one should drive an economy-class car rather than a luxury vehicle; live in a modest house rather than a mansion; fly coach rather than first class; and not cultivate a taste for expensive pleasures like fine wines, country club surroundings, and overseas vacations. If an affluent person lives by such rules, he'll have a lot more money to donate at year's end.

And now comes the rub: If you want to lead the most generous kind of life, then the most important decision you'll ever make is whether to have kids. Having kids—with all the financial and emotional commitments that parenthood involves—is the single greatest impediment to the realization of the benevolent ideal. To put this point another way: if you wish to help others, then the worst decision you can make is to become a parent, because your child will tie up most of your spare time and resources for the next two decades. This is the deepest connection between Singer's Famine Relief Argument and the Famine Relief Argument against Having Children: my argument tries to expose the most important practical implication of Singer's argument—namely, that it requires us to be childless. . . .

4. FIVE OBJECTIONS

My argument endorses a two-part plan for moral living: *Don't have kids*, and *spend the money you'll save on the poor*. Some readers might dislike the whole tenor of this. They might think, "Even if I were rich and childless, I wouldn't be obligated to use my money benevolently." That outlook, however, raises questions that are beyond the scope of this paper. In general, I am assuming a viewpoint friendly to Singer's Famine Relief Argument. It would be too much, and too boringly familiar, to review all of the standard objections to Singer's position. Instead, I'll focus on what's distinctive to this paper—namely, its application of Singer's perspective to parenthood. So let's engage with the objector who believes, "Even if it would be immoral for me to spend $227,000 on a yacht, it would *not* be immoral for me to have a child knowing that I will spend $227,000 on her; children are relevantly different from yachts."

I'll consider five objections to the Famine Relief Argument against Having Children.

1. Some objections point to disastrous consequences that would ensue if everyone remained childless. If nobody had kids, then the human race would die out, and before it did, there would be the Era of the Elderly, when every living person would be over 70. After that would come the Era of the Very Elderly, the Era of the Half Dead, and, finally, the Era of Please Kill Me but There's No One Still Around Able to Do That. A different objection laments the prospect of taking all the good people out of parenting. It says that if every *good* person were to refrain from procreating, then tomorrow's parents would come only from the Pool of Scoundrels, and the future of humankind would be bleak. The first objection is of the form, "What if everybody did that?" The second objection is of the form, "What if all the good people did that?"

It would be fair, if un-philosophical-sounding, to respond by saying, "But they won't." Both objections are fallacious. Consider the principle underlying them: it would be wrong to do x if some very large number of people's doing x would have bad consequences. On this principle, it would be wrong for the cable guy to come to my house, because if billions of people came to my house, then there would be no place for anyone to park. Or, it would be wrong for me to go to law school, because if everyone did that, then who would teach the classes? The principle is indefensible.

I have not been arguing that *we should all refrain from having kids*; I've only been arguing that *you, the reader, shouldn't have kids*. Or, to put the thesis more generally: *anyone in our position shouldn't have kids* (where "our position" includes facts about how others will behave as well as facts about our own economic situation). There is nothing paradoxical in saying that *you* should do something but that it might be bad if *everyone* or if *many people* did it. In deciding what to do, we need to be realistic about what others will do. If we become saints, then we do so alone. The rest of the world won't follow our lead, nor will all the people whom we think would make good parents. . . .

2. The second objection says that having children isn't wrong because having children is so *natural* for human beings. But showing that some behavior is natural is a poor moral defense of it. If we were created in the image of a perfect God, then what's natural for us might always be good—indeed, might always be god-like. But, as the world attests, we have no such nature. Rather, we evolved by the morally blind forces of natural selection, and what's natural for us is what promoted our ancestors' reproductive fitness. Yet what promoted their fitness might have been something horrible, like rape. Rape might be a natural consequence of males being sexually voracious, aggressive, and physically stronger than females. However, this is no defense of sexual assault.

In general, what's natural bears no regular relation to what's good. Leukemia, failing eyesight, and aggression in males are all natural for human beings, yet all are bad. Nor does saying that something is "natural" entail that it is inevitable. Men can choose whether to assault women, despite the "naturalness" of wanting sex. Similarly, a couple can choose whether to have a baby, even if desiring children is natural.

3. Some people will say that an ethic which prohibits parenthood is too demanding. On this view, a moral system that forbids procreation forbids too much: it is too intrusive, or it expects too much of us, or something like that.

How exactly is the objection supposed to go? The thesis that *having children is immoral* is not literally intrusive; stating the thesis does not, for example, involve going inside somebody's house and looking around to see whether they have kids. Nor does the thesis "expect too much of people"—to say that x is immoral is not to predict or expect that people won't do x. So I think the objection must instead go something like this: "to require that people remain childless is to require them to make a big sacrifice, and we cannot rightfully require big sacrifices of people, even if we can rightfully demand small things from them." The principle behind this objection is that you can't be obliged to do x if x requires you to make a large sacrifice.

In response, one might wonder why morality can't demand big sacrifices of us. Is there any good reason to think such a thing, or do we believe it merely because we imagine ourselves *making* the sacrifice instead of *benefitting* from it, and we are too selfish to like what we imagine? However, I won't pursue that response. Instead, I'll argue that remaining childless is not a big sacrifice.

What is a "big sacrifice?" In my [way of speaking], a big sacrifice involves giving something up for someone else's benefit, at a great cost to one's own happiness. What is sacrificed is not the thing given so much as the happiness attending it. Others might say that a sacrifice counts as "big" if it involves a lot of effort or a change in lifestyle, even if making the sacrifice doesn't greatly diminish one's welfare.

None of these ideas implies that remaining childless is a big sacrifice. First, not having kids requires no effort at all—it is *the having of kids* that requires great effort. Similarly, not having kids requires no lifestyle change—rather, it is *the having of kids* that requires a lifestyle change. Asking people not to have children is, in a sense, asking them to do nothing at all (except, perhaps, to use birth control). Thus, the Famine Relief Argument against Having Children is not "demanding" of people in these ways. . . .

But the main question is whether being childless greatly reduces one's happiness. Until recently, such questions were left to common-sense observation and good judgment. In the last fifteen years, however, a new academic subfield has emerged, variously called "positive psychology," "the economics of happiness," or "happiness studies." This new subfield uses survey data and statistical analyses to investigate the causes of happiness and unhappiness. At root, happiness is hard to study because it cannot be directly measured; instead, we must rely on self-reports, and those reports might be inaccurate for various reasons. Thus, the findings of happiness studies are rarely conclusive. However, they probably represent our best-supported beliefs on the subject.

Happiness researchers have studied how children affect parental well-being. The details of these studies are fascinating, but we needn't delve into them, because the upshot is clear: being childless does *not* have a large negative impact on happiness. Instead, the data suggest that childless couples are actually happier than parents. In part, this is because children hurt marital relations[9]—relations that improve once the children leave home. "Despite what we read in the popular press," writes Daniel Gilbert, "the only known symptom of 'empty nest syndrome' is increased smiling."[10] Another expert summarized the overall picture like this: "Parents experience lower levels of emotional well-being, less frequent positive emotions and more frequent negative emotions than their childless peers."[11] Not all researchers draw such depressing conclusions for parents, however; another said, "The broad message is not that children make you less happy; it's just that children don't make you *more* happy" (unless, he adds, you have more than one child: "Then the studies show a more negative impact").[12]

The range of current expert opinion on the impact of children on parental happiness thus extends from "very little impact" to "a medium-sized negative impact." *No* expert believes what the third objection requires, namely, that parenting makes people *much* happier, and so an ethic that forbids it could be too demanding. Nor can one object that these studies focus on happiness but ignore meaning. The studies ask respondents such broad questions about their well-being that the respondents' feelings of pride and fulfillment and belonging (or, conversely, their feelings of despair and listlessness and isolation) are taken into account alongside more traditional hedonistic elements.

Some people find these conclusions incredible. In his best-selling book, *Stumbling on Happiness*, Daniel Gilbert devotes only three pages to the topic, yet most of the skeptical questions he receives at his lectures concern it. "I've never met anyone who didn't argue with me about this," he says.[13] Given Gilbert's experience, I'll say a little more about the drawbacks of parenting—not to prove that parenting is miserable (it isn't), but just to combat any incredulous stares at the data. Gilbert writes: "Careful studies of how women feel as they go about their daily activities show that they are less happy when taking care of their children than when eating, exercising, shopping, napping, or watching television. Indeed, looking after the kids appears to be only slightly more pleasant than doing housework."[14] Gilbert, himself a parent, adds: "None of this should surprise us. Every parent knows that children are a lot of work—a lot of really *hard* work—and although parenting has many rewarding moments, the vast majority of its moments involve dull and selfless service to people who will take decades to become even begrudgingly grateful for what we are doing." Another parent laments that children are "all joy and no fun." Still another says that kids are "a huge source of joy, but they turn every other source of joy to shit."[15] And now consider the alternative. If you don't have children, then what will you do with the time that you would have spent changing diapers, constructing science fair projects, cleaning up spills, purchasing school supplies, acting as a chauffeur, and responding to toddler tantrums and adolescent freeze-outs? Answer: *anything you want*. Even if it's not obvious that having children diminishes parental happiness, it's obvious that it might. . . .

As I said, happiness-study findings are rarely conclusive. However, overall, there is little reason to think that being childless is such a deprivation that an ethic which requires it could be too demanding. Yet I do recognize one type of exception. Some people want kids *really* badly; their desire for children is like a desperate thirst that needs quenching.

For them, it may be psychologically impossible to choose childlessness. I don't think it makes sense, either as social policy or as abstract philosophy, to hold people accountable for choices that are psychologically forced on them (even if they could physically do otherwise). For that reason, even though it would be regrettable for such people to have children (because their $227,000 could be better spent), I would not regard their decision to have children as immoral. Indeed, I'm not even sure I would regard it as a decision.

4. The fourth objection goes something like this: "What if we raise our children to care about others, and to have the right values? My child might give *more* than $227,000 to charity. And what if my child becomes the next great inventor or finds the cure for malaria? My child might achieve goods far greater than I could achieve by giving $227,000 to charity."

This objection might be called the "Wishful Thinking Objection" or the "Pass-the-Buck-and-Hope Objection." Of course it is *possible* that our child would become a great humanitarian. But if we compare the number of well-meaning parents to the number of great humanitarians, then we can see how improbable this is. Moreover, we must also consider the possibility of less welcome outcomes. For example, there's around a 1-in-68 chance that a child born today will be autistic.[16] Also, one's child might have a tremendously bad effect on the world—not necessarily due to malice; maybe just due to causal bad luck.

We could try to improve the utility calculation by self-consciously raising our child to become a great humanitarian. However, that would probably do more harm than good. Children tend to respond to unusual parental pressure either by developing neuroses or by rebelling as soon as they can. Our child might even decide that we were right: the best way to improve the world *is* to have children and to raise them properly. Thus, they might do exactly what we did. And so might their children. . . .

Sometimes people think that *their* child would have a decent chance of becoming a great benefactor, even though they'd admit that a randomly selected child would have little such chance. But that's just vanity. Realistically, our children are probably going to be like us: thoughtful and caring but also selfish and susceptible to rationalization.

5. Finally, one might say that I have drawn the wrong conclusion from my arguments. Instead of not procreating, shouldn't we have children but raise them on less than $227,000? If we do, then we'll have more money than our neighbors to be generous with, and our children can more easily right the scales later by benefiting the world more than we could have done by not having them.

In response, I should begin by agreeing that, *if* you have children, then you should raise them frugally, for two reasons: you'll have more money to be generous with, and your children won't cultivate expensive tastes. *Live simply so that others can simply live, and raise your children to do the same.* However, I reject the fifth objection for three reasons.

First, I have been assuming that raising a child costs around $227,000. Yet I would defend the Famine Relief Argument against Having Children even if the cost were much less—say, $100,000. Thus, I am not sure whether raising a child frugally would bring the cost down enough to invalidate my argument—especially because $227,000 was a conservative estimate.

Second, for simplicity I have focused on how much *money* it takes to raise a child, but I could also have focused on the *time* and *energy* that parenting consumes. If you have a child, then raising that child will take up time and energy that you could have spent doing volunteer work and/or making more money to give to the poor. Thus, one advantage of not having kids, as compared to frugal parenting, is that childless adults have more time and energy to spend on others.

Finally, if you become a parent, then your love for your children may impel you to spend more money on them than you had intended. Love, though itself a great good, conflicts with benevolence. The great altruist Zell Kravinsky understands this. Kravinsky, who gave his entire $45-million fortune to charity, once lamented that "The sacrosanct commitment to the family is the rationalization for all manner of greed and selfishness."[17] In practical terms, it might be easier to remain childless than to deny one's children luxuries that other children enjoy.

NOTES

1. The exact estimate is $25,631, according to the May, 2012, *Harper's Index* (source: The Wedding Report [Tucson]).

2. See, for example, Murtaugh, P. A. and Schlax, M. G., "Reproduction and the Carbon Legacies of Individuals," *Global Environmental Change* 19 (2009), pp. 14–20.

3. See Table 1 in "Unintended Pregnancy in the United States," *Family Planning Perspectives* 30(1) (1998), pp. 24–29 and p. 46.

4. Genesis 1:28, *The Holy Bible*, English Standard Version. U.S.A.: Good News Publishers, 2001.

5. See Lino, M., U.S. Department of Agriculture / Center for Nutrition Policy and Promotion, *Expenditures on Children by Families, 2010*, released May 2011. The $226,920 figure is in today's dollars; given projections about inflation, one is likely to actually pay $286,860.

6. At the end of 2011, 29% of American adults aged 25 to 34 lived at home—see Parker, K., Pew Research Center, "The Boomerang Generation: Feeling OK about Living with Mom and Dad," released March 15, 2012.

7. See Schoeni, R. F. and Ross, K. E., "Material Assistance from Families during the Transition to Adulthood," in R. A. Settersten Jr., F. F. Furstenberg Jr., and R. G. Rumbaut (eds.), *On the Frontier of Adulthood: Theory, Research, and Public Policy*, 2nd edition (Chicago: University of Chicago Press, 2005), pp. 396–417.

8. See Singer, P., "Famine, Affluence and Morality," *Philosophy and Public Affairs* 1 (1972), pp. 229–43.

9. See, for example, the National Marriage Project's 2011 "State of Our Unions" report as well as Twenge, J. M., Campbell, W. K., and Foster, C. A., "Parenthood and Marital Satisfaction: A Meta-Analytic Review," *Journal of Marriage and Family* 65(3) (2003), pp. 574–83.

10. Gilbert, D., *Stumbling on Happiness* (New York: Vintage Books, 2006), p. 243.

11. Robin Simon, quoted in Ali, L., "Having Kids Makes You Happy," *Newsweek*, July 7, 2008.

12. Andrew Oswald, quoted in Senior, J., "All Joy and No Fun: Why Parents Hate Parenting," *New York Times Magazine*, July 4, 2010.

13. Quoted in J. Senior.

14. D. Gilbert, pp. 244–45. The next quote is from p. 245.

15. The last two quotes come from J. Senior.

16. According to the Centers for Disease Control and Prevention (CDC), March 2014.

17. Parker, I., "The Gift," *The New Yorker*, August 2, 2004, pp. 54–63 (p. 60).

RACE

Chapter 21

The Case for Reparations

Ta-Nehisi Coates

The history of racism in America is not just a history of bigoted individuals and unjust laws; it is also a history of discriminatory business practices. When this essay first appeared, in *The Atlantic*, the caption at the top read: *Two hundred fifty years of slavery. Ninety years of Jim Crow. Sixty years of separate but equal. Thirty-five years of racist housing policy. Until we reckon with our compounding moral debts, America will never be whole.*

Ta-Nehisi Coates is an American historian, journalist, cultural critic, and best-selling author. He also writes Marvel comics.

By our unpaid labor and suffering, we have earned the right to the soil, many times over and over, and now we are determined to have it.

—Anonymous, 1861

SO THAT'S JUST ONE OF MY LOSSES

Clyde Ross was born in 1923, the seventh of 13 children, near Clarksdale, Mississippi, the home of the blues. Ross's parents owned and farmed a 40-acre tract of land, flush with cows, hogs, and mules. Ross's mother would drive to Clarksdale to do her shopping in a horse and buggy, in which she invested all the pride one might place in a Cadillac. The family owned another horse, with a red coat, which they gave to Clyde. The Ross family wanted for little, save that which all black families in the Deep South then desperately desired—the protection of the law.

In the 1920s, Jim Crow Mississippi was, in all facets of society, a kleptocracy. The majority of the people in the state were perpetually robbed of the vote—a hijacking engineered through the trickery of the poll tax and the muscle of the lynch mob. Between 1882 and 1968, more black people were lynched in Mississippi than in any other state. "You and I know what's the best way to keep the nigger from voting," blustered Theodore Bilbo, a Mississippi senator and a proud Klansman. "You do it the night before the election."

The state's regime partnered robbery of the franchise with robbery of the purse. Many of Mississippi's black farmers lived in debt peonage, under the sway of cotton kings who were at once their landlords, their employers, and their primary merchants. Tools and necessities were advanced against the return on the crop, which was determined by the employer. When farmers were deemed to be in debt—and they often were—the negative balance was then carried over to the next season. A man or woman who protested this arrangement did so at the risk of grave injury or death. Refusing to work meant arrest under vagrancy laws and forced labor under the state's penal system.

Well into the twentieth century, black people spoke of their flight from Mississippi in much the same manner as their runagate ancestors had. In her 2010 book, *The Warmth of Other Suns*, Isabel Wilkerson tells the story of Eddie Earvin, a spinach picker who fled Mississippi in 1963, after being made to work at gunpoint. "You didn't talk about it or tell nobody," Earvin said. "You had to sneak away."

When Clyde Ross was still a child, Mississippi authorities claimed his father owed $3,000 in back taxes. The elder Ross could not read. He did not have a lawyer. He did not know anyone at the local courthouse. He could not expect the police to be impartial. Effectively, the Ross family had no way to contest the claim and no protection under the law. The authorities seized the land. They seized the buggy. They took the cows, hogs, and mules. And so for the upkeep of separate but equal, the entire Ross family was reduced to sharecropping.

This was hardly unusual. In 2001, the Associated Press published a three-part investigation into the theft of black-owned land stretching back to the antebellum period. The series documented some 406 victims and 24,000 acres of land valued at tens of millions of dollars. The land was taken through means ranging from legal chicanery to terrorism. "Some of the land taken from black families has become a country club in Virginia," the AP reported, as well as "oil fields in Mississippi" and "a baseball spring training facility in Florida."

Clyde Ross was a smart child. His teacher thought he should attend a more challenging school. There was very little support for educating black people in Mississippi. But Julius Rosenwald, a part owner of Sears, Roebuck, had begun an ambitious effort to build schools for black children throughout the South. Ross's teacher believed he should attend the local Rosenwald school. It was too far for Ross to walk and get back in time to work in the fields. Local white children had a school bus. Clyde Ross did not, and thus lost the chance to better his education.

Then, when Ross was 10 years old, a group of white men demanded his only childhood possession—the horse with the red coat. "You can't have this horse. We want it," one of the white men said. They gave Ross's father $17.

"I did everything for that horse," Ross told me. "Everything. And they took him. Put him on the racetrack. I never did know what happened to him after that, but I know they didn't bring him back. So that's just one of my losses."

The losses mounted. As sharecroppers, the Ross family saw their wages treated as the landlord's slush fund. Landowners were supposed to split the profits from the cotton fields with sharecroppers. But bales would often disappear during the count, or the split might be altered on a whim. If cotton was selling for 50 cents a pound, the Ross family might get 15 cents, or only five. One year Ross's mother promised to buy him a $7 suit for a summer program at their church. She ordered the suit by mail. But that year Ross's family was paid only five cents a pound for cotton. The mailman arrived with the suit. The Rosses could not pay. The suit was sent back. Clyde Ross did not go to the church program.

It was in these early years that Ross began to understand himself as an American—he did not live under the blind decree of justice, but under the heel of a regime that elevated armed robbery to a governing principle. He thought about fighting. "Just be quiet," his father told him. "Because they'll come and kill us all."

Clyde Ross grew. He was drafted into the Army. The draft officials offered him an exemption if he stayed home and worked. He preferred to take his chances with war. He was stationed in California. He found that he could go into stores without being bothered. He could walk the streets without being harassed. He could go into a restaurant and receive service.

Ross was shipped off to Guam. He fought in World War II to save the world from tyranny. But when he returned to Clarksdale, he found that tyranny had followed him home. This was 1947, eight years before Mississippi lynched Emmett Till and tossed his broken body into the Tallahatchie River. The Great Migration, a mass exodus of 6 million African-Americans that spanned most of the twentieth century, was now in its second wave. The black pilgrims did not journey north simply seeking better wages and work, or bright lights and big adventures. They were fleeing the acquisitive warlords of the South. They were seeking the protection of the law.

Clyde Ross was among them. He came to Chicago in 1947 and took a job as a taster at Campbell's Soup. He made a stable wage. He married. He had children. His paycheck was his own. No Klansmen stripped him of the vote. When he walked down the street, he did not have to move because a white man was walking past. He did not have to take off his hat or avert his gaze. His journey from peonage to full citizenship seemed near-complete. Only one item was missing—a home, that final badge of entry into the sacred order of the American middle class of the Eisenhower years.

In 1961, Ross and his wife bought a house in North Lawndale, a bustling community on Chicago's West Side. North Lawndale had long been a predominantly Jewish neighborhood, but a handful of middle-class African-Americans had lived there starting in the 1940s. The community was anchored by the sprawling Sears, Roebuck headquarters. North Lawndale's Jewish People's Institute actively encouraged blacks to move into the neighborhood, seeking to make it a "pilot community for interracial living." In the battle for integration then being fought around the country, North Lawndale seemed to offer promising terrain. But out in the tall grass, highwaymen, nefarious as any Clarksdale kleptocrat, were lying in wait.

Three months after Clyde Ross moved into his house, the boiler blew out. This would normally be a homeowner's responsibility, but in fact, Ross was not really a homeowner. His payments were made to the seller, not the bank. And Ross had not signed a normal mortgage. He'd bought "on contract": a predatory agreement that combined all the responsibilities of homeownership with all the disadvantages of renting—while offering the benefits of neither. Ross had bought his house for $27,500. The seller, not the previous homeowner but a new kind of middleman, had bought it for only $12,000 six months before selling it to Ross. In a contract sale, the seller kept the deed until the contract was paid in full—and, unlike with a normal mortgage, Ross would acquire no equity in the meantime. If he missed a single payment, he would immediately forfeit his $1,000 down payment, all his monthly payments, and the property itself.

The men who peddled contracts in North Lawndale would sell homes at inflated prices and then evict families who could not pay—taking their down payment and their monthly installments as profit. Then they'd bring in another black family, rinse, and repeat. "He loads them up with payments they can't meet," an office secretary told *The Chicago Daily News* of her boss, the speculator Lou Fushanis, in 1963. "Then he takes the property away from them. He's sold some of the buildings three or four times."

Ross had tried to get a legitimate mortgage in another neighborhood, but was told by a loan officer that there was no financing available. The truth was that there was no financing for people like Clyde Ross. From the 1930s through the 1960s, black people across the country were largely cut out of the legitimate home-mortgage market through means both legal and extralegal. Chicago whites employed every measure, from "restrictive covenants" to bombings, to keep their neighborhoods segregated.

Their efforts were buttressed by the federal government. In 1934, Congress created the Federal Housing Administration. The FHA insured private mortgages, causing a drop in interest rates and a decline in the size of the down payment required to buy a house. But an insured mortgage was not a possibility for Clyde Ross. The FHA had adopted a system of maps that rated neighborhoods according to their perceived stability. On the maps, green areas, rated "A," indicated "in demand" neighborhoods that, as one appraiser put it, lacked "a single foreigner or Negro." These neighborhoods were considered excellent prospects for insurance. Neighborhoods where black people lived were rated "D" and were usually considered ineligible for FHA backing. They were colored in red. Neither the percentage of black people living there nor their social class mattered. Black people were viewed as a contagion. Redlining went beyond FHA-backed loans and spread to the entire mortgage industry, which was already rife with racism, excluding black people from most legitimate means of obtaining a mortgage.

"A government offering such bounty to builders and lenders could have required compliance with a nondiscrimination policy," Charles Abrams, the urban-studies expert who helped create the New York City Housing Authority, wrote in 1955. "Instead, the FHA adopted a racial policy that could well have been culled from the Nuremberg laws."

The devastating effects are cogently outlined by Melvin L. Oliver and Thomas M. Shapiro in their 1995 book, *Black Wealth/White Wealth*:

> Locked out of the greatest mass-based opportunity for wealth accumulation in American history, African Americans who desired and were able to afford home ownership found themselves consigned to central-city communities where their investments were affected by the "self-fulfilling prophecies" of the FHA appraisers: cut off from sources of new investment, their homes and communities deteriorated and lost value in comparison to those homes and communities that FHA appraisers deemed desirable.

In Chicago and across the country, whites looking to achieve the American dream could rely on a legitimate credit system backed by the government. Blacks were herded into the sights of unscrupulous lenders who took them for money and for sport. "It was like people who like to go out and shoot lions in Africa. It was the same thrill," a housing attorney told the historian Beryl Satter in her 2009 book, *Family Properties*. "The thrill of the chase and the kill."

The kill was profitable. At the time of his death, Lou Fushanis owned more than 600 properties, many of them in North Lawndale, and his estate was estimated to be worth $3 million. He'd made much of this money by exploiting the frustrated hopes of black migrants like Clyde Ross. During this period, according to one estimate, 85 percent of all black home buyers who bought in Chicago bought on contract. "If anybody who is well established in this business in Chicago doesn't earn

$100,000 a year," a contract seller told *The Saturday Evening Post* in 1962, "he is loafing."

Contract sellers became rich. North Lawndale became a ghetto.

Clyde Ross still lives there. He still owns his home. He is 91, and the emblems of survival are all around him—awards for service in his community, pictures of his children in cap and gown. But when I asked him about his home in North Lawndale, I heard only anarchy.

"We were ashamed. We did not want anyone to know that we were that ignorant," Ross told me. He was sitting at his dining-room table. His glasses were as thick as his Clarksdale drawl. "I'd come out of Mississippi where there was one mess, and come up here and got in another mess. So how dumb am I? I didn't want anyone to know how dumb I was."

"When I found myself caught up in it, I said, 'How? I just left this mess. I just left no laws. And no regard. And then I come here and get cheated wide open.' I would probably want to do some harm to some people, you know, if I had been violent like some of us. I thought, 'Man, I got caught up in this stuff. I can't even take care of my kids.' I didn't have enough for my kids. You could fall through the cracks easy fighting these white people. And no law."

But fight Clyde Ross did. In 1968 he joined the newly formed Contract Buyers League—a collection of black homeowners on Chicago's South and West Sides, all of whom had been locked into the same system of predation. There was Howell Collins, whose contract called for him to pay $25,500 for a house that a speculator had bought for $14,500. There was Ruth Wells, who'd managed to pay out half her contract, expecting a mortgage, only to suddenly see an insurance bill materialize out of thin air—a requirement the seller had added without Wells's knowledge. Contract sellers used every tool at their disposal to pilfer from their clients. They scared white residents into selling low. They lied about properties' compliance with building codes, then left the buyer responsible when city inspectors arrived. They presented themselves as real-estate brokers, when in fact they were the owners. They guided their clients to lawyers who were in on the scheme.

The Contract Buyers League fought back. Members—who would eventually number more than 500—went out to the posh suburbs where the speculators lived and embarrassed them by knocking on their neighbors' doors and informing them of the details of the contract-lending trade.

They refused to pay their installments, instead holding monthly payments in an escrow account. Then they brought a suit against the contract sellers, accusing them of buying properties and reselling in such a manner "to reap from members of the Negro race large and unjust profits."

In return for the "deprivations of their rights and privileges under the Thirteenth and Fourteenth Amendments," the league demanded "prayers for relief"—payback of all moneys paid on contracts and all moneys paid for structural improvement of properties, at 6 percent interest minus a "fair, non-discriminatory" rental price for time of occupation. Moreover, the league asked the court to adjudge that the defendants had "acted willfully and maliciously and that malice is the gist of this action."

Ross and the Contract Buyers League were no longer appealing to the government simply for equality. They were no longer fleeing in hopes of a better deal elsewhere. They were charging society with a crime against their community. They wanted the crime publicly ruled as such. They wanted the crime's executors declared to be offensive to society. And they wanted restitution for the great injury brought upon them by said offenders. In 1968, Clyde Ross and the Contract Buyers League were no longer simply seeking the protection of the law. They were seeking reparations.

A DIFFERENCE OF KIND, NOT DEGREE

. . . One thread of thinking in the African-American community holds that these depressing numbers partially stem from cultural pathologies that can be altered through individual grit and exceptionally good behavior. (In 2011, Philadelphia Mayor Michael Nutter, responding to violence among young black males, put the blame on the family: "Too many men making too many babies they don't want to take care of, and then we end up dealing with your children." Nutter turned to those presumably fatherless babies: "Pull your pants up and buy a belt, because no one wants to see your underwear or the crack of your butt.") The thread is as old as black politics itself. It is also wrong. The kind of trenchant racism to which black people have persistently been subjected can never be defeated by making its victims more respectable. The essence of American racism is disrespect. And in the wake of the grim numbers, we see the grim inheritance.

The Contract Buyers League's suit brought by Clyde Ross and his allies took direct aim at this inheritance. The suit was rooted in Chicago's long history of segregation, which had created two housing markets—one legitimate and backed by the government, the other lawless and patrolled by predators. The suit dragged on until 1976, when the league lost a jury trial. Securing the equal protection of the law proved hard; securing reparations proved impossible. If there were any doubts about the mood of the jury, the foreman removed them by saying, when asked about the verdict, that he hoped it would help end "the mess Earl Warren made with *Brown v. Board of Education* and all that nonsense." . . .

THE ILLS THAT SLAVERY FREES US FROM

America begins in black plunder and white democracy, two features that are not contradictory but complementary. "The men who came together to found the independent United States, dedicated to freedom and equality, either held slaves or were willing to join hands with those who did," the historian Edmund S. Morgan wrote. "None of them felt entirely comfortable about the fact, but neither did they feel responsible for it. Most of them had inherited both their slaves and their attachment to freedom from an earlier generation, and they knew the two were not unconnected."

. . . The wealth accorded America by slavery was not just in what the slaves pulled from the land but in the slaves themselves. "In 1860, slaves as an asset were worth more than all of America's manufacturing, all of the railroads, all of the productive capacity of the United States put together," the Yale historian David W. Blight has noted. "Slaves were the single largest, by far, financial asset of property in the entire American economy." The sale of these slaves—"in whose bodies that money congealed," writes Walter Johnson, a Harvard historian—generated even more ancillary wealth. Loans were taken out for purchase, to be repaid with interest. Insurance policies were drafted against the untimely death of a slave and the loss of potential profits. Slave sales were taxed and notarized. The vending of the black body and the sundering of the black family became an economy unto themselves, estimated to have brought in tens of millions of dollars to antebellum America. In 1860 there were more millionaires per capita in the Mississippi Valley than anywhere else in the country.

Beneath the cold numbers lay lives divided. "I had a constant dread that Mrs. Moore, her mistress, would be in want of money and sell my dear wife," a freedman wrote, reflecting on his time in slavery. "We constantly dreaded a final separation. Our affection for each was very strong, and this made us always apprehensive of a cruel parting."

Forced partings were common in the antebellum South. A slave in some parts of the region stood a 30 percent chance of being sold in his or her lifetime. Twenty-five percent of interstate trades destroyed a first marriage and half of them destroyed a nuclear family.

When the wife and children of Henry Brown, a slave in Richmond, Virginia, were to be sold away, Brown searched for a white master who might buy his wife and children to keep the family together. He failed:

> The next day, I stationed myself by the side of the road, along which the slaves, amounting to three hundred and fifty, were to pass. The purchaser of my wife was a Methodist minister, who was about starting for North Carolina. Pretty soon five waggon-loads of little children passed, and looking at the foremost one, what should I see but a little child, point-ing its tiny hand towards me, exclaiming, "There's my father; I knew he would come and bid me good-bye." It was my eldest child! Soon the gang approached in which my wife was chained. I looked, and beheld her familiar face; but O, reader, that glance of agony! may God spare me ever again enduring the excruciating horror of that moment! She passed, and came near to where I stood. I seized hold of her hand, intending to bid her farewell; but words failed me; the gift of utterance had fled, and I remained speechless. I followed her for some distance, with her hand grasped in mine, as if to save her from her fate, but I could not speak, and I was obliged to turn away in silence.

In a time when telecommunications were primitive and blacks lacked freedom of movement, the parting of black families was a kind of murder. Here we find the roots of American wealth and democracy—in the for-profit destruction of the most important asset available to any people, the family. The destruction was not incidental to America's rise; it facilitated that rise. By erecting a slave society, America created the economic foundation for its great experiment in democracy. The labor strife that seeded Bacon's rebellion was sup-pressed. America's indispensable working class existed as property beyond the realm of politics, leaving white Americans free to trumpet their love of freedom and democratic values. Assessing antebellum democracy in Virginia, a visitor from England observed that the state's natives "can profess an unbounded love of liberty and of democracy in consequence of the mass of the people, who in other countries might become mobs, being there nearly altogether composed of their own Negro slaves."

A LOT OF PEOPLE FELL BY THE WAY

. . . To keep up with his payments and keep his heat on, Clyde Ross took a second job at the post office and then a third job delivering pizza. His wife took a job working at Marshall Field. He had to take some of his children out of private school. He was not able to be at home to supervise his children or help them with their homework. Money and time that Ross wanted to give his children went instead to enrich white speculators.

"The problem was the money," Ross told me. "Without the money, you can't move. You can't educate your kids. You can't give them the right kind of food. Can't make the house look good. They think this neighborhood is where they supposed to be. It changes their outlook. My kids were going to the best schools in this neighborhood, and I couldn't keep them in there."

NEGRO POVERTY IS NOT WHITE POVERTY

. . . Chicago, like the country at large, embraced policies that placed black America's most energetic, ambitious, and thrifty countrymen beyond the pale of society and marked them as rightful targets for legal theft. The effects reverberate beyond the families who were robbed to the community that beholds the spectacle. Don't just picture Clyde Ross working three jobs so he could hold on to his home. Think of his North Lawndale neighbors—their children, their nephews, and nieces—and consider how watching this affects them. Imagine yourself as a young black child watching your elders play by all the rules only to have their possessions tossed out in the street and to have their most sacred possession—their home—taken from them.

TOWARD A NEW COUNTRY

. . . Scholars have long discussed methods by which America might make reparations to those on whose labor and exclusion the country was built. In the 1970s, the Yale Law professor Boris Bittker argued in *The Case for Black Reparations* that a rough price tag for reparations could be determined by multiplying the number of African-Americans in the population by the difference in white and black per capita income. That number—$34 billion in 1973, when Bittker wrote his book—could be added to a reparations program each year for a decade or two. Today Charles Ogletree, the Harvard Law School professor, argues for something broader: a program of job training and public works that takes racial justice as its mission but includes the poor of all races.

To celebrate freedom and democracy while forgetting America's origins in a slavery economy is patriotism à la carte.

Perhaps no statistic better illustrates the enduring legacy of our country's shameful history of treating black people as sub-citizens, sub-Americans, and sub-humans than the wealth gap. Reparations would seek to close this chasm. But as surely as the creation of the wealth gap required the cooperation of every aspect of the society, bridging it will require the same.

Perhaps after a serious discussion and debate . . . we may find that the country can never fully repay African-Americans. But we stand to discover much about ourselves in such a discussion—and that is perhaps what scares us. The idea of reparations is frightening not simply because we might lack the ability to pay. The idea of reparations threatens something much deeper—America's heritage, history, and standing in the world.

. . . And so we must imagine a new country. Reparations—by which I mean the full acceptance of our collective biography and its consequences—is the price we must pay to see ourselves squarely. The recovering alcoholic may well have to live with his illness for the rest of his life. But at least he is not living a drunken lie. Reparations beckons us to reject the intoxication of hubris and see America as it is—the work of fallible humans.

. . . What I'm talking about is more than recompense for past injustices—more than a handout, a payoff, hush money, or a reluctant bribe. What I'm talking about is a national reckoning that would lead to spiritual renewal. Reparations would mean the end of scarfing hot dogs on the Fourth of July while denying the facts of our heritage. Reparations would mean the end of yelling "patriotism" while waving a Confederate flag. Reparations would mean a revolution of the American consciousness, a reconciling of our self-image as the great democratizer with the facts of our history.

Chapter 22

Is Racial Discrimination Arbitrary?

Peter Singer

When the Major League Baseball season ended in 1973, Atlanta Braves slugger Hank Aaron was just one swing away from the greatest prize in baseball: Babe Ruth's record of 714 career home runs. History was in the making; the Bambino was about to get hammered. Aaron's first at bat of the 1974 season saw number 714. Number 715 came on April 8, 1974, before a sellout crowd in Atlanta. Today, outside the Braves' stadium, there is a statue of Hank Aaron swinging a bat, and though the stadium has moved, a sign in Turner Field still commemorates the spot where home run 715 cleared the outfield fence.

There is, however, an unpleasant side to this story. Aaron later recalled those "glory" days as being the worst of his life. Why? Because Aaron is African-American, and for daring to break Babe Ruth's record, he had to endure a torrent of hatred. In 1973, he received 930,000 pieces of mail, most of it filled with racial slurs. As he got near Ruth's record, Aaron holed up in his apartment, afraid to go outside. The FBI uncovered a plot to kill his daughter, who lived in Nashville. And when he actually hit number 715, Aaron's mother, Estella, jumped out of the stands and rushed onto the field, not out of joy, but because she believed that her son was about to be shot by a sniper.

Peter Singer, "Is Racial Discrimination Arbitrary?" in *Philosophia*, vol. 8, no. 2–3 (November 1978): 185–203. Copyright © 1978 Peter Singer. Used with permission of the author.

Racial discrimination violates one of our deepest moral beliefs: that people should not be treated badly for arbitrary reasons like the color of their skin. The hatred Hank Aaron had to endure was clearly vile. However, other cases of differential treatment are less clear. Peter Singer discusses three such cases in this selection.

---

1. INTRODUCTION

There is nowadays wide agreement that racism is wrong. To describe a policy, law, movement, or nation as "racist" is to condemn it. It may be thought that since we all agree that racism is wrong, it is unnecessary to speculate on exactly what it is and why it is wrong. This indifference to moral fundamentals could, however, prove dangerous. For one thing, the fact that most people agree today that racism is wrong does not mean that this attitude will always be so widely shared. Even if we had no fears for the future, though, we need to have some understanding of what it is about racism that is wrong if we are to handle satisfactorily all the problems we face today. For instance, there is the contentious issue of "reverse discrimination" or discrimination in favor of members of oppressed minority groups. It must be granted that a university which admits members of minority groups who do not achieve the minimum standard that others must reach in order to be admitted is discriminating on racial lines. Is such discrimination therefore wrong?

Or, to take another issue, the efforts of Arab nations to have the United Nations declare Zionism a form of racism provoked an extremely hostile reaction in nations friendly to Israel, particularly the United States, but it led to virtually no discussion of whether Zionism is a form of racism. Yet the charge is not altogether without plausibility, for if Jews are a race, then Zionism promotes the idea of a state dominated by one race, and this has practical consequences in, for instance, Israel's immigration laws. Again, to consider whether this makes Zionism a form of racism we need to understand what it is that makes a policy racist and wrong. . . .

If we ask those who regard racial discrimination as wrong to say why it is wrong, it is commonly said that it is wrong to pick on race as a reason for treating one person differently from others, because race is irrelevant to whether a person should be given a job, the vote, higher education, or any benefits or burdens of this sort. The irrelevance of race, it is said, makes it quite arbitrary to give these things to people of one race while withholding them from those of another race. I shall refer to this account of what is wrong with racial discrimination as the "standard objection" to racial discrimination.

A sophisticated theory of justice can be invoked in support of this standard objection to racial discrimination. Justice requires, as Aristotle so plausibly said, that equals be treated equally and unequals be treated unequally. To this we must add the obvious proviso that the equalities or inequalities should be relevant to the treatment in question. Now when we consider things like employment, it becomes clear that the relevant inequalities between candidates for a vacant position are inequalities in their ability to carry out the duties of the position and, perhaps, inequalities in the extent to which they will benefit through being offered the position. Race does not seem to be relevant at all. Similarly with the vote, capacity for rational choice between candidates or policies might be held a relevant characteristic, but race should not be; and so on for other goods. It is hard to think of anything for which race in itself is a relevant characteristic, and hence to use race as a basis for discrimination is arbitrarily to single out an irrelevant factor, no doubt because of a bias or prejudice against those of a different race.

As we shall see, this account of why racial discrimination is wrong is inadequate because there are many situations in which, from at least one point of view, the racial factor is by no means irrelevant, and therefore it can be denied that racial discrimination in these situations is arbitrary.

One type of situation in which race must be admitted to be relevant to the purposes of the person discriminating need not delay us at this stage; this is the situation in which those purposes themselves favor a particular race. Thus if the purpose of Hitler and the other Nazi leaders was, among other things, to produce a world in which there were no Jews, it was certainly not irrelevant to their purposes that those rounded up and murdered by the SS were Jews rather than so-called "Aryans." But the fundamental wrongness of the aims of the Nazis makes the "relevance" of race to those aims totally inefficacious so far as justifying Nazi racial discrimination is concerned. While their type of racial discrimination may not have been arbitrary discrimination in the usual sense, it was no less wrong for that. *Why* it was wrong is something that I hope will become clearer later in this article. Meanwhile I shall look at some less cataclysmic forms of racial discrimination, for too much contemporary

discussion of racial discrimination has focused on the most blatant
instances: Nazi Germany, [the former situation in] South Africa, and
the American "Deep South" during the period of legally enforced racial
segregation. These forms of racism are not the type that face us now
in our own societies . . . and to discuss racial discrimination in terms
of these examples today is to present an oversimplified picture of the
problem of racial discrimination. By looking at some of the reasons for
racial discrimination that might actually be offered today in countries
all over the world I hope to show that the real situation is usually much
more complex than consideration of the more blatant instances of racial
discrimination would lead us to believe.

2. EXAMPLES

I shall start by describing an example of racial discrimination which
may at first glance seem to be an allowable exception to a general rule
that racial discrimination is arbitrary and therefore wrong; and I shall
then suggest that this case has parallels with other cases we may not be
so willing to allow as exceptions.

Case 1. A film director is making a film about the lives of blacks
living in New York's Harlem. He advertises for black actors. A white
actor turns up, but the director refuses to allow him to audition, saying
that the film is about blacks and there are no roles for whites. The actor
replies that, with the appropriate wig and make-up, he can look just like
a black; moreover he can imitate the mannerisms, gestures, and speech
of Harlem blacks. Nevertheless the director refuses to consider him for
the role, because it is essential to the director's conception of the film
that the black experience be authentically portrayed, and however good
a white actor might be, the director would not be satisfied with the
authenticity of the portrayal.

The film director is discriminating along racial lines, yet he cannot
be said to be discriminating arbitrarily. His discrimination is apt for
his purpose. Moreover his purpose is a legitimate one. So the standard
objection to racial discrimination cannot be made in this instance.

Racial discrimination may be acceptable in an area like casting for
films or the theater, when the race of a character in the film or play
is important, because this is one of the seemingly few areas in which
a person's race is directly relevant to his capacity to perform a given

task. As such, it may be thought, these areas can easily be distinguished from other areas of employment, as well as from areas like housing, education, the right to vote, and so on, where race has no relevance at all. Unfortunately there are many other situations in which race is not as totally irrelevant as this view assumes.

Case 2. The owner of a cake shop with a largely white and racially prejudiced clientele wishes to hire an assistant. The owner has no prejudice against blacks himself, but is reluctant to employ one, for fear that his customers will go elsewhere. If his fears are well-founded (and this is not impossible) then the race of a candidate for the position is, again, relevant to the purpose of the employer, which in this case is to maintain the profitability of his business.

What can we say about this case? We cannot deny the connection between race and the owner's purposes, and so we must recognize that the owner's discrimination is not arbitrary, and does not necessarily indicate a bias or prejudice on his part. Nor can we say that the owner's purpose is an illegitimate one, for making a profit from the sale of cakes is not generally regarded as wrong, at least if the amount of profit made is modest.

We can, of course, look at other aspects of the matter. We can object to the racial discrimination shown by customers who will search out shops staffed by whites only—such people do discriminate arbitrarily, for race is irrelevant to the quality of the goods and the proficiency of service in a shop—but is this not simply a fact that the shop-owner must live with, however much he may wish he could change it? We might argue that by pandering to the prejudices of his customers, the owner is allowing those prejudices to continue unchallenged; whereas if he and other shopkeepers took no notice of them, people would eventually become used to mixing with those of another race, and prejudices would be eroded. Yet it is surely too much to ask an individual shop-owner to risk his livelihood in a lone and probably vain effort to break down prejudice. Few of the most dedicated opponents of racism do as much. If there were national legislation which distributed the burden more evenly, by a general prohibition of discrimination on racial grounds (with some recognized exceptions for cases like casting for a film or play) the situation would be different. Then we could reasonably ask every shop-owner to play his part. Whether there should be such legislation is a different question from whether the shop-owner may be blamed for discriminating in the absence of legislation. I shall discuss the issue of legislation shortly, after we consider a different kind of racial discrimination that, again, is not arbitrary.

Case 3. A landlord discriminates against blacks in renting the accommodation he owns. Let us say that he is not so rigid as never to rent an apartment to a black, but if a black person and a white person appear to be equally suitable as tenants, with equally good references and so on, the landlord invariably prefers the white. He defends his policy along the following lines:

> If more than a very small proportion of my tenants get behind in their rent and then disappear without paying the arrears, I will be out of business. Over the years, I have found that more blacks do this than whites. I admit that there are many honest blacks (some of my best tenants have been black) and many dishonest whites, but, for some reason I do not claim to understand, the odds on a white tenant defaulting are longer than on a black doing so, even when their references and other credentials appear equally good. In this business you can't run a full-scale probe of every prospective tenant—and if I tried I would be abused for invading privacy—so you have to go by the average rather than the individual. That is why blacks have to have better indications of reliability than whites before I will rent to them.

Now the landlord's impression of a higher rate of default among blacks than among comparable whites may itself be the result of prejudice on his part. Perhaps in most cases when landlords say this kind of thing, there is no real factual basis to their allegations. People have grown up with racial stereotypes, and these stereotypes are reinforced by a tendency to notice occurrences which conform to the stereotype and to disregard those which conflict with it. So if unreliability is part of the stereotype of blacks held by many whites, they may take more notice of blacks who abscond without paying the rent than of blacks who are reliable tenants; and conversely they will take less notice of absconding whites and more of those whites who conform to their ideas of normal white behavior.

If it is prejudice that is responsible for the landlord's views about black and white tenants, and there is no factual basis for his claims, then the problem becomes one of eliminating this prejudice and getting the landlord to see his mistake. This is by no means an easy task, but it is not a task for philosophers, and it does not concern us here, for we are interested in attempts to justify racial discrimination, and an attempted justification based on an inaccurate description of a situation can be rejected without raising the deeper issue of justification.

On the other hand, the landlord's impression of a higher rate of default among black tenants *could* be entirely accurate. (It might be explicable in terms of the different cultural and economic circumstances in which blacks are brought up.) Whether or not we think this likely, we need to ask what its implications would be for the justifiability of the racial discrimination exercised by the landlord. To refuse even to consider this question would be to rest all one's objections to the landlord's practice on the falsity of his claims, and thereby to fail to examine the possibility that the landlord's practice could be open to objection even if his impressions on tenant reliability are accurate.

If the landlord's impressions were accurate, we would have to concede, once again, that racial discrimination in this situation is not arbitrary; that it is, instead, relevant to the purposes of the landlord. We must also admit that these purposes—making a living from letting property that one owns—are not themselves objectionable, provided the rents are reasonable, and so on. Nor can we, this time, locate the origin of the problem in the prejudices of others, except insofar as the problem has its origin in the prejudices of those responsible for the conditions of deprivation in which many of the present generation of blacks grew up—but it is too late to do anything to alter those prejudices anyway, since they belong to previous generations.

We have now looked at three examples of racial discrimination, and can begin to examine the parallels and differences between them. Many people, as I have already said, would make no objection to the discriminatory hiring practice of the film director in the first of these cases. But we can now see that if we try to justify the actions of the film director in this case on the grounds that his purpose is a legitimate one and the discrimination he uses is relevant for his purpose, we will have to accept the actions of the cake-shop owner and the landlord as well. I suspect that many of those ready to accept the discriminatory practice in the first case will be much more reluctant about the other two cases. But what morally significant difference is there between them?

It might be suggested that the difference between them lies in the nature of what blacks are being deprived of, and their title to it. The argument would run like this: No one has a right to be selected to act in a film; the director must have absolute discretion to hire whomsoever he wishes to hire. After all, no one can force the director to make the film at all, and if he didn't make it, no one would be hired to play in it; if he does decide to make it, therefore, he must be allowed to make it on his own terms. Moreover, since so few people ever get the chance to appear in a film, it would be absurd to hold that the director violates someone's rights by not giving him something which most people will never have anyway. On the other hand, people do have a right to employment, and to housing. To discriminate against blacks in an ordinary employment situation, or in the letting of accommodation, threatens their basic rights and therefore should not be tolerated.

Plausible as it appears, this way of distinguishing the first case from the other two will not do. Consider the first and second cases: almost everything that we have said about the film director applies to the cake-shop owner as well. No one can force the cake-shop owner to keep his shop open, and if he didn't, no one would be hired to work in it. If in the film director's case this was a reason for allowing him to make the film on his own terms, it must be a reason for allowing the shop-owner to run his shop on his own terms. In fact, such reasoning, which would allow unlimited discrimination in restaurants, hotels, and shops, is invalid. There are plenty of examples where we would not agree that the fact that someone did not have to make an offer or provide an opportunity at all means that if he does do it he must be allowed to make the offer or provide the opportunity on his own terms. The United States Civil Rights Act of 1965 certainly does not recognize this line of argument, for it prohibits those offering food and lodgings to the public from excluding customers on racial grounds. We may, as a society, decide that we shall not allow people to make certain offers, if the way in which the offers are made will cause hardship or offense to others. In so doing we are balancing people's freedom to do as they please against the harm this may do to others, and coming down on the side of preventing harm rather than enlarging freedom. This is a perfectly defensible position, if the harm is sufficiently serious and the restriction of freedom not grave.

Nor does it seem possible to distinguish the first and second cases by the claim that since so few people ever get the chance to appear in a film, no one's rights are violated if they are not given something that most people will never have anyway. For if the number of jobs in cake shops was small, and the demand for such jobs high, it would also be true that few people would ever have the chance to work in a cake shop.

It would be odd if such an increase in competition for the job justified an otherwise unjustifiable policy of hiring whites only. Moreover, this argument would allow a film director to discriminate on racial lines even if race was irrelevant to the roles he was casting; and that is quite a different situation from the one we have been discussing.

The best way to distinguish the situations of the film director and the shop-owner is by reference to the nature of the employment offered, and to the reasons why racial discrimination in these cases is not arbitrary. In casting for a film about blacks, the race of the actor auditioning is intrinsically significant, independently of the attitudes of those connected with the film. In the case of hiring a shop assistant, race is relevant only because of the attitudes of those connected (as customers) with the shop; it has nothing to do with the selling of cakes in itself, but only with the selling of cakes to racially prejudiced customers. This means that in the case of the shop assistant we could eliminate the relevance of race if we could eliminate the prejudices of the customers; by contrast there is no way in which we could eliminate the relevance of the race of an actor auditioning for a role in a film about blacks, without altering the nature of the film. Moreover, in the case of the shop-owner racial discrimination probably serves to perpetuate the very prejudices that make such discrimination relevant and (from the point of view of the owner seeking to maintain his profits) necessary. Thus people who can buy all their cakes and other necessities in shops staffed only by whites will never come into the kind of contact with comparable blacks which might break down their aversion to being served by blacks; whereas if shop-owners were to hire more blacks, their customers would no doubt become used to it and in time might wonder why they ever opposed the idea. . . .

Hence if we are opposed to arbitrary discrimination we have reason to take steps against racial discrimination in situations like Case 2, because such discrimination, while not itself arbitrary, both feeds on and gives support to discrimination by others which is arbitrary. In prohibiting it we would, admittedly, be preventing the employer from discriminating in a way that is relevant to his purposes; but if the causal hypothesis suggested in the previous paragraph is correct, this situation would only be temporary, and after some time the circumstances inducing the employer to discriminate racially would have been eliminated.

The case of the landlord presents a more difficult problem. If the facts he alleges are true his non-arbitrary reasons for discrimination against blacks are real enough. They do not depend on present arbitrary discrimination by others, and they may persist beyond an interval in which there is no discrimination. Whatever the roots of hypothetical racial differences in reliability as tenants might be, they would probably go too deep to be eradicated solely by a short period in which there was no racial discrimination.

We should recognize, then, that if the facts are as alleged, to legislate against the landlord's racially discriminatory practice is to impose a long-term disadvantage upon him. At the very least, he will have to take greater care in ascertaining the suitability of prospective tenants. Perhaps he will turn to data-collecting agencies for assistance, thus contributing to the growth of institutions that are threats, potential or actual, to our privacy. Perhaps, if these methods are unavailable or unavailing, the landlord will have to take greater losses than he otherwise would have, and perhaps this will lead to increased rents or even to a reduction in the amount of rentable housing available.

None of this forces us to conclude that we should not legislate against the landlord's racial discrimination. There are good reasons why we should seek to eliminate racial discrimination even when such discrimination is neither arbitrary in itself nor relevant only because of the arbitrary prejudices of others. These reasons may be so important as to make the disadvantage imposed on the landlord comparatively insignificant.

An obvious point that can be made against the landlord is that he is judging people, at least in part, as members of a race rather than as individuals. The landlord does not deny that some black prospective tenants he turns away would make better tenants than some white prospective tenants he accepts. Some highly eligible black prospective tenants are refused accommodation simply because they are black. If the landlord assessed every prospective tenant as an individual this would not happen. . . .

There are plenty of reasons why in situations like admitting people to higher education or providing them with employment or other benefits we should regard people as individuals and not as members of some larger group. For one thing we will be able to make a selection better suited for our own purposes, for selecting or discarding whole groups of people will generally result in, at best, a crude approximation to the results we hope to achieve. This is certainly true in an area like education. On the other hand it must be admitted that in some situations a crude approximation is all that can be achieved anyway. The landlord claims that his situation is one of these, and that as he cannot reliably tell which individuals will make suitable tenants, he is justified in resorting to so crude a means of selection as race. Here we need to turn our attention from the landlord to the prospective black tenant.

To be judged merely as a member of a group when it is one's individual qualities on which the verdict should be given is to be treated as less than the unique individual that we see ourselves as. Even where our individual qualities would merit less than we receive as a member of a group—if we are promoted over better-qualified people because we went to the "right" private school—the benefit is usually less welcome than it would be if it had been merited by our own attributes. Of course in this case qualms are easily stilled by the fact that a benefit has been received, never mind how. In the contrary case, however, when something of value has been lost, the sense of loss will be compounded by the feeling that one was not assessed on one's own merits, but merely as a member of a group.

To this general preference for individual as against group assessment must be added a consideration arising from the nature of the group. To be denied a benefit because one was, say, a member of the Communist Party, would be unjust and a violation of basic principles of political liberty, but if one has chosen to join the Communist Party, then one is, after all, being assessed for what one has done, and one can choose between living with the consequences of continued party membership or leaving the party. Race, of course, is not something that one chooses to adopt or that one can ever choose to give up. The person who is denied advantages because of his race is totally unable to alter this particular circumstance of his existence and so may feel with added sharpness that his life is clouded, not merely because he is not being judged as an individual, but because of something over which he has no control at all. This makes racial discrimination peculiarly invidious.

So we have the viewpoint of the victim of racial discrimination to offset against the landlord's argument in favor, and it seems that the victim has more at stake and hence should be given preference, even if the landlord's reason for discriminating is non-arbitrary and hence in a sense legitimate. The case against racial discrimination becomes stronger still when we consider the long-term social effects of discrimination.

When members of a racial minority are overwhelmingly among the poorest members of a society, living in a deprived area, holding jobs low in pay and status, or no jobs at all, and less well educated than the average member of the community, racial discrimination serves to perpetuate a divided society in which race becomes a badge of a much broader inferiority. It is the association of race with economic status and educational disadvantages which in turn gives rise to the situation in which there could be a coloring of truth to the claim that race is a relevant ground for discriminating between prospective tenants, applicants for employment, and so on. Thus there is, in the end, a parallel between the situation of the landlord and the cake-shop owner, for both, by their discrimination, contribute to the maintenance of the grounds for claiming that this discrimination is non-arbitrary. Hence prohibition of such discrimination can be justified as breaking this circle of deprivation and discrimination. The difference between the situations, as I have already said, is that in the case of the cake-shop owner it is only a prejudice against contact with blacks that needs to be broken down, and experience has shown that such prejudices do evaporate in a relatively short period of time. In the case of the landlord, however, it is the whole social and economic position of blacks that needs to be changed, and while overcoming discrimination would be an essential part of this process it may not be sufficient. That is why, if the facts are as the landlord alleges them to be, prohibition of racial discrimination is likely to impose more of a long-term disadvantage on the landlord than on the shop-owner—a disadvantage which is, however, outweighed by the costs of continuing the circle of racial discrimination and deprivation for those discriminated against; and the costs of greater social inequality and racial divisiveness for the community as a whole.

Chapter 23

In Defense of Quotas

James Rachels

Affirmative action programs began in the 1960s as a way of redressing past and current discrimination against African-Americans. Later, these programs were expanded to include other groups, such as women, Hispanics, and people with disabilities. Today, some affirmative action programs even benefit white males, because male students are in the minority on college campuses.

There are two kinds of affirmative action: quotas and racially sensitive policies. *Quotas* set numerical requirements for admission, hiring, and promotion. For example, a quota would be imposed on a country club if the club were told to admit at least five members of a specific minority group within a year's time. *Racially sensitive policies* merely consider race as one relevant factor in making a decision; no quota is imposed. For instance, some universities have policies to promote "diversity," where one kind of diversity is racial diversity. In *California v. Bakke* (1978), the U.S. Supreme Court ruled that quotas are unconstitutional but that racially sensitive policies are permitted.

In this selection, James Rachels specifies some conditions under which quotas seem justified. He begins by discussing an unfamiliar type of prejudice: "heightism," or prejudice against short males. An important study on height and salary, from 2004, confirmed

James Rachels, "In Defense of Quotas" in *Philosophia*, vol. 8, no. 1 (October 1978). Used with permission.

Rachels' belief that heightism is a serious problem—heightism, it found, affects earning power as much as racism and sexism do. However, it suggested that the problem is not prejudice against short *men*, as Rachels believes, but against short *adolescents*. Being short in grade school seems to permanently affect a male's self-esteem and economic prospects. Males who were short in grade school but then had a growth spurt in their late teens still suffer these effects. Rachels, however, does cite evidence for prejudice against short *men*, so maybe the facts are not clear.

James Rachels (1941–2003) wrote and edited thirteen books, including *Problems from Philosophy* (3rd edition, 2012), an introduction to philosophy, and *The Elements of Moral Philosophy* (9th edition, 2019), an introduction to ethics.

"Good sense," said Descartes, "is of all things in the world the most equally distributed, for everybody thinks himself so abundantly provided with it, that even those most difficult to please in all other matters do not commonly desire more of it than they already possess."[1] Much the same might be said about prejudice: everyone believes himself or herself to be objective and free of bias. We recognize that other people may be prejudiced, but we imagine that we ourselves see things as they really are.

But of course this is a mistake. We feel that we are unprejudiced only because we are unaware of our biases and how they work. This is true not only of bigots but of relatively open-minded people as well. It is a mistake for any of us to think that we are free of bias. Even when we are striving hardest to be objective, prejudices of all sorts can creep into our thinking without our noticing it.

To illustrate this, we may consider a type of example that does not often occur to us. We are familiar enough with prejudice based on race or gender. But those are not the only ways in which we discriminate. There is an impressive body of evidence that we are also prejudiced against people because of their height. I do not mean abnormally short or tall people—dwarfs or giants. That sort of prejudice is familiar enough. The less widely-recognized form of prejudice is against shorter people whose height falls within the normal range. Let me briefly mention some of the investigations that show this.[2]

In one study, 140 job-placement officers were asked to choose between two applicants with exactly the same qualifications, but one was described, parenthetically, as being 6′1″ while the other candidate was listed as 5′5″. One hundred and two of the recruiters judged the taller candidate to be better qualified, while only one preferred the shorter candidate. The rest of them—a mere 27 percent—recognized that the two were equally qualified.

Other studies have shown that a person's earning potential is affected more by height than by, say, educational performance. One study compared the starting salaries of male librarians between 6′1″ and 6′3″ with the starting salaries of male librarians less than 6′. The same comparison was then made between those who had been in the top half of their classes academically and those in the bottom half. The average difference in starting salary between the taller and shorter graduates was found to be more than three times greater than the difference between the salaries of the more and less academically gifted. Another study using a sample of over five thousand men found that after twenty-five years of pursuing their varied careers, those who were 5′6″ or 5′7″ were earning on average $2,500 per year less than those who were 6′0″ or 6′1″.

The moral seems to be: if you could choose between being tall and being smart, from a crass economic standpoint, it's better to be tall.

The same sort of prejudice influences the way we vote. Of all U.S. presidents, only two—James Madison and Benjamin Harrison—were shorter than the average height for American males at the time of their election. And since 1904, the taller candidate has emerged victorious in 80 percent of presidential elections. Another moral might be drawn: if you are trying to predict the outcome of such an election, forget the other factors and put your money on the taller man.

Prejudice against short people seems importantly different from racist or sexist prejudice, because the latter sorts of prejudice seem to be motivated, at least in part, by the fact that members of the dominant group derive advantages from the discriminatory practices. These advantages are often economic. However, this seems much less plausible where height is concerned. It seems more likely that prejudice regarding height has some other, deeper psychological source. John S. Gillis, a psychologist who has written at length about this, has speculated that the source of our association of height with ability is to be found in childhood experiences:

All of us experience a real association between height and power throughout our childhood. Adults tower over us physically as children, and they are the ones who control every single important thing in our lives. This may be the fountainhead of heightism. Each of us begins life with a dozen years or so of learning that the bigger person is more powerful and intelligent. This learning takes place not so much on an intellectual level but, more importantly, on the emotional level. Our attitudes and feelings are shaped in ways of which we are unaware.[3]

Whatever the source of these feelings, it is clear that they have deep and long-lasting effects.

The facts about "heightism" are quite remarkable. They suggest a number of points that should be of interest to anyone who is thinking about the philosophical problem of equality, especially as it relates to the formulation and assessment of social policies. First, the studies I have cited show that prejudice can have its influence quite unconsciously. No one—or so nearly no one as makes no difference—realizes that he thinks less well of shorter people. Yet the available evidence shows that this prejudice exists, and that it is widespread. The people who are affected by it are simply unaware of it.

Second, this evidence also suggests that people are very good at rationalizing their prejudiced judgments. The men and women whose actions were studied in these investigations—those who hired, promoted, and gave pay raises to the taller candidates—were, no doubt, reasonable people who could "explain" each decision by reference to the lucky employee's objective qualifications. No one believed that he was simply rewarding height. Yet the evidence shows that this is what was happening much of the time. The behavior induced by prejudice includes, importantly, the verbal behavior that "justifies" the prejudiced judgments.

These points, taken together, have a discouraging implication. They suggest that it is difficult even for people of good will to prevent such prejudice from influencing their deliberations. If I am prejudiced in ways that I do not fully realize, and if I am skilled at coming up with reasons to "justify" the decisions that such prejudice leads me to make, then my good intention to "think objectively"—no matter how sincerely I want to do this—may be depressingly ineffective.

THE JUSTIFICATION OF QUOTAS

People ought to be treated fairly. Yet we know that our assessments of people are often corrupted by prejudice. Does this make any difference in the sorts of policies that should be adopted?

Choosing Widgets

Suppose you are the president of a manufacturing company and each year in the course of your business you need a supply of widgets. Widgets vary greatly in quality, and from among the hundreds available you need to get the ten best you can find. You are not able to devote much of your own time to this task, but luckily you have an assistant who is one of the most astute widget evaluators in the land. "Examine all the available widgets," you tell her, "and bring me the ten best."

In the fullness of time your assistant brings you ten good widgets, and all seems well. But then you notice that all ten were made at the Buffalo Widget Works. This is odd, because you know that the Albany Widget Works makes an equally good product; and moreover, you know that the pool from which your assistant made her selection contained equal numbers of Albany widgets and Buffalo widgets. So why should the ten best all come from Buffalo? One would expect that, on average, five would come from Buffalo and five from Albany. But perhaps this was just a statistical fluke, and it will all average out over time.

The next year, however, much the same thing happens. You need ten widgets; you assign your assistant to identify the best; and she brings you nine made in Buffalo and only one made in Albany. "Why?" you ask, and in response she assures you that, even though the Albany company does make excellent widgets, most of the best ones available this year happened to be from Buffalo. To prove the point she gives you quite an intelligent and persuasive analysis of the merits of the widgets in this year's pool. You are so impressed that you name her Vice President for Widget Procurement (VPWP).

In subsequent years the story is repeated again and again, with only slight variations. Each year you are told that almost all the best available widgets are from Buffalo. You begin to feel sure that something peculiar is going on. Briefly, you wonder whether your VPWP is accepting bribes from the Buffalo company, but you reject that hypothesis. She is an honest woman, and you cannot help but believe that she is using her best judgment. Then you consider whether, in fact, the Buffalo widgets are simply better than the Albany widgets. But you reject this possibility also; other experts testify that they are equally good.

Finally, you make a discovery that explains everything. It turns out that your vice president was raised in Buffalo, where there is a strong sense of civic pride, and an even stronger sense of rivalry with Albany. Children in Buffalo, it seems, have it drilled into them that everything about Buffalo is better than anything about Albany. Moreover, before coming to work for you, your VPWP worked for the Buffalo Chamber of Commerce and was in charge of promoting Buffalo products. Obviously, then, she is prejudiced, and that explains why she almost always judges Buffalo widgets to be superior.

What are you to do? You could forget about it; after all, the widgets you are getting from Buffalo are pretty good. But you don't want to do that; it is important to you to have the very best widgets you can get. So you talk to your VPWP, you confront her with your suspicion that she is prejudiced, and you stress the importance of getting the best widgets regardless of whether they are from Buffalo or Albany. She is a bit offended by this because she is a good woman and believes herself to be impartial. Again, she assures you that she is selecting the best widgets available, and if they happen to be from Buffalo, she can't help it. And as time passes, nothing changes; she continues to select mostly Buffalo widgets.

Now what? You are certain she is prejudiced, but because the prejudice is entirely unconscious, your VPWP seems unable to overcome it or even to recognize it. You could get a new VPWP. But you don't want to do that, because this woman is an excellent judge of widgets, except for this one problem. Then an obvious solution occurs to you. You could simply change your instructions. Instead of saying, each year, "Bring me the ten best widgets," you could say, "Bring me the five best Buffalo widgets and the five best Albany widgets." She might not like that—she might take it as an insult to her ability to judge widgets impartially—but, if it is true that Albany widgets are equally as good as Buffalo widgets, this would result in your getting a better overall quality of widget, on average, year in and year out. . . .

The VPWP might, however, offer an interesting objection. She might point out that, in carrying out your new instructions, she would sometimes have to include in the total of ten an Albany widget that is inferior to a Buffalo widget that was also available. You will have to admit that this is so. But your problem is a practical one. You can trust the VPWP to judge which are the best Albany widgets, and you can trust her to judge which are the best Buffalo widgets. But you cannot trust her to compare objectively the relative merits of a widget from one city with a widget from the other city. In these circumstances, your new instructions give you a better chance of ending up with the best overall supply. Or to put it another way: you want the best-qualified widgets to get the jobs, and the quota system you have established will see to that more effectively than the alternative method of simply allowing your VPWP to exercise her judgment.

Hiring People

In the workplace, people ought to be treated equally, but often they are not. Among the important reasons is prejudice; after all, somebody has to decide who is to be hired, or promoted, or given a pay raise, and those who get to make such decisions are only human and might be prejudiced. Social policies ought to be devised with this in mind. Such policies should contain provisions to ensure that people are given equal treatment, insofar as this is possible, despite the fact that those policies must be administered by imperfect human beings.

Of all the kinds of policies that have been devised to combat discrimination, quotas are the most despised. Almost no one has a good word to say about them. Yet the widget example suggests that, under certain circumstances, quotas can be defensible. Can a similar argument be constructed, not for choosing widgets, but for hiring people?

Suppose you are the dean of a college, and you are concerned that only the best-qualified scholars are hired for your faculty. You notice, however, that your philosophy department never hires any women. (They did hire one woman, years ago, so they have a token female. But that's as far as it has gone.) So you investigate. You discover that there are, indeed, lots of women philosophers looking for jobs each year. And you have no reason to think that these women are, on average, any less capable than their male colleagues. So you talk to the (male) chairperson of the department and you urge him to be careful to give full and fair consideration to the female applicants. Being a good liberal fellow, he finds this agreeable enough—although he may be a little offended by the suggestion that he is not already giving the women due consideration. But the talk has little apparent effect. Whenever candidates are being considered, he continues to report, with evident sincerity, that in the particular group under review a male has emerged as the best qualified. And so, he says each year, if we want to hire the best-qualified applicant we have to hire the male, at least this time.

This is repeated annually, with minor variations. One variation is that the best female philosopher in the pool may be listed as the department's top choice. But when, predictably enough, she turns out to be unavailable (having been snapped up by a more prestigious university), no women in the second tier are considered to be good alternatives. Here you notice a disturbing asymmetry: although the very best males are also going to other universities, the males in the second tier are considered good alternatives. Momentarily, then, you consider whether the problem could be that philosophical talent is distributed in a funny way: while the very best women are equal to the very best men, at the next level down, the men suddenly dominate. But that seems unlikely.

After further efforts have been made along these lines, without result, you might eventually conclude that there is an unconscious prejudice at work. Your department, despite its good intentions and its one female member, is biased. It isn't hard to understand why this could be so. In addition to the usual sources of prejudice against women—the stereotypes, the picture of women as less rational than men, and so forth—an all-male or mostly male group enjoys a kind of camaraderie that might seem impossible if females were significantly included. In choosing a new colleague, the matter of how someone would "fit in" with the existing group will always have some influence. This will work against females, no matter their talents as teachers and scholars.

Finally, then, you may conclude that the existing prejudice cannot be countered by any measure short of issuing a new instruction, and you tell the philosophy department that it must hire some additional women, in numbers at least in proportion to the number of women in the applicant pool. The reply, of course, will be that this policy could result in hiring a less qualified woman over a better qualified man. But the answer is the same as in the example about the widgets. You are not trying to give women a special break, any more than you were trying to give Albany widgets a special break. Nor are you trying to redress the injustices that women have suffered in the past; nor are you trying to provide "role models" for female students. You may be pleased if your policy has these effects, but the purpose of your policy is not to achieve them. Your only purpose is to get the best-qualified scholars for your faculty, regardless of their gender. The fact of unconscious prejudice makes the usual system of simply allowing your experts—the philosophy department—to exercise their judgment an imperfect system for accomplishing that purpose. Allowing them to exercise their judgment within the limits of a quota system, on the other hand, may be more effective, because it reduces the influence of unconscious prejudice.

It is sure to be objected that people are not widgets, and so the two cases are not analogous. But they do seem to be analogous in the relevant respects. The features of the widget example that justified imposing a quota were: (1) There was a selection process that involved human judgment. (2) The result of the process was that individuals from a certain group were regularly rated higher than members of another group. (3) There was no reason to think that the members of the former group were in fact better than the members of the latter group. (4) There was reason to think that the human beings who were judging these individuals might have been prejudiced against members of the latter group. The case of hiring women faculty also has these four features. That is what permits the construction of a similar argument.

This argument takes into account a feature of the selection process that is often ignored when quotas (or "affirmative action," or "reverse discrimination") are discussed. Often, the question is put like this: assuming that X is better qualified than Y, is it justifiable to adopt a policy that would permit hiring or promoting Y rather than X? Then various reasons are produced that might justify this, such as that a preferential policy redresses wrongs, or that it helps to combat racism or sexism. The debate then focuses on whether such reasons are sufficient. But when the issue is approached in this way, a critical point is overlooked. People do not come pre-labeled as better or worse qualified. Before we can say that X is better qualified than Y, someone has to have made that judgment. And this is where prejudice is most likely to enter the picture. A male philosopher, judging other philosophers, might very well rate women lower, without even realizing he is doing so. The argument we are considering is intended to address this problem, which arises before the terms of the conventional discussion are even set.

Of course, this argument does not purport to show that *any* system of quotas, applied in any circumstances, is fair. The argument is only a defense of quotas used in a certain way in certain circumstances. But the circumstances I have described are not uncommon. Actual quota systems, of the sort that have been established and tested in the courts during the past three decades, often have just this character: they are instituted to counter the prejudice, conscious or otherwise, that corrupts judgments of merit. Here is a real case that illustrates this.

In 1972 there were no blacks in the Alabama State Police. In the 37-year history of the force, there had never been any. Then the NAACP brought suit to end this vestige of segregation. They won their case in the trial court when federal district Judge Frank Johnson condemned what he termed a "blatant and continuous pattern and practice of discrimination." Judge Johnson did not, however, simply order the Alabama authorities to stop discriminating and start making their decisions impartially. He knew that such an order would be treated with amused contempt; the authorities would have been only too happy to continue as before, "impartially" finding that no blacks were qualified. So in order to prevent this and to ensure that the Alabamians could not avoid hiring qualified blacks, Johnson ordered that the state hire and promote one qualified black for every white trooper hired or promoted, until 25 percent of the force was black.

Judge Johnson's order was appealed to the Eleventh Circuit Court, where it was upheld. Time went by while the state was supposed to be carrying out his instructions. In 1984, twelve years later, the district court reviewed the situation to see what progress had been made. Forced by the court to do so, the department had hired some blacks. But virtually none had been promoted. The court found that, among the six majors on the force, none was black. Of the 25 captains, none was black. Of the 35 lieutenants, none was black. Of the 65 sergeants, none was black. Of the 66 corporals, however, there were four blacks. The court declared: "This is intolerable and must not continue."

The state of Alabama's last hope was the U.S. Supreme Court, which heard the case and rendered its decision in 1987. By a five-to-four vote, the Supreme Court upheld Judge Johnson's orders, and the *Birmingham News* ran a front-page story describing the "bitter feelings" of the white troopers, who viewed the ruling as a "setback." A spokesman for the Alabama Department of Public Safety assured the newspaper, "The department will comply with this ruling." It was clear enough from the official statements, however, that "complying with the ruling" would force the department to take steps—actually promoting blacks—that it would never take voluntarily.[4]

The Circumstances in Which Quotas Are Justified

The imposition of a quota may be justified as a way of countering the effects of prejudice. As I have said, this argument does not justify just any old quota. Our argument envisions the imposition of a quota as a corrective to a "normal" decision-making process that has gone wrong. For present purposes we may define a normal process as follows: (1) The goal of the process is to identify the best-qualified individuals for the purpose at hand. (2) The nature of the qualifications is specified. (3) A pool of candidates is assembled. (4) The qualifications of the individuals in the pool are assessed, using the specified criteria, and the individuals are ranked from best to worst. (5) The jobs, promotions, or whatever are awarded to the best-qualified individuals.

This process may go wrong in any number of ways, of course, some of them not involving prejudice. We are not concerned here with all the ways in which things can go wrong. We are concerned only with the following set of circumstances: First, we notice that, as the selection process is carried out, individuals from a certain group are regularly rated higher than members of another group. Second, we can find no reason to think that the members of the former group are in fact better than the members of the latter group; on the contrary, there is reason to think the members of the two groups are, on average, equally well qualified. And third, there is reason to think that the people performing the assessments are prejudiced against members of the latter group. These are the circumstances in which our argument says the imposition of a quota may be justified.

Even in these circumstances, however, the use of a quota does not eliminate human judgment, and so it does not guarantee that prejudice will disappear from the equation. Prejudice is eliminated from one part of the process, but it may reappear at a different point.

Consider again the male philosophy professors who always recommended the hiring of other males. In our example, the dean concluded that the male philosophers were prejudiced. In order to reach this conclusion, however, the dean had to make the judgment that female philosophers are equally as talented as males. (Otherwise, there would have been no grounds for thinking that the philosophy department's preference for hiring males was the result of bias.) An analogous judgment had to be made by Judge Johnson. He had to assume that black people were as qualified as whites for employment and promotion in the Alabama State Police. But prejudice can infect these general assessments just as it can influence the specific judgments that were being made by the philosophy professors and the highway patrol officials.

Therefore, our argument seems to require the assumption that some people—the hypothetical dean and, more to the point, actual federal court judges—are less prejudiced than others.

This assumption, however, seems correct. Some people are in fact less prejudiced than others; that is why prejudiced decisions can sometimes be successfully appealed. In general, people who are a step removed from a decision-making process are in a better position to be unbiased, or at least to recognize their biases and act to correct them, than those who are close to the "front lines." Part of the reason is that they have less at stake personally. The dean does not have to live in the philosophy department, and the judge does not have to work in the highway patrol. Another part of the reason is that in many instances the officials who impose the quotas are better educated and are more practiced in dealing with prejudice than those on whom the quotas are imposed. Judge Johnson was one of the most distinguished southern jurists with long experience in handling civil rights cases. The argument that I have presented does indeed assume that he was more capable of thinking objectively about what was going on, as well as about the likely qualifications of blacks, than the officials of the Alabama highway patrol. If that assumption is false, then our argument in defense of his action collapses. But I do not think that assumption is false.

Our argument has one other limitation that should be mentioned. It does not apply in the case of decisions made solely on the basis of "objective" criteria—test scores and the like—assuming, of course, that the tests really are objective and do not contain hidden bias. We can imagine procedures that, by using only such objective criteria, leave no room for the operation of prejudice. So in such cases the "normal" procedure will work well enough. The best-qualified will win out, and quotas will be unnecessary.

But such cases will be rare. Consider the range of cases that must be dealt with in the real world. Is there any decision procedure that a rational person would adopt for hiring teachers that would not disclose that an applicant for a teaching job was female? Should we be willing to hire teachers without an interview? Is there any imaginable multiple-choice test that one would be willing to use as the sole criterion for promotion in a police department? Would we want to eliminate the use of the assessments of those who have observed the officer's performance?

Moreover, it should also be remembered that so-called objective criteria often involve the use of tainted evidence. Suppose, in order to be perfectly impartial, I resolve to make a hiring decision using only objective criteria such as college grades. In this way I prevent any prejudices that I might have from coming into play. So far, so good. But the grades themselves were handed out by teachers whose prejudices could have come into play during the grading process.

Objections and Replies

The quota policy mandated by Judge Johnson continues to cause controversy. Newspaper columnist James J. Kilpatrick summed up the case against the judge's order succinctly. In the process of complying with the judge's ruling, he wrote, "white troopers with higher test scores and objectively better qualifications lost out. They themselves had engaged in no discrimination. They were the innocent victims of a remedial process addressed to blacks as a group. Were those whites denied equal protection of the law?"[5] These familiar objections are often taken to vitiate the whole idea of quotas as such. Do they undercut the argument presented here? In the time-honored way, we may consider these objections one by one.

Objection: People ought to be hired or promoted on the basis of their qualifications, and not on the basis of their race or sex. To give preference to a black merely because he is black, or to a woman merely because she is a woman, is no more defensible than to prefer a white man because he is white or male.

Reply: The whole point of the argument is that quotas may be justified as part of a plan to make sure that people are hired or promoted on the basis of their qualifications. The sort of policy that I have discussed does not involve hiring or promoting on the basis of race or gender, but only on the basis of qualifications. Quota policies are being defended, in some circumstances, because they are the most effective policies for achieving that goal.

Objection: The white male who is passed over is not responsible for the injustices that were done to blacks in the past; therefore it is unfair to make him pay the price for it. As Kilpatrick pointed out, the Alabama state troopers who were not promoted were not responsible for the injustices that were done to blacks, so why should they now be penalized?

Reply: Again, this misses the point. The argument does not envision the use of quotas as a response to past discrimination, but as a way of preventing, or at least minimizing, *present* discrimination. Sometimes people who defend the use of quotas or other such policies defend them as only temporary measures to be used reluctantly until racism and sexism have been eliminated. It may be agreed that if racist and sexist prejudice were eliminated, there would be no need for race- or gender-based quotas. But unfortunately, despite the progress that has been made, there is little reason to expect this to happen anytime soon.

Objection: To repeat the most obvious objection: Wouldn't there be some instances of injustice (i.e., instances in which a less well qualified individual is preferred to a better-qualified individual) under a policy of quotas that otherwise wouldn't occur? And isn't this inherently unfair?

Reply: Of course this will inevitably happen. But the question is whether there would be fewer injustices under this policy than under the alternative of "hiring strictly according to qualifications," which means, in practice, hiring according to assessments of qualifications made by biased judges. Some philosophers have also urged that it is not acceptable to treat someone unjustly for the purpose of preventing other injustices, but that point, even if it is correct, doesn't apply here. The choice here is between two policies neither of which is perfect and each of which would inevitably involve some injustices. The relevant question is, which policy would involve more?

Objection: Finally, there is an objection that will surely have occurred to many readers. If our argument were accepted, wouldn't it lead to all sorts of quotas—not only to quotas favoring blacks and women, but also to quotas favoring short people, for example? After all, as has been pointed out here, short people are also the victims of bias.

Reply: If it were possible to devise practical policies that would ensure fair treatment for short people, I can see no reason to object. However, I do not know whether there are particular circumstances in which quotas would be practicable and effective, so I do not know whether such a policy would be defensible. The problem is that prejudice against short people has never been perceived as a serious social issue; consequently it has received little study, and it is less well understood and its effects are less well documented than, say, racist or sexist prejudice. But I know of no reason to rule out in advance the adoption of policies that would counter this sort of bias.

This admission might be taken to show the absurdity of our argument. The very idea of quotas in favor of short people may seem so silly that if the argument leads to this, then the argument may be thought absurd. But why? One might well fear the intrusion of the heavy hand of government in still another area. Yet, if in fact short people are being treated unfairly—if they are singled out for unfavorable treatment because of an irrelevant characteristic—this seems, on its face, just as objectionable as any other form of discrimination and just as good a cause for corrective action. "Heightism" is not now a social issue. But it could become one.

In the meantime, those who have studied the subject have made some modest suggestions. John S. Gillis, the psychologist I quoted above, has made this form of prejudice his special concern. Here are a few of the things he proposes we do:[6] Employers should become aware of height bias and try to ensure that it does not influence personnel decisions. (The effects of such individual efforts might be small and imperfect, but they are better than nothing.) To help break the psychological connection between height and worth, we should avoid using the word "stature" to refer to status, caliber, and prestige. Teachers should stop the common practice of lining up schoolchildren according to height, which suggests to the children that this correlates with something important. Gillis also urges that metric measurements be used to indicate height. This, he says, would help to break "the mystique of the six-footer"—being 6 feet tall is perceived as a grand thing for a man, but being 183 centimeters tall doesn't have the same ring. These are all modest and reasonable proposals. The imposition of quotas in hiring and the like would be a much more drastic measure, which probably would not be wise until such time as heightism is established as a more pressing social concern.

NOTES

1. Elizabeth S. Haldane and G. R. T. Ross, *The Philosophical Works of Descartes* (New York: Dover Books, 1955), 1:81.

2. The following information is drawn from John S. Gillis, *Too Tall, Too Small* (Champaign, IL: Institute for Personality and Ability Testing, 1982).

3. Gillis, *Too Tall*, 125.

4. *Birmingham News,* 26 February 1987, sec. A, p. 1.

5. James J. Kilpatrick, "Reverse Discrimination Is Still Discrimination," *Birmingham News*, 5 November 1986, sec. A, p. 9.

6. Gillis, *Too Tall,* chap. 7.

GUNS, IMMIGRATION, AND TAXES

Chapter 24

Why Guns Shouldn't Be Outlawed

Michael Huemer

In this selection, Michael Huemer argues that a complete ban on gun ownership would violate the right that individuals have to self-protection. Such a right, he allows, might be overridden if a great enough good could be achieved through its violation; however, the good that could be had by outlawing firearms would always be limited by the fact that some people would defy the law and possess guns anyway.

The author's arguments, even if they are sound, do not address the question of how guns should be regulated, given that they are legal. The wisdom of background checks, waiting periods, minimum-age requirements, mandatory record-keeping, and the banning of large-capacity magazines, for example, will have to be assessed separately.

[I will address] the two most important arguments concerning the simplest and most extreme form of gun control, which would be a complete ban on private gun ownership. The first argument is that gun prohibition would violate the right of individuals to protect themselves. The second argument is that gun prohibition will fail because criminals will disregard the law.

Michael Huemer, "Why Guns Shouldn't Be Outlawed: Two Problems of Prohibition" in *The Critique*, July/August 2016. Copyright © 2016. Used with permission of the author.

THE RIGHT TO SELF-DEFENSE

The rights of the individual often seem lost in gun policy debate, as in most policy debates—we ask "what is good for society?" but we rarely ask "what does the individual have a right to?" At the same time, we tend to ignore the factual situation of people different from ourselves, so that when asked what is best for society, we answer based on our personal circumstances, or even on the imagined circumstances of an ideal society.

I, for example, live in an incredibly safe place; I hardly need a gun. Perhaps you, reader, are in a similar situation. If so, you might be inclined to think, "No one needs a gun." But it isn't true. *I* need never walk home on streets where I fear for my life. But *many* Americans live in places where they fear for their own safety, and are completely justified in that fear. Many more have abusive lovers, ex-husbands, or other people in their lives who have beaten them or threatened them with violence. And many believe—again, with complete justification—that the government cannot or will not protect them.

Consider the case of Ruth Bunnell, who in 1972 called the San Jose Police Department to report that her estranged husband had just told her that he was coming over to her house to murder her. She requested immediate police aid, but the police refused to help, instructing her instead to call back when her husband arrived. When he arrived forty-five minutes later, she was unable to call back because the husband immediately stabbed her to death.

My point in relating this case is not the usual one; my point is not simply that Bunnell could have defended herself with a gun. My point concerns what happened after the murder. John Hartzler, the administrator of Ruth Bunnell's estate, brought a lawsuit against the city for failing to protect her. In tort law, there are four conditions for a valid civil claim: (i) the defendant must have had some duty to the plaintiff; (ii) the defendant must have breached that duty; (iii) the plaintiff must have suffered a harm; (iv) the breach of duty must have caused the harm. On this basis, you might assume that Hartzler had an open-and-shut case: surely the police were duty bound to respond to Bunnell's plea for protection; surely their failure to do so caused her death.

You would be mistaken. The court dismissed the suit without a trial. Hartzler appealed, but the appellate court affirmed the dismissal. No one disputed that Bunnell had suffered a tragic harm caused by the police's refusal to protect her. The city simply claimed that they *never had any duty to protect* Ruth Bunnell in the first place—and the court agreed. Nor was this an idiosyncratic decision; U.S. courts have consistently held to the theory that the government only has an obligation to "society" in general, to provide a general deterrent to crime—not an obligation to any individual.

My point: individuals have a right to protect themselves. I would say this even if the government had promised to protect all of us, but I think the point is especially clear given that they have not. Having refused to accept any obligation to protect you, the government cannot justly turn around and prohibit you from taking reasonable and effective measures for your own defense. For many Americans, that means a gun. Studies of defensive gun uses consistently find that gun use decreases one's chance of being injured by a criminal, compared with other methods of self-protection.[1]

. . . Imagine that a killer has broken into a house where his intended victim lies in bed. The victim has a gun, which he would use to defend himself against the killer. Unfortunately, however, the killer has an accomplice in the house. As the victim reaches for his gun, the accomplice grabs it first and runs away with it. As a result, the killer is then able to stab the victim to death. In this scenario, the killer is guilty of murder. What about the accomplice?

The accomplice's action was less bad than that of the killer; nevertheless, it was extremely wrong. By taking away the victim's means of self-defense, he violated the victim's rights in an extremely serious way and became responsible (in addition to the killer) for the victim's death. Just so, when the state deprives individuals of weapons, it can predict that some individuals will suffer murder, rape, or other serious crimes that would have been prevented if the victims had the means to defend themselves. By coercively interfering in individuals' self-defense efforts, the state becomes partly responsible (in addition to the criminals themselves) for their victimization—the state in effect becomes an accomplice to those crimes. Failing to protect people is one thing; actively intervening to stop them from protecting themselves is much worse.

Just as it would be wrong for the state to murder a certain number of innocent individuals, it is also wrong for the state to be an accomplice in their murders. This is true even if the state has reason to believe that a greater overall benefit to society would be attained. One may not, for example, murder an innocent person, even if your doing so somehow stops someone else from murdering two other innocent people. (May you murder an innocent person to prevent a *thousand* other murders? Perhaps—but that is not what is at issue here. By most accounts, the number of crimes prevented by guns is comparable to the number caused by guns.[2])

Thus, consider a famous hypothetical from the ethics literature: suppose a defendant is on trial for a crime that has caused great public outrage. If no one is punished, there will be riots, during which several innocent people will most likely be unjustly injured or killed. The jury, however, realizes that the defendant is factually innocent. Should they convict anyway—thus sacrificing the one innocent defendant to save several other innocent people from being harmed by the riots? Almost everyone answers "no" to this question. The reason seems to be that to do so would violate the rights of the one individual, and one may not do this, even to prevent other people from committing several other rights-violations.

I gave this argument in 2003. Since then, I have seen one printed response to it. It was from (anti-gun) philosopher Jeff McMahan in a 2012 editorial:

> Imposing a ban on guns, [gun rights advocates] argue, would be tanta-mount to taking a person's gun from her just as someone is about to kill her. But this is a defective analogy. [. . .] Guns are only one means of self-defense and self-defense is only one means of achieving security against attack. It is the right to security against attack that is fundamental. A policy that unavoidably deprives a person of one means of self-defense but on balance substantially reduces her vulnerability to attack is there-fore respectful of the more fundamental right from which the right of self-defense is derived.[3]

I see two ways of understanding McMahan's argument: (1) Perhaps McMahan is arguing that, even if gun prohibition causes some people to be victimized who otherwise would have defended themselves, it still decreases the total number of victimizations that occur, and therefore it is not a violation of anyone's right to security. But of course, this would just miss the central point. This would be analogous to claiming, in the example above, that punishing the innocent defendant is permissible because it will decrease the total number of rights-violations.

(2) More likely, what McMahan means is this: a ban on guns will not just increase the overall level of security for society, but will actually

increase security for *every individual*. And since the right to security is the only relevant right at stake here, the gun ban will not violate anyone's rights. If that is the argument, it is factually false. McMahan may believe that individuals only need guns because others have guns—but that just isn't the case. Take the case of the woman whose estranged husband has threatened to kill her. He has beaten her in the past—not with a gun, with his fists. If he attempts to kill her, and neither of them has a gun, he will most likely kill her. She needs a gun to defend herself. She doesn't need it because he has a gun; she needs it because he outweighs her by fifty pounds, because he might have a knife, because she doesn't know how to fight.

Or take the case of the man who has to walk home through gang territory at night. If he is accosted by a gang, he will not successfully defend himself with a knife, or a can of mace, or a phone. He needs a gun. Again, he doesn't need it because the gang has guns; if no one has a gun, the gang is going to be able to do whatever they want.

The reader will appreciate that these are hardly outlandish scenarios. These are precisely the sort of situations that make people want a gun for self-defense. Now, suppose the woman with the violent husband turns up at a gun store. And suppose they send her away, because a new law has just been passed that says only government agents are allowed to buy guns. How is she made safer by this? I am not asking how society might be made safer. I am asking about *that individual*, who went to buy a gun to protect herself—she was not worried about gun violence in society, she was worried about her abusive husband. So how is *she* more secure?

Now suppose she decides to buy a gun anyway. She gets it on the black market, as it would be in a gun prohibition regime. But the police catch her, and she is prosecuted for an illegal gun purchase. In court, she tries to explain her reasons for the purchase—she had no desire to hurt anyone, but she had to protect herself. The police could not protect her and didn't even claim that they could. These explanations are rejected in court (as they surely would be), because "the desire to protect oneself" is not accepted under the anti-gun law as a valid excuse for buying a gun, and thus the woman is sent to jail. Is this a just outcome? Could we in good conscience claim that at no point in this story were anyone's rights violated; at no point was an innocent person sacrificed for the sake of others?

If you say frankly that we *should* sacrifice innocent individuals whenever doing so is better for society, that is a position I can at least understand. And if you are also willing to say that the jury in the earlier example in fact *should* convict the innocent defendant to prevent the riots, then you have a consistent position. But even then, it is far from clear that gun prohibition will achieve its stated aim—which brings us to the other major problem with prohibition.

THE COMPLIANCE PROBLEM

Many confuse the question, "Would it be good for everyone to give up their guns?" with the question, "Would it be good to have *a law that says* everyone has to give up their guns?" These are two very different questions—for what the law prescribes is not the same as what actually happens.

Most people can appreciate this point for at least some issues. For example, the drug war. It is illegal to buy or sell marijuana, cocaine, heroin, or any of a variety of other recreational drugs. That does not mean that people do not buy and sell drugs. What it means is that they are bought and sold on the black market. It does not mean that you cannot get hold of cocaine if you want it; it means that you must buy it from criminals at high prices. It also means that the state will not enforce agreements between drug sellers and buyers, so if you feel cheated, you must enforce your rights yourself. This is why the drug trade is so prone to violence. Granted, society would be better if everyone gave up using drugs. That does not mean that society is better for having laws against using drugs.

The same was true of alcohol during the Prohibition era: massive noncompliance, expansion of organized crime, a violence-prone black market. Much the same has been true of prostitution for as long as it has been proscribed. The same will be true of guns during America's gun prohibition era, if that era ever arrives. Some Americans will give up their weapons—but many will not. America is not England; guns play practically no role in British culture, but America, for better or worse, is another matter entirely. Many Americans love guns, which is why the country now has about 270 million guns, with an adult population of only 247 million.[4] About a third of households contain at least one gun.[5] And guns are durable; a hundred-year-old gun may still be perfectly functional. So even if we completely stop producing them right now, America's gun stock is not going to run dry during this century. However you feel about America's gun culture, it is a fact that has to be contended with. Pretending that people do whatever the law says has not given us a successful drug policy; it won't give us a successful gun policy either.

The question to ask about a proposed law is never, "Would it be good if everyone followed this law?" The question is always, "Will things be better when those who are most likely to follow this law follow it, and those who can be expected to break it break it?"

There are two kinds of gun owners: criminal gun owners and noncriminal owners. Criminals (and prospective criminals) own a gun for purposes of robbing, threatening, or killing others (perhaps in addition to noncriminal purposes); noncriminal owners own a gun for purposes of self-protection, hunting, or other recreation. The ideal situation would be to disarm all the criminals, while leaving the noncriminal citizens armed. But that option is not available. In the event that private gun ownership were outlawed, who would actually be most likely to follow the law, and who would be most likely to break it?

The group most likely to follow the law would be those who own a gun for self-defense or recreation. The group most likely to break the law would be those who own a gun for criminal purposes. Why? Criminals, to put it lightly, have a lesser average level of respect for law than the rest of us. A man who is prepared to commit armed robbery or murder is unlikely to pause at the thought of committing a misdemeanor gun law violation. Therefore, restrictive gun laws affect innocent citizens much more than they affect criminals. Criminals may even welcome more restrictive gun laws: surveys show that criminals in America are more afraid of encountering armed victims than they are of encountering the police (and wisely so).[6] Restrictive gun laws help criminals by reducing their chances of encountering armed victims. In other words, they tend to have approximately the opposite of their intended effect.

The popular version of this argument is well known: "If guns are outlawed, only outlaws will have guns." This is an old argument, and gun control advocates are ready for it. Their response: it isn't only the criminals we have to worry about. It is *ordinary citizens* we should worry about. Gun control proponents fear that a perfectly normal, noncriminal person with access to a gun may one day, in the heat of argument with a neighbor or family member, suddenly "snap" and shoot the other party. To support this fear, they cite statistics about the number of murder victims who were killed by someone they knew, or the number of murders that occur after a heated argument.

This argument is a logical and empirical error. When we hear that most murder victims were killed by a family member *or someone they knew*, this does not imply that they were killed by a normal person as a result of a simple disagreement of the sort that anyone could find themselves in. Remember that the category "someone known to the victim" includes such people as the victim's drug dealer, the victim's pimp, one of the victim's fellow gang members, the victim's partner in crime. Most homicides are committed by people with prior criminal records, and they are overwhelmingly committed *against other criminals.*[7] Many are gang-related or drug-related.[8] It isn't Aunt Sally shooting Uncle Ted in an argument over the phone bill. Even the minority of cases that involve a spouse or family member of the killer do little to support the contention that it is ordinary citizens we need to worry about, rather than criminals. Criminals have acquaintances and family members too. Not surprisingly, people who have a criminal way of life—drug dealers, gang leaders, and so on—are also prone to commit crimes against their own family members, spouses, and so on. This does not show that *ordinary* people are in danger of shooting their family if they have access to a gun.

For a reality check, ask yourself how often you have seen a normal adult (say, one with no criminal record) punch a friend, acquaintance, or family member in the face as a result of a disagreement. Now consider how much stronger the inhibitions must be against *murder* than against simple punching, in the mind of a normal adult in our society. Normal people do not kill others because of a family squabble. Criminals with antisocial personality traits and poor impulse control may do so—but they are also the people least likely to actually obey restrictive gun laws.

Gun control advocates believe our society would be safer if no one had guns. Perhaps so—but that is not the relevant question. The question is whether our society would be safer if the people with the greatest disposition to follow the law gave up their weapons, and the people with the least inclination to obey the law kept theirs.

CONCLUSION

To summarize the main line of reasoning:

Premise 1: It is permissible to violate an individual's rights only if, at minimum, doing so prevents harms many times greater than the harm it causes to that individual.

Comment: This is supported by the example of the jury convicting the innocent man to prevent riots. There are many similar examples. Some believe, in fact, that it is *never* permissible to violate certain rights; that view is compatible with (but stronger than) premise 1. Premise 1 only rules out that a rights violation could be justified by its preventing harms only modestly greater than the harms it causes—and this is something that any believer in rights accepts.

Premise 2: Gun prohibition violates the self-defense rights of individuals, causing some of them to be seriously harmed or killed.

Comment: The claim that gun prohibition will result in some citizens being harmed or killed is an uncontroversial empirical claim; many surveys show that self-defense uses of firearms are very common in the United States. The claim that gun prohibition would be a *rights violation* is supported by the example of the accomplice who seizes a victim's gun just before a murderer kills the victim.

Intermediate conclusion: Gun prohibition is permissible only if, at minimum, it prevents harms many times greater than the harms it causes.

Premise 3: Gun prohibition will not prevent much greater harm than it causes.

Comment: There is a great deal of complex and mixed data on this that cannot be reviewed here. Here, I have focused on one main point: that in America, gun prohibition is not likely to succeed in keeping guns out of the hands of criminals; its largest effect will be on the behavior of innocent citizens. Thus, whether gun prohibition would even prevent more harm than it caused is at best unknown; it cannot reasonably be claimed that it would prevent many times more harm than it caused.

Conclusion: Gun prohibition is impermissible.

NOTES

1. Committee on Priorities for a Public Health Research Agenda to Reduce the Threat of Firearm-Related Violence, *Priorities for Research to Reduce the Threat of Firearm-Related Violence* (Washington, D.C.: National Academies Press, 2013), pp. 15–16, http://www.nap.edu/download.php?record_id=18319.

2. Committee on Priorities, op. cit., p. 15.

3. "Why Gun 'Control' Is Not Enough," *New York Times* (Dec. 19, 2012), http://opinionator.blogs.nytimes.com/2012/12/19/why-gun-control-is-not-enough/.

4. Madeleine Morgenstern, "How Many People Own Guns in America? And Is Gun Ownership Actually Declining?" *The Blaze* (Mar. 19, 2013), http://www.theblaze.com/stories/2013/03/19/how-many-people-own-guns-in-america-and-is-gun-ownership-actually-declining/; U.S. Census Bureau, "Quick Facts: United States," https://www.census.gov/quickfacts/table/PST0 45215/00.

5. CBS News, "Number of households with guns on the decline, study shows," Mar. 10, 2015, http://www.cbsnews.com/news/number-of-househ olds-with-guns-on-the-decline-study-shows/.

6. James D. Wright and Peter H. Rossi, *Armed and Considered Dangerous: A Survey of Felons and Their Firearms* (Hawthorne, NY: Aldine de Gruyter, 1986), pp. 144–46.

7. Michael Thompson, "Most Murder Victims in Big Cities Have Criminal Record," WorldNetDaily (Mar. 4, 2013), http://www.wnd.com/2013/03/most-murder-victims-in-big-cities-have-criminal-record/.

8. Marcus Hawkins, "Putting Gun Death Statistics in Perspective," *About. com* (Aug. 1, 2015), http://usconservatives.about.com/od/capitalpunishment/a /Putting-Gun-Death-Statistics-In-Perspective.htm.

Chapter 25

The Case for Open Immigration

Michael Huemer

Strangely absent from the American debate on immigration is a discussion of whether our borders should be closed at all. In this selection, Michael Huemer argues that keeping people out harms them unjustly and amounts to discrimination.

Michael Huemer is professor of philosophy at the University of Colorado at Boulder. His books include *Ethical Intuitionism* (2005) and *The Problem of Political Authority* (2013).

According to government estimates, 11 million people presently reside in the United States illegally. This number is up 27 percent since 2000. What should be done about this apparent problem? Demands that the government "secure the border" are increasingly prominent, with many calling on other states to follow Arizona's lead.

I have a different proposal: America should open the border, and grant amnesty to the 11 million undocumented residents. My argument is not that immigration benefits America, though that is true. My argument is that U.S. immigration policy is fundamentally unjust. It disregards the rights and interests of other human beings, merely because those persons were born in another country. It coercively imposes clear and serious harms on some people, for the sake of relatively minor

Michael Huemer, "Opinion: The Case for Open Immigration" in *The Boulder Daily Camera*, June 6, 2010. Copyright © 2010. Used with permission of the author.

or dubious benefits for others who happened to have been born in the right geographical area. The question Americans should be asking is not "What is best for current citizens?" but "What right do we have to exclude others from the same freedom and opportunity that we were given by an accident of birth?"

My premises are simple. First: it is wrong to knowingly impose severe harms on others, by force, without having a good reason for doing so. This principle holds regardless of where one's victims were born or presently reside.

Second, the U.S. government, in restricting immigration, knowingly and coercively imposes severe harms on millions of human beings. Consider a simple analogy. Marvin is desperately hungry and plans to travel to a nearby marketplace to buy food. Sam intentionally stops Marvin and coercively prevents him from reaching the marketplace, knowing that this will prevent Marvin from obtaining food. Sam did not cause Marvin to be hungry to begin with. But when he coercively intervenes to stop Marvin from obtaining food, Sam becomes responsible for what results. If Marvin dies of starvation, Sam will be responsible for the death.

That is the behavior of the U.S. government. The government hires armed guards to stop people from crossing the border, and to forcibly expel those who are found residing in the country without permission. The U.S. government knows, when it does this, that many of these would-be immigrants will suffer severe poverty, oppression, and greatly diminished life prospects as a result. The government is therefore responsible for these consequences, just as Sam would be responsible for Marvin's starvation.

Third, the U.S. government has no good reason for imposing such harms on potential immigrants. Immigration restrictions are typically defended by the claim that immigrants "steal American jobs" or dilute American culture. Now consider this analogy. After stopping Marvin from reaching the marketplace and thus causing Marvin to starve, suppose that Sam tries to defend his action by saying that it was necessary to prevent Marvin from competing with other buyers in the marketplace and thus driving up the price of bread. Or suppose Sam argues that his action was justified because Marvin has a different culture from most of the people already in the marketplace. Surely these justifications would not succeed. The desire to limit marketplace competition or cultural influence is not normally an adequate reason for coercively imposing serious harms on other people.

From these three premises, it follows that U.S. immigration policy is morally wrong. This typically goes unnoticed in the immigration debate, because most Americans are prejudiced against foreigners, in the same way that we were once prejudiced against blacks. No one today would dream of arguing that the government should stop white people from hiring blacks, so that blacks don't "steal white jobs." But we are not bothered by the prejudice displayed in arguing that the government needs to stop Americans from hiring foreign-born people so that the foreign-born don't "steal American jobs." This can only be because prejudice based on nationality has outlived prejudice based on race. But neither attitude is morally defensible.

Chapter 26

Is Taxation Theft?

Michael Huemer

According to the old cliché, only two things in life are certain: death and taxes. Does the fact that we regard taxes as inevitable—as an unavoidable part of life—make it hard for us to see that taxation is a form of theft? In this selection, Professor Michael Huemer argues that if the government is going to be justified in seizing our money each April, then they need especially good reasons for doing so, just as a person would need good reasons for doing the same thing.

1. WHY TAXATION MIGHT BE A FORM OF THEFT

Imagine that I have founded a charity organization that helps the poor.[1] But not enough people are voluntarily contributing to my charity, so many of the poor remain hungry. I decide to solve the problem by approaching well-off people on the street, pointing a gun at them, and demanding their money. I funnel the money into my charity, and the poor are fed and clothed at last.

Michael Huemer, "Is Taxation Theft?" in *Libertarianism*, March 16, 2017. Copyright © 2017. Used with permission. Originally published at Libertarianism.org.

In this scenario, I would be called a thief. Why? The answer seems to be: because I am *taking other people's property without their consent.* The italicized phrase just seems to be what "theft" means. "Taking without consent" includes taking by means of a threat of force issued against other people, as in this example. This fact is not altered by what I do with the money after taking it. You wouldn't say, "Oh, you gave the money to the poor? In that case, taking people's property without consent *wasn't* theft after all." No; you might claim that it was a socially beneficial theft, but it was still a theft.

Now compare the case of taxation. When the government "taxes" citizens, what this means is that the government demands money from each citizen, under a threat of force: if you do not pay, armed agents hired by the government will take you away and lock you in a cage. This looks like about as clear a case as any of taking people's property without consent. So the government is a thief. This conclusion is not changed by the fact that the government uses the money for a good cause (if it does so). That might make taxation a socially beneficial kind of theft, but it is still theft.

2. THREE COUNTER-ARGUMENTS

Most people are reluctant to call taxation theft. How might one avoid saying this? Following are three arguments one might try, together with the most obvious responses.

First Argument

Taxation is not theft, because citizens have agreed *to pay taxes. This is part of the "social contract," which is a kind of agreement between citizens and the government, whereby the citizens agree to pay taxes and obey the laws, in return for the government's protection. By using government services (such as roads, schools, and police), and remaining present in the government's territory, you indicate that you accept the social contract.*[2]

Reply to First Argument

There simply isn't any such contract.[3] The government has never actually written up and offered such a contract, nor has anyone signed it.

Still, the use of government services might imply agreement to pay for those services *if* people who didn't use the services were not required to pay. But in fact, the government forces citizens to pay taxes regardless of whether they use government services or not. Therefore, the fact that you use government services does not indicate anything about whether you agree to pay taxes.

Remaining present in "the government's territory" also does not indicate agreement to the putative social contract. This is because the government does not in fact own all the land that it claims as "its territory"; this land is, rather, mainly owned by private individuals. If I own some land that other people are using, I can demand that the other people either pay me money or vacate my land. But if I see some people on *their* land, I cannot demand that they either pay me money or vacate their own land. If I do that, I am a thief. Similarly, when the government demands that we either pay it money or vacate our own land, the government acts as a thief.

Second Argument

The government can't be a thief, because it is the government that defines property rights through its laws. The government can simply make laws that say that the money you are supposed to pay in taxes isn't really yours in the first place; it is the government's money.[4]

Reply to Second Argument

The Second Argument turns on the claims (i) that there are no property rights independent of government laws, and (ii) that the government can create property rights simply by declaring that something belongs to someone. There is no obvious reason to believe either (i) or (ii), and both claims are counterintuitive.

Imagine that you travel to a remote region outside any government's jurisdiction, where you find a hermit living off the land. The hermit hunts with a spear of his own making, which you find interesting. You decide (without the hermit's consent) to take the spear with you when you leave. It would seem correct to say that you "stole" the spear. This shows the implausibility of (i).

Next, imagine that you are a slave in the nineteenth-century American South. Suppose you decide to escape from your master without your master's consent. If (ii) is true, then you would be *violating your master's rights* by *stealing* yourself. Note that you would not merely be violating a *legal* right; if (ii) is true, the government creates moral rights and obligations through its laws, so you would be violating your master's *moral* rights. This shows the implausibility of (ii).

Third Argument

Taxes are just the price the government charges for providing law and order. Without taxation, the government would collapse, then all social order would break down, and then you wouldn't have any money at all. Taxation is unlike theft because thieves do not provide valuable services, let alone services that enable you to make the very money that they are taking a portion of.[5]

Reply to Third Argument

Imagine that I hold you up at gunpoint and take $20 from you. I also leave one of my books behind in exchange. When you see me later without my gun, you call me a thief and demand your money back. "Oh no," I say, "I am no thief, for I gave you something valuable in exchange. True, you never *asked* for the book, but it's a good book, worth much more than $20."

This reply on my part would be confused. It doesn't matter that I gave you a good in exchange, and it doesn't matter whether the book is really worth more than $20. What matters is that I took your money without your consent.

It also does not matter if you benefit greatly from the book. Suppose that (unable to convince me to take it back) you wind up reading my book, which turns out to contain such useful advice that you end up much better off (including *financially* better off) than before I came along. None of this changes the fact that I am a thief. The temporal order also does not matter: if I give you the unsolicited book first, then wait for you to profit from it financially, and *then* forcibly take away some of the money you earned, I will still be a thief.

The lesson: Taking people's property without consent is theft, even if you also benefit them, and even if you helped them obtain that same property.

3. SO WHAT IF TAXATION IS THEFT?

If taxation is theft, does it follow that we must abolish all taxation? Not necessarily. Some thefts might be justified. If you have to steal a loaf of bread to survive, then you are justified in doing so. Similarly, the government might be justified in taxing if this is necessary to prevent some terrible outcome, such as a breakdown of social order.

Why, then, does it matter whether taxation is theft? Because although theft *can* be justified, it is *usually* unjustified. It is wrong to steal without having a very good reason. What count as good enough reasons is beyond the scope of this short article. But as an example, you are not justified in stealing money, say, so that you can buy a nice painting for your wall. Similarly, if taxation is theft, then it would probably be wrong to tax people, say, to pay for an art museum.

In other words, the "taxation is theft" thesis has the effect of *raising the standards* for justified use of taxes. When the government plans to spend money on something (support for the arts, a space program, a national retirement program, and so on), one should ask: would it be permissible to steal from people in order to run this sort of program? If not, then it is not permissible to *tax* people in order to run the program, since taxation is theft.

NOTES

1. This example is from Michael Huemer, *The Problem of Political Authority* (New York: Palgrave Macmillan, 2013), pp. 3–4, 154.

2. See John Locke, *Second Treatise of Government*, ed. C. B. Macpherson (Indianapolis, IN: Hackett, 1980; originally published 1690), esp. sections 120–21.

3. The problems with the social contract theory are explained in detail in Huemer, *The Problem of Political Authority*, ch. 2.

4. See Liam Murphy and Thomas Nagel, *The Myth of Ownership: Taxes and Justice* (Oxford: Oxford University Press, 2002), p. 58.

5. See Murphy and Nagel, op. cit., pp. 32–33; Stephen Holmes and Cass Sunstein, *The Cost of Rights: Why Liberty Depends on Taxes* (New York: W.W. Norton, 1999), ch. 3. For a more elaborate reply, see Michael Huemer, "Is Wealth Redistribution a Rights Violation?" in *The Routledge Handbook of Libertarianism*, ed. Jason Brennan, David Schmidtz, and Bas van der Vossen (New York: Routledge, 2017).

ANIMALS

Chapter 27

All Animals Are Equal

Peter Singer

Peter Singer has written about assisted reproduction, animal rights, abortion, infanticide, the environment, and famine relief. Because of his controversial beliefs, Singer's appointment to Princeton University in 1999 created a public uproar reminiscent of 1940, when the City College of New York appointed Bertrand Russell, one of the twentieth century's greatest philosophers, to a one-year professorship. In Russell's case, the outcry culminated in a judge's ruling that canceled the state university's appointment. Commenting on the case, Albert Einstein said, "Great spirits have always found violent opposition from mediocrities." Since Princeton is a private university, Singer's ordeal stayed out of the courts.

The treatment of nonhuman animals has traditionally been regarded as a trivial matter. Until recently, almost every ethicist who wrote on the subject provided some rationale for excluding animals from moral concern. Aristotle said that, in the natural order of things, animals exist to serve human purposes. The Christian tradition added that man alone is made in God's image and that animals do not have souls. Immanuel Kant said that animals are not self-conscious, so we can have no duties to them.

The utilitarians took a different view, holding that we should consider the interests of all beings, human and nonhuman. Peter Singer (1946–) took up this argument in the mid-1970s.

Today, Professor Singer splits his time between Princeton University in the United States and Melbourne University in Australia.

"Animal Liberation" may sound more like a parody of other liberation movements than a serious objective. The idea of "The Rights of Animals" actually was once used to parody the case for women's rights. When Mary Wollstonecraft, a forerunner of today's feminists, published her *Vindication of the Rights of Woman* in 1792, her views were widely regarded as absurd, and before long an anonymous publication appeared entitled *A Vindication of the Rights of Brutes*. The author of this satirical work (now known to have been Thomas Taylor, a distinguished Cambridge philosopher) tried to refute Mary Wollstonecraft's arguments by showing that they could be carried one stage further. If the argument for equality was sound when applied to women, why should it not be applied to dogs, cats, and horses? The reasoning seemed to hold for these "brutes" too; yet to hold that brutes had rights was manifestly absurd. Therefore the reasoning by which this conclusion had been reached must be unsound, and if unsound when applied to brutes, it must also be unsound when applied to women, since the very same arguments had been used in each case.

In order to explain the basis of the case for the equality of animals, it will be helpful to start with an examination of the case for the equality of women. Let us assume that we wish to defend the case for women's rights against the attack by Thomas Taylor. How should we reply?

One way in which we might reply is by saying that the case for equality between men and women cannot validly be extended to nonhuman animals. Women have a right to vote, for instance, because they are just as capable of making rational decisions about the future as men are; dogs, on the other hand, are incapable of understanding the significance of voting, so they cannot have the right to vote. There are many other obvious ways in which men and women resemble each other closely, while humans and animals differ greatly. So, it might be said, men and women are similar beings and should have similar rights, while humans and nonhumans are different and should not have equal rights.

The reasoning behind this reply to Taylor's analogy is correct up to a point, but it does not go far enough. There are obviously important differences between humans and other animals, and these differences must give rise to some differences in the rights that each have. Recognizing this evident fact, however, is no barrier to the case for extending the basic principle of equality to nonhuman animals. The differences that exist between men and women are equally undeniable, and the supporters of Women's Liberation are aware that these differences may give rise to different rights. Many feminists hold that women have the right to an abortion on request. It does not follow that since these same feminists are campaigning for equality between men and women they must support the right of men to have abortions too. Since a man cannot have an abortion, it is meaningless to talk of his right to have one. Since dogs can't vote, it is meaningless to talk of their right to vote. There is no reason why either Women's Liberation or Animal Liberation should get involved in such nonsense. The extension of the basic principle of equality from one group to another does not imply that we must treat both groups in exactly the same way, or grant exactly the same rights to both groups. Whether we should do so will depend on the nature of the members of the two groups. The basic principle of equality does not require equal or identical *treatment*; it requires equal consideration. Equal consideration for different beings may lead to different treatment and different rights.

So there is a different way of replying to Taylor's attempt to parody the case for women's rights, a way that does not deny the obvious differences between human beings and nonhumans but goes more deeply into the question of equality and concludes by finding nothing absurd in the idea that the basic principle of equality applies to so-called brutes. At this point such a conclusion may appear odd; but if we examine more deeply the basis on which our opposition to discrimination on grounds of race or sex ultimately rests, we will see that we would be on shaky ground if we were to demand equality for blacks, women, and other groups of oppressed humans while denying equal consideration to nonhumans. To make this clear we need to see, first, exactly why racism and sexism are wrong. When we say that all human beings, whatever their race, creed, or sex, are equal, what is it that we are asserting? Those who wish to defend hierarchical, inegalitarian societies have often pointed out that by whatever test we choose it simply is not true that all humans are equal. Like it or not we must face the fact

that humans come in different shapes and sizes; they come with different moral capacities, different intellectual abilities, different amounts of
benevolent feeling and sensitivity to the needs of others, different abilities to communicate effectively, and different capacities to experience
pleasure and pain. In short, if the demand for equality were based on the
actual equality of all human beings, we would have to stop demanding
equality.

Still, one might cling to the view that the demand for equality among
human beings is based on the actual equality of the different races and
sexes. Although, it may be said, humans differ as individuals, there
are no differences between the races and sexes as such. From the mere
fact that a person is black or a woman we cannot infer anything about
that person's intellectual or moral capacities. This, it may be said, is
why racism and sexism are wrong. The white racist claims that whites
are superior to blacks, but this is false; although there are differences
among individuals, some blacks are superior to some whites in all of
the capacities and abilities that could conceivably be relevant. The
opponent of sexism would say the same: a person's sex is no guide to
his or her abilities, and this is why it is unjustifiable to discriminate on
the basis of sex.

The existence of individual variations that cut across the lines of
race or sex, however, provides us with no defense at all against a more
sophisticated opponent of equality, one who proposes that, say, the
interests of all those with IQ scores below 100 be given less consideration than the interests of those with ratings over 100. Perhaps those
scoring below the mark would, in this society, be made the slaves of
those scoring higher. Would a hierarchical society of this sort really
be so much better than one based on race or sex? I think not. But if
we tie the moral principle of equality to the factual equality of the different races or sexes, taken as a whole, our opposition to racism and
sexism does not provide us with any basis for objecting to this kind of
inegalitarianism.

There is a second important reason why we ought not to base our
opposition to racism and sexism on any kind of factual equality, even
the limited kind that asserts that variations in capacities and abilities are
spread evenly among the different races and between the sexes: we can
have no absolute guarantee that these capacities and abilities really are
distributed evenly, without regard to race or sex, among human beings.
So far as actual abilities are concerned there do seem to be certain

measurable differences both among races and between sexes. These differences do not, of course, appear in every case, but only when averages are taken. More important still, we do not yet know how many of these differences are really due to the different genetic endowments of the different races and sexes, and how many are due to poor schools, poor housing, and other factors that are the result of past and continuing discrimination. Perhaps all of the important differences will eventually prove to be environmental rather than genetic. Anyone opposed to racism and sexism will certainly hope that this will be so, for it will make the task of ending discrimination a lot easier; nevertheless, it would be dangerous to rest the case against racism and sexism on the belief that all significant differences are environmental in origin. The opponent of, say, racism who takes this line will be unable to avoid conceding that if differences in ability did after all prove to have some genetic connection with race, racism would in some way be defensible.

Fortunately there is no need to pin the case for equality to one particular outcome of a scientific investigation. The appropriate response to those who claim to have found evidence of genetically based differences in ability among the races or between the sexes is not to stick to the belief that the genetic explanation must be wrong, whatever evidence to the contrary may turn up; instead we should make it quite clear that the claim to equality does not depend on intelligence, moral capacity, physical strength, or similar matters of fact. Equality is a moral idea, not an assertion of fact. There is no logically compelling reason for assuming that a factual difference in ability between two people justifies any difference in the amount of consideration we give to their needs and interests. *The principle of the equality of human beings is not a description of an alleged actual equality among humans: it is a prescription of how we should treat human beings.*

Jeremy Bentham, the founder of the reforming utilitarian school of moral philosophy, incorporated the essential basis of moral equality into his system of ethics by means of the formula: "Each to count for one and none for more than one." In other words, the interests of every being affected by an action are to be taken into account and given the same weight as the like interests of any other being. A later utilitarian, Henry Sidgwick, put the point in this way: "The good of any one individual is of no more importance, from the point of view (if I may say so) of the Universe, than the good of any other." More recently the leading figures in contemporary moral philosophy have shown a great deal of agreement in specifying as a fundamental presupposition of their moral theories some similar requirement that works to give everyone's interests equal consideration—although these writers generally cannot agree on how this requirement is best formulated.

It is an implication of this principle of equality that our concern for others and our readiness to consider their interests ought not to depend on what they are like or on what abilities they may possess. Precisely what our concern or consideration requires us to do may vary according to the characteristics of those affected by what we do: concern for the well-being of children growing up in America would require that we teach them to read; concern for the well-being of pigs may require no more than that we leave them with other pigs in a place where there is adequate food and room to run freely. But the basic element—the taking into account of the interests of the being, whatever those interests may be—must, according to the principle of equality, be extended to all beings, black or white, masculine or feminine, human or nonhuman.

Thomas Jefferson, who was responsible for writing the principle of the equality of men into the American Declaration of Independence, saw this point. It led him to oppose slavery even though he was unable to free himself fully from his slaveholding background. He wrote in a letter to the author of a book that emphasized the notable intellectual achievements of Negroes in order to refute the then common view that they had limited intellectual capacities:

> Be assured that no person living wishes more sincerely than I do, to see a complete refutation of the doubts I myself have entertained and expressed on the grade of understanding allotted to them by nature, and to find that they are on a par with ourselves . . . but whatever be their degree of talent it is no measure of their rights. Because Sir Isaac Newton was superior to others in understanding, he was not therefore lord of the property or persons of others.

Similarly, when in the 1850s the call for women's rights was raised in the United States, a remarkable black feminist named Sojourner Truth made the same point in more robust terms at a feminist convention:

> They talk about this thing in the head; what do they call it? ["Intellect," whispered someone nearby.] That's it. What's that got to do with women's rights or Negroes' rights? If my cup won't hold but a pint and yours holds a quart, wouldn't you be mean not to let me have my little half-measure full?

It is on this basis that the case against racism and the case against sexism must both ultimately rest; and it is in accordance with this principle that the attitude that we may call "speciesism," by analogy with racism, must also be condemned. Speciesism—the word is not an attractive one, but I can think of no better term—is a prejudice or attitude of bias in favor of the interests of members of one's own species and against those of members of other species. It should be obvious that the fundamental objections to racism and sexism made by Thomas Jefferson and Sojourner Truth apply equally to speciesism. If possessing a higher degree of intelligence does not entitle one human to use another for his or her own ends, how can it entitle humans to exploit nonhumans for the same purpose?

Many philosophers and other writers have proposed the principle of equal consideration of interests, in some form or other, as a basic moral principle; but not many of them have recognized that this principle applies to members of other species as well as to our own. Jeremy Bentham was one of the few who did realize this. In a forward-looking passage written at a time when black slaves had been freed by the French but in the British dominions were still being treated in the way we now treat animals, Bentham wrote:

> The day *may* come when the rest of the animal creation may acquire those rights which never could have been withholden from them but by the hand of tyranny. The French have already discovered that the blackness of the skin is no reason why a human being should be abandoned without redress to the caprice of a tormentor. It may one day come to be recognized that the number of the legs, the villosity of the skin, or the termination of the *os sacrum* are reasons equally insufficient for abandoning a sensitive being to the same fate. What else is it that should trace the insuperable line? Is it the faculty of reason, or perhaps the faculty of discourse? But a full-grown horse or dog is beyond comparison a more rational, as well as a more conversable animal, than an infant of a day or a week or even a month, old. But suppose they were otherwise, what would it avail? The question is not, Can they *reason?* nor Can they *talk?* but, Can they *suffer?*

In this passage Bentham points to the capacity for suffering as the vital characteristic that gives a being the right to equal consideration. The capacity for suffering—or more strictly, for suffering and/or enjoyment or happiness—is not just another characteristic like the capacity for language or higher mathematics. Bentham is not saying that those who try to mark "the insuperable line" that determines whether the interests of a being should be considered happen to have chosen the wrong characteristic. By saying that we must consider the interests of all beings with the capacity for suffering or enjoyment Bentham does not arbitrarily exclude from consideration any interests at all—as those who draw the line with reference to the possession of reason or language do. The capacity for suffering and enjoyment is *a prerequisite for having interests at all*, a condition that must be satisfied before we can speak of interests in a meaningful way. It would be nonsense to say that it was not in the interests of a stone to be kicked along the road by a schoolboy. A stone does not have interests because it cannot suffer. Nothing that we can do to it could possibly make any difference to its welfare. The capacity for suffering and enjoyment is, however, not only necessary, but also sufficient for us to say that a being has interests—at an absolute minimum, an interest in not suffering. A mouse, for example, does have an interest in not being kicked along the road, because it will suffer if it is.

Although Bentham speaks of "rights" in the passage I have quoted, the argument is really about equality rather than about rights. Indeed, in a different passage, Bentham famously described "natural rights" as "nonsense" and "natural and imprescriptable rights" as "nonsense upon stilts." He talked of moral rights as a shorthand way of referring to protections that people and animals morally ought to have; but the real weight of the moral argument does not rest on the assertion of the existence of the right, for this in turn has to be justified on the basis of the possibilities for suffering and happiness. In this way we can argue for equality for animals without getting embroiled in philosophical controversies about the ultimate nature of rights.

In misguided attempts to refute the arguments of this book, some philosophers have gone to much trouble developing arguments to show that animals do not have rights. They have claimed that to have rights a being must be autonomous, or must be a member of a community, or must have the ability to respect the rights of others, or must possess a sense of justice. These claims are irrelevant to the case for Animal Liberation. The language of rights is a convenient political shorthand. It is even more valuable in the era of thirty-second TV news clips than it was in Bentham's day; but in the argument for a radical change in our attitude to animals, it is in no way necessary.

If a being suffers there can be no moral justification for refusing to take that suffering into consideration. No matter what the nature of the being, the principle of equality requires that its suffering be counted equally with the like suffering—insofar as rough comparisons can be made—of any other being. If a being is not capable of suffering, or of experiencing enjoyment or happiness, there is nothing to be taken into account. So the limit of sentience (using the term as a convenient if not strictly accurate shorthand for the capacity to suffer and/or experience enjoyment) is the only defensible boundary of concern for the interests of others. To mark this boundary by some other characteristic like intelligence or rationality would be to mark it in an arbitrary manner. Why not choose some other characteristic, like skin color?

Racists violate the principle of equality by giving greater weight to the interests of members of their own race when there is a clash between their interests and the interests of those of another race. Sexists violate the principle of equality by favoring the interests of their own sex. Similarly, speciesists allow the interests of their own species to override the greater interests of members of other species. The pattern is identical in each case. . . .

Animals can feel pain. As we saw earlier, there can be no moral justification for regarding the pain (or pleasure) that animals feel as less important than the same amount of pain (or pleasure) felt by humans. But what practical consequences follow from this conclusion? To prevent misunderstanding I shall spell out what I mean a little more fully.

If I give a horse a hard slap across its rump with my open hand, the horse may start, but it presumably feels little pain. Its skin is thick enough to protect it against a mere slap. If I slap a baby in the same way, however, the baby will cry and presumably feel pain, for its skin is more sensitive. So it is worse to slap a baby than a horse, if both slaps are administered with equal force. But there must be some kind of blow—I don't know exactly what it would be, but perhaps a blow with a heavy stick—that would cause the horse as much pain as we cause a baby by slapping it with our hand. That is what I mean by "the same amount of pain," and if we consider it wrong to inflict that much pain on a baby for no good reason then we must, unless we are speciesists, consider it equally wrong to inflict the same amount of pain on a horse for no good reason.

Other differences between humans and animals cause other complications. Normal adult human beings have mental capacities that will, in certain circumstances, lead them to suffer more than animals would in the same circumstances. If, for instance, we decided to perform extremely painful or lethal scientific experiments on normal adult humans, kidnapped at random from public parks for this purpose, adults who enjoy strolling in parks would become fearful that they would be kidnapped. The resultant terror would be a form of suffering additional to the pain of the experiment. The same experiments performed on nonhuman animals would cause less suffering since the animals would not have the anticipatory dread of being kidnapped and experimented upon. This does not mean, of course, that it would be *right* to perform the experiment on animals, but only that there is a reason, which is *not* speciesist, for preferring to use animals rather than normal adult human beings, if the experiment is to be done at all. It should be noted, however, that this same argument gives us a reason for preferring to use human infants—orphans perhaps—or severely retarded human beings for experiments, rather than adults, since infants and retarded humans would also have no idea of what was going to happen to them. So far as this argument is concerned nonhuman animals and infants and retarded humans are in the same category; and if we use this argument to justify experiments on nonhuman animals we have to ask ourselves whether we are also prepared to allow experiments on human infants and retarded adults; and if we make a distinction between animals and these humans, on what basis can we do it, other than a bare-faced—and morally indefensible—preference for members of our own species?

There are many matters in which the superior mental powers of normal adult humans make a difference: anticipation, more detailed memory, greater knowledge of what is happening, and so on. Yet these differences do not all point to greater suffering on the part of the normal human being. Sometimes animals may suffer more because of their more limited understanding. If, for instance, we are taking prisoners in wartime we can explain to them that although they must submit to capture, search, and confinement, they will not otherwise be harmed and will be set free at the conclusion of hostilities. If we capture wild animals, however, we cannot explain that we are not threatening their lives. A wild animal cannot distinguish an attempt to overpower and confine from an attempt to kill; the one causes as much terror as the other.

It may be objected that comparisons of the sufferings of different species are impossible to make and that for this reason when the interests of animals and humans clash the principle of equality gives no guidance. It is probably true that comparisons of suffering between members of different species cannot be made precisely, but precision is not essential. Even if we were to prevent the infliction of suffering on animals only when it is quite certain that the interests of humans will not be affected to anything like the extent that animals are affected, we would be forced to make radical changes in our treatment of animals that would involve our diet, the farming methods we use, experimental procedures in many fields of science, our approach to wildlife and to hunting, trapping and the wearing of furs, and areas of entertainment like circuses, rodeos, and zoos. As a result, a vast amount of suffering would be avoided.

Chapter 28

Torturing Puppies and Eating Meat

It's All in Good Taste

Alastair Norcross

Farm animals in America once grazed on open fields beside country roads. Those days, however, are gone. Today, farm animals live in smelly, crowded, automated warehouses. Every independent study has found these factories to be inhumane. The cramped conditions are stressful and unnatural for the animals; cows pumped full of food often experience internal abscesses; chickens and turkeys have their beaks cut off, and pigs and cows have their tails severed—all without anesthesia—to avoid the fighting that occurs precisely because the animals are packed in so tightly.

The number of animals that suffer under these conditions is staggering—in the billions, year after year. When people in our culture think of a moral horror, they often think of the Holocaust—the campaign of genocide in which Hitler and his Nazi thugs starved, beat, and ultimately murdered 5.7 million Jews. They do not think of factory farming. Yet for every human being who suffered under Hitler's tyranny, several thousand animals have suffered in these farms during the past twenty years. The Nobel laureate Isaac Bashevis Singer wrote, "In relation to [animals], all people are Nazis; for the animals it is an eternal Treblinka."

Alastair Norcross, "Torturing Puppies and Eating Meat: It's All in Good Taste" in *Southwest Philosophy Review*, vol. 20, no. 1 (2004): 117–23. Copyright © 2004. Used with permission of the author.

In this selection, Alastair Norcross asks how we can justify treating chickens in ways that we would never treat puppies. Despite the seriousness of the topic, Norcross's piece contains humor—some of it directed at my home state of Alabama, and some directed specifically at the city of Tuscaloosa, where I live. We Alabamians can take the ridicule—even when it's not in good taste.

Alastair Norcross is a professor of philosophy at the University of Colorado at Boulder, where many people play the banjo.

Consider the story of Fred, who receives a visit from the police one day. They have been summoned by Fred's neighbors, who have been disturbed by strange sounds emanating from Fred's basement. When they enter the basement they are confronted by the following scene: Twenty-six small wire cages, each containing a puppy, some whining, some whimpering, some howling. The puppies range in age from newborn to about six months. Many of them show signs of mutilation. Urine and feces cover the bottoms of the cages and the basement floor. Fred explains that he keeps the puppies for twenty-six weeks, and then butchers them while holding them upside-down. During their lives he performs a series of mutilations on them, such as slicing off their noses and their paws with a hot knife, all without any form of anesthesia. Except for the mutilations, the puppies are never allowed out of the cages, which are barely big enough to hold them at twenty-six weeks. The police are horrified, and promptly charge Fred with animal abuse. As details of the case are publicized, the public is outraged. Newspapers are flooded with letters demanding that Fred be severely punished. There are calls for more severe penalties for animal abuse. Fred is denounced as a vile sadist.

Finally, at his trial, Fred explains his behavior, and argues that he is blameless and therefore deserves no punishment. He is, he explains, a great lover of chocolate. A couple of years ago, he was involved in a car accident, which resulted in some head trauma. Upon his release from the hospital, having apparently suffered no lasting ill effects, he visited his favorite restaurant and ordered their famous rich dark chocolate mousse. Imagine his dismay when he discovered that his experience of the mousse was a pale shadow of its former self. The mousse tasted bland, slightly pleasant, but with none of the intense chocolaty flavor he remembered so well. The waiter assured him that the recipe was unchanged from the last time he had tasted it, just the day before his accident. In some consternation, Fred rushed out to buy a bar of his favorite Belgian chocolate. Again, he was dismayed to discover that his experience of the chocolate was barely even pleasurable. Extensive investigation revealed that his experience of other foods remained unaffected, but chocolate, in all its forms, now tasted bland and insipid. Desperate for a solution to his problem, Fred visited a renowned gustatory neurologist, Dr. T. Bud. Extensive tests revealed that the accident had irreparably damaged the godiva gland, which secretes cocoamone, the hormone responsible for the experience of chocolate. Fred urgently requested hormone replacement therapy. Dr. Bud informed him that, until recently, there had been no known source of cocoamone, other than the human godiva gland, and that it was impossible to collect cocoamone from one person to be used by another. However, a chance discovery had altered the situation. A forensic veterinary surgeon, performing an autopsy on a severely abused puppy, had discovered high concentrations of cocoamone in the puppy's brain. It turned out that puppies, who don't normally produce cocoamone, could be stimulated to do so by extended periods of severe stress and suffering. The research that led to this discovery, while gaining tenure for its authors, had not been widely publicized, for fear of antagonizing animal welfare groups. Although this research clearly gave Fred the hope of tasting chocolate again, there were no commercially available sources of puppy-derived cocoamone. Lack of demand, combined with fear of bad publicity, had deterred drug companies from getting into the puppy torturing business. Fred appeals to the court to imagine his anguish, on discovering that a solution to his severe deprivation was possible, but not readily available. But he wasn't inclined to sit around bemoaning his cruel fate. He did what any chocolate lover would do. He read the research, and set up his own cocoamone collection lab in his basement. Six months of intense puppy suffering, followed by a brutal death, produced enough cocoamone to last him a week, hence the twenty-six cages. He isn't a sadist or an animal abuser, he explains. If there were a method of collecting cocoamone without torturing puppies, he would gladly employ it. He derives no pleasure from the suffering of the puppies itself. He sympathizes with those who are horrified by the pain and misery of the animals, but the court must realize that human pleasure is at stake. The puppies, while undeniably cute, are mere animals. He admits that he would be just as healthy without chocolate, if not more so. But this isn't a matter of survival or health. His life would be unacceptably impoverished without the experience of chocolate.

End of story. Clearly, we are horrified by Fred's behavior, and unconvinced by his attempted justification. It is, of course, unfortunate for Fred that he can no longer enjoy the taste of chocolate, but that in no way excuses the imposition of severe suffering on the puppies. I expect near universal agreement with this claim (the exceptions being those who are either inhumanly callous or thinking ahead, and wish to avoid the following conclusion, to which such agreement commits them). No decent person would even contemplate torturing puppies merely to enhance a gustatory experience. However, billions of animals endure intense suffering every year for precisely this end. Most of the chicken, veal, beef, and pork consumed in the United States comes from intensive confinement facilities, in which the animals live cramped, stress-filled lives and endure un-anaesthetized mutilations. The vast majority of people would suffer no ill health from the elimination of meat from their diets. Quite the reverse. The supposed benefits from this system of factory farming, apart from the profits accruing to agribusiness, are increased levels of gustatory pleasure for those who claim that they couldn't enjoy a meat-free diet as much as their current meat-filled diets. If we are prepared to condemn Fred for torturing puppies merely to enhance his gustatory experiences, shouldn't we similarly condemn the millions who purchase and consume factory-raised meat? Are there any morally significant differences between Fred's behavior and their behavior?

The first difference that might seem to be relevant is that Fred tortures the puppies himself, whereas most Americans consume meat that comes from animals that have been tortured by others. But is this really relevant? What if Fred had been squeamish and had employed someone else to torture the puppies and extract the cocoamone? Would we have thought any better of Fred? Of course not.

Another difference between Fred and many consumers of factory-raised meat is that many, perhaps most, such consumers are unaware of the treatment of the animals, before they appear in neatly wrapped packages on supermarket shelves. Perhaps I should moderate my challenge, then. If we are prepared to condemn Fred for torturing puppies merely to enhance his gustatory experiences, shouldn't we similarly condemn those who purchase and consume factory-raised meat, in full, or even partial, awareness of the suffering endured by the animals? While many consumers are still blissfully ignorant of the appalling treatment meted out to meat, that number is rapidly dwindling, thanks to vigorous publicity campaigns waged by animal welfare groups. Furthermore, any meat-eating readers of this article are now deprived of the excuse of ignorance.

Perhaps a consumer of factory-raised animals could argue as follows: While I agree that Fred's behavior is abominable, mine is crucially different. If Fred did not consume his chocolate, he would not raise and torture puppies (or pay someone else to do so). Therefore Fred could prevent the suffering of the puppies. However, if I did not buy and consume factory-raised meat, no animals would be spared lives of misery. Agribusiness is much too large to respond to the behavior of one consumer. Therefore I cannot prevent the suffering of any animals. I may well regret the suffering inflicted on animals for the sake of human enjoyment. I may even agree that the human enjoyment doesn't justify the suffering. However, since the animals will suffer no matter what I do, I may as well enjoy the taste of their flesh.

There are at least two lines of response to this attempted defense. First, consider an analogous case. You visit a friend in an exotic location, say Alabama. Your friend takes you out to eat at the finest restaurant in Tuscaloosa. For dessert you select the house specialty, "Chocolate Mousse à la Bama," served with a small cup of coffee, which you are instructed to drink before eating the mousse. The mousse is quite simply the most delicious dessert you have ever tasted. Never before has chocolate tasted so rich and satisfying. Tempted to order a second, you ask your friend what makes this mousse so delicious. He informs you that the mousse itself is ordinary, but the coffee contains a concentrated dose of cocoamone, the newly discovered chocolate-enhancing hormone. Researchers at Auburn University have perfected a technique for extracting cocoamone from the brains of freshly slaughtered puppies, who have been subjected to lives of pain and frustration. Each puppy's brain yields four doses, each of which is effective for about fifteen minutes, just long enough to enjoy one serving of mousse. You are, naturally, horrified and disgusted. You will certainly not order another serving, you tell your friend. In fact, you are shocked that your friend, who had always seemed to be a morally decent person, could have both recommended the dessert to you and eaten one himself, in full awareness of the loathsome process necessary for the experience.

He agrees that the suffering of the puppies is outrageous, and that the gain in human pleasure in no way justifies the appalling treatment they have to endure. However, neither he nor you can save any puppies by refraining from consuming cocoamone. Cocoamone production is now Alabama's leading industry, surpassing even banjo-making and inbreeding.[1] The industry is much too large to respond to the behavior of one or two consumers. Since the puppies will suffer no matter what either of you does, you may as well enjoy the mousse.

If it is as obvious as it seems that a morally decent person, who is aware of the details of cocoamone production, couldn't order Chocolate Mousse à la Bama, it should be equally obvious that a morally decent person, who is aware of the details of factory farming, can't purchase and consume factory-raised meat. If the attempted excuse of causal impotence is compelling in the latter case, it should be compelling in the former case. But it isn't.

The second response to the claim of causal impotence is to deny it. Consider the case of chickens, the most cruelly treated of all animals raised for human consumption, with the possible exception of veal calves. In 1998, almost 8 billion chickens were slaughtered in the United States,[2] almost all of them raised on factory farms. Suppose that there are 250 million chicken eaters in the United States, and that each one consumes, on average, 25 chickens per year (this leaves a fair number of chickens slaughtered for nonhuman consumption, or for export). Clearly, if only one of those chicken eaters gave up eating chicken, the industry would not respond. Equally clearly, if they all gave up eating chicken, billions of chickens (approximately 6.25 billion per year) would not be bred, tortured, and killed. But there must also be some number of consumers, far short of 250 million, whose renunciation of chicken would cause the industry to reduce the number of chickens bred in factory farms. The industry may not be able to respond to each individual's behavior, but it must respond to the behavior of fairly large numbers. Suppose that the industry is sensitive to a reduction in demand for chicken equivalent to 10,000 people becoming vegetarians. (This seems like a reasonable guess, but I have no idea what the actual numbers are, nor is it important.) For each group of 10,000 who give up chicken, a quarter of a million fewer chickens are bred per year. It appears, then, that if you give up eating chicken, you have only a one in ten thousand chance of making any difference to the lives of chickens, unless it is certain that fewer than 10,000 people will ever give up eating chicken, in which case you have no chance. Isn't a one in ten thousand chance small enough to render your continued consumption of chicken blameless? Not at all. While the chance that your behavior is harmful may be small, the harm that is risked is enormous. The larger the numbers needed to make a difference to chicken production, the larger the difference such numbers would make. A one in ten thousand chance of saving 250,000 chickens per year from excruciating lives is morally and mathematically equivalent to the certainty of saving 25 chickens per year. We commonly accept that even small risks of great harms are unacceptable. That is why we disapprove of parents who fail to secure their children in car seats or with seat belts, who leave their small children unattended at home, or who drink or smoke heavily during pregnancy. Or consider commercial aircraft safety measures. The chances that the oxygen masks, the lifejackets, or the emergency exits on any given plane will be called on to save any lives in a given week, are far smaller than one in ten thousand. And yet we would be outraged to discover that an airline had knowingly allowed a plane to fly for a week with non-functioning emergency exits, oxygen masks, and lifejackets. So, even if it is true that your giving up factory raised chicken has only a tiny chance of preventing suffering, given that the amount of suffering that would be prevented is in inverse proportion to your chance of preventing it, your continued consumption is not thereby excused.

But perhaps it is not even true that your giving up chicken has only a tiny chance of making any difference. Suppose again that the poultry industry only reduces production when a threshold of 10,000 fresh vegetarians is reached. Suppose also, as is almost certainly true, that vegetarianism is growing in popularity in the United States (and elsewhere). Then, even if you are not the one, newly converted vegetarian, to reach the next threshold of 10,000, your conversion will reduce the time required before the next threshold is reached. The sooner the threshold is reached, the sooner production, and therefore animal suffering, is reduced. Your behavior, therefore, does make a difference. Furthermore, many people who become vegetarians influence others to become vegetarian, who in turn influence others, and so on. It appears, then, that the claim of causal impotence is mere wishful thinking, on the part of those meat lovers who are morally sensitive enough to realize that human gustatory pleasure does not justify inflicting extreme suffering on animals. . . .

I have been unable to discover any morally relevant differences between the behavior of Fred, the puppy torturer, and the behavior of the millions of people who purchase and consume factory-raised meat, at least those who do so in the knowledge that the animals live lives of suffering and deprivation. Just as morality demands that we not torture puppies merely to enhance our own eating pleasure, morality also demands that we not support factory farming by purchasing factory-raised meat.

NOTES

1. I realize that I am playing on stereotypes for comic effect. Banjo-making, of course, has never really been one of Alabama's leading industries.

2. *Livestock Slaughter 1998 Summary*, NASS, USDA (Washington, DC: March 1999), 2; and *Poultry Slaughter*, NASS, USDA (Washington, DC: February 2, 1999), 1f.

Chapter 29

Do Animals Have Rights?

Tibor R. Machan

Animals are not moral agents—they are not morally responsible for what they do, nor are they capable of moral goodness. People are moral agents—we are smarter and more valuable than animals. Professor Tibor R. Machan (1939–2016) emphasizes ideas like these. Even though we should treat animals humanely, he says, we should recognize that they have no fundamental right to life, liberty, or property. Animals have no such rights, Machan believes, because they cannot make free choices based on their own values.

Although the idea that animals have rights goes back to the eighteenth century, at least, it has only recently become something of a *cause celebre* among numerous serious and well-placed intellectuals, including moral and political philosophers. Although Jeremy Bentham seems to have suggested legislation requiring humane treatment of animals, he didn't defend animal rights, per se—not surprisingly, since Bentham himself had not been impressed with the more basic (Lockean) doctrine of natural rights—calling them "nonsense upon stilts." John Locke's idea of individual rights has had enormous influence, and even where it is not respected, it is ultimately invoked as some kind of model for what it would take for something to have rights.

Tibor R. Machan, "Do Animals Have Rights?" in *Public Affairs Quarterly*, vol. 5, no. 2 (April 1991): 163–73. Copyright © 1991. Used with permission.

In recent years the doctrine of animals rights has found champions in important circles where the general doctrine of rights is itself well respected. For example, Professor Tom Regan, in his important book *The Case for Animal Rights* (UC Press, 1983), finds the idea of natural rights intellectually congenial but then extends this idea to cover animals near humans on the evolutionary scale. The tradition from within which Regan works is clearly Lockean, only he does not agree that human nature is distinctive enough, in relevant respects, to restrict the scope of natural rights to human beings alone.

Following a different tradition, namely, utilitarianism, the idea of animal liberation has emerged. And this idea comes to roughly the same thing, practically speaking. Only the argument is different because for utilitarians what is important is not that someone or something must have a specific sphere of dominion but that they be well off in their lives. So long as the bulk of the relevant creatures enjoy a reasonably high living standard, the moral and political objectives for us will have been met. But if this goal is neglected, moral and political steps are required to improve on the situation. Animal liberation is such a step.

This essay will maintain that animals have no rights and need no liberation. I will argue that to think they do is a category mistake—it is, to be blunt, to unjustifiably anthropomorphize animals, to treat them as if they were what they are not, namely, human beings. Rights and liberty are political concepts applicable to human beings because human beings are moral agents, in need of what Harvard philosopher Robert Nozick calls "moral space," that is, a definite sphere of moral jurisdiction where their authority to act is respected and protected so it is they, not intruders, who govern themselves and either succeed or fail in their moral tasks.

Oddly, it is clearly admitted by most animal rights or liberation theorists that only human beings are moral agents—for example, they never urge animals to behave morally (by, e.g., standing up for their rights, by leading a political revolution). No animal rights theorist proposes that animals be tried for crimes and blamed for moral wrongs.

If it is true that the moral nature of human beings gives rise to the conception of basic rights and liberties, then by this alone animal rights and liberation theorists have made an admission fatal to their case.

Before getting under way I want to note that rights and liberty are certainly not the whole of moral concern to us. There are innumerable other moral issues one can raise, including about the way human beings relate to animals. In particular, there is the question of how people should treat animals. Should they be hunted even when this does not serve any vital human purpose? Should they be utilized in hurtful—indeed, evidently agonizing—fashion even for trivial human purposes? Should their pain and suffering be ignored in the process of being made use of for admittedly vital human purposes?

It is clear that once one has answered the question of whether animals have rights (or ought to be liberated from human beings) in the negative, one has by no means disposed of these other issues. In this essay I will be dealing mostly with the issue of animal rights and liberation. Yet I will also touch briefly on the other moral issues just raised. I will indicate why they may all be answered in the negative without it being the case that animals have rights or should be liberated—that is, without raising any serious political issues.

WHY MIGHT ANIMALS HAVE RIGHTS?

To have a right amounts to having those around one abstain from intruding on one within a given sphere of jurisdiction. If I have the right to the use of our community swimming pool, no one may prevent me from making the decision as to whether I do or do not use the pool. Someone's having a right is a kind of freedom from the unavoidable interference of moral agents, beings who are capable of choosing whether they will interfere or not interfere with the rights holder.

When a right is considered natural, the freedom involved in having this right is supposed to be justified by reference to the kind of being one is, one's nature as a certain kind of entity. The idea of natural rights was formulated in connection with the issue of the proper relationship between human beings, especially citizens and governments. The idea goes back many centuries. . . .

The major political thinker with an influential doctrine of natural rights was John Locke. In his *Second Treatise on Government* he argued that each human being is responsible to follow the Law of Nature, the source of morality. But to do so, each also requires a sphere of personal authority, which is identified by the principle of the natural right to property—including one's person and estate. In other words, to be a morally responsible being in the company of other persons one needs what Robert Nozick has called "moral space," that is, a sphere of sovereignty or personal jurisdiction so that one can engage in self-government—for better or for worse.

Locke made it a provision of having such a right that there be sufficient and good enough of whatever one may have a right to left for others—that is, the Lockean proviso against absolute monopoly. For Locke the reason government is necessary is "that though in the state of Nature [every human being] hath such a right [to absolute freedom], yet the enjoyment of it is very uncertain and constantly exposed to the invasion of others."[1] So we establish government to make us secure in the enjoyment of our rights.

Since Locke's time the doctrine of natural rights has undergone a turbulent intellectual history, falling into disrepute at the hands of empiricism and positivism but gaining a revival at the hands of some influential political philosophers of the second half of the twentieth century.

Ironically, at a time in recent intellectual history when natural rights theory had not been enjoying much support, the idea that animals might also have rights came under increasing discussion. Most notable among those who proposed such a notion was Thomas Taylor, whose anonymous work, *Vindication of the Rights of Brutes*, was published in 1792 but discussed animal rights only in the context of demeaning human rights. More positive (though brief) was the contribution of Jeremy Bentham, who in his *An Introduction to the Principles of Morals and Legislation* (1789) argued that those animals that can suffer are owed moral consideration, even if those that molest us or those we may make good use of may be killed—but not "tormented."

In the latter part of the nineteenth century an entire work was devoted to the idea by Henry S. Salt, entitled *Animals' Rights*.[2] And in our time numerous philosophers and social commentators have made the attempt to demonstrate that if we are able to ascribe basic rights to life, liberty, and property to human beings, we can do the same for many of the higher animals. In essentials their arguments can be broken down into two parts. First, they subscribe to Darwin's thesis that no difference of kind, only a difference of degree, can be found between other animals and human beings.[3] Second, even if there were a difference in kind between other animals—especially mammals—and human beings, since they both can be shown to have interests (e.g., the avoidance of pain or suffering), for certain moral and legal purposes the difference does not matter, only the similarity does. In connection with both of these arguments the central conclusion is that if human beings can be said to have certain basic rights—for example, to life, liberty, or consideration for their capacity to suffer—then so do (higher) animals.[4]

Now I do not wish to give the impression that no diversity exists among those who defend animal rights. Some do so from the viewpoint of natural rights, treating animals' rights as basic limiting principles which may not be ignored except when it would also make sense to disregard the rights of human beings. Even on this matter there are serious differences among defenders of animal rights—some do not allow any special regard for human beings,[5] some hold that when it comes to a choice between a person and a dog, it is ordinarily the person who should be given protection.[6] But others choose to defend animal rights on utilitarian grounds—to the extent that it amounts to furthering overall pleasure or happiness in the world, animals must be given equal consideration to what human beings receive. Thus only if there really is demonstrable contribution to the overall pleasure or happiness on earth, may an animal capable of experiencing pleasure or happiness be sacrificed for the sake of some human purpose. Barring such demonstrable contribution, animals and humans enjoy equal rights.[7]

At times the argument for animal rights begins with the rather mild point that "reason requires that other animals are as much within the scope of moral concern as are men" but then moves on to the more radical claim that therefore "we must view our entire history as well as all aspects of our daily lives from a new perspective."[8]

Of course, people have generally invoked some moral considerations as they treated animals—I can recall living on a farm in Hungary when I was 11 and getting all kinds of lectures about how I ought to treat the animals, receiving severe rebuke when I mistreated a cat and lots of praise when I took the favorite cow grazing every day and established a close bond with it over time. Hardly anyone can have escaped one or another moral lecture from parents or neighbors concerning the treatment of pets, household animals, or birds. When a young boy once tried out an air gun by shooting a pigeon sitting on a telephone wire before the apartment house in which he lived, I recall that there was no end of rebuke in response to his wanton callousness. Yet none of those who engaged in the moralizing ever entertained the need to "view our entire history as well as all aspects of our daily lives from a new perspective." Rather they seemed to have understood that reckless disregard for the life or well-being of animals shows a defect of character, lack of sensitivity, callousness—realizing, at the same time, that numerous human purposes justify our killing and using animals in the various ways most of us do use them.

And this really is the crux of the matter. But why? Why is it more reasonable to think of animals as available for our sensible use rather than owed the kind of respect and consideration we ought to extend to other human beings? It is one thing to have this as a commonsense conviction, it is another to know it as a sound viewpoint, in terms of which we may confidently conduct ourselves.

WHY WE MAY USE ANIMALS

While I will return to the arguments for animal rights, let me first place on record the case for the use of animals for human purposes. Without this case reasonably well established, it will not be possible to critically assess the case for animal rights. After all, this is a comparative matter—which viewpoint makes better sense, which is, in other words, more likely to be true?

One reason for the propriety of our use of animals is that we are more important or valuable than other animals and some of our projects may require animals for them to be successful. Notice that this is different from saying that human beings are "uniquely important," a position avidly ridiculed by Stephen R. L. Clark, who claims that "there seems no decent ground in reason or revelation to suppose that man is uniquely important or significant."[9] If man were uniquely important, that would mean that one could not assign any value to plants or nonhuman animals apart from their relationship to human beings. That is not the position I am defending. I argue that there is a scale of importance in nature, and among all the various kinds of being, human beings are the most important—even while it is true that some members of the human species may indeed prove themselves to be the most vile and worthless, as well.

How do we establish that we are more important or valuable? By considering whether the idea of lesser or greater importance or value in the nature of things makes clear sense and applying it to an understanding of whether human beings or other animals are more important. If it turns out that ranking things in nature as more or less important makes sense, and if we qualify as more important than other animals, there is at least the beginning of a reason why we may make use of other animals for our purposes.

That there are things of different degrees of value in nature is admitted by animal rights advocates, so there is no great need here to argue about that. When they insist that we treat animals differently from the way we treat, say, rocks or iron ore—so that while we may not use the former as we choose, we may use the latter—they testify, at least by implication, that animals are more important than, say, iron ore. Certainly they invoke some measure of importance or value and place animals higher in line with this measure than they place other aspects of nature. They happen, also, to deny that human beings rank higher than animals, or at least they do not admit that human beings' higher ranking warrants their using animals for their purposes. But that is a distinct issue which we can consider later.

Quite independently of the implicit acknowledgment by animal rights advocates of the hierarchy of nature, there simply is evidence through the natural world of the existence of beings of greater complexity and of higher value. For example, while it makes no sense to evaluate as good or bad such things as planets or rocks or pebbles—except as they may relate to human purposes—when it comes to plants and animals the process of evaluation commences very naturally indeed. We can speak of better or worse trees, oaks, redwoods, or zebras, foxes or chimps. While at this point we confine our evaluation to the condition or behavior of such beings without any intimation of their responsibility for being better or worse, when we start discussing human beings our evaluation takes on a moral component. Indeed, none are more ready to testify to this than animal rights advocates who, after all, do not demand any change of behavior on the part of non-human animals and yet insist that human beings conform to certain moral edicts as a matter of their own choice. This means that even animal rights advocates admit outright that to the best of our knowledge it is with human beings that the idea of moral goodness and moral responsibility enters the universe.

Clearly this shows a hierarchical structure in nature: some things do not invite evaluations at all—it is a matter of no significance or of indifference whether they are or are not or what they are or how they behave. Some things invite evaluation but without implying any moral standing with reference to whether they do well or badly. And some things—namely, human beings—invite moral evaluation. The level of importance or value may be noted to move from the inanimate to the animate world, culminating, as far as we now know, with human life. Normal human life involves moral tasks, and that is why we are more important than other beings in nature—we are subject to moral appraisal, it is a matter of our doing whether we succeed or fail in our lives.

Now when it comes to our moral task, namely, to succeed as human beings, we are dependent upon reaching sensible conclusions about what we should do. We can fail to do this and too often do so. But we can also succeed. The process that leads to our success involves learning, among other things, what it is that nature avails us with to achieve our highly varied tasks in life. Clearly among these highly varied tasks could be some that make judicious use of animals—for example, to find out whether some medicine is safe for human use, we might wish to use animals. To do this is the rational thing for us to do, so as to make the best use of nature for our success in living our lives. That does not mean there need be no guidelines involved in how we might make use of animals—any more than there need be no guidelines involved in how we use anything else.

WHY INDIVIDUAL HUMAN RIGHTS?

Where do individual *human* rights come into this picture? The rights being talked of in connection with human beings have as their source, as we have noted earlier, the human capacity to make moral choices. We have the right to life, liberty, and property—as well as more specialized rights connected with politics, the press, religion—because we have as our central task in life to act morally. And in order to be able to do this throughout the scope of our lives, we require a reasonably clear sphere of personal jurisdiction—a dominion where we are sovereign and can either succeed or fail to live well, to do right, to act properly.

If we did not have rights, we would not have such a sphere of personal jurisdiction and there would be no clear idea as to whether we are acting in our own behalf or those of other persons. No one could be blamed or praised, for we would not know clearly enough whether what the person is doing is in his or her authority to do or in someone else's. This is precisely the problem that arises in communal living and, especially, in totalitarian countries where everything is under forced collective governance. The reason moral distinctions are still possible to make under such circumstances is that in fact—as distinct from law—there is always some sphere of personal jurisdiction wherein people may exhibit courage, prudence, justice, honesty, and other virtues. But where collectivism has been successfully enforced, there is no individual responsibility at play and people's morality and immorality are submerged within the group.

Indeed the main reason for governments has for some time been recognized to be nothing other than that our individual human rights should be protected. In the past—and in many places even today—it was thought that government (or the State) has some kind of leadership role in human communities. This belief followed the view that human beings differ amongst themselves radically, some being lower, some higher class, some possessing divine rights, others lacking them, some having a personal communion with God, others lacking this special advantage.

With such views in place, it made clear enough sense to argue that government should have a patriarchal role in human communities—the view against which John Locke forcefully argued his theory of natural individual human rights.[10]

WHERE IS THERE ROOM FOR ANIMAL RIGHTS?

We have seen that the most sensible and influential doctrine of human rights rests on the fact that human beings are indeed members of a discernibly different species—the members of which have a moral life to aspire to and must have principles upheld for them in communities that make their aspiration possible. Now there is plainly no valid intellectual place for rights in the non-human world, the world in which moral responsibility is for all practical purposes absent. Some would want to argue that some measure of morality can be found within the world of at least higher animals—for example, dogs. For example, Rollin holds that "In actual fact, some animals even seem to exhibit behavior that bespeaks something like moral agency or moral agreement."[11] His argument for this is rather anecdotal but it is worth considering:

> Canids, including the domesticated dog, do not attack another when the vanquished bares its throat, showing a sign of submission. Animals

typically do not prey upon members of their own species. Elephants and porpoises will and do feed injured members of their species. Porpoises will help humans, even at risk to themselves. Some animals will adopt orphaned young of other species. (Such cross-species "morality" would certainly not be explainable by simple appeal to mechanical evolution, since there is no advantage whatever to one's own species.) Dogs will act "guilty" when they break a rule such as one against stealing food from a table and will, for the most part, learn not to take it.[12]

Animal rights advocates such as Rollin maintain that it is impossible to clearly distinguish between human and non-human animals, including on the grounds of the former's characteristic as a moral agent. Yet what they do to defend this point is to invoke borderline cases, imaginary hypotheses and anecdotes.

In contrast, in his book *The Difference of Man and the Difference It Makes,* Mortimer Adler undertakes the painstaking task of showing that even with the full acknowledgment of the merits of Darwinian and, especially, post-Darwinian evolutionary theory, there is ample reason to uphold the doctrine of species-distinction—a distinction, incidentally, that is actually presupposed within Darwin's own work.[13] Adler shows that although the theistic doctrine of radical species differences is incompatible with current evolutionary theory, the more naturalistic view that species are superficially (but non-negligibly) different is indeed necessary to it. The fact of occasional borderline cases is simply irrelevant—what is crucial is that the generalization is true that human beings are basically different from other animals—by virtue of "a crucial threshold in a continuum of degrees." As Adler explains:

> Distinct species are genetically isolated populations between which inter-breeding is impossible, arising (except in the case of polyploidy) from varieties between which interbreeding was not impossible, but between which it was prevented. Modern theorists, with more assurance than Darwin could manage, treat distinct species as natural kinds, not as man-made class distinctions.[14]

Adler adds that "Without the critical insight provided by the distinction between superficial and radical differences in kind, biologists [as well as animal rights advocates, one should add] might be tempted to follow Darwin in thinking that all differences in kind must be apparent, not real."[15]

Since Locke's admittedly incomplete—sometimes even confusing—theory had gained respect and, especially, practical import (e.g., in British and American political history), it became clear enough that the only justification for the exercise of state power—namely the force of the law—is that the rights of individuals are being or have been violated. But as with all successful doctrines, Locke's idea became corrupted by innumerable efforts to concoct rights that government must protect, rights that were actually disguised special interest objectives—values that some people, perhaps quite legitimately, wanted very badly to have secured for them.

While it is no doubt true that many animal rights advocates sincerely believe that they have found a justification for the actual existence of animal rights, it is equally likely that if the Lockean doctrine of rights had not become so influential, they would now be putting their point differently—in a way, namely, that would secure for them what they, as a special interest group, want: the protection of animals they have such love and sympathy for.

CLOSING REFLECTIONS

As with most issues on the minds of many intelligent people as well as innumerable crackpots, a discussion of whether there are animal rights and how we ought to treat animals cannot be concluded with dogmatic certainty one way or the other. Even though those who defend animal rights are certain almost beyond a shadow of doubt, all I can claim is to being certain beyond a reasonable doubt. Animals are not the sort of beings with basic rights to life, liberty, and property, whereas human beings, in the main, are just such beings. Yet we know that animals can feel pain and can enjoy themselves and this must give us pause when we consider using them for our legitimate purposes. We ought to be humane, we ought to kill them and rear them and train them and hunt them in a fashion consistent with such care about them as sentient beings.

In a review of Tom Regan's provocative book already mentioned, *The Case for Animal Rights,* John Hospers makes the following observations that I believe put the matter into the best light we can shed on our topic:

> As one reads page after page of Regan's book, one has the growing impression that his thesis is in an important way "going against nature."

It is a fact of nature that living things have to live on other living things in order to stay alive themselves. It is a fact of nature that carnivores must consume, not plants (which they can't digest), but other sentient beings capable of intense pain and suffering, and that they can survive in no other way. It is a fact of nature that animal reproduction is such that far more creatures are born or hatched than can possibly survive. It is a fact of nature that most creatures die slow lingering tortuous deaths, and that few animals in the wild ever reach old age. It is a fact of nature that we cannot take one step in the woods without killing thousands of tiny organisms whose lives we thereby extinguish. This has been the order of nature for millions of years before man came on the scene, and has indeed been the means by which any animal species has survived to the present day; to fight it is like trying to fight an atomic bomb with a dart gun. . . . This is the world as it is, nature in the raw, unlike the animals in Disney cartoons.[16]

Of course, one might then ask, why should human beings make any attempt to behave differently among themselves, why bother with morality at all?

The fact is that with human nature a problem arose in nature that had not been there before—basic choices had to be confronted, which other animals do not have to confront. The question "How should I live?" faces each human being. And that is what makes it unavoidable for human beings to dwell on moral issues as well as to see other human beings as having the same problem to solve, the same question to dwell on. For this reason we are very different from other animals—we also do terrible, horrible, awful things to each other as well as to nature, but we can also do much, much better and achieve incredible feats nothing else in nature can come close to.

Indeed, then, the moral life is the exclusive province of human beings, so far as we can tell for now. Other—lower(!)—animals simply cannot be accorded the kind of treatment that such a moral life demands, namely, respect for and protection of basic rights.

NOTES

1. John Locke, *Two Treatises on Government*, Par. 123.
2. Henry S. Salt, *Animals' Rights* (London: George Bell & Sons, Ltd., 1892; Clark Summit, PA: Society for Animal Rights, Inc., 1980). This is

perhaps *the* major philosophical effort to defend animals' rights prior to Tom Regan's treatises on the same topic.

3. Charles Darwin, *The Descent of Man*, Chpts. 3 and 4. Reprinted in Tom Regan and Peter Singer, eds., *Animal Rights and Human Obligations* (Englewood Cliffs, NJ: Prentice-Hall, 1976), pp. 72–81.

4. On these points both the deontologically oriented Tom Regan and the utilitarian Peter Singer tend to agree, although they differ considerably in their arguments.

5. Peter Singer holds that "we would be on shaky grounds if we were to demand equality for blacks, women, and other groups of oppressed humans while denying equal consideration to nonhumans." "All Animals Are Equal," op. cit., Regan and Singer, *Animal Rights*, p. 150.

6. Tom Regan contends that "[it] is not to say that practices that involve taking the lives of animals cannot possibly be justified . . . in order to seriously consider approving such a practice [it] would [have to] prevent, reduce, or eliminate a much greater amount of evil . . . there is no other way to bring about these consequences . . . and . . . we have very good reason to believe that these consequences will obtain." "Do Animals Have a Right to Life?" op. cit., Regan and Singer, *Animal Rights*, pp. 205–6.

7. This is the gist of Singer's thesis.

8. Bernard E. Rollin, *Animal Rights and Human Morality* (Buffalo, NY: Prometheus Books, 1981), p. 4.

9. Stephen R. L. Clark, *The Moral Status of Animals* (Oxford, England: Clarendon Press, 1977), p. 13.

10. John Locke, *Two Treatises.*

11. Rollin, *Animal Rights*, p. 14.

12. Ibid.

13. See a discussion of this in Mortimer Adler, *The Difference of Man and the Difference It Makes* (New York: World Publishing Co., 1968), pp. 73ff.

14. Ibid.

15. Ibid., p. 75.

16. John Hospers, "Review of the Case for Animal Rights," *Reason Papers*, No. 10, p. 123.

ABORTION

Chapter 30

On the Moral and Legal Status of Abortion *and* Postscript on Infanticide

Mary Anne Warren

Abortion was not traditionally treated as a crime in Western law. Under English common law, abortion was tolerated even late in the pregnancy, and no laws in the United States banned it until well into the nineteenth century. When such laws were enacted, they were motivated by three concerns: a desire to discourage illicit sexual activity, the belief that abortions are medically unsafe, and the feeling that it is morally wrong to kill an unborn baby.

In the twentieth century, every American state passed laws forbidding abortion. However, these laws were deemed unconstitutional by the U.S. Supreme Court in its decision in *Roe v. Wade* (1973). The Court held that states cannot ban abortion until the fetus is "viable"—that is, until the fetus is mature enough to survive outside the womb. The upshot is that women in America can get abortions until they are about six months pregnant.

Today, most Americans support the *Roe v. Wade* decision, but that decision might be overturned by the U.S. Supreme Court, which has a solid conservative majority. If the Supreme Court does overturn *Roe*, then they will probably let individual states choose their own abortion laws with minimal federal interference. States would then be free to ban abortion altogether.

Mary Anne Warren (1946–2010) believes that physical characteristics, such as genes, are never enough to make someone a person. Persons, she says, are defined by their advanced mental capacities, such as self-awareness and the ability to use a language. Fetuses lack such characteristics; so, they are not persons. Warren also rejects the idea that the fetus's *potential* might outweigh the mother's rights. Thus, she concludes that abortion is morally acceptable. However, she does not believe it is permissible to kill a baby when there are people who would want to take care of it.

We will be concerned with both the moral status of abortion, which for our purposes we may define as the act which a woman performs in voluntarily terminating, or allowing another person to terminate, her pregnancy, and the legal status which is appropriate for this act. . . . It is possible to show that, on the basis of intuitions which we may expect even the opponents of abortion to share, a fetus is not a person, and hence not the sort of entity to which it is proper to ascribe full moral rights.

Of course, while some philosophers would deny the possibility of any such proof, others will deny that there is any need for it, since the moral permissibility of abortion appears to them to be too obvious to require proof. But the inadequacy of this attitude should be evident from the fact that both the friends and the foes of abortion consider their position to be morally self-evident. Because pro-abortionists have never adequately come to grips with the conceptual issues surrounding abortion, most, if not all, of the arguments which they advance in opposition to laws restricting access to abortion fail to refute or even weaken the traditional antiabortion argument, namely, that a fetus is a human being, and therefore abortion is murder.

These arguments are typically of one of two sorts. Either they point to the terrible side effects of the restrictive laws, for example, the deaths due to illegal abortions, and the fact that it is poor women who suffer the most as a result of these laws, or else they state that to deny a woman access to abortion is to deprive her of her right to control her own body. Unfortunately, however, the fact that restricting access to abortion has tragic side effects does not, in itself, show that the restrictions are unjustified, since murder is wrong regardless of the consequences of prohibiting it; and the appeal to the right to control one's body, which is generally construed as a property right, is at best a rather feeble argument for the permissibility of abortion. Mere ownership does not give me the right to kill innocent people whom I find on my property, and indeed I am apt to be held responsible if such people injure themselves while on my property. It is equally unclear that I have any moral right to expel an innocent person from my property when I know that doing so will result in his death. . . .

The question which we must answer in order to produce a satisfactory solution to the problem of the moral status of abortion is this: How are we to define the moral community, the set of beings with full and equal moral rights, such that we can decide whether a human fetus is a member of this community or not? What sort of entity, exactly, has the inalienable rights to life, liberty, and the pursuit of happiness? Jefferson attributed these rights to all *men*, and it may or may not be fair to suggest that he intended to attribute them *only* to men. Perhaps he ought to have attributed them to all human beings. . . .

1. ON THE DEFINITION OF "HUMAN"

. . . The term "human" has two distinct, but not often distinguished, senses. This fact results in a slide of meaning, which serves to conceal the fallaciousness of the traditional argument that since (1) it is wrong to kill innocent human beings, and (2) fetuses are innocent human beings, then (3) it is wrong to kill fetuses. For if "human" is used in the same sense in both (1) and (2) then, whichever of the two senses is meant, one of these premises is question-begging. And if it is used in two different senses then of course the conclusion doesn't follow.

Thus, (1) is a self-evident moral truth, and avoids begging the question about abortion, only if "human being" is used to mean something like "a full-fledged member of the moral community." (It may or may not also be meant to refer exclusively to members of the species *Homo sapiens.*) We may call this the *moral* sense of "human." It is not to be confused with what we will call the *genetic* sense, that is, the sense in which *any* member of the species is a human being, and no member of any other species could be. If (1) is acceptable only if the moral sense is intended, (2) is non-question-begging only if what is intended is the genetic sense. . . .

2. DEFINING THE MORAL COMMUNITY

Can it be established that genetic humanity is sufficient for moral humanity? I think that there are very good reasons for not defining the moral community in this way. I would like to suggest an alternative way of defining the moral community, which I will argue for only to the extent of explaining why it is, or should be, self-evident. The suggestion is simply that the moral community consists of all and only *people*, rather than all and only human beings; and probably the best way of demonstrating its self-evidence is by considering the concept of personhood, to see what sorts of entity are and are not persons, and what the decision that a being is or is not a person implies about its moral rights.

What characteristics entitle an entity to be considered a person? This is obviously not the place to attempt a complete analysis of the concept of personhood, but we do not need such a fully adequate analysis just to determine whether and why a fetus is or isn't a person. All we need is a rough and approximate list of the most basic criteria of personhood, and some idea of which, or how many, of these an entity must satisfy in order to properly be considered a person.

In searching for such criteria, it is useful to look beyond the set of people with whom we are acquainted, and ask how we would decide whether a totally alien being was a person or not. (For we have no right to assume that genetic humanity is necessary for personhood.) Imagine a space traveler who lands on an unknown planet and encounters a race of beings utterly unlike any he has ever seen or heard of. If he wants to be sure of behaving morally toward these beings, he has to somehow decide whether they are people, and hence have full moral rights, or whether they are the sort of thing which he need not feel guilty about treating as, for example, a source of food.

How should he go about making this decision? If he has some anthropological background, he might look for such things as religion, art, and the manufacturing of tools, weapons, or shelters, since these factors have been used to distinguish our human from our pre-human ancestors, in what seems to be closer to the moral than the genetic sense of "human." And no doubt he would be right to consider the presence of such factors as good evidence that the alien beings were people, and morally human. It would, however, be overly anthropocentric of him to take the absence of these things as adequate evidence that they were not, since we can imagine people who have progressed beyond, or evolved without ever developing, these cultural characteristics.

I suggest that the traits which are most central to the concept of personhood, or humanity in the moral sense, are, very roughly, the following:

(1) consciousness (of objects and events external and/or internal to the being), and in particular the capacity to feel pain;
(2) reasoning (the *developed* capacity to solve new and relatively complex problems);
(3) self-motivated activity (activity which is relatively independent of either genetic or direct external control);
(4) the capacity to communicate, by whatever means, messages of an indefinite variety of types, that is, not just with an indefinite number of possible contents, but on indefinitely many possible topics;
(5) the presence of self-concepts, and self-awareness. . . .

Admittedly, there are apt to be a great many problems involved in formulating precise definitions of these criteria, let alone in developing universally valid behavioral criteria for deciding when they apply. But I will assume that both we and our explorer know approximately what (1)–(5) mean, and that he is also able to determine whether or not they apply. How, then, should he use his findings to decide whether or not the alien beings are people? We needn't suppose that an entity must have *all* of these attributes to be properly considered a person; (1) and (2) alone may well be sufficient for personhood, and quite probably (1)–(3) are sufficient. Neither do we need to insist that any one of these criteria is *necessary* for personhood, although once again (1) and (2) look like fairly good candidates for necessary conditions, as does (3), if "activity" is construed so as to include the activity of reasoning.

All we need to claim, to demonstrate that a fetus is not a person, is that any being which satisfies *none* of (1)–(5) is certainly not a person.

I consider this claim to be so obvious that I think anyone who denied it, and claimed that a being which satisfied none of (1)–(5) was a person all the same, would thereby demonstrate that he had no notion at all of what a person is—perhaps because he had confused the concept of a person with that of genetic humanity. If the opponents of abortion were to deny the appropriateness of these five criteria, I do not know what further arguments would convince them. We would probably have to admit that our conceptual schemes were indeed irreconcilably different, and that our dispute could not be settled objectively.

I do not expect this to happen, however, since I think that the concept of a person is one which is very nearly universal (to people), and that it is common to both pro-abortionists and antiabortionists, even though neither group has fully realized the relevance of this concept to the resolution of their dispute. Furthermore, I think that on reflection even the antiabortionists ought to agree not only that (1)–(5) are central to the concept of personhood, but also that it is a part of this concept that all and only people have full moral rights. The concept of a person is in part a moral concept; once we have admitted that *x* is a person we have recognized, even if we have not agreed to respect, *x*'s right to be treated as a member of the moral community. It is true that the claim that *x* is a *human being* is more commonly voiced as part of an appeal to treat *x* decently than is the claim that *x* is a person, but this is either because "human being" is here used in the sense which implies personhood, or because the genetic and moral senses of "human" have been confused.

Now if (1)–(5) are indeed the primary criteria of personhood, then it is clear that genetic humanity is neither necessary nor sufficient for establishing that an entity is a person. Some human beings are not people, and there may well be people who are not human beings. A man or woman whose consciousness has been permanently obliterated but who remains alive is a human being which is no longer a person; defective human beings, with no appreciable mental capacity, are not and presumably never will be people; and a fetus is a human being which is not yet a person, and which therefore cannot coherently be said to have full moral rights. Citizens of the next century should be prepared to recognize highly advanced, self-aware robots or computers, should such be developed, and intelligent inhabitants of other worlds, should such be found, as people in the fullest sense, and to respect their moral rights. But to ascribe full moral rights to an entity which is not a person is as absurd as to ascribe moral obligations and responsibilities to such an entity.

3. FETAL DEVELOPMENT AND
THE RIGHT TO LIFE

. . . It is clear that even though a seven- or eight-month fetus has features which make it apt to arouse in us almost the same powerful protective instinct as is commonly aroused by a small infant, nevertheless it is not significantly more person-like than is a very small embryo. It is *somewhat* more person-like; it can apparently feel and respond to pain, and it may even have a rudimentary form of consciousness, insofar as its brain is quite active. Nevertheless, it seems safe to say that it is not fully conscious, in the way that an infant of a few months is, and that it cannot reason, or communicate messages of indefinitely many sorts, does not engage in self-motivated activity, and has no self-awareness. Thus, in the *relevant* respects, a fetus, even a fully developed one, is considerably less person-like than is the average mature mammal, indeed the average fish. And I think that a rational person must conclude that if the right to life of a fetus is to be based upon its resemblance to a person, then it cannot be said to have any more right to life than, let us say, a newborn guppy (which also seems to be capable of feeling pain), and that a right of that magnitude could never override a woman's right to obtain an abortion, at any stage of her pregnancy. . . .

Thus, since the fact that even a fully developed fetus is not person-like enough to have any significant right to life on the basis of its person-like-ness shows that no legal restrictions upon the stage of pregnancy in which an abortion may be performed can be justified on the grounds that we should protect the rights of the older fetus; and since there is no other apparent justification for such restrictions, we may conclude that they are entirely unjustified. . . .

4. POTENTIAL PERSONHOOD
AND THE RIGHT TO LIFE

We have seen that a fetus does not resemble a person in any way which can support the claim that it has even some of the same rights. But what about its *potential*, the fact that if nurtured and allowed to develop naturally it will very probably become a person? Doesn't that alone give it at least some right to life? It is hard to deny that the fact that an entity is a potential person is a strong prima facie reason for not destroying it; but we need not conclude from this that a potential person has a right to life, by virtue of that potential. It may be that our feeling that it is better, other things being equal, not to destroy a potential person is better explained by the fact that potential people are still (felt to be) an invaluable resource, not to be lightly squandered. Surely, if every speck of dust were a potential person, we would be much less apt to conclude that every potential person has a right to become actual.

Still, we do not need to insist that a potential person has no right to life whatever. There may well be something immoral, and not just imprudent, about wantonly destroying potential people, when doing so isn't necessary to protect anyone's rights. But even if a potential person does have some prima facie right to life, such a right could not possibly outweigh the right of a woman to obtain an abortion, since the rights of any actual person invariably outweigh those of any potential person, whenever the two conflict. Since this may not be immediately obvious in the case of a human fetus, let us look at another case.

Suppose that our space explorer falls into the hands of an alien culture, whose scientists decide to create a few hundred thousand or more human beings, by breaking his body into its component cells, and using these to create fully developed human beings, with, of course, his genetic code. We may imagine that each of these newly created men will have all of the original man's abilities, skills, knowledge, and so on, and also have an individual self-concept, in short that each of them will be a bona fide (though hardly unique) person. Imagine that the whole project will take only seconds, and that its chances of success are extremely high, and that our explorer knows all of this, and also knows that these people will be treated fairly. I maintain that in such a situation he would have every right to escape if he could, and thus to deprive all of these potential people of their potential lives; for his right to life outweighs all of theirs together, in spite of the fact that they are all genetically human, all innocent, and all have a very high probability of becoming people very soon, if only he refrains from acting.

Indeed, I think he would have a right to escape even if it were not his life which the alien scientists planned to take, but only a year of his freedom, or, indeed, only a day. Nor would he be obligated to stay if he had gotten captured (thus bringing all these people-potentials into existence) because of his own carelessness, or even if he had done so deliberately, knowing the consequences. Regardless of how he got captured, he is not morally obligated to remain in captivity for *any* period of time for the sake of permitting any number of potential people to come into actuality, so great is the margin by which one actual person's right to liberty outweighs whatever right to life even a hundred thousand potential people have. And it seems reasonable to conclude that the rights of a woman will outweigh by a similar margin whatever right to life a fetus may have by virtue of its potential personhood.

Thus, neither a fetus's resemblance to a person, nor its potential for becoming a person provides any basis whatever for the claim that it has any significant right to life. Consequently, a woman's right to protect her health, happiness, freedom, and even her life, by terminating an unwanted pregnancy, will always override whatever right to life it may be appropriate to ascribe to a fetus, even a fully developed one. And thus, in the absence of any overwhelming social need for every possible child, the laws which restrict the right to obtain an abortion, or limit the period of pregnancy during which an abortion may be performed, are a wholly unjustified violation of a woman's most basic moral and constitutional rights.

POSTSCRIPT ON INFANTICIDE

One of the most troubling objections to the argument presented in this article is that it may appear to justify not only abortion but infanticide as well. A newborn infant is not a great deal more person-like than a nine-month fetus, and thus it might seem that if late-term abortion is sometimes justified, then infanticide must also be sometimes justified. Yet most people consider that infanticide is a form of murder, and thus never justified.

While it is important to appreciate the emotional force of this objection, its logical force is far less than it may seem at first glance. There are many reasons why infanticide is much more difficult to justify than abortion, even though if my argument is correct neither constitutes the killing of a person. In this country, and in this period of history, the deliberate killing of viable newborns is virtually never justified. This is in part because neonates are so very *close* to being persons that to kill them requires a very strong moral justification—as does the killing of dolphins, whales, chimpanzees, and other highly person-like creatures.

It is certainly wrong to kill such beings just for the sake of convenience, or financial profit, or "sport."

Another reason why infanticide is usually wrong, in our society, is that if the newborn's parents do not want it, or are unable to care for it, there are (in most cases) people who are able and eager to adopt it and to provide a good home for it. Many people wait years for the opportunity to adopt a child, and some are unable to do so even though there is every reason to believe that they would be good parents. The needless destruction of a viable infant inevitably deprives some person or persons of a source of great pleasure and satisfaction, perhaps severely impoverishing their lives. Furthermore, even if an infant is considered to be unadoptable (e.g., because of some extremely severe mental or physical handicap) it is still wrong in most cases to kill it. For most of us value the lives of infants, and would prefer to pay taxes to support orphanages and state institutions for the handicapped rather than to allow unwanted infants to be killed. So long as most people feel this way, and so long as our society can afford to provide care for infants which are unwanted or which have special needs that preclude home care, it is wrong to destroy any infant which has a chance of living a reasonably satisfactory life.

If these arguments show that infanticide is wrong, at least in this society, then why don't they also show that late-term abortion is wrong? After all, third trimester fetuses are also highly person-like, and many people value them and would much prefer that they be preserved, even at some cost to themselves. As a potential source of pleasure to some family, a viable fetus is just as valuable as a viable infant. But there is an obvious and crucial difference between the two cases: once the infant is born, its continued life cannot (except, perhaps, in very exceptional cases) pose any serious threat to the woman's life or health, since she is free to put it up for adoption, or, where this is impossible, to place it in a state-supported institution. While she might prefer that it die, rather than being raised by others, it is not clear that such a preference would constitute a right on her part. True, she may suffer greatly from the knowledge that her child will be thrown into the lottery of the adoption system, and that she will be unable to ensure its well-being, or even to know whether it is healthy, happy, doing well in school, etc.; for the law generally does not permit natural parents to remain in contact with their children, once they are adopted by another family. But there are surely better ways of dealing with these problems than by permitting infanticide in such cases. (It might help, for instance, if the natural parents of adopted children could at least receive some information about their progress, without necessarily being informed of the identity of the adopting family.)

In contrast, a pregnant woman's right to protect her own life and health clearly outweighs other people's desire that the fetus be preserved—just as, when a person's life or limb is threatened by some wild animal, and when the threat cannot be removed without killing the animal, the person's right to self-protection outweighs the desires of those who would prefer that the animal not be harmed. Thus, while the moment of birth may not mark any sharp discontinuity in the degree to which an infant possesses a right to life, it does mark the end of the mother's absolute right to determine its fate. Indeed, if and when a late-term abortion could be safely performed without killing the fetus, she would have no absolute right to insist on its death (e.g., if others wish to adopt it or to pay for its care), for the same reason that she does not have a right to insist that a viable infant be killed.

It remains true that according to my argument neither abortion nor the killing of neonates is properly considered a form of murder. Perhaps it is understandable that the law should classify infanticide as murder or homicide, since there is no other existing legal category which adequately or conveniently expresses the force of our society's disapproval of this action. But the moral distinction remains, and it has several important consequences.

In the first place, it implies that when an infant is born into a society which—unlike ours—is so impoverished that it simply cannot care for it adequately without endangering the survival of existing persons, killing it or allowing it to die is not necessarily wrong—provided that there is no *other* society which is willing and able to provide such care. Most human societies, from those at the hunting and gathering stage of economic development to the highly civilized Greeks and Romans, have permitted the practice of infanticide under such unfortunate circumstances, and I would argue that it shows a serious lack of understanding to condemn them as morally backward for this reason alone.

In the second place, the argument implies that when an infant is born with such severe physical anomalies that its life would predictably be a very short and/or very miserable one, even with the most heroic of medical treatment, and where its parents do not choose to bear the often crushing emotional, financial, and other burdens attendant upon the artificial prolongation of such a tragic life, it is not morally wrong to cease or withhold treatment, thus allowing the infant a painless death. It is wrong (and sometimes a form of murder) to practice involuntary euthanasia on persons, since they have the right to decide for themselves whether or not they wish to continue to live. But terminally ill neonates cannot make this decision for themselves, and thus it is incumbent upon responsible persons to make the decision for them, as best they can. The mistaken belief that infanticide is always tantamount to murder is responsible for a great deal of unnecessary suffering, not just on the part of infants which are made to endure needlessly prolonged and painful deaths, but also on the part of parents, nurses, and other involved persons, who must watch infants suffering needlessly, helpless to end that suffering in the most humane way.

I am well aware that these conclusions, however modest and reasonable they may seem to some people, strike other people as morally monstrous, and that some people might even prefer to abandon their previous support for women's right to abortion rather than accept a theory which leads to such conclusions about infanticide. But all that these facts show is that abortion is not an isolated moral issue; to fully understand the moral status of abortion we may have to reconsider other moral issues as well, issues not just about infanticide and euthanasia, but also about the moral rights of women and of nonhuman animals. It is a philosopher's task to criticize mistaken beliefs which stand in the way of moral understanding, even when—perhaps especially when—those beliefs are popular and widespread. The belief that moral strictures against killing should apply equally to *all* genetically human entities, and *only* to genetically human entities, is such an error. The overcoming of this error will undoubtedly require long and often painful struggle; but it must be done.

Chapter 31

Why Abortion Is Immoral

Don Marquis

When people discuss the morality of abortion, they usually begin by asking, Is the fetus a person, with a right to life? However, Professor Don Marquis (1935–) asks a different question: Do we have the same reasons not to kill a fetus that we have not to kill an adult? Killing adults, he says, is wrong because it deprives them of their future. But in killing a fetus, we deprive *it* of *its* future. Thus, it seems inconsistent to condemn one but not the other.

The view that abortion is, with rare exceptions, seriously immoral has received little support in the recent philosophical literature. No doubt most philosophers affiliated with secular institutions of higher education believe that the anti-abortion position is either a symptom of irrational religious dogma or a conclusion generated by seriously confused philosophical argument. The purpose of this essay is to undermine this general belief. This essay sets out an argument that purports to show, as well as any argument in ethics can show, that abortion is, except possibly in rare cases, seriously immoral, that it is in the same moral category as killing an innocent adult human being. . . .

Don Marquis, "Why Abortion Is Immoral" in *The Journal of Philosophy*, vol. 86, no. 4 (April 1989): 183–202. Copyright © 1989. Used with permission.

I

A sketch of standard anti-abortion and pro-choice arguments exhibits how those arguments possess certain symmetries that explain why partisans of those positions are so convinced of the correctness of their own positions, why they are not successful in convincing their opponents, and why, to others, this issue seems to be unresolvable. An analysis of the nature of this standoff suggests a strategy for surmounting it.

Consider the way a typical anti-abortionist argues. She will argue or assert that life is present from the moment of conception or that fetuses look like babies or that fetuses possess a characteristic such as a genetic code that is both necessary and sufficient for being human. Anti-abortionists seem to believe that (1) the truth of all of these claims is quite obvious, and (2) establishing any of these claims is sufficient to show that abortion is morally akin to murder.

A standard pro-choice strategy exhibits similarities. The pro-choicer will argue or assert that fetuses are not persons or that fetuses are not rational agents or that fetuses are not social beings. Pro-choicers seem to believe that (1) the truth of any of these claims is quite obvious, and (2) establishing any of these claims is sufficient to show that an abortion is not a wrongful killing.

In fact, both the pro-choice and the anti-abortion claims do seem to be true, although the "it looks like a baby" claim is more difficult to establish the earlier the pregnancy. We seem to have a standoff. How can it be resolved?

As everyone who has taken a bit of logic knows, if any of these arguments concerning abortion is a good argument, it requires not only some claim characterizing fetuses, but also some general moral principle that ties a characteristic of fetuses to having or not having the right to life or to some other moral characteristic that will generate the obligation or the lack of obligation not to end the life of a fetus. Accordingly, the arguments of the anti-abortionist and the pro-choicer need a bit of filling in to be regarded as adequate.

Note what each partisan will say. The anti-abortionist will claim that her position is supported by such generally accepted moral principles as "It is always prima facie seriously wrong to take a human life" or "It is always prima facie seriously wrong to end the life of a baby." Since these are generally accepted moral principles, her position is certainly not obviously wrong. The pro-choicer will claim that her position is supported by such plausible moral principles as "Being a person is what gives an individual intrinsic moral worth" or "It is only seriously prima facie wrong to take the life of a member of the human community." Since these are generally accepted moral principles, the pro-choice position is certainly not obviously wrong. Unfortunately, we have again arrived at a standoff.

Now, how might one deal with this standoff? The standard approach is to try to show how the moral principles of one's opponent lose their plausibility under analysis. It is easy to see how this is possible. On the one hand, the anti-abortionist will defend a moral principle concerning the wrongness of killing which tends to be broad in scope in order that even fetuses at an early stage of pregnancy will fall under it. The problem with broad principles is that they often embrace too much. In this particular instance, the principle "It is always prima facie wrong to take a human life" seems to entail that it is wrong to end the existence of a living human cancer-cell culture, on the grounds that the culture is both living and human. Therefore, it seems that the anti-abortionist's favored principle is too broad.

On the other hand, the pro-choicer wants to find a moral principle concerning the wrongness of killing which tends to be narrow in scope in order that fetuses will *not* fall under it. The problem with narrow principles is that they often do not embrace enough. Hence, the needed principles such as "It is prima facie seriously wrong to kill only persons" or "It is prima facie wrong to kill only rational agents" do not explain why it is wrong to kill infants or young children or the severely retarded or even perhaps the severely mentally ill. Therefore, we seem again to have a standoff. The anti-abortionist charges, not unreasonably, that pro-choice principles concerning killing are too narrow to be acceptable; the pro-choicer charges, not unreasonably, that anti-abortionist principles concerning killing are too broad to be acceptable. . . .

. . . All this suggests that a necessary condition of resolving the abortion controversy is a more theoretical account of the wrongness of killing. After all, if we merely believe, but do not understand, why killing adult human beings such as ourselves is wrong, how could we conceivably show that abortion is either immoral or permissible?

II

In order to develop such an account, we can start from the following unproblematic assumption concerning our own case: it is wrong to kill *us.* Why is it wrong? Some answers can be easily eliminated. It might be said that what makes killing us wrong is that a killing brutalizes the one who kills. But the brutalization consists of being inured to the performance of an act that is hideously immoral; hence, the brutalization does not explain the immorality. It might be said that what makes killing us wrong is the great loss others would experience due to our absence. Although such hubris is understandable, such an explanation does not account for the wrongness of killing hermits, or those whose lives are relatively independent and whose friends find it easy to make new friends.

A more obvious answer is better. What primarily makes killing wrong is neither its effect on the murderer nor its effect on the victim's friends and relatives, but its effect on the victim. The loss of one's life is one of the greatest losses one can suffer. The loss of one's life deprives one of all the experiences, activities, projects, and enjoyments that would otherwise have constituted one's future. Therefore, killing someone is wrong, primarily because the killing inflicts (one of) the greatest possible losses on the victim. To describe this as the loss of life can be misleading, however. The change in my biological state does not by itself make killing me wrong. The effect of the loss of my biological life is the loss to me of all those activities, projects, experiences, and enjoyments which would otherwise have constituted my future personal life. These activities, projects, experiences, and enjoyments are either valuable for their own sakes or are means to something else that is valuable for its own sake. Some parts of my future are not valued by me now, but will come to be valued by me as I grow older and as my values and capacities change. When I am killed, I am deprived both of what I now value which would have been part of my future personal life, but also what I would come to value. Therefore, when I die, I am deprived of all of the value of my future. Inflicting this loss on me is ultimately what makes killing me wrong. This being the case, it would seem that what makes killing *any* adult human being prima facie seriously wrong is the loss of his or her future.[1] . . .

The claim that what makes killing wrong is the loss of the victim's future is directly supported by two considerations. In the first place, this theory explains why we regard killing as one of the worst of crimes. Killing is especially wrong, because it deprives the victim of more than perhaps any other crime. In the second place, people with AIDS or cancer who know they are dying believe, of course, that dying is a very bad thing for them. They believe that the loss of a future to them that they would otherwise have experienced is what makes their premature death a very bad thing for them. A better theory of the wrongness of killing would require a different natural property associated with killing which better fits with the attitudes of the dying. What could it be?

The view that what makes killing wrong is the loss to the victim of the value of the victim's future gains additional support when some of its implications are examined. In the first place, it is incompatible with the view that it is wrong to kill only beings who are biologically human. It is possible that there exists a different species from another planet whose members have a future like ours. Since having a future like that is what makes killing someone wrong, this theory entails that it would be wrong to kill members of such a species. Hence, this theory is opposed to the claim that only life that is biologically human has great moral worth, a claim which many anti-abortionists have seemed to adopt. This opposition, which this theory has in common with personhood theories, seems to be a merit of the theory.

In the second place, the claim that the loss of one's future is the wrong-making feature of one's being killed entails the possibility that the futures of some actual nonhuman mammals on our own planet are sufficiently like ours that it is seriously wrong to kill them also. Whether some animals do have the same right to life as human beings depends on adding to the account of the wrongness of killing some additional account of just what it is about my future or the futures of other adult human beings which makes it wrong to kill us. No such additional account will be offered in this essay. Undoubtedly, the provision of such an account would be a very difficult matter. Undoubtedly, any such account would be quite controversial. Hence, it surely should not reflect badly on this sketch of an elementary theory of the wrongness of killing that it is indeterminate with respect to some very difficult issues regarding animal rights.

In the third place, the claim that the loss of one's future is the wrong-making feature of one's being killed does not entail, as sanctity of human life theories do, that active euthanasia is wrong. Persons who are severely and incurably ill, who face a future of pain and despair, and who wish to die will not have suffered a loss if they are killed. It is, strictly speaking, the value of a human's future which makes killing wrong in this theory. This being so, killing does not necessarily wrong some persons who are sick and dying. Of course, there may be other

reasons for a prohibition of active euthanasia, but that is another matter. Sanctity-of-human-life theories seem to hold that active euthanasia
is seriously wrong even in an individual case where there seems to be
good reason for it independently of public policy considerations. This
consequence is most implausible, and it is a plus for the claim that the
loss of a future of value is what makes killing wrong that it does not
share this consequence.

In the fourth place, the account of the wrongness of killing defended
in this essay does straightforwardly entail that it is prima facie seriously
wrong to kill children and infants, for we do presume that they have
futures of value. Since we do believe that it is wrong to kill defenseless
little babies, it is important that a theory of the wrongness of killing easily account for this. Personhood theories of the wrongness of killing, on
the other hand, cannot straightforwardly account for the wrongness of
killing infants and young children. Hence, such theories must add special ad hoc accounts of the wrongness of killing the young. The plausibility of such ad hoc theories seems to be a function of how desperately
one wants such theories to work. The claim that the primary wrong-
making feature of a killing is the loss to the victim of the value of its
future accounts for the wrongness of killing young children and infants
directly; it makes the wrongness of such acts as obvious as we actually
think it is. This is a further merit of this theory. Accordingly, it seems
that this value of a future-like-ours theory of the wrongness of killing
shares strengths of both sanctity-of-life and personhood accounts while
avoiding weaknesses of both. In addition, it meshes with a central intuition concerning what makes killing wrong.

The claim that the primary wrong-making feature of a killing is the
loss to the victim of the value of its future has obvious consequences
for the ethics of abortion. The future of a standard fetus includes a set
of experiences, projects, activities, and such which are identical with
the futures of adult human beings and are identical with the futures of
young children. Since the reason that is sufficient to explain why it is
wrong to kill human beings after the time of birth is a reason that also
applies to fetuses, it follows that abortion is prima facie seriously morally wrong.

This argument does not rely on the invalid inference that, since
it is wrong to kill persons, it is wrong to kill potential persons also.
The category that is morally central to this analysis is the category of

having a valuable future like ours; it is not the category of personhood. The argument to the conclusion that abortion is prima facie seriously morally wrong proceeded independently of the notion of person or potential person or any equivalent. Someone may wish to start with this analysis in terms of the value of a human future, conclude that abortion is, except perhaps in rare circumstances, seriously morally wrong, infer that fetuses have the right to life, and then call fetuses "persons" as a result of their having the right to life. Clearly, in this case, the category of person is being used to state the *conclusion* of the analysis rather than to generate the *argument* of the analysis. . . .

Of course, this value of a future-like-ours argument, if sound, shows only that abortion is prima facie wrong, not that it is wrong in any and all circumstances. Since the loss of the future to a standard fetus, if killed, is, however, at least as great a loss as the loss of the future to a standard adult human being who is killed, abortion, like ordinary killing, could be justified only by the most compelling reasons. The loss of one's life is almost the greatest misfortune that can happen to one. Presumably abortion could be justified in some circumstances, only if the loss consequent on failing to abort would be at least as great. Accordingly, morally permissible abortions will be rare indeed unless, perhaps, they occur so early in pregnancy that a fetus is not yet definitely an individual. Hence, this argument should be taken as showing that abortion is presumptively very seriously wrong, where the presumption is very strong—as strong as the presumption that killing another adult human being is wrong.

NOTE

1. I have been most influenced on this matter by Jonathan Glover, *Causing Death and Saving Lives* (New York: Penguin, 1977), ch. 3; and Robert Young, "What Is So Wrong with Killing People?" *Philosophy* 54, no. 210 (1979): 515–28.

Chapter 32

A Defense of Abortion

Judith Jarvis Thomson

For the sake of argument, Judith Jarvis Thomson grants that a
fetus is a person, with a right to life, from the moment of conception. Given that assumption, can we conclude that abortion is
immoral? The answer turns out to be surprisingly complicated.
Thomson's discussion not only throws light on the abortion issue,
it also illuminates the nature of rights.

Readers of this essay who are unfamiliar with Henry Fonda may
instead think of Ryan Reynolds, Channing Tatum, or Michael B.
Jordan. The philosophical point will be the same.

Judith Jarvis Thomson (1929–) is professor emerita at the Massachusetts Institute of Technology (MIT).

Most opposition to abortion relies on the premise that the fetus is a
human being, a person, from the moment of conception. . . .

. . . I think that the premise is false, that the fetus is not a person from
the moment of conception. A newly fertilized ovum, a newly implanted
clump of cells, is no more a person than an acorn is an oak tree. But I
shall not discuss any of this. For it seems to me to be of great interest
to ask what happens if, for the sake of argument, we allow the premise.
How, precisely, are we supposed to get from there to the conclusion that

abortion is morally impermissible? Opponents of abortion commonly spend most of their time establishing that the fetus is a person, and hardly any time explaining the step from there to the impermissibility of abortion. Perhaps they think the step too simple and obvious to require much comment. . . . Whatever the explanation, I suggest that the step they take is neither easy nor obvious, that it calls for closer examination than it is commonly given, and that when we do give it this closer examination we shall feel inclined to reject it.

I propose, then, that we grant that the fetus is a person from the moment of conception. How does the argument go from here? Something like this, I take it. Every person has a right to life. So the fetus has a right to life. No doubt the mother has a right to decide what shall happen in and to her body; everyone would grant that. But surely a person's right to life is stronger and more stringent than the mother's right to decide what happens in and to her body, and so outweighs it. So the fetus may not be killed; an abortion may not be performed.

It sounds plausible. But now let me ask you to imagine this. You wake up in the morning and find yourself back to back in bed with an unconscious violinist. A famous unconscious violinist. He has been found to have a fatal kidney ailment, and the Society of Music Lovers has canvassed all the available medical records and found that you alone have the right blood type to help. They have therefore kidnapped you, and last night the violinist's circulatory system was plugged into yours, so that your kidneys can be used to extract poisons from his blood as well as your own. The director of the hospital now tells you, "Look, we're sorry the Society of Music Lovers did this to you—we would never have permitted it if we had known. But still, they did it, and the violinist now is plugged into you. To unplug you would be to kill him. But never mind, it's only for nine months. By then he will have recovered from his ailment, and can safely be unplugged from you." Is it morally incumbent on you to accede to this situation? No doubt it would be very nice of you if you did, a great kindness. But do you *have* to accede to it? What if it were not nine months, but nine years? Or longer still? What if the director of the hospital says, "Tough luck, I agree, but you've now got to stay in bed, with the violinist plugged into you, for the rest of your life. Because remember this. All persons have a right to life, and violinists are persons. Granted you have a right to decide what happens in and to your body, but a person's right to life outweighs your right to decide what happens in and to your body. So you cannot ever be unplugged from him." I imagine you would regard this as outrageous, which suggests that something really is wrong with that plausible-sounding argument I mentioned a moment ago.

In this case, of course, you were kidnapped; you didn't volunteer for the operation that plugged the violinist into your kidneys. Can those who oppose abortion on the ground I mentioned make an exception for a pregnancy due to rape? Certainly. They can say that persons have a right to life only if they didn't come into existence because of rape; or they can say that all persons have a right to life, but that some have less of a right to life than others, in particular, that those who came into existence because of rape have less. But these statements have a rather unpleasant sound. Surely the question of whether you have a right to life at all, or how much of it you have, shouldn't turn on the question of whether or not you are the product of a rape. And in fact the people who oppose abortion on the ground I mentioned do not make this distinction, and hence do not make an exception in case of rape.

Nor do they make an exception for a case in which the mother has to spend the nine months of her pregnancy in bed. They would agree that would be a great pity, and hard on the mother; but all the same, all persons have a right to life, the fetus is a person, and so on. I suspect, in fact, that they would not make an exception for a case in which, miraculously enough, the pregnancy went on for nine years, or even the rest of the mother's life.

Some won't even make an exception for a case in which continuation of the pregnancy is likely to shorten the mother's life; they regard abortion as impermissible even to save the mother's life. Such cases are nowadays very rare, and many opponents of abortion do not accept this extreme view. All the same, it is a good place to begin: a number of points of interest come out in respect to it.

1. Let us call the view that abortion is impermissible even to save the mother's life "the extreme view." I want to suggest first that it does not issue from the argument I mentioned earlier without the addition of some fairly powerful premises. Suppose a woman has become pregnant, and now learns that she has a cardiac condition such that she will die if she carries the baby to term. What may be done for her? The fetus, being a person, has a right to life, but as the mother is a person too, so has she a right to life. Presumably they have an equal right to life.

How is it supposed to come out that an abortion may not be performed? If mother and child have an equal right to life, shouldn't we perhaps flip a coin? Or should we add to the mother's right to life her right to decide what happens in and to her body, which everybody seems to be ready to grant—the sum of her rights now outweighing the fetus' right to life?

The most familiar argument here is the following. We are told that performing the abortion would be directly killing the child, whereas doing nothing would not be killing the mother, but only letting her die. Moreover, in killing the child, one would be killing an innocent person, for the child has committed no crime, and is not aiming at his mother's death. And then there are a variety of ways in which this might be continued. (1) But as directly killing an innocent person is always and absolutely impermissible, an abortion may not be performed. Or, (2) as directly killing an innocent person is murder, and murder is always and absolutely impermissible, an abortion may not be performed. Or, (3) as one's duty to refrain from directly killing an innocent person is more stringent than one's duty to keep a person from dying, an abortion may not be performed. Or, (4) if one's only options are directly killing an innocent person or letting a person die, one must prefer letting the person die, and thus an abortion may not be performed.

Some people seem to have thought that these are not further premises which must be added if the conclusion is to be reached, but that they follow from the very fact that an innocent person has a right to life. But this seems to me to be a mistake, and perhaps the simplest way to show this is to bring out that while we must certainly grant that innocent persons have a right to life, the theses in (1) through (4) are all false. Take (2), for example. If directly killing an innocent person is murder, and thus is impermissible, then the mother's directly killing the innocent person inside her is murder, and thus is impermissible. But it cannot seriously be thought to be murder if the mother performs an abortion on herself to save her life. It cannot seriously be said that she *must* refrain, that she *must* sit passively by and wait for her death. Let us look again at the case of you and the violinist. There you are, in bed with the violinist, and the director of the hospital says to you, "It's all most distressing, and I deeply sympathize, but you see this is putting an additional strain on your kidneys, and you'll be dead within the month. But you *have* to stay where you are all the same. Because unplugging you would be directly killing an innocent violinist, and that's murder, and that's impermissible." If anything in the world is true, it is that you do not commit murder, you do not do what is impermissible, if you reach around to your back and unplug yourself from that violinist to save your life.

The main focus of attention in writings on abortion has been on what a third party may or may not do in answer to a request from a woman for an abortion. This is in a way understandable. Things being as they are, there isn't much a woman can safely do to abort herself. So the question asked is what a third party may do, and what the mother may do, if it is mentioned at all, is deduced, almost as an afterthought, from what it is concluded that third parties may do. But it seems to me that to treat the matter in this way is to refuse to grant to the mother that very status of person which is so firmly insisted on for the fetus. For we cannot simply read off what a person may do from what a third party may do. Suppose you find yourself trapped in a tiny house with a growing child. I mean a very tiny house, and a rapidly growing child—you are already up against the wall of the house and in a few minutes you'll be crushed to death. The child on the other hand won't be crushed to death; if nothing is done to stop him from growing he'll be hurt, but in the end he'll simply burst open the house and walk out a free man. Now I could well understand it if a bystander were to say, "There's nothing we can do for you. We cannot choose between your life and his, we cannot be the ones to decide who is to live, we cannot intervene." But it cannot be concluded that you too can do nothing, that you cannot attack it to save your life. However innocent the child may be, you do not have to wait passively while it crushes you to death. Perhaps a pregnant woman is vaguely felt to have the status of house, to which we don't allow the right of self-defense. But if the woman houses the child, it should be remembered that she is a person who houses it.

I should perhaps stop to say explicitly that I am not claiming that people have a right to do anything whatever to save their lives. I think, rather, that there are drastic limits to the right of self-defense. If someone threatens you with death unless you torture someone else to death, I think you have not the right, even to save your life, to do so. But the case under consideration here is very different. In our case there are only two people involved, one whose life is threatened, and one who threatens it. Both are innocent: the one who is threatened is not threatened because of any fault, the one who threatens does not threaten because of any fault. For this reason we may feel that we bystanders cannot intervene. But the person threatened can.

In sum, a woman surely can defend her life against the threat to it posed by the unborn child, even if doing so involves its death. And this shows not merely that the theses in (1) through (4) are false; it shows also that the extreme view of abortion is false, and so we need not canvass any other possible ways of arriving at it from the argument I mentioned at the outset.

2. The extreme view could of course be weakened to say that while abortion is permissible to save the mother's life, it may not be performed by a third party, but only by the mother herself. But this cannot be right either. For what we have to keep in mind is that the mother and the unborn child are not like two tenants in a small house which has, by an unfortunate mistake, been rented to both: the mother *owns* the house. The fact that she does adds to the offensiveness of deducing that the mother can do nothing from the supposition that third parties can do nothing. But it does more than this: it casts a bright light on the supposition that third parties can do nothing. Certainly it lets us see that a third party who says "I cannot choose between you" is fooling himself if he thinks this is impartiality. If Jones has found and fastened on a certain coat, which he needs to keep him from freezing, but which Smith also needs to keep him from freezing, then it is not impartiality that says "I cannot choose between you" when Smith owns the coat. Women have said again and again "This body is *my* body!" and they have reason to feel angry, reason to feel that it has been like shouting into the wind. Smith, after all, is hardly likely to bless us if we say to him, "Of course it's your coat, anybody would grant that it is. But no one may choose between you and Jones who is to have it." . . .

I suppose that in some views of human life the mother's body is only on loan to her, the loan not being one which gives her any prior claim to it. One who held this view might well think it impartiality to say "I cannot choose." But I shall simply ignore this possibility. My own view is that if a human being has any just, prior claim to anything at all, he has a just, prior claim to his own body. And perhaps this needn't be argued for here anyway, since, as I mentioned, the arguments against abortion we are looking at do grant that the woman has a right to decide what happens in and to her body.

But although they do grant it, I have tried to show that they do not take seriously what is done in granting it. I suggest the same thing will reappear even more clearly when we turn away from cases in which the mother's life is at stake, and attend, as I propose we now do, to the vastly more common cases in which a woman wants an abortion for some less weighty reason than preserving her own life.

3. Where the mother's life is not at stake, the argument I mentioned at the outset seems to have a much stronger pull. "Everyone has a right to life, so the unborn person has a right to life." And isn't the child's right to life weightier than anything other than the mother's own right to life, which she might put forward as ground for an abortion?

This argument treats the right to life as if it were unproblematic. It is not, and this seems to me to be precisely the source of the mistake.

For we should now, at long last, ask what it comes to, to have a right to life. In some views having a right to life includes having a right to be given at least the bare minimum one needs for continued life. But suppose that what in fact *is* the bare minimum a man needs for continued life is something he has no right at all to be given? If I am sick unto death, and the only thing that will save my life is the touch of Henry Fonda's cool hand on my fevered brow, then all the same, I have no right to be given the touch of Henry Fonda's cool hand on my fevered brow. It would be frightfully nice of him to fly in from the West Coast to provide it. It would be less nice, though no doubt well meant, if my friends flew out to the West Coast and carried Henry Fonda back with them. But I have no right at all against anybody that he should do this for me. Or again, to return to the story I told earlier, the fact that for continued life that violinist needs the continued use of your kidneys does not establish that he has a right to be given the continued use of your kidneys. He certainly has no right against you that *you* should give him continued use of your kidneys. For nobody has any right to use your kidneys unless you give him such a right; and nobody has the right against you that you shall give him this right—if you do allow him to go on using your kidneys, this is a kindness on your part, and not something he can claim from you as his due. Nor has he any right against anybody else that *they* should give him continued use of your kidneys. Certainly he had no right against the Society of Music Lovers that they should plug him into you in the first place. And if you now start to unplug yourself, having learned that you will otherwise have to spend nine years in bed with him, there is nobody in the world who must try to prevent you, in order to see to it that he is given something he has a right to be given.

Some people are rather stricter about the right to life. In their view, it does not include the right to be given anything, but amounts to, and only to, the right not to be killed by anybody. But here a related difficulty arises. If everybody is to refrain from killing that violinist, then everybody must refrain from doing a great many different sorts of things. Everybody must refrain from slitting his throat, everybody must refrain from shooting him—and everybody must refrain from unplugging you from him. But does he have a right against everybody that they shall refrain from unplugging you from him? To refrain from doing this is to allow him to continue to use your kidneys. It could be argued that he has a right against us that *we* should allow him to continue to use your kidneys. That is, while he had no right against us that we should give him the use of your kidneys, it might be argued that he anyway has a right against us that we shall not now intervene and deprive him of the use of your kidneys. I shall come back to third-party interventions later. But certainly the violinist has no right against you that *you* shall allow him to continue to use your kidneys. As I said, if you do allow him to use them, it is a kindness on your part, and not something you owe him.

. . . I would stress that I am not arguing that people do not have a right to life—quite to the contrary, it seems to me that the primary control we must place on the acceptability of an account of rights is that it should turn out in that account to be a truth that all persons have a right to life. I am arguing only that having a right to life does not guarantee having either a right to be given the use of or a right to be allowed continued use of another person's body—even if one needs it for life itself. So the right to life will not serve the opponents of abortion in the very simple and clear way in which they seem to have thought it would.

4. There is another way to bring out the difficulty. In the most ordinary sort of case, to deprive someone of what he has a right to is to treat him unjustly. Suppose a boy and his small brother are jointly given a box of chocolates for Christmas. If the older boy takes the box and refuses to give his brother any of the chocolates, he is unjust to him, for the brother has been given a right to half of them. But suppose that, having learned that otherwise it means nine years in bed with that violinist, you unplug yourself from him. You surely are not being unjust to him, for you gave him no right to use your kidneys, and no one else can have given him any such right. But we have to notice that in unplugging yourself, you are killing him; and violinists, like everybody else, have a right to life, and thus in the view we were considering just now, the right not to be killed. So here you do what he supposedly has a right you shall not do, but you do not act unjustly to him in doing it.

The emendation which may be made at this point is this: the right to life consists not in the right not to be killed, but rather in the right not to be killed unjustly. This runs a risk of circularity, but never mind: it would enable us to square the fact that the violinist has a right to life with the fact that you do not act unjustly toward him in unplugging yourself, thereby killing him. For if you do not kill him unjustly, you do not violate his right to life, and so it is no wonder you do him no injustice.

But if this emendation is accepted, the gap in the argument against abortion stares us plainly in the face: it is by no means enough to show that the fetus is a person, and to remind us that all persons have a right to life—we need to be shown also that killing the fetus violates its right to life, that is, that abortion is unjust killing. And is it?

I suppose we may take it as a datum that in a case of pregnancy due to rape the mother has not given the unborn person a right to the use of her body for food and shelter. Indeed, in what pregnancy could it be supposed that the mother has given the unborn person such a right? It is not as if there were unborn persons drifting about the world, to whom a woman who wants a child says "I invite you in."

But it might be argued that there are other ways one can have acquired a right to the use of another person's body than by having been invited to use it by that person. Suppose a woman voluntarily indulges in intercourse, knowing of the chance it will issue in pregnancy, and then she does become pregnant; is she not in part responsible for the presence, in fact the very existence, of the unborn person inside her? No doubt she did not invite it in. But doesn't her partial responsibility for its being there itself give it a right to the use of her body? If so, then her aborting it would be more like the boy's taking away the chocolates, and less like your unplugging yourself from the violinist—doing so would be depriving it of what it does have a right to, and thus would be doing it an injustice.

And then, too, it might be asked whether or not she can kill it even to save her own life: If she voluntarily called it into existence, how can she now kill it, even in self-defense?

The first thing to be said about this is that it is something new. Opponents of abortion have been so concerned to make out the independence of the fetus, in order to establish that it has a right to life, just as its mother does, that they have tended to overlook the possible support they might gain from making out that the fetus is *dependent* on the mother, in order to establish that she has a special kind of responsibility for it, a responsibility that gives it rights against her which are not possessed by any independent person—such as an ailing violinist who is a stranger to her.

On the other hand, this argument would give the unborn person a right to its mother's body only if her pregnancy resulted from a voluntary act, undertaken in full knowledge of the chance a pregnancy might result from it. It would leave out entirely the unborn person whose existence is due to rape. Pending the availability of some further argument, then, we would be left with the conclusion that unborn persons whose existence is due to rape have no right to the use of their mothers' bodies, and thus that aborting them is not depriving them of anything they have a right to and hence is not unjust killing.

And we should also notice that it is not at all plain that this argument really does go even as far as it purports to. For there are cases and cases, and the details make a difference. If the room is stuffy, and I therefore open a window to air it, and a burglar climbs in, it would be absurd to say, "Ah, now he can stay, she's given him a right to the use of her house—for she is partially responsible for his presence there, having voluntarily done what enabled him to get in, in full knowledge that there are such things as burglars, and that burglars burgle." It would be still more absurd to say this if I had had bars installed outside my windows, precisely to prevent burglars from getting in, and a burglar got in only because of a defect in the bars. It remains equally absurd if we imagine it is not a burglar who climbs in, but an innocent person who blunders or falls in. Again, suppose it were like this: people-seeds drift about in the air like pollen, and if you open your windows, one may drift in and take root in your carpets or upholstery. You don't want children, so you fix up your windows with fine mesh screens, the very best you can buy. As can happen, however, and on very, very rare occasions does happen, one of the screens is defective; and a seed drifts in and takes root. Does the person-plant who now develops have a right to the use of your house? Surely not—despite the fact that you voluntarily opened your windows, you knowingly kept carpets and upholstered furniture, and you knew that screens were sometimes defective. Someone may argue that you are responsible for its rooting, that it does have a right to your house, because after all you *could* have lived out your life with bare floors and furniture, or with sealed windows and doors. But this won't do—for by the same token anyone can avoid a pregnancy due to rape by having a hysterectomy, or anyway by never leaving home without a (reliable!) army.

It seems to me that the argument we are looking at can establish at most that there are *some* cases in which the unborn person has a right to the use of its mother's body, and therefore *some* cases in which abortion is unjust killing. There is room for much discussion and argument as to precisely which, if any. But I think we should sidestep this issue and leave it open, for at any rate the argument certainly does not establish that all abortion is unjust killing.

5. There is room for yet another argument here, however. We surely must all grant that there may be cases in which it would be morally indecent to detach a person from your body at the cost of his life. Suppose you learn that what the violinist needs is not nine years of your life, but only one hour: all you need do to save his life is to spend one hour in that bed with him. Suppose also that letting him use your kidneys for that one hour would not affect your health in the slightest. Admittedly you were kidnapped. Admittedly you did not give anyone permission to plug him into you. Nevertheless it seems to me plain you *ought* to allow him to use your kidneys for that hour—it would be indecent to refuse.

Again, suppose pregnancy lasted only an hour, and constituted no threat to life or health. And suppose that a woman becomes pregnant as a result of rape. Admittedly she did not voluntarily do anything to bring about the existence of a child. Admittedly she did nothing at all which would give the unborn person a right to the use of her body. All the same it might well be said, as in the newly emended violinist story, that she *ought* to allow it to remain for that hour—that it would be indecent of her to refuse.

Now some people are inclined to use the term "right" in such a way that it follows from the fact that you ought to allow a person to use your body for the hour he needs, that he has a right to use your body for the hour he needs, even though he has not been given that right by any person or act. They may say that it follows also that if you refuse, you act unjustly toward him. This use of the term is perhaps so common that it cannot be called wrong; nevertheless it seems to me to be an unfortunate loosening of what we would do better to keep a tight rein on. Suppose that box of chocolates I mentioned earlier had not been given to both boys jointly, but was given only to the older boy. There he sits, stolidly eating his way through the box, his small brother watching enviously. Here we are likely to say "You ought not to be so mean. You ought to give your brother some of those chocolates." My own view is that it just does not follow from the truth of this that the brother has any right to any of the chocolates. If the boy refuses to give his brother any, he is greedy, stingy, callous—but not unjust. I suppose that the people I have in mind will say it does follow that the brother has a right to some of the chocolates, and thus that the boy does act unjustly if he refuses to give his brother any. But the effect of saying this is to obscure what we should keep distinct, namely the difference between the boy's refusal in this case and the boy's refusal in the earlier case, in which the box was given to both boys jointly, and in which the small brother thus had what was from any point of view clear title to half.

A further objection to so using the term "right" that from the fact that A ought to do a thing for B, it follows that B has a right against A that A do it for him, is that it is going to make the question of whether or not a man has a right to a thing turn on how easy it is to provide him with it; and this seems not merely unfortunate, but morally unacceptable. Take the case of Henry Fonda again. I said earlier that I had no right to the touch of his cool hand on my fevered brow, even though I needed it to save my life. I said it would be frightfully nice of him to fly in from the West Coast to provide me with it, but that I had no right against him that he should do so. But suppose he isn't on the West Coast. Suppose he has only to walk across the room, place a hand briefly on my brow—and lo, my life is saved. Then surely he ought to do it, it would be indecent to refuse. Is it to be said "Ah, well, it follows that in this case she has a right to the touch of his hand on her brow, and so it would be an injustice in him to refuse"? So that I have a right to it when it is easy for him to provide it, though no right when it's hard? It's rather a shocking idea that anyone's rights should fade away and disappear as it gets harder and harder to accord them to him.

So my own view is that even though you ought to let the violinist use your kidneys for the one hour he needs, we should not conclude that he has a right to do so—we should say that if you refuse, you are, like the boy who owns all the chocolates and will give none away, self-centered and callous, indecent in fact, but not unjust. And similarly, that even supposing a case in which a woman pregnant due to rape ought to allow the unborn person to use her body for the hour he needs, we should not conclude that he has a right to do so; we should conclude that she is self-centered, callous, indecent, but not unjust, if she refuses. The complaints are no less grave; they are just different. However, there is no need to insist on this point. If anyone does wish to deduce "he has a right" from "you ought," then all the same he must surely grant that there are cases in which it is not morally required of you that you allow that violinist to use your kidneys, and in which he does not have a right to use them, and in which you do not do him an injustice if you refuse. And so also for mother and unborn child. Except in such cases as the unborn person has a right to demand it—and we were leaving open the possibility that there may be such cases—nobody is morally *required* to make large sacrifices, of health, of all other interests and concerns, of all other duties and commitments, for nine years, or even for nine months, in order to keep another person alive.

6. We have in fact to distinguish between two kinds of Samaritan: the Good Samaritan and what we might call the Minimally Decent Samaritan. The story of the Good Samaritan, you will remember, goes like this:

> A certain man went down from Jerusalem to Jericho, and fell among thieves, which stripped him of his raiment, and wounded him, and departed, leaving him half dead.
>
> And by chance there came down a certain priest that way; and when he saw him, he passed by on the other side.
>
> And likewise a Levite, when he was at the place, came and looked on him, and passed by on the other side.
>
> But a certain Samaritan, as he journeyed, came where he was; and when he saw him he had compassion on him.
>
> And went to him, and bound up his wounds, pouring in oil and wine, and set him on his own beast, and brought him to an inn, and took care of him.
>
> And on the morrow, when he departed, he took out two pence, and gave them to the host, and said unto him, "Take care of him; and

whatsoever thou spendest more, when I come again, I will repay thee."
(Luke 10:30–35)

The Good Samaritan went out of his way, at some cost to himself, to
help one in need of it. We are not told what the options were, that is,
whether or not the priest and the Levite could have helped by doing less
than the Good Samaritan did, but assuming they could have, then the
fact they did nothing at all shows they were not even Minimally Decent
Samaritans, not because they were not Samaritans, but because they
were not even minimally decent.

These things are a matter of degree, of course, but there is a difference, and it comes out perhaps most clearly in the story of Kitty
Genovese, who, as you will remember, was murdered while thirty-eight
people watched or listened, and did nothing at all to help her. A Good
Samaritan would have rushed out to give direct assistance against the
murderer. Or perhaps we had better allow that it would have been a
Splendid Samaritan who did this, on the ground that it would have
involved a risk of death for himself. But the thirty-eight not only did not
do this, they did not even trouble to pick up a phone to call the police.
Minimally Decent Samaritanism would call for doing at least that, and
their not having done it was monstrous.

After telling the story of the Good Samaritan, Jesus said "Go, and do
thou likewise." Perhaps he meant that we are morally required to act as
the Good Samaritan did. Perhaps he was urging people to do more than
is morally required of them. At all events it seems plain that it was not
morally required of any of the thirty-eight that he rush out to give direct
assistance at the risk of his own life, and that it is not morally required
of anyone that he give long stretches of his life—nine years or nine
months—to sustaining the life of a person who has no special right (we
were leaving open the possibility of this) to demand it.

Indeed, with one rather striking class of exceptions, no one in any
country in the world is *legally* required to do anywhere near as much
as this for anyone else. The class of exceptions is obvious. My main
concern here is not the state of the law in respect to abortion, but it is
worth drawing attention to the fact that in no state in this country is any
man compelled by law to be even a Minimally Decent Samaritan to any
person; there is no law under which charges could be brought against
the thirty-eight who stood by while Kitty Genovese died. By contrast,

in most states in this country women are compelled by law to be not merely Minimally Decent Samaritans, but Good Samaritans to unborn persons inside them. This doesn't by itself settle anything one way or the other, because it may well be argued that there should be laws in this country—as there are in many European countries—compelling at least Minimally Decent Samaritanism. But it does show that there is a gross injustice in the existing state of the law. And it shows also that the groups currently working against liberalization of abortion laws, in fact working toward having it declared unconstitutional for a state to permit abortion, had better start working for the adoption of Good Samaritan laws generally, or earn the charge that they are acting in bad faith.

I should think, myself, that Minimally Decent Samaritan laws would be one thing, Good Samaritan laws quite another, and in fact highly improper. But we are not here concerned with the law. What we should ask is not whether anybody should be compelled by law to be a Good Samaritan, but whether we must accede to a situation in which some-body is being compelled—by nature, perhaps—to be a Good Samaritan. We have, in other words, to look now at third-party interventions. I have been arguing that no person is morally required to make large sacrifices to sustain the life of another who has no right to demand them, and this even where the sacrifices do not include life itself; we are not morally required to be Good Samaritans or anyway Very Good Samaritans to one another. But what if a man cannot extricate himself from such a situation? What if he appeals to us to extricate him? It seems to me plain that there are cases in which we can, cases in which a Good Samaritan would extricate him. There you are, you were kidnapped, and nine years in bed with that violinist lie ahead of you. You have your own life to lead. You are sorry, but you simply cannot see giving up so much of your life to the sustaining of his. You cannot extricate yourself, and ask us to do so. I should have thought that—in light of his having no right to the use of your body—it was obvious that we do not have to accede to your being forced to give up so much. We can do what you ask. There is no injustice to the violinist in our doing so.

7. Following the lead of the opponents of abortion, I have throughout been speaking of the fetus merely as a person, and what I have been asking is whether or not the argument we began with, which proceeds only from the fetus' being a person, really does establish its conclusion. I have argued that it does not.

But of course there are arguments and arguments, and it may be said that I have simply fastened on the wrong one. It may be said that what is important is not merely the fact that the fetus is a person, but that it is a person for whom the woman has a special kind of responsibility issuing from the fact that she is its mother. And it might be argued that all my analogies are therefore irrelevant—for you do not have that special kind of responsibility for that violinist, Henry Fonda does not have that special kind of responsibility for me. And our attention might be drawn to the fact that men and women both *are* compelled by law to provide support for their children.

I have in effect dealt (briefly) with this argument in section 4 above; but a (still briefer) recapitulation now may be in order. Surely we do not have any such "special responsibility" for a person unless we have assumed it, explicitly or implicitly. If a set of parents do not try to prevent pregnancy, do not obtain an abortion, and then at the time of birth of the child do not put it out for adoption, but rather take it home with them, then they have assumed responsibility for it, they have given it rights, and they cannot *now* withdraw support from it at the cost of its life because they now find it difficult to go on providing for it. But if they have taken all reasonable precautions against having a child, they do not simply by virtue of their biological relationship to the child who comes into existence have a special responsibility for it. They may wish to assume responsibility for it, or they may not wish to. And I am suggesting that if assuming responsibility for it would require large sacrifices, then they may refuse. A Good Samaritan would not refuse—or anyway, a Splendid Samaritan, if the sacrifices that had to be made were enormous. But then so would a Good Samaritan assume responsibility for that violinist; so would Henry Fonda, if he is a Good Samaritan, fly in from the West Coast and assume responsibility for me.

8. My argument will be found unsatisfactory on two counts by many of those who want to regard abortion as morally permissible. First, while I do argue that abortion is not impermissible, I do not argue that it is always permissible. There may well be cases in which carrying the child to term requires only Minimally Decent Samaritanism of the mother, and this is a standard we must not fall below. I am inclined to think it a merit of my account precisely that it does *not* give a general yes or a general no. It allows for and supports our sense that, for example, a sick and desperately frightened fourteen-year-old schoolgirl, pregnant due to rape, may *of course* choose abortion, and that any law which rules this out is an insane law. And it also allows for and supports our sense that in other cases resort to abortion is even positively indecent. It would be indecent in the woman to request an abortion, and indecent in a doctor to perform it, if she is in her seventh month, and wants the abortion just to avoid the nuisance of postponing a trip abroad. The very fact that the arguments I have been drawing attention to treat all cases of abortion, or even all cases of abortion in which the mother's life is not at stake, as morally on a par ought to have made them suspect at the outset.

Secondly, while I am arguing for the permissibility of abortion in some cases, I am not arguing for the right to secure the death of the unborn child. It is easy to confuse these two things in that up to a certain point in the life of the fetus it is not able to survive outside the mother's body; hence removing it from her body guarantees its death. But they are importantly different. I have argued that you are not morally required to spend nine months in bed, sustaining the life of that violinist; but to say this is by no means to say that if, when you unplug yourself, there is a miracle and he survives, you then have a right to turn around and slit his throat. You may detach yourself even if this costs him his life; you have no right to be guaranteed his death, by some other means, if unplugging yourself does not kill him. There are some people who will feel dissatisfied by this feature of my argument. A woman may be utterly devastated by the thought of a child, a bit of herself, put out for adoption and never seen or heard of again. She may therefore want not merely that the child be detached from her, but more, that it die. Some opponents of abortion are inclined to regard this as beneath contempt—thereby showing insensitivity to what is surely a powerful source of despair. All the same, I agree that the desire for the child's death is not one which anybody may gratify, should it turn out to be possible to detach the child alive.

At this place, however, it should be remembered that we have only been pretending throughout that the fetus is a human being from the moment of conception. A very early abortion is surely not the killing of a person, and so is not dealt with by anything I have said here.

BIOETHICS: EUTHANASIA, HEALTHCARE, AND CLONING

Chapter 33

The Morality of Euthanasia

James Rachels

James Rachels wrote *The End of Life: Euthanasia and Morality* (1986). Here he defends the "argument from mercy." Euthanasia, he thinks, is justified when death is the only way to escape awful pain. In Rachels' main example, the pain is suffered by someone dying from cancer.

Rachels himself died of cancer in 2003. At the end of his life, nothing persuaded him to change his view of euthanasia. But he did wonder whether the argument from mercy would require less intentional killing than he had thought. Often a humane death occurs via "permanent sedation." This is when a dying patient is given more and more pain medication for pain relief, which causes the patient to lose consciousness (or "go to sleep") before dying. Under such circumstances, the intention to kill is unnecessary.

The single most powerful argument in support of euthanasia is the argument from mercy. It is also an exceptionally simple argument, at least in its main idea, which makes one uncomplicated point. Terminally ill patients sometimes suffer pain so horrible that it is beyond the comprehension of those who have not actually experienced it. Their suffering can be so terrible that we do not even like to read about it or

James Rachels, "The Morality of Euthanasia" in *Philosophy and Public Affairs*, vol. 1, no. 1 (autumn 1971): 47–66. Used with permission.

think about it; we recoil even from the description of such agony. The argument from mercy says euthanasia is justified because it provides an end to *that*.

The great Irish satirist Jonathan Swift took eight years to die, while, in the words of Joseph Fletcher, "His mind crumbled to pieces." At times the pain in his blinded eyes was so intense he had to be restrained from tearing them out with his own hands. Knives and other potential instruments of suicide had to be kept from him. For the last three years of his life, he could do nothing but sit and drool; and when he finally died it was only after convulsions that lasted thirty-six hours.

Swift died in 1745. Since then, doctors have learned how to eliminate much of the pain that accompanies terminal illness, but the victory has been far from complete. So, here is a more modern example.

Stewart Alsop was a respected journalist who died in 1975 of a rare form of cancer. Before he died, he wrote movingly of his experiences as a terminal patient. Although he had not thought much about euthanasia before, he came to approve of it after rooming briefly with someone he called Jack:

> The third night that I roomed with Jack in our tiny double room in the solid-tumor ward of the cancer clinic of the National Institutes of Health in Bethesda, Md., a terrible thought occurred to me.
>
> Jack had a melanoma in his belly, a malignant solid tumor that the doctors guessed was about the size of a softball. The cancer had started a few months before with a small tumor in his left shoulder, and there had been several operations since. The doctors planned to remove the softball-sized tumor, but they knew Jack would soon die. The cancer had metastasized—it had spread beyond control.
>
> Jack was good-looking, about 28, and brave. He was in constant pain, and his doctor had prescribed an intravenous shot of a synthetic opiate—a pain-killer, or analgesic—every four hours. His wife spent many of the daylight hours with him, and she would sit or lie on his bed and pat him all over, as one pats a child, only more methodically, and this seemed to help control the pain. But at night, when his pretty wife had left (wives cannot stay overnight at the NIH clinic) and darkness fell, the pain would attack without pity.
>
> At the prescribed hour, a nurse would give Jack a shot of the synthetic analgesic, and this would control the pain for perhaps two hours or a bit more. Then he would begin to moan, or whimper, very low, as though he didn't want to wake me. Then he would begin to howl, like a dog.

When this happened, either he or I would ring for a nurse, and ask for a pain-killer. She would give him some codeine or the like by mouth, but it never did any real good—it affected him no more than half an aspirin might affect a man who had just broken his arm. Always the nurse would explain as encouragingly as she could that there was not long to go before the next intravenous shot—"Only about 50 minutes now." And always poor Jack's whimpers and howls would become more loud and frequent until at last the blessed relief came.

     The third night of this routine, the terrible thought occurred to me. "If Jack were a dog," I thought, "what would be done with him?" The answer was obvious: the pound, and chloroform. No human being with a spark of pity could let a living thing suffer so, to no good end.

The NIH clinic is, of course, one of the most modern and best-equipped hospitals we have. Jack's suffering was not the result of poor treatment in some backward rural facility; it was the inevitable product of his disease, which medical science was powerless to prevent.

I have quoted Alsop at length not for the sake of indulging in gory details but to give a clear idea of the kind of suffering we are talking about. We should not gloss over these facts with euphemistic language or squeamishly avert our eyes from them. For only by keeping them firmly and vividly in mind can we appreciate the full force of the argument from mercy: If a person prefers—and even begs for—death as the only alternative to lingering on *in this kind of torment*, only to die anyway after a while, then surely it is not immoral to help this person die sooner. As Alsop put it, "No human being with a spark of pity could let a living thing suffer so, to no good end."

THE UTILITARIAN VERSION OF THE ARGUMENT

In connection with this argument, the utilitarians deserve special mention. They argued that actions and social policies should be judged right or wrong *exclusively* according to whether they cause happiness or misery; and they argued that when judged by this standard, euthanasia turns out to be morally acceptable. The utilitarian argument may be elaborated as follows:

(1) Any action or social policy is morally right if it serves to increase the amount of happiness in the world or to decrease the amount of

misery. Conversely, an action or social policy is morally wrong if it serves to decrease happiness or to increase misery.

(2) The policy of killing, at their own request, hopelessly ill patients who are suffering great pain would decrease the amount of misery in the world. (An example could be Alsop's friend Jack.)

(3) Therefore, such a policy would be morally right.

The first premise of this argument, (1), states the Principle of Utility, which is the basic utilitarian assumption. Today most philosophers think that this principle is wrong, because they think that the promotion of happiness and the avoidance of misery are not the *only* morally important things. Happiness, they say, is only one among many values that should be promoted: freedom, justice, and a respect for people's rights are also important. To take one example: people *might* be happier if there were no freedom of religion, for if everyone adhered to the same religious beliefs, there would be greater harmony among people. There would be no unhappiness caused within families by Jewish girls marrying Catholic boys, and so forth. Moreover, if people were brainwashed well enough, no one would mind not having freedom of choice. Thus happiness would be increased. But, the argument continues, even if happiness *could* be increased this way, it would not be right to deny people freedom of religion, because people have a right to make their own choices. Therefore, the first premise of the utilitarian argument is unacceptable.

There is a related difficulty for utilitarianism, which connects more directly with the topic of euthanasia. Suppose a person is leading a miserable life—a life containing more unhappiness than happiness—but does *not* want to die. This person thinks that a miserable life is better than none at all. Now I assume that we would all agree that the person should not be killed; that would be plain, unjustifiable murder. Yet it *would* decrease the amount of misery in the world if we killed this person—it would lead to an increase in the balance of happiness over unhappiness—and so it is hard to see how, on strictly utilitarian grounds, it could be wrong. Again, the Principle of Utility seems to be an inadequate guide for determining right and wrong. So we are on shaky ground if we rely on *this* version of the argument from mercy for a defense of euthanasia.

DOING WHAT IS IN EVERYONE'S
BEST INTERESTS

Although the foregoing utilitarian argument is faulty, it is nevertheless based on a sound idea. For even if the promotion of happiness and avoidance of misery are not the *only* morally important things, they are still very important. So, when an action or a social policy would decrease misery, that is *a* very strong reason in its favor. In the cases of voluntary euthanasia we are now considering, great suffering is eliminated, and since the patient requests it, there is no question of violating individual rights. That is why, regardless of the difficulties of the Principle of Utility, the utilitarian version of the argument still retains considerable force.

I want now to present a somewhat different version of the argument from mercy, which is inspired by utilitarianism but which avoids the difficulties of the foregoing version by not making the Principle of Utility a premise of the argument. I believe that the following argument is sound and proves that euthanasia *can* be justified:

(1) If an action promotes the best interests of *everyone* concerned and violates *no one's* rights, then that action is morally acceptable.
(2) In at least some cases, active euthanasia promotes the best interests of everyone concerned and violates no one's rights.
(3) Therefore, in at least some cases, active euthanasia is morally acceptable.

It would have been in everyone's best interests if active euthanasia had been employed in the case of Stewart Alsop's friend Jack. First, and most important, it would have been in Jack's own interests, since it would have provided him with an easier, better death, without pain. (Who among us would choose Jack's death, if we had a choice, rather than a quick painless death?) Second, it would have been in the best interests of Jack's wife. Her misery, helplessly watching him suffer, must have been almost unbearable. Third, the hospital staff's best interests would have been served, since if Jack's dying had not been prolonged, they could have turned their attention to other patients whom they could have helped. Fourth, other patients would have benefited, since medical resources would no longer have been used in the sad, pointless maintenance of Jack's physical existence. Finally, if Jack himself requested to be killed, the act would not have violated his rights. Considering all this, how can active euthanasia in this case be wrong? How can it be wrong to do an action that is merciful, that benefits everyone concerned, and that violates no one's rights?

Chapter 34

The Wrongfulness of Euthanasia

J. Gay-Williams

In this selection, J. Gay-Williams offers several standard objections to euthanasia: that it goes against our natural instincts; that it violates human dignity; that it forecloses the possibility of miraculous cures; that the critically ill, and their caretakers, might give up too easily if euthanasia were an option; and, finally, that the legalization of euthanasia might lead to horrific abuses.

"J. Gay-Williams" is a pseudonym. We are not told the author's real name.

My impression is that euthanasia—the idea, if not the practice—is slowly gaining acceptance within our society. Cynics might attribute this to an increasing tendency to devalue human life, but I do not believe this is the major factor. The acceptance is much more likely to be the result of unthinking sympathy and benevolence. Well-publicized, tragic stories like that of Karen Quinlan elicit from us deep feelings of compassion. We think to ourselves, "She and her family would be better off if she were dead." It is an easy step from this very human response to the view that if someone (and others) would be better off dead, then it might be all right to kill that person. Although I respect the compassion that leads to this conclusion, I believe the conclusion is wrong.

I want to show that euthanasia is wrong. It is inherently wrong, but it is also wrong judged from the standpoints of self-interest and of practical effects.

Before presenting my arguments to support this claim, it would be well to define "euthanasia." An essential aspect of euthanasia is that it involves taking a human life, either one's own or that of another. Also, the person whose life is taken must be someone who is believed to be suffering from some disease or injury from which recovery cannot reasonably be expected. Finally, the action must be deliberate and intentional. Thus, euthanasia is intentionally taking the life of a presumably hopeless person. Whether the life is one's own or that of another, the taking of it is still euthanasia.

It is important to be clear about the deliberate and intentional aspect of the killing. If a hopeless person is given an injection of the wrong drug by mistake and this causes his death, this is wrongful killing but not euthanasia. The killing cannot be the result of accident. Furthermore, if the person is given an injection of a drug that is believed to be necessary to treat his disease or better his condition and the person dies as a result, then this is neither wrongful killing nor euthanasia. The intention was to make the patient well, not kill him. Similarly, when a patient's condition is such that it is not reasonable to hope that any medical procedures or treatments will save his life, a failure to implement the procedures or treatments is not euthanasia. If the person dies, this will be as a result of his injuries or disease and not because of his failure to receive treatment.

The failure to continue treatment after it has been realized that the patient has little chance of benefiting from it has been characterized by some as "passive euthanasia." This phrase is misleading and mistaken. In such cases, the person involved is not killed (the first essential aspect of euthanasia), nor is the death of the person intended by the withholding of additional treatment (the third essential aspect of euthanasia). The aim may be to spare the person additional and unjustifiable pain, to save him from the indignities of hopeless manipulations, and to avoid increasing the financial and emotional burden on his family. When I buy a pencil it is so that I can use it to write, not to contribute to an increase in the gross national product (GNP). This may be the unintended consequence of my action, but it is not the aim of my action. So it is with failing to continue the treatment of a dying person. I intend his death no more than I intend to reduce the GNP by not using medical supplies. His is an unintended dying, and so-called "passive euthanasia" is not euthanasia at all.

1. THE ARGUMENT FROM NATURE

Every human being has a natural inclination to continue living. Our reflexes and responses fit us to fight attackers, flee wild animals, and dodge out of the way of trucks. In our daily lives we exercise the caution and care necessary to protect ourselves. Our bodies are similarly structured for survival right down to the molecular level. When we are cut, our capillaries seal shut, our blood clots, and fibrinogen is produced to start the process of healing the wound. When we are invaded by bacteria, antibodies are produced to fight against the alien organisms, and their remains are swept out of the body by special cells designed for clean-up work.

Euthanasia does violence to this natural goal of survival. It is literally acting against nature because all the processes of nature are bent towards the end of bodily survival. Euthanasia defeats these subtle mechanisms in a way that, in a particular case, disease and injury might not.

It is possible, but not necessary, to make an appeal to revealed religion in this connection. Man as trustee of his body acts against God, its rightful possessor, when he takes his own life. He also violates the commandment to hold life sacred and never to take it without just and compelling cause. But since this appeal will persuade only those who are prepared to accept that religion has access to revealed truths, I shall not employ this line of argument.

It is enough, I believe, to recognize that the organization of the human body and our patterns of behavioral responses make the continuation of life a natural goal. By reason alone, then, we can recognize that euthanasia sets us against our own nature. Furthermore, in doing so, euthanasia does violence to our dignity. Our dignity comes from seeking our ends. When one of our goals is survival, and actions are taken that eliminate that goal, then our natural dignity suffers. Unlike animals, we are conscious through reason of our nature and our ends. Euthanasia involves acting as if this dual nature—inclination towards survival and awareness of this as an end—did not exist. Thus, euthanasia denies our basic human character and requires that we regard ourselves or others as something less than fully human.

2. THE ARGUMENT FROM SELF-INTEREST

The above arguments are, I believe, sufficient to show that euthanasia is inherently wrong. But there are reasons for considering it wrong when judged by standards other than reason. Because death is final and irreversible, euthanasia contains within it the possibility that we will work against our own interest if we practice it or allow it to be practiced on us.

Contemporary medicine has high standards of excellence and a proven record of accomplishment, but it does not possess perfect and complete knowledge. A mistaken diagnosis is possible, and so is a mistaken prognosis. Consequently, we may believe that we are dying of a disease when, as a matter of fact, we may not be. We may think that we have no hope of recovery when, as a matter of fact, our chances are quite good. In such circumstances, if euthanasia were permitted, we would die needlessly. Death is final and the chance of error too great to approve the practice of euthanasia.

Also, there is always the possibility that an experimental procedure or a hitherto untried technique will pull us through. We should at least keep this option open, but euthanasia closes it off. Furthermore, spontaneous remission does occur in many cases. For no apparent reason, a patient simply recovers when those all around him, including his physicians, expected him to die. Euthanasia would just guarantee their expectations and leave no room for the "miraculous" recoveries that frequently occur.

Finally, knowing that we can take our life at any time (or ask another to take it) might well incline us to give up too easily. The will to live is strong in all of us, but it can be weakened by pain and suffering and feelings of hopelessness. If during a bad time we allow ourselves to be killed, we never have a chance to reconsider. Recovery from a serious illness requires that we fight for it, and anything that weakens our determination by suggesting that there is an easy way out is ultimately against our own interest. Also, we may be inclined towards euthanasia because of our concern for others. If we see our sickness and suffering as an emotional and financial burden on our family, we may feel that to leave our life is to make their lives easier. The very presence of the possibility of euthanasia may keep us from surviving when we might.

3. THE ARGUMENT FROM PRACTICAL EFFECTS

Doctors and nurses are, for the most part, totally committed to saving lives. A life lost is, for them, almost a personal failure, an insult to their skills and knowledge. Euthanasia as a practice might well alter this. It could have a corrupting influence so that in any case that is severe, doctors and nurses might not try hard enough to save the patient. They might decide that the patient would simply be "better off dead" and take the steps necessary to make that come about. This attitude could then carry over to their dealings with patients less seriously ill. The result would be an overall decline in the quality of medical care.

Finally, euthanasia as a policy is a slippery slope. A person apparently hopelessly ill may be allowed to take his own life. Then he may be permitted to deputize others to do it for him should he no longer be able to act. The judgment of others then becomes the ruling factor. Already at this point euthanasia is not personal and voluntary, for others are acting "on behalf of" the patient as they see fit. This may well incline them to act on behalf of other patients who have not authorized them to exercise their judgment. It is only a short step, then, from voluntary euthanasia (self-inflicted or authorized) to directed euthanasia administered to a patient who has given no authorization, to involuntary euthanasia conducted as part of a social policy. Recently many psychiatrists and sociologists have argued that we define as "mental illness" those forms of behavior that we disapprove of. This gives us license then to lock up those who display the behavior. The category of the "hopelessly ill" provides the possibility of even worse abuse. Embedded in a social policy, it would give society or its representatives the authority to eliminate all those who might be considered too "ill" to function normally any longer. The dangers of euthanasia are too great to all to run the risk of approving it in any form. The first slippery step may well lead to a serious and harmful fall.

I hope that I have succeeded in showing why the benevolence that inclines us to give approval of euthanasia is misplaced. Euthanasia is inherently wrong because it violates the nature and dignity of human beings. But even those who are not convinced by this must be persuaded that the potential personal and social dangers inherent in euthanasia are sufficient to forbid our approving it either as a personal practice or as a public policy.

Suffering is surely a terrible thing, and we have a clear duty to comfort those in need and to ease their suffering when we can. But suffering is also a natural part of life with values for the individual and for others that we should not overlook. We may legitimately seek for others and for ourselves an easeful death, as Arthur Dyck has pointed out. Euthanasia, however, is not just an easeful death. It is a wrongful death. Euthanasia is not just dying. It is killing.

Chapter 35

Letting Go

What Should Medicine Do When It Can't Save Your Life?

Atul Gawande

When the point is put abstractly, almost everyone would agree that society shouldn't spend vast sums of money trying to extend the lives of the dying, when those lives are of poor quality and the effort to prolong them usually fails, succeeding only in harming the patient. Yet American society now does exactly that. In Dr. Atul Gawande's real-life examples, we can see how this happens; we can see how easy it is for well-meaning people to make a series of decisions that produce a result that nobody wants: neither the patient, nor the doctor, nor the rest of society. But this is not inevitable.

Atul Gawande is a surgeon in Boston and a professor at Harvard University. Since 1998, he has also written regularly for *The New Yorker* magazine, where this essay first appeared.

I

The soaring cost of health care is the greatest threat to the country's long-term solvency, and the terminally ill account for a lot of it. Twenty-five percent of all Medicare spending is for the 5 percent of patients who are in their final year of life, and most of that money goes for care in their last couple of months which is of little apparent benefit.

Spending on a disease like cancer tends to follow a particular pattern. There are high initial costs as the cancer is treated, and then, if all goes well, these costs taper off. Medical spending for a breast-cancer survivor, for instance, averaged an estimated $54,000 in 2003, the vast majority of it for the initial diagnostic testing, surgery, and, where necessary, radiation and chemotherapy. For a patient with a fatal version of the disease, though, the cost curve is U-shaped, rising again toward the end—to an average of $63,000 during the last six months of life with an incurable breast cancer. Our medical system is excellent at trying to stave off death with $8,000-a-month chemotherapy, $3,000-a-day intensive care, $5,000-an-hour surgery. But, ultimately, death comes, and no one is good at knowing when to stop.

The subject seems to reach national awareness mainly as a question of who should "win" when the expensive decisions are made: the insurers and the taxpayers footing the bill or the patient battling for his or her life. Budget hawks urge us to face the fact that we can't afford everything. Demagogues shout about rationing and death panels. Market purists blame the existence of insurance: if patients and families paid the bills themselves, those expensive therapies would all come down in price. But they're debating the wrong question. The failure of our system of medical care for people facing the end of their life runs much deeper. To see this, you have to get close enough to grapple with the way decisions about care are actually made.

Recently, while seeing a patient in an intensive-care unit at my hospital, I stopped to talk with the critical-care physician on duty, someone I'd known since college. "I'm running a warehouse for the dying," she said bleakly. Out of the ten patients in her unit, she said, only two were likely to leave the hospital for any length of time. More typical was an almost 80-year-old woman at the end of her life, with irreversible congestive heart failure, who was in the I.C.U. for the second time in three weeks, drugged to oblivion and tubed in most natural orifices and a few artificial ones. Or the 70-year-old with a cancer that had metastasized to her lungs and bone, and a fungal pneumonia that arises only in the final phase of the illness. She had chosen to forgo treatment, but her oncologist pushed her to change her mind, and she was put on a ventilator and antibiotics. Another woman, in her eighties, with end-stage respiratory and kidney failure, had been in the unit for two weeks. Her husband had died after a long illness, with a feeding tube and a tracheotomy, and she had mentioned that she didn't want to die that way. But her children couldn't let her go, and asked to proceed with the placement of various devices: a permanent tracheotomy, a feeding tube, and a dialysis catheter. So now she just lay there tethered to her pumps, drifting in and out of consciousness.

Almost all these patients had known, for some time, that they had a terminal condition. Yet they—along with their families and doctors—were unprepared for the final stage. "We are having more conversation now about what patients want for the end of their life, by far, than they have had in all their lives to this point," my friend said. "The problem is that's way too late." In 2008, the national Coping with Cancer project published a study showing that terminally ill cancer patients who were put on a mechanical ventilator, given electrical defibrillation or chest compressions, or admitted, near death, to intensive care had a substantially worse quality of life in their last week than those who received no such interventions. And, six months after their death, their caregivers were three times as likely to suffer major depression. Spending one's final days in an I.C.U. because of terminal illness is for most people a kind of failure. You lie on a ventilator, your every organ shutting down, your mind teetering on delirium and permanently beyond realizing that you will never leave this borrowed, fluorescent place. The end comes with no chance for you to have said goodbye or "It's O.K." or "I'm sorry" or "I love you."

People have concerns besides simply prolonging their lives. Surveys of patients with terminal illness find that their top priorities include, in addition to avoiding suffering, being with family, having the touch of others, being mentally aware, and not becoming a burden to others. Our system of technological medical care has utterly failed to meet these needs, and the cost of this failure is measured in far more than dollars. The hard question we face, then, is not how we can afford this system's expense. It is how we can build a health-care system that will actually help dying patients achieve what's most important to them at the end of their lives.

II

For all but our most recent history, dying was typically a brief process. Whether the cause was childhood infection, difficult childbirth, heart attack, or pneumonia, the interval between recognizing that you had a life-threatening ailment and death was often just a matter of days or weeks. Consider how our presidents died before the modern era. George Washington developed a throat infection at home on December 13, 1799, that killed him by the next evening. John Quincy Adams, Millard Fillmore, and Andrew Johnson all succumbed to strokes, and died within two days. Rutherford Hayes had a heart attack and died three days later. Some deadly illnesses took a longer course: James Monroe and Andrew Jackson died from the months-long consumptive process of what appears to have been tuberculosis; Ulysses Grant's oral cancer took a year to kill him; and James Madison was bedridden for two years before dying of "old age." But, as the end-of-life researcher Joanne Lynn has observed, people usually experienced life-threatening illness the way they experienced bad weather—as something that struck with little warning—and you either got through it or you didn't.

. . . These days, swift catastrophic illness is the exception; for most people, death comes only after long medical struggle with an incurable condition—advanced cancer, progressive organ failure (usually the heart, kidney, or liver), or the multiple debilities of very old age. In all such cases, death is certain, but the timing isn't. So everyone struggles with this uncertainty—with how, and when, to accept that the battle is lost. . . .

I once cared for a woman in her sixties who had severe chest and abdominal pain from a bowel obstruction that had ruptured her colon, caused her to have a heart attack, and put her into septic shock and renal failure. I performed an emergency operation to remove the damaged length of colon and give her a colostomy. A cardiologist stented her coronary arteries. We put her on dialysis, a ventilator, and intravenous feeding, and stabilized her. After a couple of weeks, though, it was clear that she was not going to get much better. The septic shock had left her with heart and respiratory failure as well as dry gangrene of her foot, which would have to be amputated. She had a large, open abdominal wound with leaking bowel contents, which would require twice-a-day cleaning and dressing for weeks in order to heal. She would not be able to eat. She would need a tracheotomy. Her kidneys were gone, and she would have to spend three days a week on a dialysis machine for the rest of her life.

She was unmarried and without children. So I sat with her sisters in the I.C.U. family room to talk about whether we should proceed with the amputation and the tracheotomy. "Is she dying?" one of the sisters asked me. I didn't know how to answer the question. I wasn't even sure what the word "dying" meant anymore. In the past few decades, medical science has rendered obsolete centuries of experience, tradition, and language about our mortality, and created a new difficulty for mankind: how to die.

III

. . . This is a modern tragedy, replayed millions of times over. When there is no way of knowing exactly how long our skeins will run—and when we imagine ourselves to have much more time than we do—our every impulse is to fight, to die with chemo in our veins or a tube in our throats or fresh sutures in our flesh. The fact that we may be shortening or worsening the time we have left hardly seems to register. We imagine that we can wait until the doctors tell us that there is nothing more they can do. But rarely is there *nothing* more that doctors can do. They can give toxic drugs of unknown efficacy, operate to try to remove part of the tumor, put in a feeding tube if a person can't eat: there's always something. We want these choices. We don't want anyone—certainly not bureaucrats or the marketplace—to limit them. But that doesn't mean we are eager to make the choices ourselves. Instead, most often, we make no choice at all. We fall back on the default, and the default is: Do Something. Is there any way out of this?

In late 2004, executives at Aetna, the insurance company, started an experiment. They knew that only a small percentage of the terminally ill ever halted efforts at curative treatment and enrolled in hospice, and that, when they did, it was usually not until the very end. So Aetna decided to let a group of policyholders with a life expectancy of less than a year receive hospice services *without* forgoing other treatments. A patient . . . could continue to try chemotherapy and radiation, and go to the hospital when she wished—but also have a hospice team at home focussing on what she needed for the best possible life now and for that morning when she might wake up unable to breathe. A two-year study of this "concurrent care" program found that enrolled patients were much more likely to use hospice: the figure leaped from 26 percent to 70 percent. That was no surprise, since they weren't forced to give up anything. The surprising result was that they did give up things. They visited the emergency room almost half as often as the control patients did. Their use of hospitals and I.C.U.s dropped by more than two-thirds. Over-all costs fell by almost a quarter.

This was stunning, and puzzling: it wasn't obvious what made the approach work. Aetna ran a more modest concurrent-care program for a broader group of terminally ill patients. For these patients, the traditional hospice rules applied—in order to qualify for home hospice, they had to give up attempts at curative treatment. But, either way, they received phone calls from palliative-care nurses who offered to check in regularly and help them find services for anything from pain control to making out a living will. For these patients, too, hospice enrollment jumped to 70 percent, and their use of hospital services dropped sharply. Among elderly patients, use of intensive-care units fell by more than 85 percent. Satisfaction scores went way up. What was going on here? The program's leaders had the impression that they had simply given patients someone experienced and knowledgeable to talk to about their daily needs. And somehow that was enough—just talking.

The explanation strains credibility, but evidence for it has grown in recent years. Two-thirds of the terminal-cancer patients in the Coping with Cancer study reported having had no discussion with their doctors about their goals for end-of-life care, despite being, on average, just four months from death. But the third who did were far less likely to undergo cardiopulmonary resuscitation or be put on a ventilator or end up in an intensive-care unit. Two-thirds enrolled in hospice. These patients suffered less, were physically more capable, and were better able, for a longer period, to interact with others. Moreover, six months after the patients died their family members were much less likely to experience persistent major depression. In other words, people who had substantive discussions with their doctor about their end-of-life preferences were far more likely to die at peace and in control of their situation, and to spare their family anguish.

Can mere discussions really do so much? Consider the case of La Crosse, Wisconsin. Its elderly residents have unusually low end-of-life hospital costs. During their last six months, according to Medicare data, they spend half as many days in the hospital as the national average, and there's no sign that doctors or patients are halting care prematurely. Despite average rates of obesity and smoking, their life expectancy outpaces the national mean by a year.

I spoke to Dr. Gregory Thompson, a critical-care specialist at Gundersen Lutheran Hospital, while he was on I.C.U. duty one recent evening, and he ran through his list of patients with me. In most respects, the patients were like those found in any I.C.U.—terribly sick and living through the most perilous days of their lives. There was a young woman with multiple organ failure from a devastating case of pneumonia, a man in his mid-sixties with a ruptured colon that had caused a rampaging infection and a heart attack. Yet these patients were completely different from those in other I.C.U.s I'd seen: none had a terminal disease; none battled the final stages of metastatic cancer or untreatable heart failure or dementia.

To understand La Crosse, Thompson said, you had to go back to 1991, when local medical leaders headed a systematic campaign to get physicians and patients to discuss end-of-life wishes. Within a few years, it became routine for all patients admitted to a hospital, nursing home, or assisted-living facility to complete a multiple-choice form that boiled down to four crucial questions. At this moment in your life, the form asked:

1. Do you want to be resuscitated if your heart stops?
2. Do you want aggressive treatments such as intubation and mechanical ventilation?
3. Do you want antibiotics?
4. Do you want tube or intravenous feeding if you can't eat on your own?

By 1996, 85 percent of La Crosse residents who died had written advanced directives, up from 15 percent, and doctors almost always knew of and followed the instructions. Having this system in place, Thompson said, has made his job vastly easier. But it's not because the specifics are spelled out for him every time a sick patient arrives in his unit.

"These things are not laid out in stone," he told me. Whatever the yes/no answers people may put on a piece of paper, one will find nuances and complexities in what they mean. "But, instead of having the discussion when they get to the I.C.U., we find many times it has already taken place."

Answers to the list of questions change as patients go from entering
the hospital for the delivery of a child to entering for complications of
Alzheimer's disease. But, in La Crosse, the system means that people
are far more likely to have talked about what they want and what they
don't want before they and their relatives find themselves in the throes
of crisis and fear. When wishes aren't clear, Thompson said, "families
have also become much more receptive to having the discussion."
The discussion, not the list, was what mattered most. Discussion had
brought La Crosse's end-of-life costs down to just over half the national
average. It was that simple—and that complicated.

IV

. . . I spoke to an oncologist who told me about a twenty-nine-year-old
patient she had recently cared for who had an inoperable brain tumor
that continued to grow through second-line chemotherapy. The patient
elected not to attempt any further chemotherapy, but getting to that
decision required hours of discussion—for this was not the decision he
had expected to make. First, the oncologist said, she had a discussion
with him alone. They reviewed the story of how far he'd come, the
options that remained. She was frank. She told him that in her entire
career she had never seen third-line chemotherapy produce a significant
response in his type of brain tumor. She had looked for experimental
therapies, and none were truly promising. And, although she was willing to proceed with chemotherapy, she told him how much strength and
time the treatment would take away from him and his family.

He did not shut down or rebel. His questions went on for an hour.
He asked about this therapy and that therapy. And then, gradually, he
began to ask about what would happen as the tumor got bigger, the
symptoms he'd have, the ways they could try to control them, how the
end might come.

The oncologist next met with the young man together with his family. That discussion didn't go so well. He had a wife and small children,
and at first his wife wasn't ready to contemplate stopping chemo. But
when the oncologist asked the patient to explain in his own words what
they'd discussed, she understood. It was the same with his mother, who
was a nurse. Meanwhile, his father sat quietly and said nothing the
entire time.

A few days later, the patient returned to talk to the oncologist. "There should be something. There *must* be something," he said. His father had shown him reports of cures on the Internet. He confided how badly his father was taking the news. No patient wants to cause his family pain. According to Block, about two-thirds of patients are willing to undergo therapies they don't want if that is what their loved ones want.

The oncologist went to the father's home to meet with him. He had a sheaf of possible trials and treatments printed from the Internet. She went through them all. She was willing to change her opinion, she told him. But either the treatments were for brain tumors that were very different from his son's or else he didn't qualify. None were going to be miraculous. She told the father that he needed to understand: time with his son was limited, and the young man was going to need his father's help getting through it.

The oncologist noted wryly how much easier it would have been for her just to prescribe the chemotherapy. "But that meeting with the father was the turning point," she said. The patient and the family opted for hospice. They had more than a month together before he died. Later, the father thanked the doctor. That last month, he said, the family simply focussed on being together, and it proved to be the most meaningful time they'd ever spent.

Given how prolonged some of these conversations have to be, many people argue that the key problem has been the financial incentives: we pay doctors to give chemotherapy and to do surgery, but not to take the time required to sort out when doing so is unwise. This certainly is a factor. . . . But the issue isn't merely a matter of financing. It arises from a still unresolved argument about what the function of medicine really is—what, in other words, we should and should not be paying for doctors to do.

The simple view is that medicine exists to fight death and disease, and that is, of course, its most basic task. Death is the enemy. But the enemy has superior forces. Eventually, it wins. And, in a war that you cannot win, you don't want a general who fights to the point of total annihilation. You don't want Custer. You want Robert E. Lee, someone who knew how to fight for territory when he could and how to surrender when he couldn't, someone who understood that the damage is greatest if all you do is fight to the bitter end.

More often, these days, medicine seems to supply neither Custers nor Lees. We [doctors] are increasingly the generals who march the soldiers onward, saying all the while, "You let me know when you want to stop." All-out treatment, we tell the terminally ill, is a train you can get off at any time—just say when. But for most patients and their families this is asking too much. They remain riven by doubt and fear and desperation; some are deluded by a fantasy of what medical science can achieve. But our responsibility, in medicine, is to deal with human beings as they are. People die only once. They have no experience to draw upon. They need doctors and nurses who are willing to have the hard discussions and say what they have seen, who will help people prepare for what is to come—and to escape a warehoused oblivion that few really want.

Chapter 36

Human Cloning and the Challenge of Regulation

John A. Robertson

When Ian Wilmut and his colleagues in Scotland announced in 1997 that they had successfully cloned an adult sheep, everyone started thinking about human cloning, and there was an immediate clamor for laws—and even international treaties—to forbid it. Intellectuals produced some outlandish arguments in support of this. Will the clone have the same soul as the original? they asked. What will stop rich people from cloning themselves? Do we want "rooms full of human clones, silently growing spare parts for the person from whom they had been copied"? It would be the worst thing in human history, said one critic; the people originated by cloning would be our slaves. All of these arguments had their intended effect. Today, a large majority of Americans believe that human cloning is wrong.

Yet cloning would only reproduce a common occurrence in nature. A clone would be the genetic duplicate of someone else, but so are monozygotic twins, and no one abhors the birth of twins. The question, then, is this: if having twins "naturally" is okay, then why should it be wrong to bring about the delayed birth of a twin using cloning? John A. Robertson (1943–2017), who taught law at the University of Texas at Austin, thinks that

John A. Robertson, "Human Cloning and the Challenge of Regulation" in the *New England Journal of Medicine*, vol. 339, no. 2 (July 9, 1998): 119–22. Copyright © 1998 Massachusetts Medical Society. Used with permission.

cloning humans is not wrong. Cloning has legitimate purposes, he
believes, and we should focus on doing it well.

The birth of Dolly, the sheep cloned from a mammary cell of an adult
ewe, has initiated a public debate about human cloning. Although
cloning of humans may never be clinically feasible, discussion of the
ethical, legal, and social issues raised is important. Cloning is just one
of several techniques potentially available to select, control, or alter the
genome of offspring. The development of such technology poses an
important social challenge: how to ensure that the technology is used to
enhance, rather than limit, individual freedom and welfare.

A key ethical question is whether a responsible couple, interested
in rearing healthy offspring biologically related to them, might ethically choose to use cloning (or other genetic-selection techniques) for
that purpose. The answer should take into account the benefits sought
through the use of the techniques and any potential harm to offspring
or to other interests.

The most likely uses of cloning would be far removed from the
bizarre or horrific scenarios that initially dominated media coverage.
Theoretically, cloning would enable rich or powerful persons to clone
themselves several times over, and commercial entrepreneurs might
hire women to bear clones of sports or entertainment celebrities to be
sold to others to rear. But current reproductive techniques can also be
abused, and existing laws against selling children would apply to those
created by cloning.

There is no reason to think that the ability to clone humans will cause
many people to turn to cloning when other methods of reproduction
would enable them to have healthy children. Cloning a human being by
somatic-cell nuclear transfer, for example, would require a consenting
person as a source of DNA, eggs to be enucleated and then fused with
the DNA, a woman who would carry and deliver the child, and a person
or couple to raise the child. Given this reality, cloning is most likely to be
sought by couples who, because of infertility, a high risk of severe genetic
disease, or other factors, cannot or do not wish to conceive a child.

Several plausible scenarios can be imagined. Rather than use sperm,
egg, or embryo from anonymous donors, couples who are infertile as
a result of gametic insufficiency might choose to clone one of the partners. If the husband were the source of the DNA and the wife provided

the egg that received the nuclear transfer and then gestated the fetus, they would have a child biologically related to each of them and would not need to rely on anonymous gamete or embryo donation. Of course, many infertile couples might still prefer gamete or embryo donation or adoption. But there is nothing inherently wrong in wishing to be biologically related to one's children, even when this goal cannot be achieved through sexual reproduction.

A second plausible application would be for a couple at high risk of having offspring with a genetic disease. Couples in this situation must now choose whether to risk the birth of an affected child, to undergo prenatal or pre-implantation diagnosis and abortion or the discarding of embryos, to accept gamete donation, to seek adoption, or to remain childless. If cloning were available, however, some couples, in line with prevailing concepts of kinship, family, and parenting, might strongly prefer to clone one of themselves or another family member. Alternatively, if they already had a healthy child, they might choose to use cloning to create a later-born twin of that child. In the more distant future, it is even possible that the child whose DNA was replicated would not have been born healthy but would have been made healthy by gene therapy after birth.

A third application relates to obtaining tissue or organs for transplantation. A child who needed an organ or tissue transplant might lack a medically suitable donor. Couples in this situation have sometimes conceived a child coitally in the hope that he or she would have the correct tissue type to serve, for example, as a bone marrow donor for an older sibling. If the child's disease was not genetic, a couple might prefer to clone the affected child to be sure that the tissue would match.

It might eventually be possible to procure suitable tissue or organs by cloning the source DNA only to the point at which stem cells or other material might be obtained for transplantation, thus avoiding the need to bring a child into the world for the sake of obtaining tissue. Cloning a person's cells up to the embryo stage might provide a source of stem cells or tissue for the person cloned. Cloning might also be used to enable a couple to clone a dead or dying child so as to have that child live on in some closely related form, to obtain sufficient numbers of embryos for transfer and pregnancy, or to eliminate mitochondrial disease.

Most, if not all, of the potential uses of cloning are controversial, usually because of the explicit copying of the genome. As the National

Bioethics Advisory Commission noted, in addition to concern about physical safety and eugenics, somatic-cell cloning raises issues of the individuality, autonomy, objectification, and kinship of the resulting children. In other instances, such as the production of embryos to serve as tissue banks, the ethical issue is the sacrifice of embryos created solely for that purpose.

Given the wide leeway now granted couples to use assisted reproduction and prenatal genetic selection in forming families, cloning should not be rejected in all circumstances as unethical or illegitimate. The manipulation of embryos and the use of gamete donors and surrogates are increasingly common. Most fetuses conceived in the United States and Western Europe are now screened for genetic or chromosomal anomalies. Before conception, screening to identify carriers of genetic diseases is widespread. Such practices also deviate from conventional notions of reproduction, kinship, and medical treatment of infertility, yet they are widely accepted.

Despite the similarity of cloning to current practices, however, the dissimilarities should not be overlooked. The aim of most other forms of assisted reproduction is the birth of a child who is a descendant of at least one member of the couple, not an identical twin. Most genetic selection acts negatively to identify and screen out unwanted traits such as genetic disease, not positively to choose or replicate the genome as in somatic-cell cloning. It is not clear, however, why a child's relation to his or her rearing parents must always be that of sexually reproduced descendant when such a relationship is not possible because of infertility or other factors. Indeed, in gamete donation and adoption, although sexual reproduction is involved, a full descendant relation between the child and both rearing parents is lacking. Nor should the difference between negative and positive means of selecting children determine the ethical or social acceptability of cloning or other techniques. In both situations, a deliberate choice is made so that a child is born with one genome rather than another or is not born at all.

Is cloning sufficiently similar to current assisted reproduction and genetic-selection practices to be treated similarly as a presumptively protected exercise of family or reproductive liberty? Couples who request cloning in the situations I have described are seeking to rear healthy children with whom they will have a genetic or biologic tie, just as couples who conceive their children sexually do. Whether described as "replication" or as "reproduction," the resort to cloning is similar enough in purpose and effects to other reproduction and genetic-selection practices that it should be treated similarly. Therefore, a couple should be free to choose cloning unless there are compelling reasons for thinking that this would create harm that the other procedures would not cause.

The concern of the National Bioethics Advisory Commission about the welfare of the clone reflects two types of fear. The first is that a child with the same nuclear DNA as another person, who is thus that person's later-born identical twin, will be so severely harmed by the identity of nuclear DNA between them that it is morally preferable, if not obligatory, that the child not be born at all. In this case the fear is that the later-born twin will lack individuality or the freedom to create his or her own identity because of confusion or expectations caused by having the same DNA as another person.

This claim does not withstand the close scrutiny that should precede interference with a couple's freedom to bear and rear biologically related children. Having the same genome as another person is not in itself harmful, as widespread experience with monozygotic twins shows. Being a twin does not deny either twin his or her individuality or freedom, and twins often have a special intimacy or closeness that few non-twin siblings can experience. There is no reason to think that being a later-born identical twin resulting from cloning would change the overall assessment of being a twin.

Differences in mitochondria and the uterine and childhood environment will undercut problems of similarity and minimize the risk of over-identification with the first twin. A clone of Smith may look like Smith, but he or she will not be Smith and will lack many of Smith's phenotypic characteristics. The effects of having similar DNA will also depend on the length of time before the second twin is born, on whether the twins are raised together, on whether they are informed that they are genetic twins, on whether other people are so informed, on the beliefs that the rearing parents have about genetic influence on behavior, and on other factors. Having a previously born twin might in some circumstances also prove to be a source of support or intimacy for the later-born child.

The risk that parents or the child will overly identify the child with the DNA source also seems surmountable. Would the child invariably be expected to match the phenotypic characteristics of the DNA source, thus denying the second twin an "open future" and the freedom to develop his or her own identity? In response to this question, one must ask whether couples who choose to clone offspring are more likely to want a child who is a mere replica of the DNA source or a child who is unique and valued for more than his or her genes. Couples may use cloning in order to ensure that the biologic child they rear is healthy, to maintain a family connection in the face of gametic infertility, or to obtain matched tissue for transplantation and yet still be responsibly committed to the welfare of their child, including his or her separate identity and interests and right to develop as he or she chooses.

The second type of fear is that parents who choose their child's genome through somatic-cell cloning will view the child as a commodity or an object to serve their own ends. We do not view children born through coital or assisted reproduction as "mere means" just because people reproduce in order to have company in old age, to fulfill what they see as God's will, to prove their virility, to have heirs, to save a relationship, or to serve other selfish purposes. What counts is how a child is treated after birth. Self-interested motives for having children do not prevent parents from loving children for themselves once they are born.

The use of cloning to form families in the situations I have described, though closely related to current assisted-reproduction and genetic-selection practices, does offer unique variations. The novelty of the relation—cloning in lieu of sperm donation, for example, produces a later-born identical twin raised by the older twin and his spouse—will create special psychological and social challenges. Can these challenges be successfully met, so that cloning produces net good for families and society? Given the largely positive experience with assisted-reproduction techniques that initially appeared frightening, cautious optimism is justified. We should be able to develop procedures and guidelines for cloning that will allow us to obtain its benefits while minimizing its problems and dangers.

In the light of these considerations, I would argue that a ban on privately funded cloning research is unjustified and likely to hamper important types of research. . . .

Rather than seek to prohibit all uses of human cloning, we should focus our attention on ensuring that cloning is done well. No physician or couple should embark on cloning without careful thought about the novel relational issues and child-rearing responsibilities that will ensue. We need regulations or guidelines to ensure safety and efficacy, fully informed consent and counseling for the couple, the consent of any person who may provide DNA, guarantees of parental rights and duties, and a limit on the number of clones from any single source. It may also be important to restrict cloning to situations where there is a strong likelihood that the couple or individual initiating the procedure will also rear the resulting child. This principle will encourage a stable parenting situation and minimize the chance that cloning entrepreneurs will create clones to be sold to others. As our experience grows, some restrictions on who may serve as a source of DNA for cloning (e.g., a ban on cloning one's parents) may also be defensible.

Cloning is important because it is the first of several positive means of genetic selection that may be sought by families seeking to have and rear healthy, biologically related offspring. In the future, mitochondrial transplantation, germ-line gene therapy, genetic enhancement, and other forms of prenatal genetic alteration may be possible. With each new technique, as with cloning, the key question will be whether it serves important health, reproductive, or family needs and whether its benefits outweigh any likely harm. Cloning illustrates the principle that when legitimate uses of a technique are likely, regulatory policy should avoid prohibition and focus on ensuring that the technique is used responsibly for the good of those directly involved. As genetic knowledge continues to grow, the challenge of regulation will occupy us for some time to come.

THE DEATH PENALTY

Chapter 37

A Defense of the Death Penalty

Louis P. Pojman

Louis P. Pojman (1935–2005) was a professor at the United States
Military Academy. Here Pojman argues that the death penalty is
justified for two reasons: It gives killers what they deserve, and
it deters potential killers. However, he does not believe that the
death penalty should be used *only* on murderers.

There is an ancient tradition, going back to biblical times, but endorsed
by the mainstream of philosophers, from Plato to Thomas Aquinas,
from Thomas Hobbes to Immanuel Kant, Thomas Jefferson, John Stuart Mill, and C. S. Lewis, that a fitting punishment for murder is the
execution of the murderer. One prong of this tradition, the *backward-
looking* or deontological position, epitomized in Aquinas and Kant,
holds that because human beings, as rational agents, have dignity, one
who with malice aforethought kills a human being forfeits his right to
life and deserves to die. The other, the *forward-looking* or consequen-
tialist tradition, exemplified by Jeremy Bentham, Mill, and Ernest van
den Haag, holds that punishment ought to serve as a deterrent, and that
capital punishment is an adequate deterrent to prospective murderers. . . . I will argue that both traditional defenses are sound and together

Louis P. Pojman, "A Defense of the Death Penalty" in *International Journal of Applied
Philosophy*, vol. 11, no. 2 (winter/spring 1997). Copyright © 1997. Used with permission.

they make a strong case for retaining the death penalty. That is, I hold a combined theory of punishment. A backward-looking judgment that the criminal has committed a heinous crime plus a forward-looking judgment that a harsh punishment will deter would-be murderers is sufficient to justify the death penalty. I turn first to the retributivist theory in favor of capital punishment.

RETRIBUTION

. . . I remember the grocer's wife. She was a plump, happy woman who enjoyed the long workday she shared with her husband in their ma-and-pa store. One evening, two young men came in and showed guns, and the grocer gave them everything in the cash register.

For no reason, almost as an afterthought, one of the men shot the grocer in the face. The woman stood only a few feet from her husband when he was turned into a dead, bloody mess.

She was about 50 when it happened. In a few years her mind was almost gone, and she looked 80. They might as well have killed her too. . . .

Human beings have dignity as self-conscious rational agents who are able to act morally. One could maintain that it is precisely their moral goodness or innocence that bestows dignity and a right to life on them. Intentionally taking the life of an innocent human being is so evil that absent mitigating circumstances, the perpetrator forfeits his own right to life. He or she deserves to die.

The retributivist holds three propositions: (1) that all the guilty deserve to be punished; (2) that only the guilty deserve to be punished; and (3) that the guilty deserve to be punished in proportion to the severity of their crime. . . .

Criminals like Steven Judy, Jeffrey Dahmer, Timothy McVeigh, Ted Bundy (who is reported to have raped and murdered over 100 women), John Muhammad and John Lee Malvo, who murdered 12 people in the killing spree of 2002, and the two men who gunned down the grocer have committed capital offenses and deserve nothing less than capital punishment. No doubt malicious acts like the ones committed by these criminals deserve worse punishment than death, and I would be open to suggestions of torture (why not?), but at a minimum, the death penalty seems warranted.

People often confuse *retribution* with *revenge*. . . . While moral people will feel outrage at acts of heinous crimes, the moral justification of punishment is not *vengeance*, but *desert*. Vengeance signifies inflicting harm on the offender out of anger because of what he has done. Retribution is the rationally supported theory that the criminal deserves a punishment fitting the gravity of his crime. . . .

Our natural instinct is for *vengeance*, but civilization demands that we restrain our anger and go through a legal process, letting the outcome determine whether and to what degree to punish the accused. Civilization demands that we not take the law into our own hands, but it should also satisfy our deepest instincts when they are consonant with reason. Our instincts tell us that some crimes, like McVeigh's, Judy's, and Bundy's, should be severely punished, but we refrain from personally carrying out those punishments, committing ourselves to the legal processes. The death penalty is supported by our gut animal instincts as well as our sense of justice as desert.

The death penalty reminds us that there are consequences to our actions, that we are responsible for what we do, so that dire consequences for immoral actions are eminently appropriate. The death penalty is such a fitting response to evil.

DETERRENCE

The second tradition justifying the death penalty is the utilitarian theory of deterrence. This holds that by executing convicted murderers we will deter would-be murderers from killing innocent people. The evidence for deterrence is controversial. . . . However, one often hears abolitionists claiming the evidence shows that the death penalty fails to deter homicide. This is too strong a claim. The sociological evidence doesn't show either that the death penalty deters or that it fails to deter. The evidence is simply inconclusive. But a commonsense case can be made for deterrence.

Imagine that every time someone intentionally killed an innocent person he was immediately struck down by lightning. When mugger Mike slashed his knife into the neck of the elderly pensioner, lightning struck, killing Mike. His fellow muggers witnessed the sequence of events. When burglar Bob pulled his pistol out and shot the bank teller through her breast, a bolt leveled Bob, his compatriots beholding the spectacle.

Soon men with their guns lying next to them were found all across the world in proximity to the corpses of their presumed victims. Do you think that the evidence of cosmic retribution would go unheeded?

We can imagine the murder rate in the United States and everywhere else plummeting. The close correlation between murder and cosmic retribution would serve as a deterrent to would-be murderers. If this thought experiment is sound, we have a prima facie argument for the deterrent effect of capital punishment. In its ideal, prompt performance, the death penalty would likely deter. . . . The question then becomes how do we institute the death penalty so as to have the maximal deterrent effect without violating the rights of the accused.

We would have to bring the accused to trial more quickly and limit the appeals process of those found guilty "beyond reasonable doubt." Having DNA evidence should make this more feasible than hitherto. Furthermore, public executions of the convicted murderer would serve as a reminder that crime does not pay. Public executions of criminals seem an efficient way to communicate the message that if you shed innocent blood, you will pay a high price. . . .

Common sense informs us that most people would prefer to remain out of jail, that the threat of public humiliation is enough to deter some people, that a sentence of 20 years will deter most people more than a sentence of two years, that a life sentence will deter most would-be criminals more than a sentence of 20 years. I think that we have commonsense evidence that the death penalty is a better deterrent than prison sentences. For one thing, as Richard Herrnstein and James Q. Wilson have argued in *Crime and Human Nature*, a great deal of crime is committed on a cost-benefit schema, wherein the criminal engages in some form of risk assessment as to his or her chances of getting caught and punished in some manner. If he or she estimates the punishment mild, the crime becomes inversely attractive, and vice versa. The fact that those who are condemned to death do everything in their power to get their sentences postponed or reduced to long-term prison sentences, in the way *lifers* do not, shows that they fear death more than life in prison. . . .

Former prosecuting attorney for the State of Florida, Richard Gernstein, has set forth the commonsense case for deterrence. First of all, he claims, the death penalty certainly deters the murderer from any further murders, including those he or she might commit within the prison where he is confined. Second, statistics cannot tell us how many potential criminals have refrained from taking another's life through fear of the death penalty. He quotes Judge Hyman Barshay of New York: "The death penalty is a warning, just like a lighthouse throwing its beams out to sea. We hear about shipwrecks, but we do not hear about the ships the lighthouse guides safely on their way. We do not have proof of the number of ships it saves, but we do not tear the lighthouse down."

Some of the commonsense evidence is anecdotal. . . . Growing up in the infamous Cicero, Illinois, home of Al Capone and the Mafia, I had friends who went into crime, mainly burglary, and larceny. It was common knowledge that one stopped short of killing in the act of robbery. A prison sentence could be dealt with—especially with a good lawyer—but being convicted of murder, which at that time included a reasonable chance of being electrocuted, was an altogether different matter. No doubt exists in my mind that the threat of the electric chair saved the lives of some of those who were robbed in my town. . . .

It seems likely that the death penalty does not deter as much as it could due to its inconsistent and rare use. For example, . . . in 1994, there were 23,305 cases of murder and non-negligent manslaughter and only 31 executions—for a ratio of better than 750 to 1. The average length of stay for a prisoner executed in 1994 was 10 years and two months. If potential murderers perceived the death penalty as a highly probable outcome of murder, would they not be more reluctant to kill? . . .

The late Ernest van den Haag has set forth what he called the Best Bet Argument. He argued that even though we don't know for certain whether the death penalty deters or prevents other murders, we should bet that it does. Indeed, due to our ignorance, any social policy we take is a gamble. Not to choose capital punishment for first-degree murder is as much a bet that capital punishment doesn't deter as choosing the policy is a bet that it does. There is a significant difference in the betting, however, in that to bet against capital punishment is to bet against the innocent and for the murderer, while to bet for it is to bet against the murderer and for the innocent. . . .

Suppose that we choose a policy of capital punishment for capital crimes. In this case we are betting that the death of some murderers will be more than compensated for by the lives of some innocents not being murdered (either by these murderers or others who would have murdered). If we're right, we have saved the lives of the innocent. If we're wrong, unfortunately, we've sacrificed the lives of some murderers. But say we choose not to have a social policy of capital punishment. If capital punishment doesn't work as a deterrent, we've come out ahead, but if it does work, then we've missed an opportunity to save innocent lives. If we value the saving of innocent lives more highly than the loss of the guilty, then to bet on a policy of capital punishment turns out to be rational. Since the innocent have a greater right to life than the guilty, it is our moral duty to adopt a policy that has a chance of protecting them from potential murderers. . . .

If the Best Bet Argument is sound, or if the death penalty does deter would-be murderers, as common sense suggests, then we should support some uses of the death penalty. It should be used for those who commit first-degree murder, for whom no mitigating factors are present, and especially for those who murder police officers, prison guards, and political leaders. Many states rightly favor it for those who murder while committing another crime, such as burglary or rape. It should be used in cases of treason and terrorist bombings. It should also be considered for the perpetrators of egregious white collar crimes such as bank managers embezzling the savings of the public. . . .

Let me consider two objections often made to the implementation of the death penalty: that it sometimes leads to the death of innocents and that it discriminates against blacks.

Objection 1: Miscarriages of justice occur. Capital punishment is to be rejected because of human fallibility in convicting innocent parties and sentencing them to death. In a survey done in 1985, Hugo Adam Bedau and Michael Radelet found that of the 7,000 persons executed in the United States between 1900 and 1985, 25 were innocent of capital crimes. While some compensation is available to those unjustly imprisoned, the death sentence is irrevocable. We can't compensate the dead. As John Maxton, a member of the British Parliament puts it, "If we allow one innocent person to be executed, morally we are committing the same, or, in some ways, a worse crime than the person who committed the murder."

Response: Mr. Maxton is incorrect in saying that mistaken judicial execution is morally the same as or worse than murder, for a deliberate intention to kill the innocent occurs in a murder, whereas no such intention occurs in wrongful capital punishment.

Sometimes the objection is framed this way: It is better to let ten criminals go free than to execute one innocent person. If this dictum is a call for safeguards, then it is well taken; but somewhere there seems to be a limit on the tolerance of society toward capital offenses. Would these abolitionists argue that it is better that 50 or 100 or 1,000 murderers go free than that one innocent person be executed? Society has a right to protect itself from capital offenses even if this means taking a finite chance of executing an innocent person. If the basic activity or process is justified, then it is regrettable, but morally acceptable, that some mistakes are made. Fire trucks occasionally kill innocent pedestrians while racing to fires, but we accept these losses as justified by the greater good of the activity of using fire trucks. We judge the use of automobiles to be acceptable even though such use causes an average of 50,000 traffic fatalities each year. We accept the morality of a defensive war even though it will result in our troops accidentally or mistakenly killing innocent people. . . .

The abolitionist is incorrect in arguing that death is different from long-term prison sentences because it is irrevocable. Imprisonment also takes good things away from us that may never be returned. We cannot restore to the inmate the freedom or opportunities he or she lost. Suppose an innocent 25-year-old man is given a life sentence for murder. Thirty years later the error is discovered and he is set free. Suppose he values three years of freedom to every one year of life. That is, he would rather live 10 years as a free man than 30 as a prisoner. Given this man's values, the criminal justice system has taken the equivalent of 10 years of life from him. If he lives until he is 65, he has, as far as his estimation is concerned, lost 10 years, so that he may be said to have lived only 55 years.

The numbers in this example are arbitrary, but the basic point is sound. Most of us would prefer a shorter life of higher quality to a longer one of low quality. Death prevents all subsequent quality, but imprisonment also irrevocably harms one by diminishing the quality of life of the prisoner.

Objection 2: The second objection made against the death penalty is that it is unjust because it discriminates against the poor and minorities, particularly African Americans, over rich people and whites. . . .

Response: First of all, it is not true that a law that is applied in a discriminatory manner is unjust. . . . The discriminatory application, not the law itself, is unjust. . . . For example, a friend once got two speeding tickets during a 100-mile trip (having borrowed my car). He complained to the police officer who gave him his second ticket that many drivers were driving faster than he was at the time. They had escaped detection, he argued, so it wasn't fair for him to get two tickets on one trip. The officer acknowledged the imperfections of the system but, justifiably, had no qualms about giving him the second ticket. . . . Discriminatory practices should be reformed, and in many cases they can be. But imperfect practices in themselves do not entail that the laws engendering these practices themselves are unjust. . . .

. . . If we concluded that we should abolish a rule or practice, unless we treated everyone exactly by the same rules all the time, we would have to abolish, for example, traffic laws and laws against imprisonment for rape, theft, and even murder. Carried to its logical limits, we would also have to refrain from saving drowning victims if a number of people were drowning but we could only save a few of them. Imperfect justice is the best that we humans can attain. We should reform our practices as much as possible to eradicate unjust discrimination wherever we can, but if we are not allowed to have a law without perfect application, we will be forced to have no laws at all.

Nathanson . . . argues that the case of death is different. "Because of its finality and extreme severity of the death penalty, we need to be more scrupulous in applying it as punishment than is necessary with any other punishment." The retentionist agrees that the death penalty is a severe punishment and that we need to be scrupulous in applying it. The difference between the abolitionist and the retentionist seems to lie in whether we are wise and committed enough as a nation to reform our institutions so that they approximate fairness. Apparently, Nathanson is pessimistic here, whereas I have faith in our ability to learn from our mistakes and reform our systems. If we can't reform our legal system, what hope is there for us?

More specifically, the charge that a higher percentage of blacks than whites are executed was once true but is no longer so. Many states have made significant changes in sentencing procedures, with the result that currently whites convicted of first-degree murder are sentenced to death at a higher rate than blacks. . . .

Abolitionists often make the complaint that only the poor get death sentences for murder. If their trials are fair, then they deserve the death penalty, but rich murderers may be equally deserving. At the moment only first-degree murder and treason are crimes deemed worthy of the death penalty. Perhaps our notion of treason should be expanded to include those who betray the trust of the public: corporation executives who have the trust of ordinary people, but who, through selfish and dishonest practices, ruin their lives. As noted above, my proposal is to consider broadening, not narrowing, the scope of capital punishment, to include business personnel who unfairly harm the public. The executives in the recent corporation scandals who bailed out of sinking corporations with golden, million-dollar lifeboats while the pension plans of thousands of employees went to the bottom of the economic ocean, may deserve severe punishment, and if convicted, they should receive what they deserve. My guess is that the threat of the death sentence would have a deterrent effect here. Whether it is feasible to apply the death penalty for horrendous white-collar crimes is debatable. But there is something to be said in its favor. It would remove the impression that only the poor get executed.

Chapter 38

Why the United States Will Join the Rest of the World in Abandoning Capital Punishment

Stephen B. Bright

As a nation that executes prisoners, the United States is in poor company. Most countries that have the death penalty are terrible violators of human rights. In 2017, only twenty-three countries performed executions, and the top executors were China, Iran, Saudi Arabia, and Iraq. The United States carried out only twenty-five executions in 2018. Most of the more than 2,700 death-row inmates in America will never be put to death; they will die of natural causes.

Stephen B. Bright (1948–) believes that the United States should and will get out of the execution business. Mr. Bright teaches at Yale Law School, Georgetown, and Georgia State University College of Law.

The United States will inevitably join other industrialized nations in abandoning the death penalty, just as it has abandoned whipping, the stocks, branding, cutting off appendages, maiming, and other primitive forms of punishment. It remains to be seen how long it will be until the use of the death penalty becomes so infrequent as to be pointless, and it is eventually abandoned. In the meantime, capital punishment is arbitrarily and unfairly imposed, undermines the standing and moral authority of the United States in the community of nations, and diminishes the credibility and legitimacy of the courts within the United States.

Although death may intuitively seem to be an appropriate punishment for a person who kills another person and polls show strong support for the death penalty, most Americans know little about realities of capital punishment, past and present. The death penalty is a direct descendant of the darkest aspects of American history—slavery, lynching, racial oppression, and perfunctory capital trials known as "legal lynchings"— and racial discrimination remains a prominent feature of capital punishment. The death penalty is not imposed to avenge every killing and—as some contend—to bring "closure" to the family of every victim, but is inflicted in less than 1 percent of all murder cases. Of more than 20,000 murders in the United States annually, an average of fewer than 300 people are sentenced to death, and only 55 are executed each year. Only 19 states actually carried out executions between 1976, when the U.S. Supreme Court authorized the resumption of capital punishment after declaring it unconstitutional in 1972, and the end of 2002. Eighty-six percent of those executions were in the South. Just two states—Texas and Virginia—carried out 45 percent of them.

Any assessment of the death penalty must not be based on abstract theories about how it should work in practice or the experiences of states like Oregon, which seldom impose the death penalty and carry it out even less. To understand the realities of the death penalty, one must look to the states that sentence people to death by the hundreds and have carried out scores of executions. In those states, innocent people have been sentenced to die based on such things as mistaken eyewitness identifications, false confessions, the testimony of partisan experts who render opinions that are not supported by science, failure of police and prosecutors to turn over evidence of innocence, and testimony of prisoners who get their own charges dismissed by testifying that the accused admitted the crime to them. Even the guilty are sentenced to death as opposed to life imprisonment without the possibility of parole not because they committed the worst crimes but because of where they happen to be prosecuted, the incompetence of their court-appointed lawyers, their race, or the race of their victim. . . .

Further experimentation with lethal punishment after centuries of failure has no place in a conservative society that is wary of too much government power and skeptical of the government's ability to do things well. Further experimentation might be justified if it served some purpose. But capital punishment is not needed to protect society or to punish offenders, as shown by over 100 countries around the world that do not have the death penalty and states such as Michigan and Wisconsin, neither of which have had the death penalty since the mid-1800s. It can be argued that capital punishment was necessary when America was a frontier society and had no prisons. But today the United States has not only maximum security prisons, but "super maximum" prisons where serial killers, mass murderers, and sadistic murderers can be severely punished and completely isolated from guards and other inmates.

Nor is crime deterred by the executions in fewer than half the states of an arbitrarily selected 1 percent of those who commit murders, many of whom are mentally ill or have limited intellectual functioning. The South, which has carried out 85 percent of the nation's executions since 1976, has the highest murder rate of any region of the country. The Northeast, which has the fewest executions by far—only 3 executions between 1976 and the end of 2002—has the lowest murder rate.

The United States does not need to keep this relic of the past to show its abhorrence of murder. As previously noted, 99 percent of the murders in the United States are not punished by death. Even at war crimes trials in The Hague, genocide and other crimes against humanity are not punished with the death penalty. The societies that do not have capital punishment surely abhor murder as much as any other, but they do not find it necessary to engage in killing in order to punish, protect, or show their abhorrence with killing.

Finally, capital punishment has no place in a decent society that places some practices, such as torture, off limits—not because some individuals have not done things so bad that they arguably deserved to be tortured, but because a civilized society simply does not engage in such acts. It can be argued that rapists deserve to be raped, that mutilators deserve to be mutilated. Most societies, however, refrain from responding in this way because the punishment is not only degrading to those on whom it is imposed, but it is also degrading to the society that engages in the same behavior as the criminals. When death sentences are carried out, small groups of people gather in execution chambers and watch as a human being is tied down and put down. Some make no effort to suppress their glee when the sentence is carried out and celebrations occur inside and outside the prison. These celebrations of death reflect the dark side of the human spirit—an arrogant, vengeful, unforgiving, uncaring side that either does not admit the possibility of innocence or redemption or is willing to kill people despite those possibilities.

A HUMAN RIGHTS VIOLATION THAT UNDERMINES THE STANDING AND MORAL AUTHORITY OF THE UNITED STATES

If people were asked 50 years ago which one of the following three countries—Russia, South Africa, or the United States—would be most likely to have the death penalty at the turn of the century, few people would have answered the United States. And yet, the United States was one of four countries that accounted for 90 percent of all the executions in the world in 2001 (the others were China, Iran, and Saudi Arabia), while Russia and South Africa are among the nations that no longer practice capital punishment. Since 1985, over 40 countries have abandoned capital punishment whereas only four countries that did not have it have adopted it. One of those, Nepal, has since abolished it. Turkey abolished the death penalty in 2001 in its efforts to join the European Union, leaving the United States the only NATO country that still has the death penalty. . . .

The retention of capital punishment in the United States draws harsh criticism from throughout the world. . . . Capital punishment also affects the United States's relations with other countries in other ways. Canada and Mexico have repeatedly protested when their nationals are executed by the United States, as have other countries. Canada, Mexico, and most European countries will not extradite suspects to the United States if they are subject to capital punishment and will not assist in the prosecution of people facing the death penalty. Just as the United States could not assert moral leadership in the world as long as it allowed segregation, it will not be a leader on human rights as long as it allows capital punishment.

ARBITRARY AND UNFAIR INFLICTION

Regardless of the practices of the rest of the world or the morality of capital punishment, the process leading to a death sentence is so unfair and influenced by so many improper factors and the infliction of death sentences is so inconsistent that this punishment should be abandoned.

The exoneration of many people who spent years of their lives in prisons for crimes they did not commit—many of them on death row—has dramatically brought to light defects in the criminal justice system that have surprised and appalled people who do not observe the system every day and assumed that it was working properly. The average person has little or no contact with the criminal courts, which deal primarily with crimes committed against and by poor people and members of racial minorities. It is a system that is overworked and underfunded, and particularly underfunded when it comes to protecting the rights of those accused.

Law enforcement officers, usually overworked and often under tremendous public pressure to solve terrible crimes, make mistakes, fail to pursue all lines of investigation, and, on occasion, overreach or take shortcuts in pursuing arrests. Prosecutors exercise vast and unchecked discretion in deciding which cases are to be prosecuted as capital cases. The race of the victim and the defendant, political considerations, and other extraneous factors influence whether prosecutors seek the death penalty and whether juries or judges impose it.

A person facing the death penalty usually cannot afford to hire an attorney and is at the mercy of the system to provide a court-appointed lawyer. While many receive adequate representation (and often are not sentenced to death as a result), many others are assigned lawyers who lack the knowledge, skill, resources—and sometimes even the inclination—to handle a serious criminal case. People who would not be sentenced to death if properly represented are sentenced to death because of incompetent court-appointed lawyers. In many communities, racial minorities are still excluded from participation as jurors, judges, prosecutors, and lawyers in the system. In too many cases, defendants are convicted on flimsy evidence, such as eyewitness identifications, which are notoriously unreliable but are seen as very credible by juries; the testimony of convicts who, in exchange for lenient treatment in their own cases, testify that the accused admitted to them that he or she committed the crime; and confessions obtained from people of limited intellect through lengthy and overbearing interrogations.

. . . These are not minor, isolated incidents; they are long-standing, pervasive, systemic deficiencies in the criminal justice system that are not being corrected and, in some places, are even becoming worse. . . . Law enforcement agencies have been unwilling to videotape interrogations and use identification procedures that are more reliable than those presently employed. People who support capital punishment as a concept are unwilling to spend millions of tax dollars to provide competent legal representation for those accused of crimes. And courts have yet to find ways to overcome centuries of racial discrimination that often influence, consciously or subconsciously, the decisions of prosecutors, judges, and juries.

A WARNING THAT SOMETHING IS TERRIBLY WRONG: INNOCENT PEOPLE CONDEMNED TO DEATH

Over 100 people condemned to death in the last 30 years have been exonerated and released after new evidence established their innocence or cast such doubt on their guilt that they could not be convicted. The 100th of those people, Ray Krone, was convicted and sentenced to death in Arizona based on the testimony of an expert witness that his teeth matched bite marks on the victim. During the ten years that Krone spent on death row, scientists developed the ability to compare biological evidence recovered at crime scenes with the DNA of suspects. DNA testing established that Krone was innocent. On Krone's release, the prosecutor said, "[Krone] deserves an apology from us, that's for sure. A mistake was made here. . . . What do you say to him? An injustice was done and we will try to do better. And we're sorry." Although unfortunate to be wrongfully convicted, Krone was very fortunate that there was DNA evidence in his case. In most cases, there is no biological evidence for DNA testing.

Other defendants had their death sentences commuted to life imprisonment without the possibility of parole because of questions about their innocence. For example, in 1994, the governor of Virginia commuted the death sentence of a mentally retarded man, Earl Washington, to life imprisonment without parole because of questions regarding his guilt. Washington, an easily persuaded, somewhat childlike special-education dropout, had been convicted of murder and rape based on a confession he gave to police, even though it was full of inconsistencies. For example, at one point in the confession Washington said that the victim was white and at another that the victim was black. Six years later, DNA evidence—not available at the time of Washington's trial or the commutation—established that Washington was innocent and he was released.

Although DNA testing has been available only in cases where there was biological evidence and the evidence has been preserved, it has established the innocence of many people who were not sentenced to death. A Michigan judge in 1984 lamented the fact that the state did not have the death penalty, saying that life imprisonment was inadequate for Eddie Joe Lloyd for the rape and murder of a 16-year-old girl. Police had obtained a confession from Lloyd while he was in a mental hospital. Seventeen years later, DNA evidence established that Lloyd did not commit the crime. On his release, Lloyd commented, "If Michigan had the death penalty, I would have been through, the angels would have sung a long time ago."

Sometimes evidence of innocence has surfaced only at the last minute. Anthony Porter, sentenced to death in Illinois, went through all the appeals and review that are available for one so sentenced. Every court upheld his conviction and sentence. As Illinois prepared to put him to death, a question arose as to whether Porter, who was brain damaged and mentally retarded, understood what was happening to him. A person who lacks the mental ability to understand that he is being put to death in punishment for a crime cannot be executed unless he is treated and becomes capable of understanding why he is being executed. Just two days before Porter was to be executed, a court stayed his execution in order to examine his mental condition. After the stay was granted, a journalism class at Northwestern University and a private investigator examined the case and proved that Anthony Porter was innocent. They obtained a confession from the person who committed the crime. Anthony Porter was released, becoming the third person released from Illinois's death row after being proven innocent by a journalism class at Northwestern.

Some people have been executed despite questions of their innocence. Gary Graham was sentenced to death in Texas based on the identification of a witness who said she saw a murder from 40 feet away. Studies have demonstrated that such identifications are often unreliable. But Graham had the misfortune to be assigned a notoriously incompetent lawyer, Ron Mock, who had so many clients sentenced to death that some refer to the "Mock Wing" of death row. Mock failed to seriously contest the state's case, conduct an independent investigation, and present witnesses at the scene who would have testified that Graham was not the person who committed the crime and that the perpetrator was much shorter than Graham. Although it was apparent that Graham did not receive a fair trial and adequate legal representation, he was executed by Texas in 2000. Whether Graham was innocent or guilty will never be resolved because in his case, like most others, there was no DNA evidence that would conclusively establish guilt or innocence.

Some proponents of capital punishment argue that the exoneration of Porter and others shows that the system works and that no innocent people have been executed. However, someone spending years on death row for a crime he did not commit is not an example of the system working. When journalism students prove that police, prosecutors, judges, defense lawyers, and the entire legal system failed to discover the perpetrator of a crime and instead condemned the wrong person to die, the system is not working. Porter and others were spared, as Chief Justice Moses Harrison of the Illinois Supreme Court observed, "only because of luck and the dedication of the attorneys, reporters, family members and volunteers who labored to win their release. They survived despite the criminal justice system, not because of it. . . ."

. . . Courts will always be fallible and reversible, while death will always be final and irreversible.

THE TWO MOST IMPORTANT
DECISIONS—MADE BY PROSECUTORS

The two most important decisions in every death penalty case are made not by juries or judges, but by prosecutors. No state or federal law ever requires prosecutors to seek the death penalty or take a capital case to trial. A prosecutor has complete discretion in deciding whether to seek the death penalty and, even if death is sought, whether to offer a sentence less than death in exchange for the defendant's guilty plea. The overwhelming majority of all criminal cases, including capital cases, are resolved not by trials but by plea bargains. Whether death is sought or imposed is based on the discretion and proclivities of the thousands of people who occupy the offices of prosecutor in judicial districts throughout the nation. . . . Some prosecutors seek the death penalty at every opportunity, and others never seek it; some seldom seek it; some

frequently seek it. There is no requirement that individual prosecutors—who, in most states, are elected by districts—be consistent in their
practices in seeking the death penalty.

As a result of this discretion, there are great geographical disparities in where death is imposed within states. Prosecutors in Houston
and Philadelphia have sought the death penalty in virtually every case
in which it can be imposed. As a result of aggressive prosecutors and
inept court-appointed lawyers, Houston and Philadelphia have each
condemned over 100 people to death—more than most states. Harris
County, which includes Houston, has had more executions in the last
30 years than any *state* except Texas and Virginia. . . .

Whether death is sought may depend on the side of the county line
where the crime was committed. A murder was committed in a parking
lot that contained the boundary between Lexington County, South Car-
olina, which at the time had sentenced 12 people to death, and Richland
County, which had sent only one person to death row. The crime was
determined to have occurred a few feet on the Lexington County side of
the line. The defendant was tried in Lexington County and sentenced to
death. Had the crime occurred a few feet in the other direction, the death
penalty almost certainly would not have been imposed. . . .

Thus, whether the death sentence is imposed may depend more on
the personal predilections and politics of local prosecutors than the hei-
nousness of the crime or the incorrigibility of the defendant.

The Role of Racial Bias

The complete discretion given to prosecutors in deciding whether
to seek the death penalty and whether to drop the death penalty in
exchange for guilty pleas also contributes to racial disparities in the
infliction of the death penalty. In the 38 states that have the death penalty, 97.5 percent of the chief prosecutors are white. In 18 of the states,
all of the chief prosecutors are white. Even the most conscientious
prosecutors who have had little experience with people of other races
may be influenced in their decisions by racial stereotypes and attitudes
they have developed over their lives.

But the rest of the criminal justice system is almost as unrepresenta-
tive of Americans' racial diversity as prosecutors' offices. In the South,
where the death penalty is most often imposed and carried out, over

half the victims of crime are people of color, well over 60 percent of the prison population is made up of people of color, and half of those sentenced to death are members of racial minorities. Yet people of color are seldom involved as judges, jurors, prosecutors, and lawyers in the courts. . . .

Although African Americans constitute only 12 percent of the national population, they are victims of half the murders that are committed in the United States. Yet 80 percent of those on death row were convicted of crimes against white people. The discrepancy is even greater in the Death Belt states of the South. In Georgia and Alabama, for example, African Americans are the victims of 65 percent of the homicides, yet 80 percent of those on death row are there for crimes against white persons. . . .

Study after study has confirmed what lawyers practicing in the criminal courts observe every day: People of color are treated more harshly than white people. A person of color is more likely than a white person to be stopped by the police, to be abused by the police during that stop, to be arrested, to be denied bail when taken to court, to be charged with a serious crime as opposed to a less serious one that could be charged, to be convicted, and to receive a harsher sentence. But a person of color is much *less* likely to be a participant in the criminal justice system as a judge, juror, prosecutor, or lawyer.

It would be quite remarkable if race affected every aspect of the criminal justice system except with regard to the death penalty—the area in which decision makers have the broadest discretion and base their decisions on evidence with tremendous emotional impact. The sad reality is that race continues to influence who is sentenced to death as it has throughout American history.

The Death Sentence for Being Assigned the Worst Lawyer

Capital cases—complex cases with the highest stakes of any in the legal system—should be handled by the most capable lawyers, with the resources to conduct thorough investigations and consult with various experts on everything from the prosecution's scientific evidence to psychologists and psychiatrists to investigate the defendant's mental health. The right to counsel is the most fundamental constitutional right of a person charged with a crime. A person accused of a crime depends on a lawyer to investigate the prosecution's case; to present any facts that may be helpful to the accused and necessary for a fair and reliable determination of guilt or innocence and, if guilty, a proper sentence; and to protect every other right of the accused. However, U.S. Supreme Court Justice Ruth Bader Ginsburg observed in 2001 that she had "yet to see a death case among the dozens coming to the Supreme Court . . . in which the defendant was well represented at trial. People who are well represented at trial do not get the death penalty."

Those receiving the death penalty are not well represented because many states do not provide the structure, resources, independence, and accountability that is required to insure competent representation in an area of such specialization. . . .

In states with no public defender offices, lawyers in private practice are assigned to defend capital cases and paid well below market rates. Lawyers, like many people, are attracted to work that pays well. Few lawyers are willing to take the most difficult and emotionally demanding cases with the highest stakes for wages that are among the lowest in the legal profession. A paralegal who works on a federal bankruptcy case is compensated at a higher hourly rate than a lawyer who defends a capital case in Alabama, Georgia, Mississippi, Virginia, and many other states that send many people to death row. . . .

In several states where journalists have investigated—Illinois, Kentucky, Tennessee, and Texas—they have found that a fourth to a third of those sentenced to death were represented at their trials by lawyers who were later disbarred, suspended, or convicted of crimes. . . .

Many courts continue to operate on the fiction that anyone licensed to practice law—even someone whose practice is mostly real estate or divorce law—is competent to handle capital cases. This is like saying that every doctor is competent to do brain surgery. . . .

Justice Hugo Black wrote for the U.S. Supreme Court in 1956 that "[t]here can be no equal justice where the kind of trial a [person] gets depends on the amount of money he [or she] has." But today, no one seriously doubts that the kind of trial, and the kind of justice, a person receives depends very much on the amount of money he or she has. The quality of legal representation tolerated by some courts shocks the conscience of a person of average sensibilities. But poor representation resulting from lack of funding and structure has been accepted as the best that can be done with the limited resources available. The commitment of many states to providing lawyers for those who cannot afford them was aptly described by a Chief Justice of the Georgia Supreme Court: "[W]e set our sights on the embarrassing target of mediocrity. I guess that means about halfway. And that raises a question. Are we willing to put up with halfway justice? To my way of thinking, one-half justice must mean one-half injustice, and one-half injustice is no justice at all."

The proponents of capital punishment are always quick to say that people facing the death penalty *should* receive better legal representation. But they do not explain how this is going to be accomplished—whether by a sudden burst of altruism on the part of members of the legal profession, who are going to suddenly start taking capital cases for a fraction of what they can make doing other work; a massive infusion of funding from state legislatures that are searching for revenue for education, transportation, and other areas that have a constituency; or some other miracle. The right to competent representation is celebrated in the abstract, but most states—and most supporters of capital punishment—are unwilling to pay for it. As a result the death penalty will continue to be imposed not upon those who commit the worst crimes, but upon those who have the misfortune to be assigned the worst lawyers. . . .

CONCLUSION

. . . We should have the humility to admit that the legal system is not infallible and that mistakes are made. We should have the honesty to admit that our society is unwilling to pay the price of providing every poor person with competent legal representation, even in capital cases. We should have the courage to acknowledge the role that race plays in the criminal justice system and make a commitment to do something about it instead of pretending that racial prejudice no longer exists. And we should have the compassion and decency to recognize the dignity of every person, even those who have offended us most grievously. The Constitutional Court of South Africa addressed many of these issues in deciding whether the death penalty violated that country's constitution. Despite a staggering crime rate and a long history of racial violence and oppression, the Court unanimously concluded that in a society in transition from hatred to understanding, from vengeance to reconciliation, there was no place for the death penalty. The American people will ultimately reach the same conclusion, deciding that, like slavery and segregation, the death penalty is a relic of another era, and that this society of such vast wealth is capable of more constructive approaches to crime. And the United States will join the rest of the civilized world in abandoning capital punishment.

SOLITARY CONFINEMENT AND TORTURE

Chapter 39

Hellhole

Atul Gawande

The Eighth Amendment of the U.S. Constitution forbids "cruel and unusual punishment." Over the years, the U.S. Supreme Court has made it clear that a punishment does not need to be both cruel and unusual in order to be disallowed—simply being cruel is enough. Here, Atul Gawande argues that tens of thousands of American prisoners are treated cruelly by virtue of being held in long-term solitary confinement. Since Dr. Gawande wrote this article, it has come to light that around half of the suicides in American prisons are committed by the less than 4 percent of inmates being held in solitary confinement.

Human beings are social creatures. We are social not just in the trivial sense that we like company, and not just in the obvious sense that we each depend on others. We are social in a more elemental way: simply to exist as a normal human being requires interaction with other people.

Children provide the clearest demonstration of this fact, although it was slow to be accepted. Well into the 1950s, psychologists were encouraging parents to give children *less* attention and affection, in order to encourage independence. Then Harry Harlow, a professor of psychology at the University of Wisconsin at Madison, produced a series of influential studies involving baby rhesus monkeys.

Atul Gawande, "Hellhole" in *The New Yorker* (March 30, 2009). Copyright © 2009. Used with permission of the author.

He happened upon the findings in the mid-fifties, when he decided to save money for his primate-research laboratory by breeding his own lab monkeys instead of importing them from India. Because he didn't know how to raise infant monkeys, he cared for them the way hospitals of the era cared for human infants—in nurseries, with plenty of food, warm blankets, some toys, and in isolation from other infants to prevent the spread of infection. The monkeys grew up sturdy, disease-free, and larger than those from the wild. Yet they were also profoundly disturbed, given to staring blankly and rocking in place for long periods, circling their cages repetitively, and mutilating themselves.

At first, Harlow and his graduate students couldn't figure out what the problem was. They considered factors such as diet, patterns of light exposure, even the antibiotics they used. Then, as Deborah Blum recounts in a fascinating biography of Harlow, "Love at Goon Park," one of his researchers noticed how tightly the monkeys clung to their soft blankets. Harlow wondered whether what the monkeys were missing in their Isolettes was a mother. So, in an odd experiment, he gave them an artificial one.

In the studies, one artificial mother was a doll made of terry cloth; the other was made of wire. He placed a warming device inside the dolls to make them seem more comforting. The babies, Harlow discovered, largely ignored the wire mother. But they became deeply attached to the cloth mother. They caressed it. They slept curled up on it. They ran to it when frightened. They refused replacements: they wanted only "their" mother. If sharp spikes were made to randomly thrust out of the mother's body when the rhesus babies held it, they waited patiently for the spikes to recede and returned to clutching it. No matter how tightly they clung to the surrogate mothers, however, the monkeys remained psychologically abnormal.

In a later study on the effect of total isolation from birth, the researchers found that the test monkeys, upon being released into a group of ordinary monkeys, "usually go into a state of emotional shock, characterized by . . . autistic self-clutching and rocking." Harlow noted, "One of six monkeys isolated for three months refused to eat after release and died five days later." After several weeks in the company of other monkeys, most of them adjusted—but not those who had been isolated for longer periods. "Twelve months of isolation almost obliterated the animals socially," Harlow wrote. They became permanently withdrawn, and they lived as outcasts—regularly set upon, as if inviting abuse.

The research made Harlow famous (and infamous, too—revulsion at his work helped spur the animal-rights movement). Other psychologists produced evidence of similarly deep and sustained damage in neglected and orphaned children. Hospitals were made to open up their nurseries to parents. And it became widely accepted that children require nurturing human beings not just for food and protection but also for the normal functioning of their brains.

We have been hesitant to apply these lessons to adults. Adults, after all, are fully formed, independent beings, with internal strengths and knowledge to draw upon. We wouldn't have anything like a child's dependence on other people, right? Yet it seems that we do. We don't have a lot of monkey experiments to call upon here. But mankind has produced tens of thousands of human ones, including in our prison system. And the picture that has emerged is profoundly unsettling.

Among our most benign experiments are those with people who voluntarily isolate themselves for extended periods. Long-distance solo sailors, for instance, commit themselves to months at sea. They face all manner of physical terrors: thrashing storms, fifty-foot waves, leaks, illness. Yet, for many, the single most overwhelming difficulty they report is the "soul-destroying loneliness," as one sailor called it. Astronauts have to be screened for their ability to tolerate long stretches in tightly confined isolation, and they come to depend on radio and video communications for social contact.

The problem of isolation goes beyond ordinary loneliness, however. Consider what we've learned from hostages who have been held in solitary confinement—from the journalist Terry Anderson, for example, whose extraordinary memoir, "Den of Lions," recounts his seven years as a hostage of Hezbollah in Lebanon.

Anderson was the chief Middle East correspondent for the Associated Press when, on March 16, 1985, three bearded men forced him from his car in Beirut at gunpoint. He was pushed into a Mercedes sedan, covered head to toe with a heavy blanket, and made to crouch head down in the footwell behind the front seat. His captors drove him to a garage, pulled him out of the car, put a hood over his head, and bound his wrists and ankles with tape. For half an hour, they grilled him for the names of other Americans in Beirut, but he gave no names and they did not beat him or press him further. They threw him in the trunk of the car, drove him to another building, and put him in what would be the first of a succession of cells across Lebanon. He was soon placed in what seemed to be a dusty closet, large enough for only a mattress. Blindfolded, he could make out the distant sounds of other hostages. (One was William Buckley, the C.I.A. station chief who was kidnapped and tortured repeatedly until he weakened and died.) Peering around his blindfold, Anderson could see a bare light bulb dangling from the ceiling. He received three unpalatable meals a day—usually a sandwich of bread and cheese, or cold rice with canned vegetables, or soup. He had a bottle to urinate in and was allotted one five- to ten-minute trip each day to a rotting bathroom to empty his bowels and wash with water at a dirty sink. Otherwise, the only reprieve from isolation came when the guards made short visits to bark at him for breaking a rule or to threaten him, sometimes with a gun at his temple.

He missed people terribly, especially his fiancée and his family. He was despondent and depressed. Then, with time, he began to feel something more. He felt himself disintegrating. It was as if his brain were grinding down. A month into his confinement, he recalled in his memoir, "The mind is a blank. Jesus, I always thought I was smart. Where are all the things I learned, the books I read, the poems I memorized? There's nothing there, just a formless, gray-black misery. My mind's gone dead. God, help me."

He was stiff from lying in bed day and night, yet tired all the time. He dozed off and on constantly, sleeping twelve hours a day. He craved activity of almost any kind. He would watch the daylight wax and wane on the ceiling, or roaches creep slowly up the wall. He had a Bible and tried to read, but he often found that he lacked the concentration to do so. He observed himself becoming neurotically possessive about his little space, at times putting his life in jeopardy by flying into a rage if a guard happened to step on his bed. He brooded incessantly, thinking back on all the mistakes he'd made in life, his regrets, his offenses against God and family.

His captors moved him every few months. For unpredictable stretches of time, he was granted the salvation of a companion—sometimes he shared a cell with as many as four other hostages—and he noticed that his thinking recovered rapidly when this occurred. He could read and concentrate longer, avoid hallucinations, and better control his emotions. "I would rather have had the worst companion than no companion at all," he noted.

In September, 1986, after several months of sharing a cell with another hostage, Anderson was, for no apparent reason, returned to solitary confinement, this time in a six-by-six-foot cell, with no windows, and light from only a flickering fluorescent lamp in an outside corridor. The guards refused to say how long he would be there. After a few weeks, he felt his mind slipping away again.

"I find myself trembling sometimes for no reason," he wrote. "I'm afraid I'm beginning to lose my mind, to lose control completely."

One day, three years into his ordeal, he snapped. He walked over to a wall and began beating his forehead against it, dozens of times. His head was smashed and bleeding before the guards were able to stop him.

Some hostages fared worse. Anderson told the story of Frank Reed, a fifty-four-year-old American private-school director who was taken hostage and held in solitary confinement for four months before being put in with Anderson. By then, Reed had become severely withdrawn. He lay motionless for hours facing a wall, semi-catatonic. He could not follow the guards' simplest instructions. This invited abuse from them, in much the same way that once isolated rhesus monkeys seemed to invite abuse from the colony. Released after three and a half years, Reed ultimately required admission to a psychiatric hospital.

"It's an awful thing, solitary," John McCain wrote of his five and a half years as a prisoner of war in Vietnam—more than two years of it spent in isolation in a fifteen-by-fifteen-foot cell, unable to communicate with other P.O.W.s except by tap code, secreted notes, or by speaking into an enamel cup pressed against the wall. "It crushes your spirit and weakens your resistance more effectively than any other form of mistreatment." And this comes from a man who was beaten regularly; denied adequate medical treatment for two broken arms, a broken leg, and chronic dysentery; and tortured to the point of having an arm broken again. A U.S. military study of almost a hundred and fifty naval aviators returned from imprisonment in Vietnam, many of whom were treated even worse than McCain, reported that they found social isolation to be as torturous and agonizing as any physical abuse they suffered.

And what happened to them *was* physical. EEG studies going back to the 1960s have shown diffuse slowing of brain waves in prisoners after a week or more of solitary confinement. In 1992, fifty-seven prisoners of war, released after an average of six months in detention camps in the former Yugoslavia, were examined using EEG-like tests. The recordings revealed brain abnormalities months afterward; the most severe were found in prisoners who had endured either head trauma sufficient to render them unconscious or, yes, solitary confinement. Without sustained social interaction, the human brain may become as impaired as one that has incurred a traumatic injury.

On December 4, 1991, Terry Anderson was released from captivity. He had been the last and the longest-held American hostage in Lebanon. I spoke to Keron Fletcher, a former British military psychiatrist who had been on the receiving team for Anderson and many other hostages, and followed them for years afterward. Initially, Fletcher said, everyone experiences the pure elation of being able to see and talk to people again, especially family and friends. They can't get enough of other people, and talk almost non-stop for hours. They are optimistic and hopeful. But, afterward, normal sleeping and eating patterns prove difficult to reestablish. Some have lost their sense of time. For weeks, they have trouble managing the sensations and emotional complexities of their freedom.

For the first few months after his release, Anderson said when I reached him by phone recently, "it was just kind of a fog." He had done many television interviews at the time. "And if you look at me in the pictures? Look at my eyes. You can tell. I look drugged."

Most hostages survived their ordeal, Fletcher said, although relationships, marriages, and careers were often lost. Some found, as John McCain did, that the experience even strengthened them. Yet none saw solitary confinement as anything less than torture. This presents us with an awkward question: If prolonged isolation is—as research and experience have confirmed for decades—so objectively horrifying, so intrinsically cruel, how did we end up with a prison system that may subject more of our own citizens to it than any other country in history has?

Recently, I met a man who had spent more than five years in isolation at a prison in the Boston suburb of Walpole, Massachusetts, not far from my home. Bobby Dellelo was, to say the least, no Terry Anderson or John McCain. Brought up in the run-down neighborhoods of Boston's West End, in the 1940s, he was caught burglarizing a shoe store at the age of ten. At thirteen, he recalls, he was nabbed while robbing a Jordan Marsh department store. (He and his friends learned to hide out in stores at closing time, steal their merchandise, and then break out during the night.) The remainder of his childhood was spent mostly in the state reform school. That was where he learned how to fight, how to hot-wire a car with a piece of foil, how to pick locks, and how to make a zip gun using a snapped-off automobile radio antenna, which, in those days, was just thick enough to barrel a .22-calibre bullet. Released upon turning eighteen, Dellelo returned to stealing. Usually, he stole from office buildings at night. But some of the people he hung out with did stickups, and, together with one of them, he held up a liquor store in Dorchester.

"What a disaster that thing was," he recalls, laughing. They put the store's owner and the customers in a walk-in refrigerator at gunpoint, took their wallets, and went to rob the register. But more customers came in. So they robbed them and put them in the refrigerator, too. Then still more customers arrived, the refrigerator got full, and the whole thing turned into a circus. Dellelo and his partner finally escaped. But one of the customers identified him to the police. By the time he was caught, Dellelo had been fingered for robbing the Commander Hotel in Cambridge as well. He served a year for the first conviction and two and a half years for the second.

Three months after his release, in 1963, at the age of twenty, he and a friend tried to rob the Kopelman jewelry store, in downtown Boston. But an alarm went off before they got their hands on anything. They separated and ran. The friend shot and killed an off-duty policeman while trying to escape, then killed himself. Dellelo was convicted of first-degree murder and sentenced to life in prison. He ended up serving forty years. Five years and one month were spent in isolation.

The criteria for the isolation of prisoners vary by state but typically include not only violent infractions but also violation of prison rules or association with gang members. The imposition of long-term isolation—which can be for months or years—is ultimately at the discretion of prison administrators. One former prisoner I spoke to, for example, recalled being put in solitary confinement for petty annoyances like refusing to get out of the shower quickly enough. Bobby Dellelo was put there for escaping.

It was an elaborate scheme. He had a partner, who picked the lock to a supervisor's office and got hold of the information manual for the microwave-detection system that patrolled a grassy no man's land between the prison and the road. They studied the manual long enough to learn how to circumvent the system and returned it. On Halloween Sunday, 1993, they had friends stage a fight in the prison yard. With all the guards in the towers looking at the fight through binoculars, the two men tipped a picnic table up against a twelve-foot wall and climbed it like a ladder. Beyond it, they scaled a sixteen-foot fence. To get over the razor wire on top, they used a Z-shaped tool they'd improvised from locker handles. They dropped down into the no man's land and followed an invisible path that they'd calculated the microwave system would not detect. No alarm sounded. They went over one more fence, walked around a parking lot, picked their way through some woods, and emerged onto a four-lane road. After a short walk to a convenience store, they called a taxi from a telephone booth and rolled away before anyone knew they were gone.

They lasted twenty-four days on the outside. Eventually, somebody ratted them out, and the police captured them on the day before Thanksgiving, at the house of a friend in Cambridge. The prison administration gave Dellelo five years in the Departmental Disciplinary Unit of the Walpole prison, its hundred-and-twenty-four-cell super-maximum segregation unit.

Wearing ankle bracelets, handcuffs, and a belly chain, Dellelo was marched into a thirteen-by-eight-foot off-white cell. A four-inch-thick concrete bed slab jutted out from the wall opposite the door. A smaller slab protruding from a side wall provided a desk. A cylindrical concrete block in the floor served as a seat. On the remaining wall was a toilet and a metal sink. He was given four sheets, four towels, a blanket, a bedroll, a toothbrush, toilet paper, a tall clear plastic cup, a bar of soap, seven white T-shirts, seven pairs of boxer shorts, seven pairs of socks, plastic slippers, a pad of paper, and a ballpoint pen. A speaker with a microphone was mounted on the door. Cells used for solitary confinement are often windowless, but this one had a ribbon like window that was seven inches wide and five feet tall. The electrically controlled door was solid steel, with a seven-inch-by-twenty-eight-inch aperture and two wickets—little door slots, one at ankle height and one at waist height, for shackling him whenever he was let out and for passing him meal trays.

As in other supermaxes—facilities designed to isolate prisoners from social contact—Dellelo was confined to his cell for at least twenty-three hours a day and permitted out only for a shower or for recreation in an outdoor cage that he estimated to be fifty feet long and five feet wide, known as "the dog kennel." He could talk to other prisoners through the steel door of his cell, and during recreation if a prisoner was in an adjacent cage. He made a kind of fishing line for passing notes to adjacent cells by unwinding the elastic from his boxer shorts, though it was contraband and would be confiscated. Prisoners could receive mail and as many as ten reading items. They were allowed one phone call the first month and could earn up to four calls and four visits per month if they followed the rules, but there could be no physical contact with anyone, except when guards forcibly restrained them. Some supermaxes even use food as punishment, serving the prisoners nutra-loaf, an unpalatable food brick that contains just enough nutrition for survival. Dellelo was spared this. The rules also permitted him to have a radio after thirty days, and, after sixty days, a thirteen-inch black-and-white television.

"This is going to be a piece of cake," Dellelo recalls thinking when the door closed behind him. Whereas many American supermax prisoners—and most P.O.W.s and hostages—have no idea when they might get out, he knew exactly how long he was going to be there. He drew a calendar on his pad of paper to start counting down the days. He would get a radio and a TV. He could read. No one was going to bother him. And, as his elaborate escape plan showed, he could be patient. "This is their sophisticated security?" he said to himself. "They don't know what they're doing."

After a few months without regular social contact, however, his experience proved no different from that of the P.O.W.s or hostages, or the majority of isolated prisoners whom researchers have studied: he started to lose his mind. He talked to himself. He paced back and forth compulsively, shuffling along the same six-foot path for hours on end. Soon, he was having panic attacks, screaming for help. He hallucinated that the colors on the walls were changing. He became enraged by routine noises—the sound of doors opening as the guards made their hourly checks, the sounds of inmates in nearby cells. After a year or so, he was hearing voices on the television talking directly to him. He put the television under his bed, and rarely took it out again.

One of the paradoxes of solitary confinement is that, as starved as people become for companionship, the experience typically leaves them unfit for social interaction. Once, Dellelo was allowed to have an in-person meeting with his lawyer, and he simply couldn't handle it. After so many months in which his primary human contact had been an occasional phone call or brief conversations with an inmate down the tier, shouted through steel doors at the top of their lungs, he found himself unable to carry on a face-to-face conversation. He had trouble following both words and hand gestures and couldn't generate them himself. When he realized this, he succumbed to a full-blown panic attack.

Craig Haney, a psychology professor at the University of California at Santa Cruz, received rare permission to study a hundred randomly selected inmates at California's Pelican Bay supermax, and noted a number of phenomena. First, after months or years of complete isolation, many prisoners "begin to lose the ability to initiate behavior of any kind—to organize their own lives around activity and purpose," he writes. "Chronic apathy, lethargy, depression, and despair often result. . . . In extreme cases, prisoners may literally stop behaving," becoming essentially catatonic.

Second, almost 90 percent of these prisoners had difficulties with "irrational anger," compared with just 3 percent of the general population. Haney attributed this to the extreme restriction, the totality of control, and the extended absence of any opportunity for happiness or joy. Many prisoners in solitary become consumed with revenge fantasies.

"There were some guards in D.D.U. who were decent guys," Dellelo told me. They didn't trash his room when he was let out for a shower, or try to trip him when escorting him in chains, or write him up for contraband if he kept food or a salt packet from a meal in his cell. "But some of them were evil, evil pricks." One correctional officer became a particular obsession. Dellelo spent hours imagining cutting his head off and rolling it down the tier. "I mean, I know this is insane thinking," he says now. Even at the time, he added, "I had a fear in the background— like how much of this am I going to be able to let go? How much is this going to affect who I am?"

He was right to worry. Everyone's identity is socially created: it's through your relationships that you understand yourself as a mother or a father, a teacher or an accountant, a hero or a villain. But, after years of isolation, many prisoners change in another way that Haney observed. They begin to see themselves primarily as combatants in the world, people whose identity is rooted in thwarting prison control.

As a matter of self-preservation, this may not be a bad thing. According to the Navy P.O.W. researchers, the instinct to fight back against the enemy constituted the most important coping mechanism for the prisoners they studied. Resistance was often their sole means of maintaining a sense of purpose, and so their sanity. Yet resistance is precisely what we wish to destroy in our supermax prisoners. As Haney observed in a review of research findings, prisoners in solitary confinement must be able to withstand the experience in order to be allowed to return to the highly social world of mainline prison or free society. Perversely, then, the prisoners who can't handle profound isolation are the ones who are forced to remain in it. "And those who have adapted," Haney writes, "are prime candidates for release to a social world to which they may be incapable of ever fully readjusting."

Dellelo eventually found a way to resist that would not prolong his ordeal. He fought his battle through the courts, filing motion after motion in an effort to get his conviction overturned. He became so good at submitting his claims that he obtained a paralegal certificate along the way. And, after forty years in prison, and more than five years in solitary, he got his first-degree-homicide conviction reduced to manslaughter. On November 19, 2003, he was freed.

Bobby Dellelo is sixty-seven years old now. He lives on Social Security in a Cambridge efficiency apartment that is about four times larger than his cell. He still seems to be adjusting to the world outside. He lives alone. To the extent that he is out in society, it is, in large measure, as a combatant. He works for prisoners' rights at the American Friends Service Committee. He also does occasional work assisting prisoners with their legal cases. Sitting at his kitchen table, he showed me how to pick a padlock—you know, just in case I ever find myself in trouble.

But it was impossible to talk to him about his time in isolation without seeing that it was fundamentally no different from the isolation that Terry Anderson and John McCain had endured. Whether in Walpole or Beirut or Hanoi, all human beings experience isolation as torture.

The main argument for using long-term isolation in prisons is that it provides discipline and prevents violence. When inmates refuse to follow the rules—when they escape, deal drugs, or attack other inmates and corrections officers—wardens must be able to punish and contain the misconduct. Presumably, less stringent measures haven't worked, or the behavior would not have occurred. And it's legitimate to incapacitate violent aggressors for the safety of others. So, advocates say, isolation is a necessary evil, and those who don't recognize this are dangerously naïve.

The argument makes intuitive sense. If the worst of the worst are removed from the general prison population and put in isolation, you'd expect there to be markedly fewer inmate shankings and attacks on corrections officers. But the evidence doesn't bear this out. Perhaps the most careful inquiry into whether supermax prisons decrease violence and disorder was a 2003 analysis examining the experience in three states—Arizona, Illinois, and Minnesota—following the opening of their supermax prisons. The study found that levels of inmate-on-inmate violence were unchanged, and that levels of inmate-on-staff violence changed unpredictably, rising in Arizona, falling in Illinois, and holding steady in Minnesota.

Prison violence, it turns out, is not simply an issue of a few belligerents. In the past thirty years, the United States has quadrupled its incarceration rate but not its prison space. Work and education programs have been cancelled, out of a belief that the pursuit of rehabilitation is pointless. The result has been unprecedented overcrowding, along with unprecedented idleness—a nice formula for violence. Remove a few prisoners to solitary confinement, and the violence doesn't change. So you remove some more, and still nothing happens. Before long, you find yourself in the position we are in today. The United States now has 5 percent of the world's population, 25 percent of its prisoners, and probably the vast majority of prisoners who are in long-term solitary confinement.

It wasn't always like this. The wide-scale use of isolation is, almost exclusively, a phenomenon of the past twenty years. In 1890, the U.S. Supreme Court came close to declaring the punishment to be unconstitutional. Writing for the majority in the case of a Colorado murderer who had been held in isolation for a month, Justice Samuel Miller noted that experience had revealed "serious objections" to solitary confinement:

> A considerable number of the prisoners fell, after even a short confinement, into a semi-fatuous condition, from which it was next to impossible to arouse them, and others became violently insane; others, still, committed suicide; while those who stood the ordeal better were not generally reformed, and in most cases did not recover sufficient mental activity to be of any subsequent service to the community.

Prolonged isolation was used sparingly, if at all, by most American prisons for almost a century. Our first supermax—our first institution specifically designed for mass solitary confinement—was not established until 1983, in Marion, Illinois. In 1995, a federal court reviewing California's first supermax admitted that the conditions "hover on the edge of what is humanly tolerable for those with normal resilience." But it did not rule them to be unconstitutionally cruel or unusual, except in cases of mental illness. The prison's supermax conditions, the court stated, did not pose "a sufficiently high risk to all inmates of incurring a serious mental illness." In other words, there could be no legal objection to its routine use, given that the isolation didn't make *everyone* crazy. The ruling seemed to fit the public mood. By the end of the 1990s, some sixty supermax institutions had opened across the country. And new solitary-confinement units were established within nearly all of our ordinary maximum-security prisons.

The number of prisoners in these facilities has since risen to extraordinary levels. America now holds at least twenty-five thousand inmates in isolation in supermax prisons. An additional fifty to eighty thousand are kept in restrictive segregation units, many of them in isolation, too, although the government does not release these figures. By 1999, the practice had grown to the point that Arizona, Colorado, Maine, Nebraska, Nevada, Rhode Island, and Virginia kept between 5 and 8 percent of their prison population in isolation, and, by 2003, New York had joined them as well. Mississippi alone held eighteen hundred prisoners in supermax—12 percent of its prisoners over all. At the same time, other states had just a tiny fraction of their inmates in solitary confinement. In 1999, for example, Indiana had eighty-five supermax beds; Georgia had only ten. Neither of these two states can be described as being soft on crime.

Advocates of solitary confinement are left with a single argument for subjecting thousands of people to years of isolation: What else are we supposed to do? How else are we to deal with the violent, the disruptive, the prisoners who are just too dangerous to be housed with others?

As it happens, only a subset of prisoners currently locked away for long periods of isolation would be considered truly dangerous. Many are escapees or suspected gang members; many others are in solitary for nonviolent breaches of prison rules. Still, there are some highly dangerous and violent prisoners who pose a serious challenge to prison discipline and safety. In August, I met a man named Robert Felton, who had spent fourteen and a half years in isolation in the Illinois state correctional system. He is now thirty-six years old. He grew up in the predominantly black housing projects of Danville, Illinois, and had been a force of mayhem from the time he was a child.

His crimes were mainly impulsive, rather than planned. The first time he was arrested was at the age of eleven, when he and a relative broke into a house to steal some Atari video games. A year later, he was sent to state reform school after he and a friend broke into an abandoned building and made off with paint cans, irons, and other property that they hardly knew what to do with. In reform school, he got into fights and screamed obscenities at the staff. When the staff tried to discipline him by taking away his recreation or his television privileges, his behavior worsened. He tore a pillar out of the ceiling, a sink and mirrors off the wall, doors off their hinges. He was put in a special cell, stripped of nearly everything. When he began attacking counselors, the authorities transferred him to the maximum-security juvenile facility at Joliet, where he continued to misbehave.

Felton wasn't a sociopath. He made friends easily. He was close to his family, and missed them deeply. He took no pleasure in hurting others. Psychiatric evaluations turned up little more than attention-deficit disorder. But he had a terrible temper, a tendency to escalate rather than to defuse confrontations, and, by the time he was released, just before turning eighteen, he had achieved only a ninth-grade education.

Within months of returning home, he was arrested again. He had walked into a Danville sports bar and ordered a beer. The barman took his ten-dollar bill.

"Then he says, 'Naw, man, you can't get no beer. You're underage,'" Felton recounts. "I says, 'Well, give me my ten dollars back.' He says, 'You ain't getting shit. Get the hell out of here.'"

Felton stood his ground. The bartender had a pocket knife on the counter. "And, when he went for it, I went for it," Felton told me. "When I grabbed the knife first, I turned around and spinned on him. I said, 'You think you're gonna cut me, man? You gotta be fucked up.'"

The barman had put the ten-dollar bill in a Royal Crown bag behind the counter. Felton grabbed the bag and ran out the back door. He forgot his car keys on the counter, though. So he went back to get the keys— "the stupid keys," he now says ruefully—and in the fight that ensued he left the barman severely injured and bleeding. The police caught Felton fleeing in his car. He was convicted of armed robbery, aggravated unlawful restraint, and aggravated battery, and served fifteen years in prison.

He was eventually sent to the Stateville Correctional Center, a maximum-security facility in Joliet. Inside the overflowing prison, he got into vicious fights over insults and the like. About three months into his term, during a shakedown following the murder of an inmate, prison officials turned up a makeshift knife in his cell. (He denies that it was his.) They gave him a year in isolation. He was a danger, and he had to be taught a lesson. But it was a lesson that he seemed incapable of learning.

Felton's Stateville isolation cell had gray walls, a solid steel door, no window, no clock, and a light that was kept on twenty-four hours a day. As soon as he was shut in, he became claustrophobic and had a panic attack. Like Dellelo, Anderson, and McCain, he was soon pacing back and forth, talking to himself, studying the insects crawling around his cell, reliving past events from childhood, sleeping for as much as sixteen hours a day. But, unlike them, he lacked the inner resources to cope with his situation.

Many prisoners find survival in physical exercise, prayer, or plans for escape. Many carry out elaborate mental exercises, building entire houses in their heads, board by board, nail by nail, from the ground up, or memorizing team rosters for a baseball season. McCain recreated in his mind movies he'd seen. Anderson reconstructed complete novels from memory. Yuri Nosenko, a K.G.B. defector whom the C.I.A. wrongly accused of being a double agent and held for three years in total isolation (no reading material, no news, no human contact except with interrogators) in a closet-size concrete cell near Williamsburg, Virginia, made chess sets from threads and a calendar from lint (only to have them discovered and swept away).

But Felton would just yell, "Guard! Guard! Guard! Guard! Guard!," or bang his cup on the toilet, for hours. He could spend whole days hallucinating that he was in another world, that he was a child at home in Danville, playing in the streets, having conversations with imaginary people. Small cruelties that others somehow bore in quiet fury—getting no meal tray, for example—sent him into a rage. Despite being restrained with handcuffs, ankle shackles, and a belly chain whenever he was taken out, he managed to assault the staff at least three times. He threw his food through the door slot. He set his cell on fire by tearing his mattress apart, wrapping the stuffing in a sheet, popping his light bulb, and using the exposed wires to set the whole thing ablaze. He did this so many times that the walls of his cell were black with soot.

After each offense, prison officials extended his sentence in isolation. Still, he wouldn't stop. He began flooding his cell, by stuffing the door crack with socks, plugging the toilet, and flushing until the water was a couple of feet deep. Then he'd pull out the socks and the whole wing would flood with wastewater.

"Flooding the cell was the last option for me," Felton told me. "It was when I had nothing else I could do. You know, they took everything out of my cell, and all I had left was toilet water. I'd sit there and I'd say, 'Well, let me see what I can do with this toilet water.'"

Felton was not allowed out again for fourteen and a half years. He spent almost his entire prison term, from 1990 to 2005, in isolation. In March, 1998, he was among the first inmates to be moved to Tamms, a new, high-tech supermax facility in southern Illinois.

"At Tamms, man, it was like a lab," he says. Contact even with guards was tightly reduced. Cutoff valves meant that he couldn't flood his cell. He had little ability to force a response—negative or positive—from a human being. And, with that gone, he began to deteriorate further. He ceased showering, changing his clothes, brushing his teeth. His teeth rotted and ten had to be pulled. He began throwing his feces around his cell. He became psychotic.

It is unclear how many prisoners in solitary confinement become psychotic. Stuart Grassian, a Boston psychiatrist, has interviewed more than two hundred prisoners in solitary confinement. In one in-depth study, prepared for a legal challenge of prisoner-isolation practices, he concluded that about a third developed acute psychosis with hallucinations. The markers of vulnerability that he observed in his interviews were signs of cognitive dysfunction—a history of seizures, serious mental illness, mental retardation, illiteracy, or, as in Felton's case, a diagnosis such as attention-deficit hyperactivity disorder, signaling difficulty with impulse control. In the prisoners Grassian saw, about a third had these vulnerabilities, and these were the prisoners whom solitary confinement had made psychotic. They were simply not cognitively equipped to endure it without mental breakdowns.

A psychiatrist tried giving Felton anti-psychotic medication. Mostly, it made him sleep—sometimes twenty-four hours at a stretch, he said. Twice he attempted suicide. The first time, he hanged himself in a noose made from a sheet. The second time, he took a single staple from a legal newspaper and managed to slash the radial artery in his left wrist with it. In both instances, he was taken to a local emergency room for a few hours, patched up, and sent back to prison.

Is there an alternative? Consider what other countries do. Britain, for example, has had its share of serial killers, homicidal rapists, and prisoners who have taken hostages and repeatedly assaulted staff. The British also fought a seemingly unending war in Northern Ireland, which brought them hundreds of Irish Republican Army prisoners committed to violent resistance. The authorities resorted to a harshly punitive approach to control, including, in the mid-seventies, extensive use of solitary confinement. But the violence in prisons remained unchanged, the costs were phenomenal (in the United States, they reach more than fifty thousand dollars a year per inmate), and the public outcry became intolerable. British authorities therefore looked for another approach.

Beginning in the 1980s, they gradually adopted a strategy that focused on preventing prison violence rather than on delivering an ever more brutal series of punishments for it. The approach starts with the simple observation that prisoners who are unmanageable in one setting often behave perfectly reasonably in another. This suggested that violence might, to a critical extent, be a function of the conditions of incarceration. The British noticed that problem prisoners were usually people for whom avoiding humiliation and saving face were fundamental and instinctive. When conditions maximized humiliation and confrontation, every interaction escalated into a trial of strength. Violence became a predictable consequence.

So the British decided to give their most dangerous prisoners more control, rather than less. They reduced isolation and offered them opportunities for work, education, and special programming to increase social ties and skills. The prisoners were housed in small, stable units of fewer than ten people in individual cells, to avoid conditions of social chaos and unpredictability. In these reformed "Close Supervision Centres," prisoners could receive mental-health treatment and earn rights for more exercise, more phone calls, "contact visits," and even access to cooking facilities. They were allowed to air grievances. And the government set up an independent body of inspectors to track the results and enable adjustments based on the data.

The results have been impressive. The use of long-term isolation in England is now negligible. In all of England, there are now fewer prisoners in "extreme custody" than there are in the state of Maine. And the other countries of Europe have, with a similar focus on small units and violence prevention, achieved a similar outcome.

In this country, in June of 2006, a bipartisan national task force, the Commission on Safety and Abuse in America's Prisons, released its recommendations after a yearlong investigation. It called for ending long-term isolation of prisoners. Beyond about ten days, the report noted, practically no benefits can be found and the harm is clear—not just for inmates but for the public as well. Most prisoners in long-term isolation are returned to society, after all. And evidence from a number of studies has shown that supermax conditions—in which prisoners have virtually no social interactions and are given no programmatic support—make it highly likely that they will commit more crimes when they are released. Instead, the report said, we should follow the preventive approaches used in European countries.

The recommendations went nowhere, of course. Whatever the evidence in its favor, people simply did not believe in the treatment.

I spoke to a state-prison commissioner who wished to remain unidentified. He was a veteran of the system, having been either a prison warden or a commissioner in several states across the country for more than twenty years. He has publicly defended the use of long-term isolation everywhere that he has worked. Nonetheless, he said, he would remove most prisoners from long-term isolation units if he could and provide programming for the mental illnesses that many of them have.

"Prolonged isolation is not going to serve anyone's best interest," he told me. He still thought that prisons needed the option of isolation. "A bad violation should, I think, land you there for about ninety days, but it should not go beyond that."

He is apparently not alone among prison officials. Over the years, he has come to know commissioners in nearly every state in the country. "I believe that today you'll probably find that two-thirds or three-fourths of the heads of correctional agencies will largely share the position that I articulated with you," he said.

Commissioners are not powerless. They could eliminate prolonged isolation with the stroke of a pen. So, I asked, why haven't they? He told me what happened when he tried to move just one prisoner out of isolation. Legislators called for him to be fired and threatened to withhold basic funding. Corrections officers called members of the crime victim's family and told them that he'd gone soft on crime. Hostile stories appeared in the tabloids. It is pointless for commissioners to act unilaterally, he said, without a change in public opinion.

This past year, both the Republican and the Democratic presidential candidates came out firmly for banning torture and closing the facility in Guantánamo Bay, where hundreds of prisoners have been held in years-long isolation. Neither Barack Obama nor John McCain, however, addressed the question of whether prolonged solitary confinement is torture. For a presidential candidate, no less than for the prison commissioner, this would have been political suicide. The simple truth is that public sentiment in America is the reason that solitary confinement has exploded in this country, even as other Western nations have taken steps to reduce it. This is the dark side of American exceptionalism. With little concern or demurral, we have consigned tens of thousands of our own citizens to conditions that horrified our highest court a century ago. Our willingness to discard these standards for American prisoners made it easy to discard the Geneva Conventions prohibiting similar treatment of foreign prisoners of war, to the detriment of America's moral stature in the world. In much the same way that a previous generation of Americans countenanced legalized segregation, ours has countenanced legalized torture. And there is no clearer manifestation of this than our routine use of solitary confinement—on our own people, in our own communities, in a supermax prison, for example, that is a thirty-minute drive from my door.

Chapter 40

Liberalism, Torture, and the Ticking Bomb

David Luban

After September 11, 2001, many Americans were afraid that terrorists would strike again. Ordinary citizens were wary about riding on airplanes; rumors spread that terrorists might use a "dirty
bomb" to destroy an American city; and Muslim-Americans
dressed patriotically to avoid angry confrontations with strangers.
Meanwhile, President George W. Bush's popularity soared—
Americans wanted to believe in their leader.

In this climate of patriotism and fear, the Bush administration
began using torture in its "War on Terror." The torturing was done
in secret, because torture violates both international law and official American policy. Word began to leak out, however, and many
people opposed this new development. But others defended the
president: If a terrorist has planted a bomb in midtown Manhattan
and won't tell you where it is, they said, then surely you would be
willing to torture him until he revealed this information.

In this selection, David Luban describes how unrealistic this
"ticking bomb" scenario is and how dangerous a policy of torture
is in practice. Luban makes a strong case without even mentioning
a number of military and geopolitical reasons not to torture: (1)
If you torture the enemy, the enemy will be more likely to torture

David Luban, "Liberalism, Torture, and the Ticking Bomb" in *Virginia Law Review*, vol. 91,
no. 6 (2005). Copyright © 2005. Used with permission.

you; (2) the enemy will be less likely to surrender if they fear being tortured, and so the battle will go on; (3) the enemy may cite your harsh tactics in recruiting volunteers; (4) in a military occupation, torturing the enemy will turn the local population against you, thus resulting in more enemies and fewer informants; (5) a country that violates human rights will find other countries less cooperative, both economically and militarily; (6) a country that breaks international law cannot rightfully object when other countries do the same; (7) someone being severely interrogated will answer a question, regardless of whether he knows the answer—he might make a guess; he might say what he thinks the interrogator wants to hear; or he might have been trained to tell a particular lie; (8) a country that tortures will find it difficult to prosecute terrorists for crimes, because the defendants can say that the evidence was obtained illegally, through torture; and (9) to obtain useful information, bribes often work better than torture—but once you start torturing, it's hard to develop a cooperative relationship with the enemy.

David Luban (1949–) is a professor at the Georgetown University Law Center in Washington, D.C.

Torture used to be incompatible with American values. Our Bill of Rights forbids cruel and unusual punishment, and that has come to include all forms of corporal punishment except prison and death by methods purported to be painless. Americans and our government have historically condemned states that torture; we have granted asylum or refuge to those who fear it. The Senate ratified the Convention Against Torture, Congress enacted anti-torture legislation, and judicial opinions spoke of "the dastardly and totally inhuman act of torture."

Then came September 11. Less than one week later, a feature story reported that a quiz in a university ethics class "gave four choices for the proper U.S. response to the terrorist attacks: A.) execute the perpetrators on sight; B.) bring them back for trial in the United States; C.) subject the perpetrators to an international tribunal; or D.) torture and interrogate those involved." Most students chose A and D—execute them on sight and torture them. Six weeks after September 11, the press reported that frustrated FBI interrogators were considering harsh interrogation tactics; a few weeks after that, the *New York Times* reported that torture had become a topic of conversation "in bars, on commuter trains, and at dinner tables." By mid-November 2001, the *Christian Science Monitor* found that 32 percent of surveyed Americans favored torturing terror suspects. Alan Dershowitz reported in 2002 that "[d] uring numerous public appearances since September 11, 2001, I have asked audiences for a show of hands as to how many would support the use of nonlethal torture in a ticking-bomb case. Virtually every hand is raised." American abhorrence to torture now appears to have extraordinarily shallow roots.

To an important extent, one's stance on torture runs independent of progressive or conservative ideology. Alan Dershowitz suggests that torture should be regulated by a judicial warrant requirement. Liberal Senator Charles Schumer has publicly rejected the idea "that torture should never, ever be used." He argues that most U.S. senators would back torture to find out where a ticking time bomb is planted. By contrast, William Safire, a self-described "conservative . . . and card-carrying hard-liner," expresses revulsion at "phony-tough" pro-torture arguments, and forthrightly labels torture "barbarism." Examples like these illustrate how vital it is to avoid a simple left-right reductionism. For the most part, American conservatives belong no less than progressives to liberal culture, broadly understood. Henceforth, when I speak of "liberalism," I mean it in the broad sense used by political philosophers from John Stuart Mill on, a sense that includes conservatives as well as progressives, so long as they believe in limited government and the importance of human dignity and individual rights. . . .

I. THE FIVE AIMS OF TORTURE

What makes torture, the deliberate infliction of suffering and pain, especially abhorrent to liberals? This may seem like a bizarre question, because the answer seems self-evident: making people suffer is a horrible thing. Pain hurts and bad pain hurts badly. But let me pose the question in different terms. Realistically, the abuses of detainees at Abu Ghraib, Baghram, and Guantanamo pale by comparison with the death, maiming, and suffering in collateral damage during the Afghan and Iraq wars. Bombs crush limbs and burn people's faces off; nothing even remotely as horrifying has been reported in American prisoner abuse cases. Yet as much as we may regret or in some cases decry the wartime suffering of innocents, we do not seem to regard it with the special abhorrence that we do torture. This seems hypocritical and irrational, almost fetishistic, and it raises the question of what makes torture more illiberal than bombing and killing. The answer lies in the relationship between torturer and victim. The self-conscious aim of torture is to turn its victim into someone who is isolated, overwhelmed, terrorized, and humiliated. Torture aims to strip away from its victim all the qualities of human dignity that liberalism prizes. The torturer inflicts pain one-on-one, deliberately, up close and personal, in order to break the spirit of the victim—in other words, to tyrannize and dominate the victim. The relationship between them becomes a perverse parody of friendship and intimacy: intimacy transformed into its inverse image, where the torturer focuses on the victim's body with the intensity of a lover, except that every bit of that focus is bent to causing pain and tyrannizing the victim's spirit.

I am arguing that torture is a microcosm, raised to the highest level of intensity, of the tyrannical political relationships that liberalism hates the most. I have said that torture isolates and privatizes. Pain forcibly severs our concentration on anything outside of us; it collapses our horizon to our own body and the damage we feel in it. Even much milder sensations of prolonged discomfort can distract us so much that it becomes impossible to pay attention to anything else, as anyone knows who has had to go to the bathroom in a situation where it cannot be done. . . . The world of the man or woman in great pain is a world without relationships or engagements, a world without an exterior. It is a world reduced to a point, a world that makes no sense and in which the human soul finds no home and no repose.

And torture terrorizes. The body in pain winces; it trembles. The muscles themselves register fear. This is rooted in pain's biological function of impelling us in the most urgent way possible to escape from the source of pain—for that impulse is indistinguishable from panic. U.S. interrogators have reportedly used the technique of "waterboarding" to break the will of detainees. Waterboarding involves immersing the victim's face in water or wrapping it in a wet towel to induce drowning sensations. As anyone who has ever come close to drowning or suffocating knows, the oxygen-starved brain sends panic signals that overwhelm everything else. . . .

And torture humiliates. It makes the victim scream and beg; the terror makes him lose control of his bowels and bladder. The essence of cruelty is inflicting pain for the purpose of lording it over someone—we sometimes say "breaking" them—and the mechanism of cruelty is making the victim the audience of your own mastery. Cruelty always aims at humiliation. . . .

The predominant setting for torture has always been military victory. The victor captures the enemy and tortures him. . . .

Underneath whatever religious significance that attaches to torturing the vanquished, the victor tortures captives for the simplest of motives: to relive the victory, to demonstrate the absoluteness of his mastery, to rub the loser's face in it, and to humiliate the loser by making him scream and beg. For the victorious warrior, it's fun; it's entertainment. . . .

Already we can see why liberals abhor torture. Liberalism incorporates a vision of engaged, active human beings possessing an inherent dignity regardless of their social station. The victim of torture is in every respect the opposite of this vision. The torture victim is isolated and reduced instead of engaged and enlarged, terrified instead of active, humiliated instead of dignified. And, in the paradigm case of torture, the victor's torment of defeated captives, liberals perceive the living embodiment of their worst nightmare: tyrannical rulers who take their pleasure from the degradation of those unfortunate enough to be subject to their will.

There are at least four other historically significant reasons for torture besides victor's cruelty. . . .

First, there is torture for the purpose of terrorizing people into submission. Dictators from Hitler to Pinochet to Saddam Hussein tortured their political prisoners so that their enemies, knowing that they might face a fate far worse than death, would be afraid to oppose them. . . .

Second, until the last two centuries, torture was used as a form of criminal punishment. . . .

Curiously, when Beccaria writes explicitly about the subject of torture, he does not mention torture as punishment. Rather, he polemicizes against judicial torture in order to extract confessions from criminal suspects. This is the third historically significant use of torture, distinct from punishment, even though judges administer both. . . .

These, then, are the four illiberal motives for torture: victor's pleasure, terror, punishment, and extracting confessions. That leaves only one rationale for torture that might conceivably be acceptable to a liberal: torture as a technique of intelligence gathering from captives who will not talk. This may seem indistinguishable from torture to extract confessions, because both practices couple torture with interrogation. The crucial difference lies in the fact that the confession is backward-looking, in that it aims to document and ratify the past for purposes of retribution, while intelligence gathering is forward-looking because it aims to gain information to forestall future evils like terrorist attacks.

It is striking, and in obvious ways reassuring, that this is the only rationale for torture that liberal political culture admits could even possibly be legitimate. To speak in a somewhat perverse and paradoxical way, liberalism's insistence on limited governments that exercise their power only for . . . pragmatic purposes creates the possibility of seeing torture as a civilized . . . practice, provided that its sole purpose is preventing future harms. . . . But more importantly, the liberal rationale for torture as intelligence gathering in gravely dangerous situations transforms and rationalizes the motivation for torture. Now, for the first time, it becomes possible to think of torture as a last resort of men and women who are profoundly reluctant to torture. And in that way, liberals can for the first time think of torture dissociated from cruelty—torture authorized and administered by decent human beings who abhor what circumstances force them to do. Torture to gather intelligence and save lives seems almost heroic. For the first time, we can think of kindly torturers rather than tyrants. . . .

Let me summarize this part of my argument. Liberals, I have said, rank cruelty first among vices—not because liberals are more compassionate than anyone else, but because of the close connection between cruelty and tyranny. Torture is the living manifestation of cruelty, and the peculiar horror of torture within liberalism arises from the fact that torture is tyranny in microcosm, at its highest level of intensity. . . . It should hardly surprise us that liberals wish to ban torture absolutely—a wish that became legislative reality in the Torture Convention's insistence that nothing can justify torture.

But what about torture as intelligence gathering, torture to forestall greater evils? I suspect that throughout history this has been the least common motivation for torture, and thus the one most readily overlooked. And yet it alone bears no essential connection with tyranny. This is not to say that the torture victim experiences it as any less terrifying, humiliating, or tyrannical. . . . But the torturer's goal of forestalling greater evils is one that liberals share. It seems like a rational motivation, far removed from cruelty and power-lust. In fact, the liberal may for the first time find it possible to view torture from the torturer's point of view rather than the victim's.

Thus, even though absolute prohibition remains liberalism's primary teaching about torture, and the basic liberal stance is empathy for the torture victim, a more permissive stance remains an unspoken possibility. . . . As long as the intelligence needs of a liberal society are slight, this possibility within liberalism remains dormant. . . . But when a catastrophe like 9/11 happens, liberals may cautiously conclude that, in the words of a well-known *Newsweek* article, it is "Time to Think About Torture."

But the pressure of liberalism will compel them to think about it in a highly stylized and artificial way, what I will call the "liberal ideology of torture." The liberal ideology insists that the sole purpose of torture must be intelligence gathering to prevent a catastrophe; that torture is necessary to prevent the catastrophe; that torturing is the exception, not the rule, so that it has nothing to do with state tyranny; that those who inflict the torture are motivated solely by the looming catastrophe, with no tincture of cruelty; that torture in such circumstances is, in fact, little more than self-defense; and that, because of the associations of torture with the horrors of yesteryear, perhaps one should not even call harsh interrogation "torture."

And the liberal ideology will crystallize all of these ideas in a single, mesmerizing example: the ticking time bomb.

II. THE TICKING BOMB

Suppose the bomb is planted somewhere in the crowded heart of an American city, and you have custody of the man who planted it. He won't talk. Surely, the hypothetical suggests, we shouldn't be too squeamish to torture the information out of him and save hundreds of lives. Consequences count, and abstract moral prohibitions must yield to the calculus of consequences.

Everyone argues the pros and cons of torture through the ticking time bomb. Senator Schumer and Professor Dershowitz, the Israeli Supreme Court and indeed every journalist devoting a think-piece to the unpleasant question of torture, begins with the ticking time bomb and ends there as well. . . . I mean to disarm the ticking time bomb and argue that it is the wrong thing to think about. If so, then the liberal ideology of torture begins to unravel.

But before beginning these arguments, I want to pause and ask why this jejune example has become the alpha and omega of our thinking about torture. I believe the answer is this: The ticking time bomb is proffered against liberals who believe in an absolute prohibition against torture. The idea is to force the liberal prohibitionist to admit that yes, even he or even she would agree to torture in at least this one situation. Once the prohibitionist admits that, then she has conceded that her opposition to torture is not based on principle. Now that the prohibitionist has admitted that her moral principles can be breached, all that is left is haggling about the price. No longer can the prohibitionist claim the moral high ground; no longer can she put the burden of proof on her opponent. She is down in the mud with them, and the only question left is how much further down she will go. Dialectically, getting the prohibitionist to address the ticking time bomb is like getting the vegetarian to eat just one little oyster because it has no nervous system. Once she does that—*gotcha!*

The ticking time-bomb scenario serves a second rhetorical goal, one that is equally important to the proponent of torture. It makes us see the torturer in a different light. . . . Now, he is not a cruel man or a sadistic man or a coarse, insensitive brutish man. The torturer is instead a conscientious public servant, heroic the way that New York firefighters were heroic, willing to do desperate things only because the plight is so desperate and so many innocent lives are weighing on the public servant's conscience. . . .

Wittgenstein once wrote that confusion arises when we become bewitched by a picture. He meant that it's easy to get seduced by simplistic examples that look compelling but actually misrepresent the world in which we live. If the subject is the morality of torture, philosophical confusions can have life-or-death consequences. I believe the ticking time bomb is the picture that bewitches us.

I don't mean that the time-bomb scenario is completely unreal. To take a real-life counterpart: in 1995, an al-Qaeda plot to bomb eleven U.S. airliners and assassinate the Pope was thwarted by information tortured out of a Pakistani bomb-maker by the Philippine police. According to journalists Marites Dañguilan Vitug and Glenda M. Gloria, the police had received word of possible threats against the Pope. They went to work. "For weeks, agents hit him with a chair and a long piece of wood, forced water into his mouth, and crushed lighted cigarettes into his private parts. . . . His ribs were almost totally broken, and his captors were surprised that he survived. . . ." Grisly, to be sure—but if they hadn't done it, thousands of innocent travelers might have died horrible deaths.

But look at the example one more time. The Philippine agents were surprised he survived—in other words, they came close to torturing him to death *before* he talked. And they tortured him *for weeks*, during which time they didn't know about any specific al-Qaeda plot. What if he too didn't know? Or what if there had been no al-Qaeda plot? Then they would have tortured him for weeks, possibly tortured him to death, for nothing. For all they knew at the time, that is exactly what they were doing. You cannot use the argument that preventing the al-Qaeda attack justified the decision to torture, because *at the moment the decision was made* no one knew about the al-Qaeda attack.

The ticking-bomb scenario cheats its way around these difficulties by stipulating that the bomb is there, ticking away, and that officials know it and know they have the man who planted it. Those conditions will seldom be met. Let us try some more realistic hypotheticals and the questions they raise:

1. The authorities know there may be a bomb plot in the offing, and they have captured a man who may know something about it, but may not. Torture him? How much? For weeks? For months? The chances are considerable that you are torturing a man with nothing to tell you. If he doesn't talk, does that mean it's time to stop, or time to ramp up the level of torture? How likely does it have to be that he knows something important? Fifty-fifty? Thirty-seventy? Will one out of a hundred suffice to land him on the waterboard?

2. Do you really want to make the torture decision by running the numbers? A 1-percent chance of saving a thousand lives yields ten statistical lives. Does that mean that you can torture up to nine people on a 1-percent chance of finding crucial information?

3. The authorities think that one out of a group of fifty captives in Guantanamo might know where Osama bin Laden is hiding, but they do not know which captive. Torture them all? That is: Do you torture forty-nine captives with nothing to tell you on the uncertain chance of capturing bin Laden?

4. For that matter, would capturing Osama bin Laden demonstrably save a single human life? . . . Or does it not matter whether torture is intended to save human lives from a specific threat, as long as it furthers some goal in the War on Terror? This last question is especially important once we realize that the interrogation of al-Qaeda suspects will almost never be employed to find out where the ticking bomb is hidden. Instead, interrogation is a more general fishing expedition for any intelligence that might be used to help "unwind" the terrorist organization. Now one might reply that al-Qaeda is itself the ticking time bomb, so that unwinding the organization meets the formal conditions of the ticking-bomb hypothetical. This is equivalent to asserting that any intelligence that promotes victory in the War on Terror justifies torture. . . . But at this point, we verge on declaring all military threats and adversaries that menace American civilians to be ticking bombs whose defeat justifies torture. The limitation of torture to emergency exceptions, implicit in the ticking-bomb story, now threatens to unravel, making torture a legitimate instrument of military policy. And then the question becomes inevitable: Why not torture in pursuit of any worthwhile goal?

5. Indeed, if you are willing to torture forty-nine innocent people to get information from the one who has it, why stop there? If suspects will not break under torture, why not torture their loved ones in front of them? They are no more innocent than the forty-nine you have already shown you are prepared to torture. In fact, if only the numbers matter, torturing loved ones is almost a no-brainer if you think it will work. Of course, you won't know until you try whether torturing his child will break the suspect. But that just changes the odds; it does not alter the argument.

The point of the examples is that in a world of uncertainty and imperfect knowledge, the ticking-bomb scenario should not form the point of reference. The ticking bomb is the picture that bewitches us. The real debate is not between one guilty man's pain and hundreds of innocent lives. It is the debate between the certainty of anguish and the mere possibility of learning something vital and saving lives. And, above all, it is the question about whether a responsible citizen must unblinkingly think the unthinkable and accept that the morality of torture should be decided purely by totaling up costs and benefits. Once you accept that only the numbers count, then anything, no matter how gruesome, becomes possible. . . .

III. TORTURE AS A PRACTICE

There is a second, insidious, error built into the ticking-bomb hypothetical. It assumes a single, ad hoc decision about whether to torture, by officials who ordinarily would do no such thing except in a desperate emergency. But in the real world of interrogations, decisions are not made one-off. The real world is a world of policies, guidelines, and directives. It is a world of *practices*, not of ad hoc emergency measures. Therefore, any responsible discussion of torture must address the practice of torture, not the ticking-bomb hypothetical. I am not saying anything original here; other writers have made exactly this point. But somehow, we always manage to forget this and circle back to the ticking time bomb. . . .

   Treating torture as a practice rather than as a desperate improvisation in an emergency means changing the subject from the ticking bomb to other issues like these: Should we create a professional cadre of trained torturers? That means a group of interrogators who know the techniques, who learn to overcome their instinctive revulsion against causing physical pain, and who acquire the legendary surgeon's arrogance about their own infallibility. . . . Should universities create an undergraduate course in torture? Or should the subject be offered only in police and military academies? Do we want federal grants for research to devise new and better techniques? Patents issued on high-tech torture devices? Companies competing to manufacture them? Trade conventions in Las Vegas? Should there be a medical sub-specialty of torture doctors, who ensure that captives do not die before they talk? The questions amount to this: Do we really want to create a torture culture and the kind of people who inhabit it? The ticking time bomb distracts us from the real issue, which is not about emergencies, but about the normalization of torture.

   Perhaps the solution is to keep the practice of torture secret in order to avoid the moral corruption that comes from creating a public culture of torture. But this so-called "solution" does not reject the normalization of torture. It accepts it, but layers on top of it the normalization of state secrecy. The result would be a shadow culture of torturers and those who train and support them, operating outside the public eye and accountable only to other insiders of the torture culture.

Just as importantly: Who guarantees that case-hardened torturers, inured to levels of violence and pain that would make ordinary people vomit at the sight, will know where to draw the line on when torture should be used? They rarely have in the past. They didn't in Algeria. They didn't in Israel, where in 1999, the Israeli Supreme Court back-pedaled from an earlier consent to torture lite because the interrogators were running amok and torturing two-thirds of their Palestinian captives. In the Argentinian Dirty War, the tortures began because terrorist cells had a policy of fleeing when one of their members had disappeared for forty-eight hours, leaving authorities two days to wring the information out of the captive. Mark Osiel, who has studied the Argentinean military in the Dirty War, reports that many of the torturers initially had qualms about what they were doing, until their priests reassured them that they were fighting God's fight. By the end of the Dirty War, the qualms were gone, and, as John Simpson and Jana Bennett report, hardened young officers were placing bets on who could kidnap the prettiest girl to rape and torture. Escalation is the rule, not the aberration.

There are two fundamental reasons for this: one rooted in the nature of bureaucracy and the other in social psychology. The liberal ideology of torture presupposes a torturer impelled by the desire to stop a looming catastrophe, not by cruelty. Implicitly, this image presumes that the interrogator and the decision-maker are the same person. But the defining fact about real organizations is the division of labor. The person who decides whether this prisoner presents a genuine ticking-bomb case is not the interrogator. The decision about what counts as a ticking-bomb case—one where torture is the lesser evil—depends on complex value judgments, and these are made further up the chain of command. The interrogator simply executes decisions made elsewhere.

Interrogators do not inhabit a world of loving kindness, or of equal concern and respect for all human beings. Interrogating resistant prisoners non-violently and non-abusively still requires a relationship that in any other context would be morally abhorrent. It requires tricking information out of the subject, and the interrogator does this by setting up elaborate scenarios to disorient the subject and propel him into an alternative reality. The subject must be deceived into thinking that his high-value intelligence has already been revealed by someone else, so that it is no longer of any value. He must be fooled into thinking that his friends have betrayed him or that the interrogator is his friend. The interrogator disrupts his sense of time and place, disorients him with sessions that never take place at predictable times or intervals, and manipulates his emotions. The very names of interrogation techniques show this: "Emotional Love," "Emotional Hate," "Fear Up Harsh," "Fear Up Mild," "Reduced Fear," "Pride and Ego Up," "Pride and Ego Down," "Futility." The interrogator may set up a scenario to make the subject think he is in the clutches of a much-feared secret police organization from a different country ("False Flag"). Every bit of the subject's environment is fair game for manipulation and deception, as the interrogator aims to create the total lie that gets the subject talking.

. . . The liberal fiction that interrogation can be done by people who are neither cruel nor tyrannical runs aground on the fact that regardless of the interrogator's character off the job, on the job, every fiber of his concentration is devoted to dominating the mind of the subject.

Only one thing prevents this from turning into abuse and torture, and that is a clear set of bright-line rules, drummed into the interrogator with the intensity of a religious indoctrination, complete with warnings of fire and brimstone. . . .

But what happens when the line is breached? When, as in Afghanistan, the interrogator gets mixed messages about whether Geneva applies, or hears rumors of ghost detainees, of high-value captives held for years of interrogation in the top-secret facility known as "Hotel California," located in some nation somewhere? Or when the interrogator observes around him the move from deception to abuse, from abuse to torture lite, from torture lite to beatings and waterboarding? Without clear lines, the tyranny innate in the interrogator's job has nothing to hold it in check. Perhaps someone, somewhere in the chain of command, is wringing hands over whether this interrogation qualifies as a ticking-bomb case; but the interrogator knows only that the rules of the road have changed and the posted speed limits no longer apply. The liberal fiction of the conscientious interrogator overlooks a division of moral labor in which the person with the fastidious conscience and the person doing the interrogation are not the same.

The fiction must presume, therefore, that the interrogator operates only under the strictest supervision, in a chain of command where his every move gets vetted and controlled by the superiors who are actually doing the deliberating. The trouble is that this assumption flies in the face of everything that we know about how organizations work. The basic rule in every bureaucratic organization is that operational details and the guilty knowledge that goes with them get pushed down the chain of command as far as possible. . . .

We saw this phenomenon at Abu Ghraib, where military intelligence officers gave military police vague orders like: "'Loosen this guy up for us;' 'Make sure he has a bad night.' 'Make sure he gets the treatment.'" Suppose that the eighteen-year-old guard interprets "[m]ake sure he has a bad night" to mean, simply, "keep him awake all night." How do you do that without physical abuse? Furthermore, personnel at Abu Ghraib witnessed far harsher treatment of prisoners by "other governmental agencies" (OGA), a euphemism for the Central Intelligence Agency. They saw OGA spirit away the dead body of an interrogation subject, and allegedly witnessed a contract employee rape a youthful prisoner. When that is what you see, abuses like those in the Abu Ghraib photos will not look outrageous. Outrageous compared with what?

This brings me to the point of social psychology. Simply stated, it is this: we judge right and wrong against the baseline of whatever we have come to consider "normal" behavior, and if the norm shifts in the direction of violence, we will come to tolerate and accept violence as a normal response. . . . I will illustrate the point with the most salient example. This is the famous Stanford Prison Experiment. Male volunteers were divided randomly into two groups who would simulate the guards and inmates in a mock prison. Within a matter of days, the inmates began acting like actual prison inmates—depressed, enraged, and anxious. And the guards began to abuse the inmates to such an alarming degree that the researchers had to halt the two-week experiment after just seven days. . . . It took only five days before a guard, who prior to the experiment described himself as a pacifist, was forcing greasy sausages down the throat of a prisoner who refused to eat; and in less than a week, the guards were placing bags over prisoners' heads, making them strip, and sexually humiliating them in ways reminiscent of Abu Ghraib.

My conclusion is very simple. Abu Ghraib is the fully predictable image of what a torture culture looks like. Abu Ghraib is not a few bad apples—it is the apple tree. And you cannot reasonably expect that interrogators in a torture culture will be the fastidious and well-meaning torturers that the liberal ideology fantasizes. . . .

For all these reasons, the ticking-bomb scenario is an intellectual fraud. In its place, we must address the real questions about torture—questions about uncertainty, questions about the morality of consequences, and questions about what it does to a culture and the torturers themselves to introduce the practice. Once we do so, I suspect that few Americans will be willing to accept that everything is possible.

WAR AND TERRORISM

Chapter 41

Fifty Years after Hiroshima

John Rawls

In the spring of 1945, the Allies finally captured land so close to Japan that they could start a bombing campaign against the Japanese home islands. Many of the bombs were incendiary, designed to spread fires that the Japanese cities were not constructed to withstand. Hundreds of thousands of civilians perished in those infernos.

On August 6 and August 9 of 1945, the United States dropped atomic bombs on Hiroshima and Nagasaki, killing tens of thousands of people instantly and leaving many more to die horrible deaths. Hiroshima and Nagasaki were chosen mostly for a pragmatic reason: few other Japanese cities were still standing.

John Rawls was an infantryman in the Pacific during World War II, and fifty years after the bombings, he wrote this essay about the conduct of war. According to Rawls, the Americans' actions violated the rights of Japanese civilians. President Harry Truman, who ordered the atomic bombings, acted like a politician but not like a statesman.

John Rawls (1921–2002) taught for many years at Harvard University. He will long be remembered as the author of *A Theory of Justice* (1971), the most influential work in political philosophy of the twentieth century.

The fiftieth year since the bombing of Hiroshima is a time to reflect about what one should think of it. Is it really a great wrong, as many now think, and many also thought then, or is it perhaps justified after all? I believe that both the fire-bombing of Japanese cities beginning in the spring of 1945 and the later atomic bombing of Hiroshima on August 6 were very great wrongs, and rightly seen as such. In order to support this opinion, I set out what I think to be the principles governing the conduct of war—*jus in bello*—of democratic peoples. These peoples have different ends of war than nondemocratic, especially totalitarian, states, such as Germany and Japan, which sought the domination and exploitation of subjected peoples, and in Germany's case, their enslavement if not extermination.

Although I cannot properly justify them here, I begin by setting out six principles and assumptions in support of these judgments. I hope they seem not unreasonable; and certainly they are familiar, as they are closely related to much traditional thought on this subject.

1. The aim of a just war waged by a decent democratic society is a just and lasting peace between peoples, especially with its present enemy.

2. A decent democratic society is fighting against a state that is not democratic. This follows from the fact that democratic peoples do not wage war against each other; and since we are concerned with the rules of war as they apply to such peoples, we assume the society fought against is nondemocratic and that its expansionist aims threatened the security and free institutions of democratic regimes and caused the war.

3. In the conduct of war, a democratic society must carefully distinguish three groups: the state's leaders and officials, its soldiers, and its civilian population. The reason for these distinctions rests on the principle of responsibility: since the state fought against is not democratic, the civilian members of the society cannot be those who organized and brought on the war. This was done by its leaders and officials assisted by other elites who control and staff the state apparatus. They are responsible, they willed the war, and for doing that, they are criminals. But civilians, often kept in ignorance and swayed by state propaganda, are not. And this is so even if some civilians knew better and were enthusiastic for the war. In a nation's conduct of war many such marginal cases may exist, but they are

irrelevant. As for soldiers, they, just as civilians, and leaving aside the upper ranks of an officer class, are not responsible for the war, but are conscripted or in other ways forced into it, their patriotism often cruelly and cynically exploited. The grounds on which they may be attacked directly are not that they are responsible for the war but that a democratic people cannot defend itself in any other way, and defend itself it must do. About this there is no choice.

4. A decent democratic society must respect the human rights of the members of the other side, both civilians and soldiers, for two reasons. One is because they simply have these rights by the law of peoples. The other reason is to teach enemy soldiers and civilians the content of those rights by the example of how they hold in their own case. In this way their significance is best brought home to them. They are assigned a certain status, the status of the members of some human society who possess rights as human persons. In the case of human rights in war the aspect of status as applied to civilians is given a strict interpretation. This means, as I understand it here, that they can never be attacked directly except in times of extreme crisis, the nature of which I discuss below.

5. Continuing with the thought of teaching the content of human rights, the next principle is that just peoples by their actions and proclamations are to foreshadow during war the kind of peace they aim for and the kind of relations they seek between nations. By doing so, they show in an open and public way the nature of their aims and the kind of people they are. These last duties fall largely on the leaders and officials of the governments of democratic peoples, since they are in the best position to speak for the whole people and to act as the principle applies. Although all the preceding principles also specify duties of statesmanship, this is especially true of 4 and 5. The way a war is fought and the actions ending it endure in the historical memory of peoples and may set the stage for future war. This duty of statesmanship must always be held in view.

6. Finally, we note the place of practical means-end reasoning in judging the appropriateness of an action or policy for achieving the aim of war or for not causing more harm than good. This mode of thought—whether carried on by (classical) utilitarian reasoning, or by cost-benefit analysis, or by weighing national interests, or in other ways—must always be framed within and strictly limited by

the preceding principles. The norms of the conduct of war set up certain lines that bound just action. War plans and strategies, and the conduct of battles, must lie within their limits. (The only exception, I repeat, is in times of extreme crisis.)

In connection with the fourth and fifth principles of the conduct of war, I have said that they are binding especially on the leaders of nations. They are in the most effective position to represent their people's aims and obligations, and sometimes they become statesmen. But who is a statesman? There is no office of statesman, as there is of president, or chancellor, or prime minister. The statesman is an ideal, like the ideal of the truthful or virtuous individual. Statesmen are presidents or prime ministers who become statesmen through their exemplary performance and leadership in their office in difficult and trying times and manifest strength, wisdom, and courage. They guide their people through turbulent and dangerous periods for which they are esteemed always, as one of their great statesmen.

The ideal of the statesman is suggested by the saying: the politician looks to the next election, the statesman to the next generation. It is the task of the student of philosophy to look to the permanent conditions and the real interests of a just and good democratic society. It is the task of the statesman, however, to discern these conditions and interests in practice; the statesman sees deeper and further than most others and grasps what needs to be done. The statesman must get it right, or nearly so, and hold fast to it. Washington and Lincoln were statesmen. Bismarck was not. He did not see Germany's real interests far enough into the future, and his judgment and motives were often distorted by his class interests and his wanting himself alone to be chancellor of Germany. Statesmen need not be selfless and may have their own interests when they hold office, yet they must be selfless in their judgments and assessments of society's interests and not be swayed, especially in war and crisis, by passions of revenge and retaliation against the enemy.

Above all, they are to hold fast to the aim of gaining a just peace, and avoid the things that make achieving such a peace more difficult. Here the proclamations of a nation should make clear (the statesman must see to this) that the enemy people are to be granted an autonomous regime of their own and a decent and full life once peace is securely reestablished. Whatever they may be told by their leaders, whatever reprisals they may reasonably fear, they are not to be held as slaves or serfs after surrender, or denied in due course their full liberties; and they may well achieve freedoms they did not enjoy before, as the Germans and the Japanese eventually did. The statesman knows, if others do not, that all descriptions of the enemy people (not their rulers) inconsistent with this are impulsive and false.

Turning now to Hiroshima and the fire-bombing of Tokyo, we find that neither falls under the exemption of extreme crisis. One aspect of this is that since (let's suppose) there are no absolute rights—rights that must be respected in all circumstances—there are occasions when civilians can be attacked directly by aerial bombing. Were there times during the war when Britain could properly have bombed Hamburg and Berlin? Yes, when Britain was alone and desperately facing Germany's superior might; moreover, this period would extend until Russia had clearly beat off the first German assault in the summer and fall of 1941, and would be able to fight Germany until the end. Here the cutoff point might be placed differently, say the summer of 1942, and certainly by Stalingrad. I shall not dwell on this, as the crucial matter is that under no conditions could Germany be allowed to win the war, and this for two basic reasons: first, the nature and history of constitutional democracy and its place in European culture; and second, the peculiar evil of Nazism and the enormous and uncalculable moral and political evil it represented for civilized society.

The peculiar evil of Nazism needs to be understood, since in some circumstances a democratic people might better accept defeat if the terms of peace offered by the adversary were reasonable and moderate, did not subject them to humiliation, and looked forward to a workable and decent political relationship. Yet characteristic of Hitler was that he accepted no possibility at all of a political relationship with his enemies. They were always to be cowed by terror and brutality, and ruled by force. From the beginning the campaign against Russia, for example, was a war of destruction against Slavic peoples, with the original inhabitants remaining, if at all, only as serfs. When Goebbels and others protested that the war could not be won that way, Hitler refused to listen.

Yet it is clear that while the extreme crisis exemption held for Britain in the early stages of the war, it never held at any time for the United States in its war with Japan. The principles of the conduct of war were always applicable to it. Indeed, in the case of Hiroshima many involved in higher reaches of the government recognized the questionable character of the bombing and that limits were being crossed. Yet during the discussions among allied leaders in June and July 1945, the weight of the practical means-end reasoning carried the day. Under the continuing pressure of war, such moral doubts as there were failed to gain an express and articulated view. As the war progressed, the heavy fire-bombing of civilians in the capitals of Berlin and Tokyo and elsewhere was increasingly accepted on the allied side. Although after the outbreak of war Roosevelt had urged both sides not to commit the inhuman barbarism of bombing civilians, by 1945 allied leaders came to assume that Roosevelt would have used the bomb on Hiroshima. The bombing grew out of what had happened before.

The practical means-end reasons to justify using the atomic bomb on Hiroshima were the following:

The bomb was dropped to hasten the end of the war. It is clear that Truman and most other allied leaders thought it would do that. Another reason was that it would save lives where the lives counted are the lives of American soldiers. The lives of Japanese, military or civilian, presumably counted for less. Here the calculations of least time and most lives saved were mutually supporting. Moreover, dropping the bomb would give the Emperor and the Japanese leaders a way to save face, an important matter given Japanese samurai culture. Indeed, at the end a few top Japanese leaders wanted to make a last sacrificial stand but were overruled by others supported by the Emperor, who ordered surrender on August 12, having received word from Washington that the Emperor could stay provided it was understood that he had to comply with the orders of the American military commander. The last reason I mention is that the bomb was dropped to impress the Russians with American power and make them more agreeable with our demands. This reason is highly disputed but is urged by some critics and scholars as important.

The failure of these reasons to reflect the limits on the conduct of war is evident, so I focus on a different matter: the failure of statesmanship on the part of allied leaders and why it might have occurred. Truman once described the Japanese as beasts and to be treated as such; yet how foolish it sounds now to call the Germans or the Japanese barbarians and beasts! Of the Nazis and Tojo militarists, yes, but they are not the German and the Japanese people. Churchill later granted that he carried the bombing too far, led by passion and the intensity of the conflict. A duty of statesmanship is not to allow such feelings, natural and inevitable as they may be, to alter the course a democratic people should best follow in striving for peace. The statesman understands that relations with the present enemy have special importance: for as I have said, war must be openly and publicly conducted in ways that make a lasting and amicable peace possible with a defeated enemy, and prepare its people for how they may expect to be treated. Their present fears of being subjected to acts of revenge and retaliation must be put to rest; present enemies must be seen as associates in a shared and just future peace.

These remarks make it clear that, in my judgment, both Hiroshima and the fire-bombing of Japanese cities were great evils that the duties of statesmanship require political leaders to avoid in the absence of the crisis exemption. I also believe this could have been done at little cost in further casualties. An invasion was unnecessary at that date, as the war was effectively over. However, whether that is true or not makes no difference. Without the crisis exemption, those bombings are great evils. Yet it is clear that an articulate expression of the principles of just war introduced at that time would not have altered the outcome. It was simply too late. A president or prime minister must have carefully considered these questions, preferably long before, or at least when they had the time and leisure to think things out. Reflections on just war cannot be heard in the daily round of the pressure of events near the end of the hostilities; too many are anxious and impatient, and simply worn out.

Similarly, the justification of constitutional democracy and the basis of the rights and duties it must respect should be part of the public political culture and discussed in the many associations of civic society as part of one's education. It is not clearly heard in day-to-day ordinary politics, but must be presupposed as the background, not the daily subject of politics, except in special circumstances. In the same way, there was not sufficient prior grasp of the fundamental importance of the principles of just war for the expression of them to have blocked the appeal of practical means-end reasoning in terms of a calculus of lives, or of the least time to end the war, or of some other balancing of costs and benefits. This practical reasoning justifies too much, too easily, and provides a way for a dominant power to quiet any moral worries that may arise. If the principles of war are put forward at that time, they easily become so many more considerations to be balanced in the scales.

Another failure of statesmanship was not to try to enter into negotiations with the Japanese before any drastic steps such as the fire-bombing of cities or the bombing of Hiroshima were taken. A conscientious attempt to do so was morally necessary. As a democratic people, we owed that to the Japanese people—whether to their government is another matter. There had been discussions in Japan for some time about finding a way to end the war, and on June 26 the government had been instructed by the Emperor to do so. It must surely have realized that with the navy destroyed and the outer islands taken, the war was lost. True, the Japanese were deluded by the hope that the Russians might prove to be their allies, but negotiations are precisely to disabuse the other side of delusions of that kind. A statesman is not free to consider that such negotiations may lessen the desired shock value of subsequent attacks.

Truman was in many ways a good, at times a very good president. But the way he ended the war showed he failed as a statesman. For him it was an opportunity missed, and a loss to the country and its armed forces as well. It is sometimes said that questioning the bombing of Hiroshima is an insult to the American troops who fought the war. This is hard to understand. We should be able to look back and consider our faults after fifty years. We expect the Germans and the Japanese to do that. . . . Why shouldn't we? It can't be that we think we waged the war without moral error!

None of this alters Germany's and Japan's responsibility for the war nor their behavior in conducting it. Emphatically to be repudiated are two nihilist doctrines. One is expressed by Sherman's remark, "War is hell," so anything goes to get it over with as soon as one can. The other says that we are all guilty so we stand on a level and no one can blame anyone else. These are both superficial and deny all reasonable distinctions; they are invoked falsely to try to excuse our misconduct or to plead that we cannot be condemned.

The moral emptiness of these nihilisms is manifest in the fact that just and decent civilized societies—their institutions and laws, their civil life and background culture and mores—all depend absolutely on making significant moral and political distinctions in all situations. Certainly war is a kind of hell, but why should that mean that all moral distinctions cease to hold? And granted also that sometimes all or nearly all may be to some degree guilty, that does not mean that all are equally so. There is never a time when we are free from all moral and political principles and restraints. These nihilisms are pretenses to be free of those principles and restraints that always apply to us fully.

Chapter 42

What Is Wrong with Terrorism?

Thomas Nagel

After the terrorist attacks of September 11, 2001, Professor Thomas Nagel of New York University wrote this short piece about why terrorism is wrong.

The attacks of 9/11 were committed by Islamic extremists. Since then, however, most of the terrorist attacks in the United States have been committed by far-right extremists, motivated by various hatreds: of blacks, of gays, of Jews, of foreigners, and of the government. According to the Anti-Defamation League, during the last decade, 71 percent of terrorist murders were committed by right-wing extremists, as opposed to 26 percent by Islamic extremists. In 2017, white supremacists alone were responsible for more than half of the murders.

Nonetheless, the total number of murders is relatively small. The chance of any particular American being killed by a terrorist in a given year is only about one in forty million.

Thomas Nagel (1937–) has written twelve books and over one hundred articles.

People all over the world react with visceral horror to attacks on civilians by Al-Qaeda, by Palestinian suicide bombers, by Basque or

---

Thomas Nagel, "What Is Wrong with Terrorism?" in *Project Syndicate*, November 19, 2002. Copyright © 2002 Project Syndicate. Used with permission.

Chechen separatists, or by IRA militants. As there now seems to be a pause in the spate of suicide bombings and other terrorist acts—if only momentary—perhaps now is a moment to grapple with a fundamental question: What makes *terrorist* killings any more worthy of condemnation than other forms of murder?

The special opprobrium associated with the word "terrorism" must be understood as a condemnation of means, not ends. Of course, those who condemn terrorist attacks on civilians often also reject the ends that the attackers are trying to achieve. They think that a separate Basque state, or the withdrawal of U.S. forces from the Middle East, for example, are not aims that anyone should be pursuing, let alone by violent means.

But the condemnation does not depend on rejecting the aims of the terrorists. The reaction to the attacks of September 11, 2001 on New York and Washington and their like underscores that such means are outrageous whatever the end; they should not be used to achieve even a good end—indeed, even if there is no other way to achieve it. The normal balancing of costs against benefits is not allowable here.

This claim is not as simple as it appears because it does not depend on a general moral principle forbidding all killing of non-combatants. Similarly, those who condemn terrorism as beyond the pale are usually not pacifists. They believe not only that it is all right to kill soldiers and bomb munitions depots in times of war, but that inflicting "collateral damage" on non-combatants is sometimes unavoidable—and morally permissible.

But if that is permissible, why is it wrong to aim *directly* at non-combatants if killing them will have a good chance of inducing the enemy to cease hostilities, withdraw from occupied territory, or grant independence? Dying is bad, however one is killed. So why should a civilian death be acceptable if it occurs as a side effect of combat that serves a worthy end, whereas a civilian death that is inflicted deliberately as a means to the *same* end is a terrorist outrage?

The distinction is not universally accepted—certainly not by the major belligerents in World War II. Hiroshima is the most famous example of terror bombing, but the Germans, the Japanese, and the British as well as the Americans deliberately slaughtered civilian non-combatants in large numbers. Today, however, terrorism inspires widespread revulsion, which in turn helps to justify military action against it. So it is essential that the reason for that revulsion become better understood.

The core moral idea is a prohibition against *aiming* at the death of a harmless person. Everyone is presumed to be inviolable in this way until he himself becomes a danger to others; so we are permitted to kill in self-defense, and to attack enemy combatants in war. But this is an exception to a general and strict requirement of respect for human life. So long as we are not doing any harm, no one may kill us just because it would be useful to do so. This minimal basic respect is owed to *every* individual, and it may not be violated even to achieve valuable long-term goals.

However, there are some activities, including legitimate self-defense or warfare, that create an unavoidable risk of harm to innocent parties. This is true not only of violent military or police actions but also of peaceful projects like major construction in densely populated cities. In those cases, if the aim is important enough, the activity is not morally prohibited provided due care is taken to minimize the risk of harm to innocent parties, consistent with the achievement of the aim.

The moral point is that we are obliged to do our best to avoid or minimize civilian casualties in warfare, even if we know that we cannot avoid them completely. Those deaths do not violate the strictest protection of human life—that we may not *aim* to kill a harmless person. On the contrary, our aim is if possible to avoid such collateral deaths.

Of course, the victim ends up dead whether killed deliberately by a terrorist or regrettably as the side effect of an attack on a legitimate military target. But in our sense of what we are owed morally by our fellow human beings, there is a huge difference between these two acts, and the attitudes they express toward human life.

So long as it remains an effective means for weak parties to exert pressure on their more powerful enemies, terrorism cannot be expected to disappear. But we should hope nonetheless that the recognition of its special form of contempt for humanity will spread, rather than being lost as a result of its recent successes.

THE MEANING OF LIFE

Chapter 43

The Meaning of Life

Richard Taylor

Richard Taylor (1919–2003) taught at Brown University, Columbia University, and the University of Rochester in upstate New York. Taylor wrote books on metaphysics and also on beekeeping. In *Good and Evil: A New Direction* (2000), he endorsed a subjectivist view of ethics but ended the book with this reflection on the meaning of life.

The question whether life has any meaning is difficult to interpret, and the more one concentrates his critical faculty on it the more it seems to elude him, or to evaporate as any intelligible question. One wants to turn it aside, as a source of embarrassment, as something that, if it cannot be abolished, should at least be decently covered. And yet I think any reflective person recognizes that the question it raises is important, and that it ought to have a significant answer.

If the idea of meaningfulness is difficult to grasp in this context, so that we are unsure what sort of thing would amount to answering the question, the idea of meaninglessness is perhaps less so. If, then, we can bring before our minds a clear image of meaningless existence, then perhaps we can take a step toward coping with our original question by seeing to what extent our lives, as we actually find them, resemble that image, and draw such lessons as we are able to from the comparison.

MEANINGLESS EXISTENCE

A perfect image of meaninglessness, of the kind we are seeking, is found in the ancient myth of Sisyphus. Sisyphus, it will be remembered, betrayed divine secrets to mortals, and for this he was condemned by the gods to roll a stone to the top of a hill, the stone then immediately to roll back down, again to be pushed to the top by Sisyphus, to roll down once more, and so on again and again, *forever.* Now in this we have the picture of meaningless, pointless toil, of a meaningless existence that is absolutely *never* redeemed. It is not even redeemed by a death that, if it were to accomplish nothing more, would at least bring this idiotic cycle to a close. If we were invited to imagine Sisyphus struggling for a while and accomplishing nothing, perhaps eventually falling from exhaustion, so that we might suppose him then eventually turning to something having some sort of promise, then the meaninglessness of that chapter of his life would not be so stark. It would be a dark and dreadful dream, from which he eventually awakens to sunlight and reality. But he does not awaken, for there is nothing for him to awaken to. His repetitive toil is his life and reality, and it goes on forever, and it is without any meaning whatever. Nothing ever comes of what he is doing, except simply, more of the same. Not by one step, nor by a thousand, nor by ten thousand does he even expiate by the smallest token the sin against the gods that led him into this fate. Nothing comes of it, nothing at all.

This ancient myth has always enchanted men, for countless meanings can be read into it. Some of the ancients apparently thought it symbolized the perpetual rising and setting of the sun, and others the repetitious crashing of the waves upon the shore. Probably the commonest interpretation is that it symbolizes man's eternal struggle and unquenchable spirit, his determination always to try once more in the face of overwhelming discouragement. This interpretation is further supported by that version of the myth according to which Sisyphus was commanded to roll the stone *over* the hill, so that it would finally roll down the other side, but was never quite able to make it.

I am not concerned with rendering or defending any interpretation of this myth, however. I have cited it only for the one element it does unmistakably contain, namely, that of a repetitious, cyclic activity that never comes to anything. We could contrive other images of this that would serve just as well, and no myth-makers are needed to supply the materials of it. Thus, we can imagine two persons transporting a stone—or even a precious gem, it does not matter—back and forth, relay style. One carries it to a near or distant point where it is received by the other; it is returned to its starting point, there to be recovered by the first, and the process is repeated over and over. Except in this relay nothing counts as winning, and nothing brings the contest to any close, each step only leads to a repetition of itself. Or we can imagine two groups of prisoners, one of them engaged in digging a prodigious hole in the ground that is no sooner finished than it is filled in again by the other group, the latter then digging a new hole that is at once filled in by the first group, and so on and on endlessly.

Now what stands out in all such pictures as oppressive and dejecting is not that the beings who enact these roles suffer any torture or pain, for it need not be assumed that they do. Nor is it that their labors are great, for they are no greater than the labors commonly undertaken by most men most of the time. According to the original myth, the stone is so large that Sisyphus never quite gets it to the top and must groan under every step, so that his enormous labor is all for naught. But this is not what appalls. It is not that his great struggle comes to nothing, but that his existence itself is without meaning. Even if we suppose, for example, that the stone is but a pebble that can be carried effortlessly, or that the holes dug by the prisoners are but small ones, not the slightest meaning is introduced into their lives. The stone that Sisyphus moves to the top of the hill, whether we think of it as large or small, still rolls back every time, and the process is repeated forever. Nothing comes of it, and the work is simply pointless. That is the element of the myth that I wish to capture.

Again, it is not the fact that the labors of Sisyphus continue forever that deprives them of meaning. It is, rather, the implication of this: that they come to nothing. The image would not be changed by our supposing him to push a different stone up every time, each to roll down again. But if we supposed that these stones, instead of rolling back to their places as if they had never been moved, were assembled at the top of the hill and there incorporated, say, in a beautiful and enduring temple, then the aspect of meaninglessness would disappear. His labors would then have a point, something would come of them all, and although one could perhaps still say it was not worth it, one could not say that the life of Sisyphus was devoid of meaning altogether. Meaningfulness would at least have made an appearance, and we could see what it was.

That point will need remembering. But in the meantime, let us note another way in which the image of meaninglessness can be altered by making only a very slight change. Let us suppose that the gods, while condemning Sisyphus to the fate just described, at the same time, as an afterthought, waxed perversely merciful by implanting in him a strange and irrational impulse; namely, a compulsive impulse to roll stones. We may if we like, to make this more graphic, suppose they accomplish this by implanting in him some substance that has this effect on his character and drives. I call this perverse, because from our point of view there is clearly no reason why anyone should have a persistent and insatiable desire to do something so pointless as that. Nevertheless, suppose that is Sisyphus's condition. He has but one obsession, which is to roll stones, and it is an obsession that is only for the moment appeased by his rolling them—he no sooner gets a stone rolled to the top of the hill than he is restless to roll up another.

Now it can be seen why this little afterthought of the gods, which I called perverse, was also in fact merciful. For they have by this device managed to give Sisyphus precisely what he wants—by making him want precisely what they inflict on him. However it may appear to us, Sisyphus's fate now does not appear to him as a condemnation, but the very reverse. His one desire in life is to roll stones, and he is absolutely guaranteed its endless fulfillment. Where otherwise he might profoundly have wished surcease, and even welcomed the quiet of death to release him from endless boredom and meaninglessness, his life is now filled with mission and meaning, and he seems to himself to have been given an entry to heaven. Nor need he even fear death, for the gods have promised him an endless opportunity to indulge his single purpose, without concern or frustration. He will be able to roll stones *forever*.

What we need to mark most carefully at this point is that the picture with which we began has not really been changed in the least by adding this supposition. Exactly the same things happen as before. The only change is in Sisyphus's view of them. The picture before was the image of meaningless activity and existence. It was created precisely to be an image of that. It has not lost that meaninglessness, it has now gained not the least shred of meaningfulness. The stones still roll back as before, each phase of Sisyphus's life still exactly resembles all the others, the task is never completed, nothing comes of it, no temple ever begins to rise, and all this cycle of the same pointless thing over and over goes on forever in this picture as in the other. The *only* thing that has happened is this: Sisyphus has been reconciled to it, and indeed more, he has been led to embrace it. Not, however, by reason or persuasion, but by nothing more rational than the potency of a new substance in his veins.

THE MEANINGLESSNESS OF LIFE

I believe the foregoing provides a fairly clear content to the idea of meaninglessness and, through it, some hint of what meaningfulness, in this sense, might be. Meaninglessness is essentially endless pointlessness, and meaningfulness is therefore the opposite. Activity, and even long, drawn-out and repetitive activity, has a meaning if it has some significant culmination, some more or less lasting end that can be considered to have been the direction and purpose of the activity. But the descriptions so far also provide something else; namely, the suggestion of how an existence that is objectively meaningless, in this sense, can nevertheless acquire a meaning for him whose existence it is.

Now let us ask: Which of these pictures does life in fact resemble? And let us not begin with our own lives, for here both our prejudices and wishes are great, but with the life in general that we share with the rest of creation. We shall find, I think, that it all has a certain pattern, and that this pattern is by now easily recognized.

We can begin anywhere, only saving human existence for our last consideration. We can, for example, begin with any animal. It does not matter where we begin, because the result is going to be exactly the same.

Thus, for example, there are caves in New Zealand, deep and dark, whose floors are quiet pools and whose walls and ceilings are covered with soft light. As one gazes in wonder in the stillness of these caves it seems that the Creator has reproduced there in microcosm the heavens themselves, until one scarcely remembers the enclosing presence of the walls. As one looks more closely, however, the scene is explained.

Each dot of light identifies an ugly worm, whose luminous tail is meant
to attract insects from the surrounding darkness. As from time to time
one of these insects draws near it becomes entangled in a sticky thread
lowered by the worm, and is eaten. This goes on month after month, the
blind worm lying there in the barren stillness waiting to entrap an occasional bit of nourishment that will only sustain it to another bit of nourishment until. . . . Until what? What great thing awaits all this long and
repetitious effort and makes it worthwhile? Really nothing. The larva
just transforms itself finally to a tiny winged adult that lacks even mouth
parts to feed and lives only a day or two. These adults, as soon as they
have mated and laid eggs, are themselves caught in the threads and are
devoured by the cannibalist worms, often without having ventured into
the day, the only point to their existence having now been fulfilled. This
has been going on for millions of years, and to no end other than that
the same meaningless cycle may continue for another millions of years.

All living things present essentially the same spectacle. The larva
of a certain cicada burrows in the darkness of the earth for seventeen
years, through season after season, to emerge finally into the daylight
for a brief flight, lay its eggs, and die—this all to repeat itself during the
next seventeen years, and so on to eternity. We have already noted, in
another connection, the struggles of fish, made only that others may do
the same after them and that this cycle, having no other point than itself,
may never cease. Some birds span an entire side of the globe each year
and then return, only to insure that others may follow the same incredibly long path again and again. One is led to wonder what the point of
it all is, with what great triumph this ceaseless effort, repeating itself
through millions of years, might finally culminate, and why it should
go on and on for so long, accomplishing nothing, getting nowhere. But
then one realizes that there is no point to it at all, that it really culmi-
nates in nothing, that each of these cycles, so filled with toil, is to be
followed only by more of the same. The point of any living thing's life
is, evidently, nothing but life itself.

This life of the world thus presents itself to our eyes as a vast
machine, feeding on itself, running on and on forever to nothing. And
we are part of that life. To be sure, we are not just the same, but the differences are not so great as we like to think; many are merely invented,
and none really cancels the kind of meaninglessness that we found in
Sisyphus and that we find all around, wherever anything lives. We are

conscious of our activity. Our goals, whether in any significant sense we choose them or not, are things of which we are at least partly aware and can therefore in some sense appraise. More significantly, perhaps, men have a history, as other animals do not, such that each generation does not precisely resemble all those before. Still, if we can in imagination disengage our wills from our lives and disregard the deep interest each man has in his own existence, we shall find that they do not so little resemble the existence of Sisyphus. We toil after goals, most of them— indeed every single one of them—of transitory significance and, having gained one of them, we immediately set forth for the next, as if that one had never been, with this next one being essentially more of the same. Look at a busy street any day, and observe the throng going hither and thither. To what? Some office or shop, where the same things will be done today as were done yesterday, and are done now so they may be repeated tomorrow. And if we think that, unlike Sisyphus, these labors do have a point, that they culminate in something lasting and, inde- pendently of our own deep interests in them, very worthwhile, then we simply have not considered the thing closely enough. Most such effort is directed only to the establishment and perpetuation of home and fam- ily; that is, to the begetting of others who will follow in our steps to do more of the same. Each man's life thus resembles one of Sisyphus's climbs to the summit of his hill, and each day of it one of his steps; the difference is that whereas Sisyphus himself returns to push the stone up again, we leave this to our children. We at one point imagined that the labors of Sisyphus finally culminated in the creation of a temple, but for this to make any difference it had to be a temple that would at least endure, adding beauty to the world for the remainder of time. Our achievements, even though they are often beautiful, are mostly bubbles; and those that do last, like the sand-swept pyramids, soon become mere curiosities while around them the rest of mankind continues its perpetual toting of rocks, only to see them roll down. Nations are built upon the bones of their founders and pioneers, but only to decay and crumble before long, their rubble then becoming the foundation for others directed to exactly the same fate. The picture of Sisyphus is the picture of existence of the individual man, great or unknown, of nations, of the race of men, and of the very life of the world.

On a country road one sometimes comes upon the ruined hulks of a house and once extensive buildings, all in collapse and spread over with weeds. A curious eye can in imagination reconstruct from what is left a once warm and thriving life, filled with purpose. There was the hearth, where a family once talked, sang, and made plans; there were the rooms, where people loved, and babes were born to a rejoicing mother; there are the musty remains of a sofa, infested with bugs, once bought at a dear price to enhance an ever-growing comfort, beauty, and warmth. Every small piece of junk fills the mind with what once, not long ago, was utterly real, with children's voices, plans made, and enterprises embarked upon. That is how these stones of Sisyphus were rolled up, and that is how they became incorporated into a beautiful temple, and that temple is what now lies before you. Meanwhile other buildings, institutions, nations, and civilizations spring up all around, only to share the same fate before long. And if the question "What for?" is now asked, the answer is clear: so that just this may go on forever.

The two pictures—of Sisyphus and of our own lives, if we look at them from a distance—are in outline the same and convey to the mind the same image. It is not surprising, then, that men invent ways of denying it, their religions proclaiming a heaven that does not crumble, their hymnals and prayer books declaring a significance to life of which our eyes provide no hint whatever.[1] Even our philosophies portray some permanent and lasting good at which all may aim, from the changeless forms invented by Plato to the beatific vision of St. Thomas and the ideals of permanence contrived by the moderns. When these fail to convince, then earthly ideals such as universal justice and brotherhood are conjured up to take their places and give meaning to man's seemingly endless pilgrimage, some final state that will be ushered in when the last obstacle is removed and the last stone pushed to the hilltop. No one believes, of course, that any such state will be final, or even wants it to be in case it means that human existence would then cease to be a struggle; but in the meantime, such ideas serve a very real need.

THE MEANING OF LIFE

We noted that Sisyphus's existence would have meaning if there were some point to his labors, if his efforts ever culminated in something that was not just an occasion for fresh labors of the same kind. But that is precisely the meaning it lacks. And human existence resembles his in that respect. Men do achieve things—they scale their towers and raise their stones to their hilltops—but every such accomplishment fades, providing only an occasion for renewed labors of the same kind.

But here we need to note something else that has been mentioned, but its significance not explored, and that is the state of mind and feeling with which such labors are undertaken. We noted that if Sisyphus had a keen and unappeasable desire to be doing just what he found himself doing, then, although his life would in no way be changed, it would nevertheless have a meaning for him. It would be an irrational one, no doubt, because the desire itself would be only the product of the substance in his veins, and not any that reason could discover, but a meaning nevertheless.

And would it not, in fact, be a meaning incomparably better than the other? For let us examine again the first kind of meaning it could have. Let us suppose that, without having any interest in rolling stones, as such, and finding this, in fact, a galling toil, Sisyphus did nevertheless have a deep interest in raising a temple, one that would be beautiful and lasting. And let us suppose he succeeded in this, that after ages of dreadful toil, all directed at this final result, he did at last complete his temple, such that now he could say his work was done, and he could rest and forever enjoy the result. Now what? What picture now presents itself to our minds? It is precisely the picture of infinite boredom! Of Sisyphus doing nothing ever again, but contemplating what he has already wrought and can no longer add anything to, and contemplating it for an eternity! Now in this picture we have a meaning for Sisyphus's existence, a point for his prodigious labor, because we have put it there; yet, at the same time, that which is really worthwhile seems to have slipped away entirely. Where before we were presented with the nightmare of eternal and pointless activity, we are now confronted with the hell of its eternal absence.

Our second picture, then, wherein we imagined Sisyphus to have had inflicted on him the irrational desire to be doing just what he found himself doing, should not have been dismissed so abruptly. The meaning that picture lacked was no meaning that he or anyone could crave, and the strange meaning it had was perhaps just what we were seeking.

At this point, then, we can reintroduce what has been until now, it is hoped, resolutely pushed aside in an effort to view our lives and human existence with objectivity; namely, our own wills, our deep interest in what we find ourselves doing. If we do this we find that our lives do indeed still resemble that of Sisyphus, but that the meaningfulness they thus lack is precisely the meaningfulness of infinite boredom. At the same time, the strange meaningfulness they possess is that of the inner compulsion to be doing just what we were put here to do, and to go on doing it forever. This is the nearest we may hope to get to heaven, but the redeeming side of that fact is that we do thereby avoid a genuine hell.

If the builders of a great and flourishing ancient civilization could somehow return now to see archaeologists unearthing the trivial remnants of what they had once accomplished with such effort—see the fragments of pots and vases, a few broken statues, and such tokens of another age and greatness—they could indeed ask themselves what the point of it all was, if this is all it finally came to. Yet, it did not seem so to them then, for it was just the building, and not what was finally built, that gave their life meaning. Similarly, if the builders of the ruined home and farm that I described a short while ago could be brought back to see what is left, they would have the same feelings. What we construct in our imaginations as we look over these decayed and rusting pieces would reconstruct itself in their very memories, and certainly with unspeakable sadness. The piece of a sled at our feet would revive in them a warm Christmas. And what rich memories would there be in the broken crib? And the weed-covered remains of a fence would reproduce the scene of a great herd of livestock, so laboriously built up over so many years. What was it all worth, if this is the final result? Yet, again, it did not seem so to them through those many years of struggle and toil, and they did not imagine they were building a Gibraltar. The things to which they bent their backs day after day, realizing one by one their ephemeral plans, were precisely the things in which their wills were deeply involved, precisely the things in which their interests lay, and there was no need then to ask questions. There is no more need of them now—the day was sufficient to itself, and so was the life.

This is surely the way to look at all of life—at one's own life, and each day and moment it contains; of the life of a nation; of the species; of the life of the world; and of everything that breathes. Even the glow worms I described, whose cycles of existence over the millions of years seem so pointless when looked at by us, will seem entirely different to us if we can somehow try to view their existence from within. Their endless activity, which gets nowhere, is just what it is their will to pursue. This is its whole justification and meaning. Nor would it be any salvation to the birds who span the globe every year, back and forth, to have a home made for them in a cage with plenty of food and protection, so that they would not have to migrate any more. It would be their condemnation, for it is the doing that counts for them, and not what they hope to win by it. Flying these prodigious distances, never ending, is what it is in their veins to do, exactly as it was in Sisyphus's veins to roll stones, without end, after the gods had waxed merciful and implanted this in him.

A human being no sooner draws his first breath than he responds to the will that is in him to live. He no more asks whether it will be worthwhile, or whether anything of significance will come of it, than the worms and the birds. The point of his living is simply to be living, in the manner that it is his nature to be living. He goes through his life building his castles, each of these beginning to fade into time as the next is begun; yet, it would be no salvation to rest from all this. It would be a condemnation, and one that would in no way be redeemed were he able to gaze upon the things he has done, even if these were beautiful and absolutely permanent, as they never are. What counts is that one should be able to begin a new task, a new castle, a new bubble. It counts only because it is there to be done and he has the will to do it. The same will be the life of his children, and of theirs; and if the philosopher is apt to see in this a pattern similar to the unending cycles of the existence of Sisyphus, and to despair, then it is indeed because the meaning and point he is seeking is not there—but mercifully so. The meaning of life is from within us, it is not bestowed from without, and it far exceeds in both its beauty and permanence any heaven of which men have ever dreamed or yearned for.

NOTE

1. A popular Christian hymn, sung often at funerals and typical of many hymns, expresses this thought:

Swift to its close ebbs out life's little day;
Earth's joys grow dim, its glories pass away;
Change and decay in all around I see:
O thou who changest not, abide with me.

Index

About the Authors

James Rachels (1941–2003) wrote *The End of Life: Euthanasia and Morality* (1986), *Created from Animals: The Moral Implications of Darwinism* (1990), *Can Ethics Provide Answers? And Other Essays in Moral Philosophy* (1997), *Problems from Philosophy* (first edition, 2005), and *The Legacy of Socrates: Essays in Moral Philosophy* (2007). His website is www.jamesrachels.org.

Stuart Rachels is associate professor of philosophy at the University of Alabama. He has revised several of James Rachels' books, including *The Elements of Moral Philosophy* and *Problems from Philosophy*. Stuart won the United States Chess Championship at the age of twenty, in 1989, and is a Bronze Life Master at bridge. He lives in Tuscaloosa, Alabama, and is currently writing a book about chess.